Sebastian Haumann, Martin Knoll, Detlev Mares (eds.)
Concepts of Urban-Environmental History

Environmental and Climate History | Volume 1

Sebastian Haumann, born in 1981, teaches urban-environmental history at Darmstadt University of Technology. He completed his PhD in urban history in 2010.

Martin Knoll, born in 1969, is a professor for European regional history at the University of Salzburg, Austria. His research focuses on environmental history, cultural history of the early modern period, the historical development of city-hinterland-relations, and the history of tourism.

Detlev Mares, born in 1965, teaches modern history and history didactics at Darmstadt University of Technology. His research deals with British history, popular political culture, and the didactics of history.

Sebastian Haumann, Martin Knoll, Detlev Mares (eds.)
Concepts of Urban-Environmental History

[transcript]

Drucklegung unterstützt aus Mitteln der Universität Salzburg (Rektorat und Fachbereich Geschichte)

Bibliographic information published by the Deutsche Nationalbibliothek
The Deutsche Nationalbibliothek lists this publication in the Deutsche Nationalbibliografie; detailed bibliographic data are available in the Internet at http://dnb.d-nb.de

© 2020 transcript Verlag, Bielefeld

All rights reserved. No part of this book may be reprinted or reproduced or utilized in any form or by any electronic, mechanical, or other means, now known or hereafter invented, including photocopying and recording, or in any information storage or retrieval system, without permission in writing from the publisher.

Cover layout: Maria Arndt, Bielefeld
Typeset by Justine Buri, Bielefeld
Printed by Majuskel Medienproduktion GmbH, Wetzlar
Print-ISBN 978-3-8376-4375-6
PDF-ISBN 978-3-8394-4375-0
https://doi.org/10.14361/9783839443750

This volume is dedicated to
Dieter Schott
upon his retirement from the
chair of Urban and Environmental History
at Darmstadt University of Technology.

Contents

Urban-Environmental History as a Field of Research
Sebastian Haumann, Martin Knoll and Detlev Mares 9

Technosphere
Chris Otter 21

Socio-Natural Sites
Verena Winiwarter and Martin Schmid 33

Materiality and Practice Theory
Sebastian Haumann 51

Path-Dependency and Trajectories
Christoph Bernhardt 65

Risk and Resilience
Dominik Collet 79

Sustainability
Ansgar Schanbacher 95

Urban Metabolism
Sabine Barles 109

Material Flows and Circular Thinking
Heike Weber 125

Urban Infrastructure and the Cultural Turn
Martin V. Melosi 145

Cities and Rivers
Uwe Lübken 155

Urban Energy Consumption, Mobility and Environmental Legacies
Christian Zumbrägel 167

Animals in Urban-Environmental History
Dorothee Brantz 191

Mobilities, Migration and Demography
Martin Knoll and Reinhold Reith 203

Heritage, Renewal and the Construction of Identity in Urban History
Michael Toyka-Seid 221

Urban Heritage and Urban Development
Rebecca Madgin 235

Village—Small Town—Metropolis
Clemens Zimmermann 253

European Periphery
Rainer Liedtke 265

Urban-Environmental Perspectives in History Teaching
Noyan Dinçkal and Detlev Mares 275

Authors 287

Acknowledgements 291

Urban-Environmental History as a Field of Research

Sebastian Haumann, Martin Knoll and Detlev Mares

Urban history and environmental history have been considered as two separate fields of research. In their long tradition, studies on past urban societies have predominantly been the domain of social and cultural history, concerned with spheres explicitly understood to be distinct from 'nature'. Meanwhile, environmental history, as it emerged during the last decades of the 20th century, has tended to conceive the city as a disruptive force and a cause of all kinds of threats to the environment. Although this juxtaposition may seem to rest on a rather crude simplification of the two strands of research, it has shaped the outlook and historians' interpretations of phenomena at the boundary of the urban and the environment.

However, in recent years, historians have increasingly linked both fields of research. Urban-environmental history contends that city and nature are inseparably intertwined. It understands the city as environment and the natural environment as an essentially urbanised phenomenon (Soens et al. 2019). It questions the very relevance of the boundary between the allegedly separated spheres and explores the many ways in which natural and social processes converge to form the city. This is more than to recognise that the city and the environment are interconnected, and yet these interconnections are important pathways into the inquiry of urban-environmental history. Infrastructures, the flow of matter, or cities as distinctive ecosystems, key topics in urban-environmental history, show cities as social *and* environmental entities, as objects of co-construction and co-evolution. The present volume provides the first systematic overview of the key concepts in this field of research.

Challenging the Nature-Culture Dichotomy

In Western thought, 'city' and 'nature' are conventionally understood as opposites. This has deep roots in judeo-christian traditions, in which humanity was conceived of as holding a divine mandate over 'nature', a 'mind' separated from the mundane constraints of the material world. From a materialist perspective,

Marxism also contributed to dichotomous thinking by explaining culture and history as the outcome of social forces, such as capital accumulation and class formation. Most recently, the 'cultural turn' has reinforced this separation from the opposite end. As Chris Otter states, the 'cultural turn' has produced a "radical form of dematerialization" (Otter 2010: 41). The intellectual separation is reflected in popular accounts, where the city is often portrayed as epitomising culture and modernisation. Urbanites have developed a particular lifestyle that is detached from the impositions of surrounding nature, so the argument goes. On this premise, urbanisation is either interpreted as overcoming restraints—as in the narrative of the mastery over nature—or endangering the environment—as declensionist narratives have it.

Over the last three decades, the dichotomy of a 'cultural' and a 'natural' sphere has come under attack. Conceiving human capacities as uncoupled from and superseding environmental constraints is seen as the root of severe misinterpretations (McNeill 2003; LeCain 2017). The development of cities, in particular, is found not to be a self-contained 'cultural' phenomenon, but to be dependent on and enmeshed with factors that have previously been idealised as 'natural'. Consequently, urban-environmental history has been at the forefront of what has been dubbed the 'material turn'. In an attempt to reconceptualise urbanisation processes, the material qualities of the environment have moved from being considered merely as a backdrop of urban development to a constituent force in the design and operation of essential functions of the city (Melosi 1993, 2010).

The assumption that city and nature are inseparably intertwined leads to a particular understanding of modernisation that breaks with both the idea of mastery over nature and declensionist narratives. Instead, urban-environmental history tends to assert that mutual interdependencies grew stronger over the past centuries and urban development "made them both broader and deeper—broader because more environments and natural resources were integrated [...], deeper because the range of linkages between humans and the natural world multiplied and expanded" (Pritchard/Zeller 2010: 85). Modernisation therefore is characterised by an ever more complex web of interrelations with the environment, which might be understood as 'Technosphere' (Otter in this volume). The increasing interdependence had a double sided effect. Human activities had a markedly increasing impact on the urbanised environment, while at the same time human life in cities became the more vulnerable the more it hinged on the integration of nature. The history of urban development and modernisation thus appears as quite the opposite of an increased separation of a 'cultural' from a 'natural' sphere, while seen from the angle of recent debates on the 'Anthropocene', human and non-human, urban and extra-urban agency have created a powerful 'urban stratum', in which the human species will leave its "mark as a major planetary event", even after its extinction (Otter 2019: 324).

Key Topics

The ever more complex interdependencies between cities and the environment first became evident in the context of research on pollution, hygiene and epidemics, which often took its questions from social history. As early as 1967, Ilja Mieck analysed urban air pollution during the first half of the 19th century and described the attempts to regulate emissions. Similarly, scholars working on the history of urban planning, such as Anthony Sutcliffe (1981), included environmental issues in their studies from the angle of regulation. Other studies concerned with the socio-spatial organisation of cities revealed the impact of environmental factors which humans did not fully understand or control. This was the central point in Richard Evans' (1987) study on the Hamburg cholera epidemic of 1892. As research showed, even the consequences of man-made pollution proved difficult to counteract precisely because they resulted from social as well as chemical and biological processes (Mosley 2001; Platt 2005). The subsequent measures to cope with these challenges through sanitary reform and technological fixes, in particular infrastructural solutions, have become recurring topics of urban-environmental history (Melosi in this volume).

Beginning with William Cronon's *Nature's Metropolis* (1991), in which he analysed the symbiosis of Chicago's urban development and the ecological change of its hinterland, urban-environmental history has scrutinised how cities and their environments have shaped each other in reciprocal relationships. The provision of water and disposal of waste, the movement and distribution of foodstuff and livestock, prominent in Cronon's study, but also the consumption of energy and the transformation of matter are important issues. Methodologically, this interest was backed by approaches to account for energy and material flows and circulation (Weber in this volume), in particular in the concept of 'urban metabolism' (Fischer-Kowalski/Haberl 1993; Barles in this volume). Thus, the flow and circulation of materials from extraction and production through conversion and consumption and all the way down to recycling and the 'ultimate sink' (Tarr 1996) have become key topics of urban-environmental history.

To a significant degree, 'urban metabolism' is organised through infrastructure, in a sense which connects the issue of sanitation with that of circulation of matter and energy more generally. Taking a cue from the history of technology, the city appears as a node of networks through which the flows of water, foodstuff, waste, raw materials, but also gas and electricity were channelled. For the history of urban energy consumption Thomas Hughes' (1987) concept of 'large technological systems' proved particularly influential (Zumbrägel in this volume). Following up on Hughes, Dieter Schott (1999) aptly characterised modern settlements as 'networked cities', pointing to the essential role of infrastructure for the functioning of urban societies in both a cultural and material sense.

The focus on infrastructure highlighted questions about how social processes relate to material forces. On the one hand, the provision of water, for example, is governed by the built structure of water mains and reservoirs, which are capable of altering the hydrology of entire watersheds. Within the cities, the provision of water and other amenities often reflected and reinforced social stratification (Gandy 2002). Therefore, urban-environmental historians often assert that infrastructures are the materialisation of social relations and that they constitute strong path dependencies (Bernhardt in this volume). On the other hand, material forces frequently disrupted the normal operation of infrastructures and necessitated their continuous maintenance. But even the breakdown of infrastructures as well as other recurring threats, such as floods or harvest failures, were never the result of natural causes alone, but always socially constructed. Through the way urban societies interacted with the environment they produced specific risks (Collet in this volume).

The fact that risks were distributed unequally has become the focus of a broad debate on 'environmental justice'. Originally a political claim, historians have adopted the concept and raised questions about the unequal exposure to environmental hazards according to race, class and gender (Flanagan 2000; Luckin 2005; Pichler-Baumgartner 2015). In urban contexts, such inequalities are not only evident in the exposure to pollution, but also in the more intricate relationship of cities and their rivers. While rivers offer significant opportunities to urban societies, they also create formidable risks, in particular for those who had to settle in the floodplains. The ambivalent character of city-river relations makes them a pre-eminent topic of urban-environmental history (Lübken in this volume). In a pioneering project on the history of the Danube in Vienna, a research group around Verena Winiwarter has analysed the many facets in which fluvial dynamics were appropriated but also counteracted human intentions (Winiwarter et al. 2013). Studies which focus on rivers are particularly apt to reveal how natural forces are inseparably intertwined with humans' decisions and power relations.

In analysing the myriad ways in which social and environmental dynamics were enmeshed, urban-environmental historians did not lose sight of how cultural constructions structured these relationships. The aim to overcome the nature-culture dichotomy notwithstanding, most studies explicitly reflect on the very concepts that were and are applied to judge, evaluate and form the urban environment. Tim Soens et al. (2019: 19) recently acknowledged that "at some points in history, the city might have existed as an imaginary category, and from this imaginary idea of a 'city' (and of 'nature'), policies were conceived and technologies applied, 'as if the city (and nature) existed'". Because the cultural construction of 'the city' and 'nature' has been formative, e. g. in the creation of urban parks, it remains important to look into processes in which the relevant understandings and conceptions were constructed. Scholars have therefore begun to historicise the ways in which past and present societies think about the relationship of urban development and the environment. They present notions such as 'circulation' (Weber in this volume) and 'sustainability' (Schanbacher in this volume) as constructions with a long history and reveal their often normative and prescriptive character—a fact that explicitly does not render them useless as analytical tools in historical research.

Just how relevant and instructive such constructions can be is evident in the current practice of conservation and urban heritage (Madgin in this volume; Toyka-Seid in this volume). In planning and governance, concepts such as 'sustainability' have gained significant influence on the ways in which a city's past and its existing urban fabric are appropriated and revaluated. The way in which we as society think about the relationship between 'city' and 'nature' continues to have a decisive impact on policies and practices. Disseminating the knowledge of non-dichotomic concepts as developed in urban-environmental history can therefore enhance debates about the future development of cities. To this end, concepts of urban-environmental history might also be usefully applied in teaching history at school and university levels (Dinçkal/Mares in this volume).

Some of the research in urban-environmental history has been criticised for predominantly representing the experiences of cities in North-Western Europe and North America. Indeed, most research does focus on these regions, whereas urbanisation in other parts of the world has often been interpreted as insufficient or 'catching up' on Western models. The emerging research on cities in Asia, Africa or Latin America might lead to a more differentiated picture, even though London, Paris, New York or Berlin remain important references (cf. Melosi 2013). When scholarly attention is extended to the so-called 'periphery' in Southern and Eastern Europe it becomes clear that urban-environmental history needs to take into account very different paths of development (Liedtke in this volume). The history of the interdependencies between cities and the environment is also complicated by the need to take into account different types and sizes of settlements beyond the well-researched metropolises (Zimmermann in this volume). Finally, the topic of mobilities has inspired a powerful new conceptual paradigm in social science debates (Urry 2007), which however is ambivalent when applied to the history of urbanisation, be it with respect to demography, urban infrastructures or reorganised city-hinterland-relations (Knoll/Reith in this volume).

The topics outlined above have been central to much of the research on cities and the environment. Focussing on these topics has proven to offer valuable insights into how the history of cities and nature are inseparably intertwined. However, they represent a particular strand of research that has evolved within an informally organised, yet highly integrated international network of scholars which has shaped the field of urban-environmental history since the 1990s.

The Historiography of Urban-Environmental History

Already in 1974, the influential French historian Emmanuel Le Roy Ladurie had identified a set of topics within the young research field of environmental history in which the urban dimension figured prominently (Bernhardt 2001: 5). The range of topics included epidemic and climatic developments, unpredicted natural events, the destruction of nature caused by demographic developments, urban and industrial emissions leading to the pollution of water and air, and finally an overload of urban space by material structures, people and noise (Le Roy Ladurie 1974: 537). Cities became an issue in environmental history throughout the 1970s and 1980s, at least in Europe, while in North America the emergence of urban-environmental history as a field of research took a different course.

In Europe, research on the city and its socio-ecological problems tied in with the wider interest in the long-term social and economic history of cities (Mosley 2006). Premodern urbanisation was already considered to be "essentially environment-driven", as David Nicholas (2003: IX) stated, and this intensified with modernisation. The socio-spatial patterns of urban development were related to environmental factors and research showed how different kinds of pollution affected urbanisation throughout the ages (Bernhardt 2001: 7). Apart from these approaches focussing on environmental problems and pollution, urban-environmental history also connected to debates about the management of resources in the 'wooden age' (Sombart 1928) and an interest in the making of networks of urban infrastructures which was established in economic history. In short, European urban-environmental history tied in into wider debates on the long-term development of urban societies.

US historiography developed in a slightly different manner (Culver 2014). What William Cronon once characterised as fundamentally "Turnerian in its implications" (Isenberg 2006: X) was a perspective in early US environmental history which predominantly focuses on land use and environmental change in extra-urban contexts. Donald Worster's (1990) 'agroecological approach' epitomised this focus. But, as Andrew Isenberg (2006: XII) aptly points out, "the disinterest of Worster and other environmental historians in urban places was equally matched by urban historians' long-standing disregard for the natural environment." Somewhat ironically, metaphors from biology and ecology were adopted in urban studies, particularly by the Chicago School, which in turn was an important influence on early urban-environmental history in the US. Martin Melosi and Joel Tarr were among the first scholars who in reaction to both environmental history's sticking with non-urban environments and urban studies' ignorance of non-human nature defined and advocated "The Place of the City in Environmental History" (Melosi 1993). Strongly influenced by William Cronon's (1991) "Nature's Metropolis", a next generation of US scholars took the interconnectedness of urban and non-urban spaces more seriously. They highlighted the relevance of these interconnections for urban *and* environmental history and advocated an approach "no longer concerned with proving the relevance of urban places to environmental history, no longer beholden to the organism or central places models of urban studies, no longer afraid that environmental history will be subsumed by other fields through greater attention to social, labor, or cultural history" (Isenberg 2006: XIV).

The integration of urban and environmental history at the beginning of the 1990s went hand in hand with an internationalisation of the scholarly debate. A group of pioneering historians around Christoph Bernhardt, Bill Luckin, Geneviève Massard-Guilbaud, Simone Neri Serneri and Dieter Schott developed the field of urban-environmental history through a series of conferences and publications. The 1998 European Association for Urban History (EAUH) conference in Venice was the first European conference on urban history to host a session dedicated to environmental history, dealing with "Urban Environmental Problems" (Bernhardt 2001). This was followed by a session on "Cities and Catastrophes" at the EAUH conference in Berlin in 2000 (Massard-Guilbaud/Platt/Schott 2002). From this emerged a series of roundtable meetings on urban-environmental history which took place in Clermont-Ferrand 2000, focusing on pollution, in Leicester 2002, with an emphasis on resources, in Siena 2004, reiterating the making of the contemporary city, in Paris 2006, focusing on milieu, material and materiality, and in Berlin 2008, once more negotiating with a broader focus the place of the city in environmental history. The results of these roundtable meetings are documented in several publications which reflect both the programmatic debate and the case studies which have been central in developing the field (Bernhardt/Massard-Guilbaud 2002; Schott/Luckin/Massard-Guilbaud 2005).

The maturation of the field led to the publication of first syntheses, namely Dieter Schott's (2014) overview of European urban-environmental history since the Middle Ages. At the same time, the ever widening horizon in terms of perspectives and interdisciplinarity resulted in a variety of research projects and publications. These, to name but a few examples, bridged the perspectives of urban-environmental history and the history of technology (Hård/Misa 2008), applied questions of environmental justice and (in)equalities to urban-environmental history (Massard-Guilbaud/Rodger 2011) or concentrated on specific sites relevant to the interconnectedness of cities and the environment, such as in city-river relations (Castonguay/Evenden 2012; Knoll/Lübken/Schott 2017).

The complexity of research topics dealt with in urban-environmental history suggests the necessarily interdisciplinary character of the field. Not only did scholars from the neighbouring fields of economic and social history, history of technology and urban planning contribute to the debate. Reaching beyond historians' usual collaborations, urban-environmental history has also been strongly influenced by disciplines such as geography, social ecology and a wide range of natural sciences. This is reflected in the prominent role of research institutions and journals which act in these interdisciplinary contexts. Interdisciplinarity has opened the community for innovations in methods and theories from various origins, but also brought with it the challenge to bridge the gap between diverse research cultures.

Currently, urban-environmental history is much inspired by the 'material turn' and concepts highlighting the hybridity of social, cultural and biophysical processes and arrangements. Under these auspices, historians from Darmstadt and Antwerp have recently taken the initiative to evaluate the role of urban agency for environmental change. Workshops in Darmstadt 2013 and Antwerp 2014 facilitated substantial debates on "Urbanizing Nature" and were the basis for a volume of the same title (Soens et al. 2019). The editors of this volume proclaimed a "'Manifesto' for the History of Urban Nature", which gives valuable inputs for further research in urban-environmental history (Soens et al.: 19-20). Based on a relativisation of the term 'city' in favour of more vague, historically changing concepts of the urban, they advocate a perspective in search of networked types of agency by human and non-human actors and actants and conceive historical change as a constantly ongoing co-evolutionary process between cities, their inhabitants and nature.

In the course of these debates, urban-environmental history has adopted theories such as Actor-Network Theory, New Materialism or praxeology to account for physical or biological forces in historical research which unfold beyond human control (Haumann in this volume). In particular the concept of Socio-Natural Sites, devised by the Viennese research group around Verena Winiwarter, has been influential in the field and inspired many empirical studies (Winiwarter/Schmid in this volume). Others have broadened the perspective to include the agency of organisms and animals in order to analyse the city as an ecosystem in which human life is integrated (Brantz in this volume). However, the attempt to include non-human actors and material forces raises many theoretical and methodological questions that still need to be discussed.

Within the overarching debates about the character of the 'Anthropocene', which has recently become a powerful reference in the humanities, urban-environmental history has gained new relevance. The concept of the 'Anthropocene' again points to the fact that social and environmental dynamics are inseparably intertwined, with cities being an important form in which this interrelationship materialised. But urban-environmental history also holds great potential with regard to the future development of a sustainability-oriented urbanism in the 21st century. Leaving aside the more general question of how far human societies are able to learn from history, the interdisciplinary research into the complex field of urban-environmental history offers a broad range of arguments informing politics, economy and urban planners—which hopefully will be heard.

The Concept of this Volume

This volume is designed as a handbook which gives a concise overview of the field of urban-environmental history with an emphasis on the theoretical and methodological concepts that have been central to the debate. Each of the chapters gives a short introduction to key issues, discusses the emergence and development of the concepts, and presents the current state of the art. In addition, they reflect on the interdisciplinary connections which are essential to urban-environmental history and indicate future challenges and unresolved questions. The handbook thus takes stock of existing research and opens up avenues for further developing the field.

In this, the volume represents a specific strand of research which has developed out of the historiographic context outlined above. It does not claim to be exhaustive, but has a strong focus on those concepts which have been influential in analysing phenomena at the intersection of urban and environmental history over the last three decades. Many other approaches from the broader fields of urban history, environmental history and beyond could have been added, some of which have been addressed in this introduction. The strong focus on the concepts at the core of urban-environmental history also shows how scholars in the field have worked on a set of often interrelated and overlapping phenomena and problems. The role of infrastructures, metabolism or material forces is discussed in many chapters of this volume. However, these phenomena and problems have been interpreted from different vantage points and under different assumptions. In combination, the chapters therefore reflect the diversity of the perspectives on urban-environmental history and yet show how these perspectives relate to each other.

This volume is dedicated to Dieter Schott on the occasion of his retirement from the chair of Urban and Environmental History at Darmstadt University of Technology. Its title does not technically carry the term 'Festschrift' since the book follows a different concept. Rather than offering a mix of contributions by friends and colleagues, the collection discusses concepts of urban-environmental history which have characterised and which have been shaped by much of Dieter Schott's work. As readers will find, Dieter Schott's ideas inform many of the following chapters, which—we hope—bear strong-voiced witness to the inspiration his research and teaching have meant for opening and establishing the field of urban-environmental history.

References

Bernhardt, Christoph (ed.) (2001): Environmental problems in European cities in the 19th and 20th century, Münster: Waxmann.

Bernhardt, Christoph/Massard-Guilbaud, Geneviève (2002) (eds.): Le démon moderne: La pollution dans les sociétés urbaines et industrielles d'Europe, Clemont-Ferrand: Presses Universitaires Blaise-Pascal.

Castonguay, Stéphane/Evenden, Matthew (eds.) (2012): Urban rivers: Remaking rivers, cities, and space in Europe and North America, Pittsburgh: University of Pittsburgh Press.

Cronon, William (1991): Nature's metropolis: Chicago and the Great West, New York: Norton.

Culver, Lawrence (2014): "Confluences of nature and culture: Cities in environmental history." In: Andrew C. Isenberg (ed.), The Oxford Handbook of Environmental History, New York: Oxford University Press, pp. 553-570.

Evans, Richard J. (1987): Death in Hamburg: Society and politics in the cholera years 1830-1910, Oxford: Oxford University Press.

Fischer-Kowalski, Marina/Haberl, Helmut (1993): "Metabolism and colonization: Modes of production and the physical exchange between societies and nature." In: Innovation: The European Journal of Social Science Research 6, pp. 415-442.

Flanagan, Maureen A. (2000): "Environmental justice in the city: A theme for urban environmental history." In: Environmental History 5, pp. 159-164.

Gandy, Matthew (2002): Concrete and clay: Reworking nature in New York City, Cambridge, Mass.: MIT Press.

Hård, Mikael/Misa, Thomas J. (eds.) (2008): Urban machinery: Inside modern European cities, Cambridge, Mass.: MIT Press.

Hughes, Thomas P. (1987): "The evolution of large technological systems." In: Thomas P. Hughes/Wiebe Bijker/Trevor Pinch (eds.), The social construction of technological systems: New directions in the sociology and history of technology, Cambridge, Mass.: MIT Press, pp. 51-82.

Isenberg, Andrew C. (ed.) (2006): The nature of cities: Culture, landscape, and urban space, Rochester, NY: University of Rochester Press.

Knoll, Martin/Lübken, Uwe/Schott, Dieter (eds.) (2017): Rivers lost—rivers regained: Rethinking city-river relationships, Pittsburgh: University of Pittsburgh Press.

Le Roy Ladurie, Emmanuel (1974): "Histoire et environnement." In: Annales Économies – Sociétés – Civilisations 29/2, p. 537.

LeCain, Timothy J. (2017): The matter of history: How things create the past, Cambridge, Mass.: Cambridge University Press.

Luckin, Bill (2005): "Environmental justice, history and the city: The United States and Britain, 1970-2000." In: Dieter Schott/Bill Luckin/Geneviève Massard-Guilbaud (eds.), Resources of the city: Contributions to an environmental history of modern Europe, Aldershot: Routledge, pp. 230-245.

Massard-Guilbaud, Geneviève/Platt, Harold/Schott, Dieter (2002) (eds.): Cities and catastrophes/villes et catastrophes: Coping with emergency in European history/Réactions à l'urgence dans l'histoire européenne, Frankfurt a.M.: Peter Lang.

Massard-Guilbaud, Geneviève/Rodger, Richard (eds.) (2011): Environmental and social justice in the city: Historical perspectives, Cambridge: White Horse Press.

McNeill, John R. (2003): "Observations on the nature and culture of environmental history." In: History and Theory 42, pp. 5-43.

Melosi, Martin V. (2013): "The urban environment." In: Peter Clark (ed.), The Oxford handbook of cities in world history, Oxford: Oxford University Press, pp. 700-719.

Melosi, Martin V. (2010): "Humans, cities, and nature: How do cities fit in the material world?" In: Journal of Urban History 36, pp. 3-21.

Melosi, Martin V. (1993): "The place of the city in environmental history." In: Environmental History Review, pp. 1-23.

Mieck, Ilja (1967): "Luftverunreinigung und Immissionsschmutz in Preußen bis zur Gewerbeordnung 1869." In: Technikgeschichte 34, pp. 36-78.

Mosley, Stephen (2006): "Common ground: integrating social and environmental history." In: Journal of Social History 39, pp. 915-933.

Mosley, Stephen (2001): The chimney of the world: A history of smoke pollution in Victorian and Edwardian Manchester, Cambridge: White Horse Press.

Nicholas, David (2003): Urban Europe, 1100-1700, Basingstoke: Palgrave Macmillan.

Otter, Chris (2019): "Beyond cities, beyond nature: Building a European urban stratum." In: Tim Soens/Dieter Schott/Michael Toyka-Seid/Bert de Munck (eds.), Urbanizing nature: Actors and agency (dis)connecting cities and nature since 1500, New York: Routledge, pp. 313-328.

Otter, Chris (2010): "Locating matter: The place of materiality in urban history." In: Tony Bennett/Patrick Joyce (eds.), Material powers: Cultural studies, history and the material turn, Milton Park: Routledge, pp. 38-59.

Pichler-Baumgartner, Luisa (2015): "'Environmental justice' als analytische Kategorie der Wirtschafts-, Sozial- und Umweltgeschichte? Schwierigkeiten und Potenziale einer Anwendung." In: Vierteljahrschrift für Sozial- und Wirtschaftsgeschichte 102, pp. 472-491.

Platt, Harold L. (2005): Shock cities: The environmental transformation and reform of Manchester and Chicago, Chicago: University of Chicago Press.

Pritchard, Sara B./Zeller, Thomas (2010): "The nature of industrialization." In: Martin Reuss/Stephen H. Cutcliffe (eds.), The illusory boundary: Environment and technology in history, Charlottesville: University of Virginia Press, pp. 69-100.

Schott, Dieter (2014): Europäische Urbanisierung (1000-2000): Eine umwelthistorische Einführung, Cologne/Weimar/Vienna: Böhlau.

Schott, Dieter (1999): Die Vernetzung der Stadt: Kommunale Energiepolitik, öffentlicher Nahverkehr und die 'Produktion' der modernen Stadt – Darmstadt – Mannheim – Mainz 1880-1918, Darmstadt: Wissenschaftliche Buchgesellschaft.

Schott, Dieter/Luckin, Bill/Massard-Guilbaud, Geneviève (eds.) (2005): Resources of the city: Contributions to an environmental history of modern Europe, Aldershot: Routledge.

Soens, Tim/Schott, Dieter/Toyka-Seid, Michael/de Munck, Bert (eds.) (2019): Urbanizing nature: Actors and agency (dis)connecting cities and nature since 1500, New York: Routledge.

Sombart, Werner (1928): Der moderne Kapitalismus, Vol. 2. Das europäische Wirtschaftsleben im Zeitalter des Frühkapitalismus, vornehmlich im 16., 17. und 18. Jahrhundert, Leipzig: Duncker & Humblot.

Sutcliffe, Anthony (1981): Towards the planned city: Germany, Britain, the United States and France, 1780-1914, Oxford: Blackwell.

Tarr, Joel (1996): The search for the ultimate sink: Urban pollution in historical perspective, Akron: University of Akron Press.

Urry, John (2007): Mobilities, Cambridge: Polity Press.

Winiwarter, Verena/Schmid, Martin/Dressel, Gert (2013): "Looking at half a millennium of co-existence: The Danube in Vienna as a socio-natural site." In: Water History 5, pp. 101-119.

Worster, Donald (1990): "Transformations of the earth: Toward an agroecological perspective in history." In: Journal of American History 76, pp. 1087-1106.

Technosphere

Chris Otter

The explosive urbanisation of the post-1945 world has stimulated a productive discussion about the concepts and object of urban studies. For some scholars, urbanisation is now a global phenomenon that has rendered the concept of 'the city' obsolete. In 1963, the urban designer Melvin Webber declared that "all space is urban space" (cited in Fard 2013: n.p.). Four years later, the Greek architect Constantinos Doxiadis argued that urbanisation appeared irreversible, with the planet destined to become a single city. He coined the term 'ecumenopolis' to refer to a future globe-encompassing universal city (Doxiadis/Papaioannou 1974). Most consequentially, in *The Urban Revolution*, Henri Lefebvre argued that "society has been completely urbanized" (2003: 1). Brenner and Schmid have expanded this Lefebvrian observation into a theory of planetary urbanisation, which argues that even putatively nonurban spaces (including mountains and the earth's atmosphere) "have become integral parts of the worldwide urban fabric" (2011: 12).

Other studies, however, have drawn contrasting conclusions. Attempts to quantify statements about boundless urbanisation, or comprehend them literally, have produced data which suggest that theories of an urban planet perhaps overstate their case. Whichever measure one utilises—urban administrative area, "places dominated by the built environment," built-up areas, artificial surfaces, impervious surface area, or population density—the data appear to confound the assertions of Webber, Lefebvre, and Brenner. Figures range as low as 0.19 per cent of the planet's surface to 3 per cent—hardly an 'urbanized planet', unless one is straining the referential capacities of the term 'urban' to breaking point (Liu et al. 2014: 765-766). *The Atlas of Urban Expansion*, produced by New York University's Urban Expansion Program, charts this phenomenon of spectacular growth in arresting detail, yet urban areas remain palpably bounded: the image is of rapid urbanisation against a backdrop of predominantly non-urbanised space.

We are presented with something of a contradiction: an urban planet that is, at least in rather strict empirical terms, far from urbanised. The word 'urban' clearly has a wide semantic reach, literal and metaphoric uses, and a multiplicity of possible material referents. Lefebvre was not implying that the whole world had become a single city. Instead, he meant that all planetary phenomena have become subordinate to the metabolic and economic demands of cities. Cities orient the world towards themselves, meaning that roads, farms, resources, economies, cultures and communications systems are all "part of the urban fabric" (Lefebvre, 2003: 4). The theory of planetary urbanisation views the urban as a kind of texture covering the planet (Brenner/Schmid 2011: 13). Its spatial imaginary emphasises not discrete, interlinked nodes but a sprawling planetary mesh. As Peter Baccini and Paul Brunner note, the problematic nature of an urban-nonurban distinction "raises the question whether the definition of urbanity needs a principal revision" (2012: 3). This question has resulted in a proliferation of neologisms which have as their referent the blurred, chaotic and expanding zones exploding between the traditional city and something roughly corresponding to the nonurban: suburbia, conurbation, edge city, Zwischenstadt, Netzstadt (Baccini/Brunner 2012: 5). The result is a tripartite conceptual schema, which solves the epistemological problem of the urban-nonurban binary by creating a hybrid third category.

The Technosphere Concept

The concept of the technosphere also abandons such binarisms. It is the latest, and arguably most conceptually useful, in a series of monistic concepts that, rather like "planetary urbanization," refer to a singular globalised space constructed by humans: technium, anthroposphere, mechanosphere, anthropostrome (Kelly 2011: 11-17; Baccini/Brunner 2012; Deleuze/Guattari 1987: 514; Passerini 1984: 211). The term 'technosphere' first appeared in the writings of systems theorists, geographers and ecologists in the 1960s and 1970s, but has been most comprehensively elaborated by the geologist Peter Haff (Milsum 1968; Nicolson 1968; Haff 2013). He defines the technosphere as

> the set of large-scale networked technologies that underlie and make possible rapid extraction from the Earth of large quantities of free energy and subsequent power generation, long-distant, nearly instantaneous communication, rapid long-distance energy and mass transport, the existence and operation of modern governmental and other bureaucracies, high-intensity industrial and manufacturing operations including regional, continental and global distribution of food and other goods, and a myriad additional 'artificial' or 'non-natural' processes without which modern civilisation and its present 7×10^9 human constituents could not exist (Haff 2013: 301-302).

Rather than focusing on what is or is not 'urban', the technosphere refers to the totality of human technologies, which, while most heavily concentrated in cities, never reaches a spatial limit and is consequently dispersed across the planet. This concept entirely sidesteps the question of what is or is not urban, instead focusing at human engineering capacity and effects, from the smallest tools and devices (paper clips, televisions) to the largest entities (dams, Tokyo, the warming climate). The technosphere is thus a multiscalar phenomenon, at once intimate and local, and "a global phenomenon, spanning the planet and absorbing into itself almost all of the world's human population" (Haff 2013: 303).

Although the technosphere dramatically expanded during the Great Acceleration, the post-1945 period when "every indicator of human activity underwent a sharp increase in rate" (Steffen et al. 2011: 849), we should not view it as simply coextensive and coterminous with planetary urbanisation. It has a long, deep and multiscalar history that is inseparable from the broader geological and biological history of Earth. Its earliest phase begins with hominid tool use around 2.6 million years ago, and the controlled use of fire around 800.000 years ago (Williams et al. 2015: 15). Tools and fire made possible the earliest technospheric nuclei—home bases, shelters and later, fragile urban settlements. The first entities we can definitively call cities appeared around 9000-6000 BCE (Douglas 2012: 8). Early urban settlements include those at Çatalhöyük and Jericho, while urban centres in Peru, such as Caral and Aspero, date back to 5000 BCE (Douglas 2012: 8-9). These urban zones had high population densities, and these people inhabited physical capsules which were bounded by walls and traversed by water infrastructures. The ground upon which they stood was reconstructed: they produced "complex burrow systems" including pipes, canals, dumps and underground buildings that were significantly larger than those created by nonhuman species (Williams et al. 2013: 146). Cities were sites of hierarchical power relations: urban populations were regulated, and surrounding agrarian space was subject to control. Grain and water were funnelled to burgeoning urban populations (Scott 2017: 205). Cities were tightly connected to their wider milieu, even if walls marked the boundary dividing urban islands from a vast nonurbanised outside.

Contemporary evolutionary theory acknowledges the active role all organisms play in constructing and modifying their environments. This co-production of dense urban zones and circumambient agrarian landscapes can be viewed as multiple acts of niche construction (Odling-Smee et al. 2003; Scott 2017: 122). Moreover, the sheer scale of this ecological engineering was several orders of magnitude beyond that of other species, and epitomised the human capacity for artefact-building on a grand scale. This artefactual sphere—encompassing fire, tools, canals, huts, granaries, city walls and scratch ploughs—belongs neither to the biological nor geological realms: it involves life interacting with nonlife to produce phenomena which neither could produce alone. While these produce the biosphere and the geosphere respectively, the human capacity for artefact-making generated the rapid emergence of the technosphere between the biotic and abiotic realms (Odling-Smee et al. 2003: 190-191). The technosphere, in turn, impacted back upon these domains, for example creating new niches within which humans, animals, microbes, and plants co-evolved in novel and unpredictable ways (Scott 2017: 73).

Expansion

This early technosphere was effectively a loose scattering of urban islands reaching into their emergent hinterlands and interconnected by waterways and trade routes. It was far from a truly globalised entity. The technosphere expanded through a series of scalar leaps through which urban centres expanded via extractive, networked relationships with their surrounding mines, fields and forests. A reliance on organic energy sources, however, limited the technosphere to relatively modest and slow growth before the 19th century. Dependence upon wood and water usually tied cities to their immediate hinterlands and limited their expansion. Estimates suggest that wood-powered cities require fifty to one hundred times their area in woodland (Smil 1994: 7). Urban areas rarely exceeded one million people. The shift to fossil fuels broke the close connection between cities and their immediate surroundings. Dense, wall-bound cities could now extend their metabolisms by drawing raw materials from many distant locations via railway and steamship and, later, trucks and planes (Barles 2009). Planetary transport and communications networks and vast urban settlements were symbiotically linked by fossil energy.

Fossil fuels powered suburbanisation, sprawl, and the phenomenon of implosion/explosion outlined by Lefebvre and furthered by Brenner. 'Implosion/explosion' is a concept Lefebvre adopted from nuclear physics, referring to the simultaneous concentration and projection of urban material across planetary space (Lefebvre 2014; Brenner 2014). The 19th and 20th centuries saw a tremendous expansion of urban areas, which ultimately became vast and often incoherent agglomerations of capsules: houses, malls, sports arenas, offices, factories, within which humans engage with a bewildering array of devices (Otter 2017). Proliferating long-distance networks provided water, heat, energy, information, food, and climate control. A central feature of the technosphere is this process of enfolding, whereby human populations are able to withdraw into artificial, capsular forms of existence precisely by virtue of the technosphere's capacity to absorb and direct materials into the densest urban areas. Such separation of urban realms from not only local land but also local climate allowed cities to explode across areas previously unsuited for large urban settlements, particularly hot and arid areas (Arizona, Dubai). Meanwhile, the biological and geological materials of the early technosphere—wood and stone—have been complemented by enhanced and synthetic matter, particularly concrete and plastics.

In other words, the phenomenological disconnection from an emergent idea of a natural domain was a product of the manifold technological connections forged between human capsules and planetary resources. Early urban sociology and ecology noted this fact (Wachsmuth 2012). However, as urban political ecologists have observed, the circulatory and metabolic connections between urban and nonurban spaces have multiplied and intensified. This multiplicity of connections itself eroded any clear sense of an urban-nonurban boundary. Urban settlements are fed, watered, powered and interlinked by a vast array of infrastructures, from food systems to fiberoptic cables. The sheer number of interconnections provided by such networks has become a central feature of technospheric space in the early 21st century. It bears repeating that this post-1800 metabolism of the technosphere, which allowed planetary urbanisation, became increasingly predicated upon the extraction of enormous quantities of fossil fuels rather than renewable energy.

Ecological and geological systems have been massively recrafted to serve urban settlements. Humans have dug and drilled far deeper into the earth than other creatures, reaching depths of over five kilometres (Zalasciewicz et al. 2014: 4). Agriculture is an active reconfiguration of ecosystems involving the modification of plants, the domestication of animals, and the maintenance of wholly artificial monocultures: hybrid corn and Holstein cows are artefacts of the technosphere as much as iPhones and SUVs. Domesticated animals also experience technospheric encapsulation, albeit within the hyperdisciplinary spaces of byres, battery farms and concentrated feeding units. Ploughing, fertilising, irrigating, and building created anthrosols or "anthropogenic soils" such as the Northwest European plaggen and the terra preta of the Amazon basin (Ellis et al. 2013: 7982). Terra preta is also composed of artefacts like broken ceramics, ash and garbage (Montgomery 2012: 143). The result has been the production of large-scale zones of non-urban anthropogenic reconfiguration: anthromes, or humanly-modified biomes. In 1700, around 95 per cent of the earth's ice-free land could be classed as wild or seminatural, but by 2000, 55 per cent of this surface had been significantly transformed by humans, into rangeland, cropland, villages and densely settled spaces (Ellis et al. 2010: 593). Remaining non-agricultural land is now embedded within anthromes, producing an overall mosaic of land, some of which is anthromic, some of which is nonanthromic (Ellis et al. 2010: 603). Anthromes, however, while humanly-modified, cannot be said to be urban in any meaningful sense of the word: their populations are dispersed and scattered, their capsular agglomerations modest, their networks distributed, and their material composition predominantly organic.

The technosphere, finally, extends above, below and beyond the earth's cultivated surface into the mountains, deserts, oceans, and atmosphere. Such areas are perhaps best characterised as anthropogenic sinks or zones of dissipation rather than anthromes: they are areas which have been far less deliberately reconfigured yet which serve as repositories (organised or otherwise) for solid, liquid and gaseous human waste. Matt Edgeworth uses the term 'archaeosphere' to refer to spaces such as landfills, soil runoff zones, rubble mounds and polluted areas, which capture the technosphere's waste and function as "platforms of occupation debris" upon which further technospheric expansion can take place (Zalasciewicz et al. 2017: 11-12; Edgeworth 2018: 159). Such anthropoturbation is apparent across aquatic space, with its ships, oil rigs, submarine cables, floating garbage patches, artificial islands, and bottom-trawled seafloors, the latter being "the submarine equivalent of terrestrial agricultural soils" (Zalasciewicz et al. 2017: 16). The earth's atmosphere is the largest anthropogenic sink of all, as the accumulation of greenhouse gases suggests. Since 1957, satellites and their debris (abandoned satellite equipment, coolant droplets) have begun orbiting the earth (Zalasciewicz et al. 2017: 17; Gärdebo et al. 2017: 46). Human detritus can be found on the moon and space junk has drifted beyond the earth-moon system.

Consequences

The gathering momentum of the technosphere has planetary repercussions at the level of the biosphere and earth systems. The technosphere appropriates and processes raw materials (coal, minerals, water, oxygen, biomass) from the lithosphere, atmosphere, and biosphere, spewing detritus into any available planetary sink (Haff 2013: 303). As Haff notes, the technosphere uses around 17 terawatts (TW) of energy per year, which is an appreciable fraction of the world's geothermal energy flux (32 TW) and biochemical energy flux (90 TW) (Haff 2013: 303). The technosphere now mediates and overdetermines hydrological patterns, atmospheric chemistry, biodiversity and the flow of reactive nitrogen (Ellis 2011: 1018-1019). Geological cycles now include entirely synthetic substances (Zalasciewicz et al. 2016: 5). The technosphere is pushing the earth over several of the nine critical boundaries identified as markers of the Anthropocene (Rockström and Klum 2015).

It is at the level of the technosphere, then, that analysis of human beings as 'geological forces' should be located. The technosphere cannot, however, be easily conceived as a singular, homogenous entity with a clear trajectory of growth or centre of force. It exists at many scales: device, machine, capsule, city, network, anthrome, anthropogenic sink. It is at its densest where tools, structures and networks form vast, complex agglomerations–phenomena which we can refer to as urban. It is thinner and patchier as we scale up to the level of anthromes and anthropogenic sinks, becomes extremely rarefied at the upper levels of the earth's atmosphere and reaches its vanishing point with Voyager 1 as it hurtles towards the outer limits of the heliosphere. These scales demarcate a gradient of artificialisation: Manhattan is extremely synthetic, the Himalayas almost entirely geological (Ingold 2007: 4).

The concept of the technosphere is by no means unproblematic. Its sheer size and complexity poses challenges for urban theories emphasising human agency. The technosphere could appear similar to what Jacques Ellul called technique: an inescapable system organising every aspect of our existence. Ellul (1964) lamented that humans were fully absorbed into a vast technological complex in which human choice was illusory and technical development irreversible. "Technique," he concluded, "is essentially independent of the modern being, who finds himself naked and disarmed before it" (Ellul, 1964: 306) Haff, despite the richness of his work on the technosphere, can veer towards determinism, arguing that the technosphere is "a system for which humans are essential but, nonetheless, subordinate parts. As shorthand we can say that the technosphere is autonomous" (Haff 2014: 127).

There is a complementary position, which views an autonomous technosphere as a cause of celebration or an opportunity for technocracy. The earliest articulations of the technosphere concept, which drew on cybernetics and systems theory, certainly had technocratic dimensions. Milsum (1968) suggested the technosphere might involve "large integrated industrial processes that are automated and computer-controlled," while Nicholson's vision of the technosphere involved the orchestration of society, land and natural resources (Milsum 1968: 77; Shleper 2016). Techno-utopians like Ray Kurzweil and Kevin Kelly regard the formation of vast technological complexes with enthusiasm, often emphasising their increasingly intelligent nature. Kelly's version of the technosphere—the technium—is a hylozoic rather than mechanical entity with "a noticeable measure of autonomy," which "wants what every living system wants: to perpetuate itself" (Kelly 2011: 12-13, 15). Finally, the technosphere might be viewed as an enormous machine which humans need to steer carefully to avoid planetary collapse. Such is the view of geoengineers and ecomodernists, who urge fuller technospheric power over earth systems in the name of a cybernetic planet whose feedback systems are amenable to technocratic control (Morton 2016).

There are, however, several compelling political and intellectual reasons for adopting the concept of the technosphere. The notion that the technosphere determines or subjugates human agency relies upon a straightforward dichotomy between the technological and the social that is no longer philosophically sustainable. The particular scales of the technosphere are linked but possess a certain level of semiautonomy from each other. Moreover, the idea that homo sapiens can exist without a technosphere is in many ways problematic. The control of fire, as Richard Wrangham (2009) has argued, allowed the evolution of larger-brained hominins which produced our species. As active niche constructors, humans have built their own environment and their neurological evolution is incomprehensible without it. The technosphere is the human niche and we cannot live without it: humans, in fact, are artefacts of the technosphere.

Niches, however, are not traps or determinants. It would be wrong to assume that the technosphere's inescapability reduces us to mere cogs in the machine. Human societies do and can exercise choices over the technologies they adopt, as Kelly (2011) notes when looking at Amish populations (217-238). However, the exercise of technological choice requires robust democratic institutions. The technosphere has to be comprehended as a political artefact. If agency is a co-production of humans and their technologies, it takes place in a field where resources, materials and opportunities are inequitably distributed, something evident from the formation of the earliest urban settlements and inseparable from the histories of slavery, racism and genocide. No account of the technosphere is complete without consideration not simply of human-formation, but subject-formation and the politics of space. Such political, subjective and psychological dimensions of the technosphere are a critical dimension of its future analysis.

The technosphere concept ultimately allows urban historians to retain a more specific and circumscribed concept of the urban. Whether one chooses population density, administrative area or artificial surfaces, or more phenomenological, quantitative variables such as culture, diversity or states of mind, the urban appears not as a planetary phenomenon but the densest, most complex and synthetic region of a vaster, more differentiated and multiscalar spatial entity. The concept of the technosphere, in short, resists the idea that everything is urban without jettisoning the critical and powerful insights of Lefebvre, Brenner, and Schmid. It does this by expanding the scope of urban studies to include ecology, environmental studies, deep history and the history and philosophy of technology. The spatial concept of the technosphere explains how and why we can have a planet that seems totally urbanised but simultaneously barely urbanised. This entity, moreover, has a history which reaches back far beyond the birth of urban settlements: it avoids the presentism evoked by excessive focus on the post-1945 period of urban expansion or the tendency to collapse the history of the engineered planet into the relatively recent history of capitalism. The technosphere thus recasts and resituates the urban in both spatial and temporal dimensions, and allows urban theorists to study the interrelation between cities and wider ecologies, particularly anthromes and anthropogenic sinks, with more conceptual specificity.

Viewed in extremely longue durée terms, the technosphere is a youthful sphere, far newer than its biological and geological cousins. Should human societies collapse or go extinct, the technosphere will become derelict and begin to rapidly decay. Shorn of fuel and humans, its animating forces will disappear. Its long-term effects on the planet are ultimately unpredictable, although they could result in global shifts comparable with giant planetary events of the past (Waters et al. 2014: 16). The technosphere's potential evanescence as an expanding domain does not, however, imply its physical disappearance. Irrespective of its future development, it will leave its mark permanently in the earth's stratigraphical record, as a thin but rich layer marking an extraordinary efflorescence of creative destruction (Zalasiewicz 2008: 241).

References

"Atlas of Urban Expansion." (http://www.atlasofurbanexpansion.org/).
Baccini, Peter/Brunner, Paul (2012): Metabolism of the anthroposphere: Analysis, evaluation, design, Cambridge, Mass.: MIT Press.
Barles, Sabine (2009): "Urban metabolism of Paris and its region." In: Journal of Industrial Ecology 13/6, 898-912.
Brenner, Neil (ed.) (2014): Implosions/explosions: Towards a study of planetary urbanization, Berlin: Jovis.
Brenner, Neil/Schmid, Christian (2011): "Planetary urbanisation." In: Matthew Gandy (ed.), Urban constellations. Berlin: Jovis, pp. 10-14.
Deleuze, Gilles/Guattari, Félix (1987): A thousand plateaus: Capitalism and schizophrenia, trans. Brian Massumi, Minneapolis: University of Minnesota Press.
Douglas, Ian (2012): Cities: An environmental history, New York: I.B. Tauris.
Doxiadis, C./Papaioannou, J. (1974): Ecumenopolis: The inevitable city of the future. New York: Norton.
Edgeworth, Matt (2018). "Humanly modified ground." In: Dominick DellaSalla/Michael Goldstein (eds.), The encyclopedia of the anthropocene. Volume 1: Geologic History and Energy. Oxford: Elsevier.
Ellis, Erle (2011). "Anthropogenic transformation of the terrestrial biosphere." In: Philosophical Transactions of the Royal Society A 369, pp. 1010-1035.
Ellis, Erle/Goldewijk, Kees Klein/Siebert, Stefan/Lightman, Deborah/Ramankutty, Navin (2010): "Anthropogenic transformation of the biomes, 1700 to 2000." In: Global Ecology and Biogeography 19, pp. 589-606.
Ellis, Erle/Kaplan, Jed O./Fuller, Dorian Q./Vavrus, Steve/Goldewijk, Kees Klein/Verburg, Peter H. (2013): "Used planet: A global history." In: PNAS 110/20, pp. 7978-7985.
Ellul, Jacques (1964): The technological society, trans. John Wilkinson, New York: Vintage.
Fard, Ali (2013): "Dissolving the city: Preliminary notes on spatial ideologies of information and communication technologies." In: MAS Context 18, Summer 2013 (http://www.mascontext.com/tag/ali-fard/).
Gärdebo, Johan/Marzecova, Agata/Knowles, Scott Gabriel (2017): "The orbital technosphere: The provision of meaning and matter by satellites." In: Anthropocene Review 4/1, pp. 44-52.

Haff, Peter (2014): "Humans and technology in the anthropocene: Six rules." In: The Anthropocene Review 1/2, pp. 126-136.

Haff, Peter (2013): "Technology as a geological phenomenon: Implications for human well-being." In: Geological Society of London Special Publications, pp. 301-309.

Ingold, Tim (2007): "Materials against materiality." In: Archaeological Dialogues 14, pp. 1-16.

Kelly, Kevin (2011): What technology wants, London: Penguin.

Lefebvre, Henri (2014): "From the city to urban society." In: Neil Brenner (ed.), Implosions/Explosions: Towards a study of planetary urbanization, Berlin: Jovis, pp. 36-52.

Lefebvre, Henri (2003): The urban revolution, trans. Robert Bononno, Minneapolis: University of Minnesota Press.

Liu, Zhifeng/He, Chunyang/Zhou, Yuyu/Wu, Jianguo (2014): "How much of the world's land has been urbanized, really? A hierarchical framework for avoiding confusion." In: Landscape Ecology 29, pp. 763-771.

Milsum, John H. (1968): "The technosphere, the biosphere, the sociosphere: Their systems modeling and optimiziation." In: IEEE Spectrum 5/6, pp. 76-82.

Montgomery, David (2012): Dirt: The erosion of civilizations, Berkeley: University of California Press.

Morton, Oliver (2016): The planet remade: How geoengineering could change the world, Princeton: Princeton University Press.

Nicholson, Max (1968). Handbook to the conservation section of the international biological programme, London: Conservation of Terrestrial Biological Communities.

Odling-Smee, John/Laland, Kevin/Feldman, Marcus (2003): Niche construction: The neglected process in evolution, Princeton: Princeton University Press.

Otter, Chris (2017): "Encapsulation: Inner worlds and their discontents." In: Journal of Literature and Science 10/2, pp. 55-66.

Passerini, Pietro (1984): "The ascent of the anthropostrome: A point of view on the man-made environment." In: Environmental Geology of Water Sciences 6/4, pp. 211-221.

Rockström, Johan/Klum, Mattias (2015): Big world, small planet: Abundance within planetary boundaries, London: Yale University Press.

Schleper, Simone (2016): "Perspectives and politics: A co-evolutionary reflection." In: Anthropocene Curriculum (https://www.anthropocene-curriculum.org/pages/root/campus-2016/co-evolutionary-perspectives-on-the-technosphere/perspectives-and-politics-a-co-evolutionary-reflection/).

Scott, James C. (2017): Against the grain: A deep history of the earliest states, New Haven: Yale University Press.

Smil, Vaclav (1994): Energy in world history, Boulder: Westview Press, 1994.

Wachsmuth, David (2012): "Three ecologies: Urban metabolism and the society-nature opposition." In: The Sociological Quarterly 53/4, pp. 506-523.
Waters, Colin/Zalasiewicz, Jan/Williams, Mark/Ellis, Michael/Snelling, Andrea (2014): "A stratigraphical basis for the anthropocene?" In: Colin Waters/ Jan Zalasiewicz/Mark Williams/Michael Ellis/Andrea Snelling (eds.), A stratigraphical basis for the anthropocene, London: Geological Society Special Publications.
Will, Steffen/Grinewald, Jacques/Crutzen, Paul/McNeil, John (2011): "The anthropocene: Conceptual and historical perspectives." In: Philosophical Transactions of the Royal Society A 369, pp. 842-867.
Williams, Mark/Zalasiewicz, Jan/Haff, P.K./Schwägerl, Christian/Bardosky, Anthony D./Ellis, Erle C. (2015): "The anthropocene biosphere." In: Anthropocene Review 2/3, pp. 196-219.
Williams, Mark/Zalasiewicz, Jan/Waters, Collin/Landing, Ed (eds.) (2013): Is the fossil record of complex animal behaviour a stratigraphical analogue for the anthropocene? London: Geological Society Special Publications.
Wrangham, Richard (2009): Catching fire: How cooking made us human, New York: Basic Books.
Zalasiewicz, Jan (2008): The earth after us: What legacy will humans leave in the rocks? Oxford: Oxford University Press.
Zalasiewicz, Jan et al. (2017): "Scale and diversity of the physical technosphere: a geological perspective." In: Anthropocene Review 4/1, pp. 9-22.
Zalasiewicz, Jan et al. (2016): "The geological cycle of plastics and their use as a stratigraphic indicator of the anthropocene." In: Anthropocene 13, pp. 4-17.
Zalasciewicz, Jan/Waters, Colin/Williams, Mark (2014): "Human bioturbation, and the subterranean landscape of the anthropocene." In: Anthropocene 6, pp. 3-9.

Socio-Natural Sites

Verena Winiwarter and Martin Schmid

The Edinburgh Philosophical Society regularly published *Proceedings of Societies* in their quarterly journal. In the issue of January 1862, the Botanical Society of Edinburgh reported on letters from Dr. Hugh Cleghorn, sent during a voyage to Alexandria in Egypt. The differences between his home and the foreign society and landscape heightened Cleghorn's awareness for the intricate web of connections between social practices and the material world, making him an astute observer of the socio-natural sites of Egypt. We can imagine the famous botanist and Indian colonial official in Shepherds' Hotel in Cairo, from where he reported on October 7, 1861.

> Immediately after arrival at Alexandria at daylight on the 5th, we received the astounding intelligence that the Nile had risen to an unusual height two days previously, overflowing the embankments, causing great destruction of life and property, and carrying away many miles of the railway between Alexandria and Cairo. [...] The whole country was flooded often as far as we could see—the usual landmarks for steering were submerged, and here and there we noticed the tops of trees in passing: while near Kafir Zayat we saw part of a railway engine and several carriages standing out of the water. On little islands and small raised embankments were long lines of villagers, with their camels, buffaloes, and sheep, and piles of furniture and goods to the water edge. I have been inquiring of the officials here as to the real state of matters, and am informed that the Nile rose 4½ feet above the usual average. The origin of the catastrophe is said to be the abolition of the establishment for watching the embankments, and whose duty it was to attend to the sluices, and repair any breach without delay. This evening the river is said to have subsided forty inches, so that it is not now more than a foot above the usual height at this season. The great question now is, to obtain an immediate and abundant supply of seed for the next crop; urgent applications have been made to the Pasha, but no reply has as yet been received. [...]
>
> I had opportunity of examining in every tumbler of water the rich deposit of the Nile, which is even more abundant than that of the Ganges in the Delta. From con-

versation in the market-place, I fear that much Egyptian cotton has been destroyed as it was ripening. The public funds have been affected, and the cost of restoring the railway will be very great. [...] I have seen great floods in India, but generally the plains were soaked with rain, which caused the flood; here a vast extent of dry, parched land was inundated with fluid mud—the very edge of the river being hot sand or baked soil of brick-like hardness. The rain evidently falls on the mountains far distant in the interior of Africa. (Cleghorn 1862: 131-132)

The letter, most probably sent from Cleghorn's honeymoon, as he had gotten married in the beginning of August, describes the observation of what we suggested to call a 'socio-natural site' (SNS) in 2008 (Winiwarter/Schmid 2008).

Socio-natural sites are the nexus of human practices on the one hand and their material precipitates and prerequisites called 'arrangements' on the other hand, as we shall discuss in detail below. Cleghorn's letter abounds with descriptions of such sites: he not only engaged in the practice of using a ship for transportation, he astutely observed that the flood had rendered the landmarks for steering invisible. One can see how unwanted changes in the landscape resulting from the river's rise made the practice of shipping more difficult and dangerous. He also describes a train stuck on submerged rails that were probably dangerously undercut by water. This allows us to observe another site where a human practice interacts with a dynamic not intended by humans.

Cleghorn's inquiries into the potential causes of the flood allow the identification of yet another socio-natural site, namely the entire Nile Valley in its human-tampered form. Whatever the reasons were for "the abolition of the establishment for watching the embankments", this organisation apparently had been necessary and useful in dealing with the Nile's changing water flow, and its abandonment led to unwanted effects. This observation is true for all interventions; investments into arrangements result in maintenance requirements that can overtax a society. We also learn of sluices and breaches that need to be repaired quickly, and hence of a socio-natural site involving technological artefacts and on-site material, such as the riverbed. The practice of agriculture has to be adapted to the situation, as Cleghorn understands; seed has to be sown while the nutrient-rich river deposit is still wet, a deposit that comes with the Nile's waters, as he establishes by investigating a water sample.

Not only can we observe Cleghorn observing the Nile at high water, thus giving us an opportunity for a second-order observation, the letter also allows us to understand that socio-natural sites are spatially nested across scales and differ in duration.

An entire river basin can be viewed as one single site for particular practices, such as Integrated River Basin Management; parts of such a basin emerge as a site only temporarily, while humans are using it, e.g. for shipping, or for a longer time, when arrangements of longer duration are built by humans, such as sluices, weirs, barrages or embankments. The concept of socio-natural sites provides an analytical tool for studies of the long-term development of the tight and multiply interwoven connections between human agency and the material realm.

Human Practices and Arrangements

Socio-natural sites are established via human practices. These practices interact with the material world, and are thus subject to natural laws. Insofar as living matter is part of the 'arrangements'—this is the notion used to denote the material parts of a socio-natural site—the development of such a site over time is also subject to evolutionary change.

But let us first define practices. According to Andreas Reckwitz,

> [...] a practice represents a pattern which can be filled out by a multitude of single and often unique actions reproducing the practice (a certain way of consuming goods can be filled out by plenty of actual acts of consumption). The single individual—as a bodily and mental agent—then acts as the 'carrier' ('Träger') of a practice—and, in fact, of many different practices which need not be coordinated with one another. (Reckwitz 2002: 249-250)

Reckwitz then explains that practices are both bodily and mental activities, based on understanding and know-how. A practice is a 'nexus of doings and sayings', understandable not only to the agent or the agents who carry it out, but also understandable to bystanders, at least within the same culture. Practices, in short, are the routinised acts that form the building blocks of everyday life. As bodily acts, practices are carried out at particular places and times. Theodore Schatzki accounts for this fact with the notion of 'social sites', as the places where practices are carried out. For him, history is constituted by the technologically-driven metamorphosis of social sites (Schatzki 2003).

Following Schatzki, we suggested in 2008 to introduce something other than just human-made technology into theories of historical change. We wanted to incorporate the role of intrinsic change of arrangements; they change because they are subject to the laws of physics and—in the case of living entities—to random mutation. The concept of arrangements acknowledges that not everything that happens when a practice is carried out is under societal control. While practices depend on arrangements, they are also restricted by them. Irrigated agriculture in the Nile Valley enabled high yields for millennia, albeit necessitating a tight schedule of planting and harvesting, the maintenance of irrigation infrastructures and yearly re-surveying and demarcation of fields after every flood. Despite those arrangements, agricultural practices in the Nile valley still depended on the process of photosynthesis, which remains beyond human control.

We conceptualise arrangements as the material precipitates of human practices, constantly changing due to changes in these practices. Arrangements are at the same time the prerequisite of practices and shape them via the opportunities they offer and the obstacles they form. Rivers like the Nile resist human practices. Floods, sedimentation, siltation, changing river arms, all pose a considerable challenge to humans, and while the hydrological and morphological specifics might be quite different at different parts of the Nile Valley, the overall pattern is very similar.

Socio-natural sites are not just functional but can be eminently political. Purposive human interventions demand particular attention if arrangements are unstable, but this is not only dreaded. Sites with highly resistant arrangements, such as flood-prone river valleys, offer the potential for groups of human actors to distinguish themselves by overcoming the resistance of 'nature', and so to gain power or at least in social status. Land surveyors, irrigation canal builders, and other proto-engineers are a case in point. Thus, resistance can lead to sites of particular political interest. The Egyptian Pasha and those in his vicinity were certainly such a group. Many 18th and 19th century rulers resorted to the 'conquest of nature' (Blackbourn 2006) to demonstrate their political power. It would be tempting to argue that a ruler's logic would be, "the more resistant the arrangements, the more powerful the lord". Instead, we suggest to emphasise the tendency of all ruling elites to underestimate the challenge of the rivers, mountains, wetlands and other ecosystems they colonise for societal purposes. As Libby Robin (2007) has pointed out, a barren and uninviting continent (Australia) created a nation by giving it the joint purpose of taming the rather unwilling nature. Petra van Dam (2016) has shown how dealing with the material and living world in the water-rich and flood-prone Netherlands had an important bearing on human history, on institutions, organisations, power distribution and conflicts. Rephrased in the terminology suggested here, environmental history abounds with socio-natural sites created and changed for political reasons. The Nile at the very latest became such a political site with President Nasser's prestige project par excellence, the Aswan Dam (Hughes 2000; Blocher 2016).

What Constitutes Socio-Natural Sites?

As we have seen, the concept of socio-natural sites uses two terms to emphasise the co-constructed quality of places. Socio-natural sites are constituted by arrangements and practices.

All practices, for example those of agriculture along the Nile, are embedded in arrangements, namely in the Nile river valley, its river sediment, waters, fields, draught animals, seeds and implements. Practices are bound by arrangements, but also change them. Every agrarian innovation changes human work as well as the fields, meadows or forests in which it takes place.

Ontologically, arrangements are themselves hybrids, in which anthropogenic and non-anthropogenic processes are inextricably interwoven. For analytical purposes, the 'natural' features of the socio-natural arrangements can be defined as those which have not been created by humans and defy full human control. But their hybrid character prevails, not least because all arrangements bear the traces of past practices. Practices and arrangements are always influenced by their precursors. This becomes obvious when one recalls that people inherit changed environments because their ancestors have intervened into them, be it in the form of fields, embankments, sluices, canals, street systems or cities.

Modern humans are not the only species that receive an ecological inheritance. All animals that build dwellings used by more than one generation experience an 'ecological inheritance', rabbit burrows, anthills, termite mounds, and beaver dams being cases in point (cf. Laland et al. 1999; Ellis 2015). While all organisms share niche construction as their capacity to modify sources of natural selection, there remains a difference between termite mounds and human arrangements. Socio-cultural human niche construction is accumulative, with new cultural traits responding to, or building on, earlier cultural traditions, making use of novel ways of transmission of information via language (Laland et al. 2000).

Practices and arrangements are connected via mutual influences. Therefore, the process of history can be understood as a consequence of transformations of socio-natural sites through *co-evolutionary* development.

The concept of the site also draws attention to the fact that observers constitute socio-natural sites by analysing historical incidents and situations. Since the analysis is mostly based on human artefacts, i.e. on materialised and preserved observations made by humans (historical sources), theirs is a second-order observation, an observation of observations. Keeping this in mind makes SNS compatible with constructivist approaches—but more importantly, with the help of such a concept, the question of the role of nature in history can be dealt with on an adequate theoretical level. As practices and arrangements are both hybrids, namely socio-natural hybrids, the dichotomy between nature and culture can be overcome, and actor-oriented and systemic observations can be coupled.

Merits of a Co-Evolutionary Concept

When we first suggested the concept of socio-natural sites, our main concern was to offer alternatives to nature-culture dichotomies and to concepts of hybridity that focus on technology and allow only a marginal role for natural processes. For us, structure and agency, cause and effect, are best understood as dialectical. This is in line with practice theory that aims for transcending the dualism of structure and agency. But while human agency and social structure are seen as mutually co-constructed (Sovacool/Hess 2017), most practice theory disregards nature's role in history.

As effects can become causes over time, the difference between agency and structure is dependent on the time of observation. However, this leaves open how interactions between entities beyond full human control (i.e. arrangements) and human practices, the focus of environmental history, should be conceptualised. As these entities are often called 'nature', Nature, natures, or nature, with a counterpart in culture, the relation between socio-natural sites and co-evolution merits attention.

The Trouble with Nature in Environmental Historiography

Environmental history has problematised the attribution of power to nature, cast in questions such as whether nature has 'agency', i.e. actor status, or whether it should better be understood as part of structures. This remains controversial.

Braudel, for example, whose concepts have been very influential in European historiography, counts nature among the structures in the form of 'longue durée' (Braudel 1960). The question of whether nature should be conceptualised as structure, as 'actant' (Latour 1996) or actor leads to a critique of the concept of the dualism of structure and action: structures are always both medium and result of social action, just as external nature is always both result and a limiting medium of social action (Giddens 1979).

Nature is a medium, since it permits certain actions, but prevents others. Nature is a result because it can only be produced if it is processed as a medium of social action (Groß 2006: 98). Reacting to this dialectic, environmental historian Linda Nash suggests that the narratives of environmental history should emphasise that human intentions do not emerge in a vacuum, that ideas are often not clearly separated or separable from actions, and that human agency cannot be separated from the environment in which it develops. "Human history", as John McNeill (2003: 6) has put it, "has always and will always unfold within a larger biological and physical context, and that context evolves in its own right". The concept of SNS focuses on the changing relationship between this 'larger context' and humans. Humans are not the motors of history, but partners in a communicative process with living and inanimate nature in which the conditions of existence are negotiated (Nash 2005).

Such considerations should not overlook an initial condition: Nature in environmental historiography—as ecological, biological, chemical and physical processes as well as landscape morphology, climate, soil, weather etc.—is set as a powerful explanandum for historical processes. Only if this setting process is not disclosed, does the question of the arbitrariness of essentialised 'nature' arise (Winiwarter/Knoll 2007: 13; cf. also Nash 2005). Environmental history pays attention to and declares natural processes as a narrative and explanandum. A dialectical approach allows tackling the question of the nature of nature. As environmental historians, we tend to accept that all humans exist in and as fundamental nature, which is not at our disposal, allowing at the same time that all nature is socially constructed. Whoever wants to explore nature or social action in nature must consider and make explicit the normative elements of his or her own position (Steinberg 2002: XI), i.e. epistemologically recognise and address the role of the scholarly observer.

SNS as a Bridging Concept to Ecology and Evolution

Focussing on practices rather than 'culture' makes SNS compatible with practice theory; focussing on arrangements rather than 'nature' or 'technology' allows for embracing the hybridity of the material world as composed of living and non-living matter and resulting in as well as influencing human practices. We suggested four 'modes', through which SNS would be constituted, namely *perception, representation* in symbolic terms, *programs* and *work*. Those engaged in practices create effects on the material world via work, what they do depends on their aims (programs), these in turn are the result of representations (e.g. in language, diagrams or maps) of what they perceive via their senses. Perception is a prerequisite for symbolic renderings of those perceptions, which are a prerequisite for the formulation of cultural programs on how to interact with the material world. The interaction itself must involve energy to have a material effect. SNS were mapped via these four modes onto the paradigm of the Vienna School of Social Ecology, an analytical, system-driven approach focussing on nature-society interactions (Fischer-Kowalski/Erb 2016)—and thus reproducing the nature-culture divide.

We soon shifted our focus towards the biological sciences, linking SNS to co-evolution, a path that seemed to support our communicative interest in becoming conversant with (historical) ecology. The cornerstone concept of the 'ecosystem', comprising living and non-living matter and made up of niches constructed by organisms and creating an ecological inheritance for them (Ellis 2015) is largely compatible with SNS. One can conceptualise niches as arrangements created and maintained by practices as well as influencing these practices. Their interaction can be described as construction of socio-natural niches, distinguished and delineated for analytical purposes as site-specific sets of practices and arrangements by scholarly observers.

Ecosystems are Governed by Biological Evolution

Recently, environmental historians have come to embrace an evolutionary approach for conceptualising the interactions between humans and other species. Edmund Russell (2003; 2011) has argued in his 'evolutionary history' that human history has to include the genetic evolution of non-human species during historical times and not just as a feature of the distant past. He draws his readers' attention to animal and microbial pests, which become resistant to the application of pesticides over time, he reminds us that domestication and breeding, along with the inadvertent zoonoses are long-term features of human co-evolution, as are plant breeding, and agents causing human diseases, even epidemics. We suggest combining these valuable insights with niche construction (Winiwarter/Groß 2015) to allow for not just evolutionary, but also ecological inheritances and co-evolutionary developments.

One way to combine evolution and ecology with human history is the conceptual framework of the 'ecological niche'. It enables to draw attention to the legacies human practices create when they intervene into ecosystems. Kevin Laland, Marcus Feldman and John Odling-Smee (1999) proposed 'cultural niche construction' as a universal principle of all species. Niches such as termite mounds or rabbit burrows form an ecological inheritance, a modification of the environment over very long periods, which impacts evolution. This is true also for the human species. Because niches can profoundly change the environment, they play an eminent role in human history. They generate 'lock-in effects' which change the relative probability of different future options for a population. Irrigated agriculture as in ancient Egypt is a case in point.

Socio-ecological niches are not just arrangements. Like the latter they have a bearing on practices, but they are also mirrored in the symbolic realm, as struggle over interpretative dominance or as competing epistemologies in the cultural construction of resources. Richard White's 'middle ground' describes an instance of competitive construction of resources between indigenous peoples and the European colonisers in the Great Plains (White 2011 [1991]).

As things stand now, our focus has both become more precise and slightly, but importantly shifted. We see SNS as a hinge concept between evolutionary ecology and history, as a contribution to a non-dichotomous perspective on interactions between humans and the rest of the world, paraphrasing Beinart and Coates' (1995) notion. But it is more than a mere bridging concept.

Arrangements and their Legacies

In a world of hybrids, SNS's main contribution lies in enabling a taxonomy of arrangements and the long-term changes in practices ('legacies') they bring about (cf. for the following paragraph Winiwarter et al. 2016). Arrangements can be categorised according to the character of the legacies they create. As arrangements consist of matter, the qualities of the materials used for a particular arrangement influence how practices will impinge on an arrangement. All matter is subject to natural laws, in particular to the laws of thermodynamics. While evolution leads to the intrinsic dynamics of living entities, the interplay between energy, exergy, dissipation and entropy causes the dynamics of inanimate arrangements. The resulting dynamic is usually called 'wear and tear'. The following table was originally developed with arrangements to harvest exergy in mind. Exergy is "the maximum work that could theoretically be done by a system as it approaches thermodynamic equilibrium with its surroundings, reversibly. Thus, exergy is effectively equivalent to potential work […], it is what most people mean when they speak of 'energy'" (Ayres/Warr 2005: 185-186). The more exergy is harvested, the more problems of wear and tear are to be expected for the arrangement. While a wooden mill wheel can be left to disintegrate without creating severe problems, leaving a nuclear reactor alone after its working life would have disastrous consequences, as wear and tear would play out on energy-rich material.

We suggest that legacies can be benign, problematic, or wicked. Hence, arrangements are wicked when they have a very long lasting legacy, in principle indefinitely long. What does indefinitely long mean? The half-life of plutonium is ca. 24.100 years. After this time, half of the plutonium is still there. Plutonium is a dangerous, pyrophoric heavy metal, not just intensely radioactive, but very poisonous. It therefore creates wicked legacies.

Exergy-rich arrangements also tend to need a lot of maintenance. The more energy society needs to invest not only into erecting an arrangement, but also into maintaining it and into dealing with its legacies, the more wicked it should be considered. More effort goes into coping with these legacies than into the original cause. Because they are so long-lasting and so difficult to deal with, the burden is shifted unequally between the builders and users on the one hand and the inheriting generations on the other. Different types of legacies have different power to transform society. Wicked legacies, because they bind society to deal with them over very long periods, transform society. A society having created a nuclear legacy has to protect it from proliferating, and one can clearly see how this transforms society. A case in point are the international politics towards Iran or Pakistan, both countries striving to or already having a nuclear industry, albeit under difficult political circumstances.

For environmental historians, it is important to understand that transformations, both those occurring thermodynamically or by biological evolution, and those humans bring about characterise the present situation. We are not living, as we might wish, in a stable world, but in a situation of great and accelerating dynamic, caused mainly by the abundance of fossil and nuclear energy. In such a situation, no single discipline has the key to address the drivers and dynamics of change adequately. We have to work together and socio-natural sites were proposed to serve as a bridging concept to foster such collaboration.

Table 1: Arrangements and their Legacies

Characteristics	Arrangements with short-lived legacies	Arrangements with stable, long-lived legacies	Arrangements with transformative legacies
Type of Legacy	Benign	Problematic	Wicked
Longevity of Legacy	Short	Middle	Long (indefinitely)
Maintenance requirements	Low	Middle	High
Energy expenditure centred on	Production	Production and Maintenance	Maintenance
Exergy harvest density	Low	Middle	High
Transformative Potential (Impact on practices)	Local, Sectoral	Local, Regional, Sectoral (one or several)	Societal, global

© Winiwarter/Schmid 2016: 164

Uses of the Concept

In our first publication, we used SNS to re-interpret an early modern agricultural textbook (Winiwarter/Schmid 2008). Thereafter, our research focussed on more 'watery' topics, namely the Danube (Schmid 2009; Winiwarter et al. 2013; Hohensinner et al. 2013; Haidvogl et al. 2018), and on other regulated rivers (Winiwarter et al. 2016). For roughly a decade, with few exceptions (Gingrich et al. 2013), we used SNS mainly to write river histories, particularly in the urban context of Vienna and with a long-term approach covering several centuries.

Consequentially, SNS met most resonance among scholars with similar interests, be it for floods on the Ohio river (Lübken 2014: 10-11), water policy and management in 20th century Czechoslovakia and Romania (Štanzel 2017: 36-37), small (Zumbrägel 2018: 49) or larger hydropower facilities in rivers (Schoder 2018). Coteli (2015: 170) referred to SNS to reconstruct what he calls the 'destruction' of the riverine landscape of the city of Kayseri in the late Ottoman period.

Apart from our own work, so far, SNS were used most intensively at TU Darmstadt, where the concept provided a common terminology for an interdisciplinary research programme in urban and sustainability studies (Engels et al. 2017: 9), again with a special interest in urban waterbodies (Toyka-Seid 2017). Recently, Dieter Schott and co-editors of a volume on urban-environmental history referenced SNS to elucidate the seeming paradox that cities change nature and are nature at the same time. In their perspective, SNS is an approach to "study historical transformations [...] in a way that avoids merely anthropocentric or naturalistic notions while acknowledging the dialectic nature of all transformation processes" (Soens et al. 2019: 8).

As a bridging concept, SNS has proven useful also in other disciplinary communities. The river geomorphologist Peter Ashmore (2015) refers to SNS to argue for what he calls a 'sociogeomorphology' of rivers. On a similar line of thinking, but from the historians' side, the concept has been applied to encompass processes of coastal erosion (De Freitas/Dias 2017). A group of environmental engineers found SNS useful to plead for a focus on the linkages between biophysical and social aspects "to better anticipate the possible future co-evolution of water systems and society" (Ceola et al. 2016). Geographers, in their pursuit to integrate the human with the physical branch of their field, have welcomed SNS as a tool to conceptualise the systemic relations between humans and the environment (von Elverfeldt/Egner 2015).

In environmental history, SNS has been applied to other than aquatic topics, too. Martin Knoll (2013) has taken up the concept and further developed it for an environmental history of Early Modern topographies. Knoll uses SNS for a thorough critique of his source type. The result is a major methodological achievement that does justice to the epistemic interests of environmental history, reconstructing historical perceptions as well as environmental realities of the past. Hahn (2014: 50), who studied early modern agricultural textbooks, focused on our initial idea of different modes (labour, programmes, perception and representation) that constitute the nexus of practices and arrangements (Winiwarter/Schmid 2008: 161-163). Our own work with similar sources on past perceptions of fluvial environments as SNS (Andraschek-Holzer/Schmid 2012) has refrained from doing so. The concept was also applied to saltworks by Martin Knoll (2016), limestone quarries (Haumann 2016), earthquakes in Italian cities (*Parrinello* 2015: 6), and for an environmental history of the Austrian Alps as they have been transformed by winter tourism (Groß 2019). Dominik Collet's recent study on European famines in the early 1770s consistently uses the German term "sozio-naturaler Schauplatz"

(Collet 2018: 18; 308) in a very similar meaning but without direct reference to our work.

Richard Hoffmann (2014) related to SNS to write his comprehensive environmental history of medieval Europe, a history that "brings the natural world into the story as an agent and object"; history occurs locally in distinct socio-natural sites while being also shaped by larger forces (Hoffmann 2014: 3-11; 372-376). Other medievalists employed SNS to reflect on the role of different forms of energy in water history and to make the point that the human body has an essential role in all socio-natural histories (Smith 2018: 15), both as performer of practices and as an element of the biophysical arrangements. Christoph Sonnlechner (2010) approached Vienna and its hinterland as a socio-natural site to reconstruct flows of wood into the medieval city and to explain conflicts over this key resource.

The concept was developed to observe and analyse changes in the material and biophysical world while emphasising, as explained above, that all historiography is second-order observation. Scholars from environmental humanities, ecocriticism in particular, have used this insight in their ways to adopt SNS (Bergthaller 2015: 22), and re-read, for example, 19th century novels as observations and descriptions of past socio-natural sites (Kneitz 2015; Kneitz 2016).

Conclusions

All these works, as diverse as they are in disciplinary terms, have in common that they appreciate SNS as a hybrid concept. Almost 25 years after Richard White's (1995) *Organic Machine*, there is obviously still an intellectual demand for conceptual tools that support radical hybrid thinking, in environmental history and beyond. As this review demonstrates, SNS have been proven useful to foster the inclusion of what usually is excluded in established disciplinary views. Broadly speaking, SNS helps to consider the 'other', being society and culture in the case of natural scientists and engineers, and nature in the case of historians and other humanities' scholars. SNS, like any other conceptual tool, aims to change the way we look at the world and how we communicate across disciplinary boundaries.

The concept has also proven fruitful in academic teaching. We have employed SNS to organise environmental history courses bridging continents (Oliveira/ Schmid 2011), students have successfully completed Master- and PhD-thesis in environmental history based on SNS under our supervision (Neundlinger 2011; Pollack 2012; Spitzbart-Glasl 2014; Veichtlbauer 2015; Schneckenleithner 2018; Schoder 2018) and at other universities (Mevissen 2013; Arrigoni Martelli 2015).

While socio-natural hybridity has so far been the core reason for many scholars to use SNS, two other features of the concept might deserve to be further elaborated and linked to each other: co-evolution and legacies. Peter Coates (2016: 152) recently told the story of a place near Denver, Colorado as that of a socio-natural site where plutonium was produced for nuclear weapons. Our world is laced with thousands of such nuclear and other scars and wounds (Storm 2014), among them post-mining sites that will constrain all life on earth deep into the future (Winiwarter/Schmid 2018). Socio-natural arrangements creating wicked legacies of transformative power emerged from co-evolutionary processes. Their existence might change co-evolution itself. To write meaningful environmental histories today, we probably need to better conceive of history as a co-evolutionary process, as the co-evolution of socio-natural sites.

References

Andraschek-Holzer, Ralph/Schmid, Martin (2012): "Umweltgeschichte und Topographische Ansichten: Zur Transformation eines österreichischen Donau-Abschnitts in der Neuzeit." In: Mitteilungen des Instituts für Österreichische Geschichtsforschung 120/1, pp. 80-115.
Arrigoni Martelli, Cristina (2015): Ducks and deer, profit and pleasure: Hunters, game and the natural landscapes of medieval Italy. PhD Thesis, Toronto: York University.
Ashmore, Peter (2015): "Towards a sociogeomorphology of rivers." In: Geomorphology 251, pp. 149-156.
Ayres, Robert U./Warr, Benjamin (2005): "Accounting for growth: The role of physical work." In: Structural Change and Economic Dynamics 16, pp. 181-209.
Bergthaller, Hannes (2015): "'No more eternal than the hills of the poets': On Rachel Carson, environmentalism, and the paradox of nature." In: Interdisciplinary Studies in Literature and Environment 22/1, pp. 9-26.
Blackbourn, David (2006): The conquest of nature: Water, landscape, and the making of modern Germany, London: Jonathan Cape.
Beinart, William/Coates, Peter (1995): Environment and history: The taming of nature in the USA and South Africa, London/New York: Routledge.
Blocher, Ewald (2016): Der Wasserbau-Staat: Die Transformation des Nils und das moderne Ägypten 1882–1971, Paderborn: Ferdinand Schöningh.
Braudel, Fernand (1960): "History and the social sciences: The long duration." In: American Behavioral Scientist 3/6, pp. 3-13.
Ceola, Serena, et al. (2016): "Adaptation of water resources systems to changing society and environment: A statement by the International Association of Hydrological Sciences." In: Hydrological Sciences Journal 61/16, pp. 2803-2817.
Cleghorn, Hugh (1862): "Extracts from letters written during a voyage to Alexandria." In: The Edinburgh Philosophical Journal 15/1, pp. 130-132.

Coates, Peter (2016): "'Get lost in the footnotes of history': The restorative afterlife of Rocky Flats, Colorado." In: Marion Hourdequin/David G. Havlick (eds.), Restoring Layered Landscapes: History, Ecology and Culture, New York: Oxford University Press, pp. 133-159.

Collet, Dominik (2018): Die doppelte Katastrophe: Klima und Kultur in der europäischen Hungerkrise 1770-1772, Göttingen: Vandenhoeck & Ruprecht.

Coteli, Methiye Gul (2015): "Urban environmental history of an Anatolian city: Destroying the riverscape of Kayseri." In: Athens Journal of Mediterranean Studies 1/2, pp. 169-186.

De Freitas, Joana Gaspar/Dias, João Alveirinho (2017): "A historical view on coastal erosion: The case of Furadouro (Portugal)." In: Environment and History 23/2, pp. 217-252.

Ellis, Erle C. (2015): "Ecology in an anthropogenic biosphere." In: Ecological Monographs 85/3, pp. 287-331.

Engels, Jens Ivo/Janich, Nina/Monstadt, Jochen/Schott, Dieter (2017): "Einleitung: Städte auf dem Weg zur nachhaltigen Entwicklung." In: Jens Ivo Engels/Nina Janich/Jochen Monstadt/Dieter Schott (eds.), Nachhaltige Stadtentwicklung: Infrastrukturen, Akteure, Diskurse, Frankfurt a.M./New York: Campus, pp. 7-25.

Fischer-Kowalski, Marina/Erb, Karl-Heinz (2016): "Core Concepts and Heuristics." In: Helmut Haberl/Marina Fischer-Kowalski/Fridolin Krausmann/Verena Winiwarter (eds.), Social ecology: Society-nature relations across time and space, Cham: Springer, pp. 29-61.

Giddens, Anthony (1979): Central problems in social theory, London: Palgrave.

Gingrich, Simone/Schmid, Martin/Gradwohl, Markus/Krausmann, Fridolin (2013): "How material and energy flows change socio-natural arrangements: The transformation of agriculture in the Eisenwurzen region, 1860-2000." In: Simron J. Singh/Helmut Haberl/Marian Chertow/Michael Mirtl/Martin Schmid (eds.), Long term socio-ecological research: Studies in society-nature interactions across spatial and temporal scales, Dordrecht: Springer, pp. 297-313.

Groß, Matthias (2006): Natur, Bielefeld: transcript.

Groß, Robert (2019): Die Beschleunigung der Berge: Eine Umweltgeschichte des Wintertourismus in Vorarlberg/Österreich (1920-2010), Cologne: Böhlau.

Hahn, Philip (2014): "Nutz, Pflicht und Vergnügen: Umweltwahrnehmung im europäischen Landwirtschaftsschrifttum des 16. und 17. Jahrhunderts." In: Manfred Jakubowski-Tiessen (ed.), Von Amtsgärten und Vogelkojen: Beiträge zum Göttinger Umwelthistorischen Kolloquium 2011-2012, Göttingen: Universitätsverlag, pp. 49-65.

Haidvogl, Gertrud/Winiwarter, Verena/Dressel, Gert/Gierlinger, Sylvia/Hauer, Friedrich/Hohensinner, Severin/Pollack, Gudrun/Spitzbart-Glasl, Christina/

Raith, Erich (2018): "Urban waters and the development of Vienna between 1683 and 1910." In: Environmental History 23/4, pp. 721-747.

Haumann, Sebastian (2016): "Konkurrenz um Kalkstein: Rohstoffsicherung der Montanindustrie und die Dynamik räumlicher Relationen um 1900." In: Jahrbuch für Wirtschaftsgeschichte/Economic History Yearbook 57/1, pp. 29-58.

Hoffmann, Richard (2014): An environmental history of medieval Europe, Cambridge: Cambridge University Press.

Hughes, J. Donald (2000): "The dams at Aswan: Does environmental history inform decisions?" In: Capitalism Nature Socialism 11/4, pp. 73-81.

Kneitz, Agnes (2016): "Pfister's spill? Narratives of failure in and around Wilhelm Raabe's 1883 Eco-novel." In: Ecozon@: European Journal of Literature, Culture and Environment 7/1, pp. 176-196.

Kneitz, Agnes (2015): "'As if the river was not meat and drink to you!': Social novels as a means of framing nineteenth-century environmental justice." In: Interdisciplinary Studies in Literature and Environment 22/1, pp. 47-62.

Knoll, Martin (2016): "Salzregionen: Der sozionaturale Schauplatz Bergbau in der topografischen Beschreibung der Frühen Neuzeit." In: Jahrbuch für Wirtschaftsgeschichte/Economic History Yearbook 57/1, pp. 143-167.

Knoll, Martin (2013): Die Natur der menschlichen Welt: Siedlung, Territorium und Umwelt in der historisch-topografischen Literatur der Frühen Neuzeit, Bielefeld: transcript.

Laland, Kevin N./Odling-Smee, F. John/Feldman, Marcus W. (2000): "Niche construction, biological evolution, and cultural change." In: Behavioral and brain sciences 23, pp. 131-175.

Laland, Kevin N./Odling-Smee, F. John/Feldman, Marcus W. (1999): "Evolutionary consequences of niche construction and their implications for ecology." In: Proceedings of the National Academy of Sciences 96/18, pp. 10242-10247.

Latour Bruno (1996): "On Actor-network-theory." In: Soziale Welt 47, pp. 369-381.

Lübken, Uwe (2014): Die Natur der Gefahr: Überschwemmungen am Ohio River im 19. und 20. Jahrhundert, Göttingen: Vandenhoeck & Ruprecht.

Mevissen, Robert S. (2013): Dynastic devotion and the Danube: Natural identities in the Habsburg Monarchy. Master Thesis, Washington, D.C.: Georgetown University.

Nash, Linda (2005): "The agency of nature or the nature of agency?" In: Environmental History 10/1, pp. 67-69.

Neundlinger, Michael (2011): Stadt-Fluss-Beziehungen als hybride Geschichte: Die Wiener Donau als sozionaturaler Schauplatz, 1700-1890, Master Thesis, Vienna: Alpen-Adria-Universität Klagenfurt.

Oliveira, Rogerio Ribeiro de/Schmid, Martin (2011): "Bridging continents in teaching environmental history: Rio de Janeiro and Vienna. Construyendo puentes entre continentes en la enseñanza de la historia ambiental: Rio de Janeiro y

Vienna." In: HALAC. Historia Ambiental Latinoamericana y Caribeña 1/1, pp. 74-85.

Parrinello, Giacomo (2015): Fault lines: Earthquakes and urbanism in modern Italy, New York/Oxford: Berghahn.

Pollack, Gudrun (2012): Verschmutzt – Verbaut – Vergessen: Eine Umweltgeschichte des Wienflusses von 1780 bis 1910. Master Thesis, Vienna: Alpen-Adria-Universität Klagenfurt.

Reckwitz, Andreas (2002): "Toward a theory of social practices: A development in culturalist theorizing." In: European Journal of Social Theory 5/2, pp. 243-263.

Robin, Libby (2007): How a continent created a nation, Sydney: University of New South Wales Press.

Russell, Edmund (2011): Evolutionary history: Uniting history and biology to understand life on earth, New York: Cambridge University Press.

Russell, Edmund (2003): "Evolutionary history: Prospectus for a new field." In: Environmental History 8/2, pp. 204-228.

Schatzki, Theodore R. (2003): "Nature and technology in history." In: History and Theory, Theme Issue 42, pp. 82-93.

Schmid, Martin (2009): "Die Donau als sozionaturaler Schauplatz: Ein konzeptueller Entwurf für umwelthistorische Studien in der Frühen Neuzeit." In: Sophie Ruppel/Aline Steinbrecher (eds.), Die Natur ist überall bei uns: Mensch und Natur in der Frühen Neuzeit, Basel: chronos, pp. 59-79.

Schneckenleithner, Clara (2018): Segenspendende Thermen und der Skiabfahrt dienende Berge: Tourismus und Umwelt in Bad Hofgastein im langen 20. Jahrhundert. Master Thesis, Vienna: Alpen-Adria-Universität Klagenfurt.

Schoder, Angelika (2018): Flow Regimes: The nature of Austrian hydropower, technical expertise, and environmental discourses in the twentieth century. PhD Thesis, Vienna: Alpen-Adria-Universität Klagenfurt.

Smith, James L. (2018): "Medieval water energies: Philosophical, hydro-social, and intellectual." In: Open Library of Humanities 4/2/28, pp. 1-27.

Soens, Tim/Dieter Schott/Michael Toyka-Seid/Bert De Munck (eds.) (2019): Urbanizing nature: Actors and agency (dis)connecting cities and nature since 1500, New York: Routledge.

Sonnlechner, Christoph (2010): "Bürger und Wald: Überlegungen zur Nutzung von Wiener Bürgerspitalwäldern im Mittelalter." In: Jahrbuch des Vereins für Geschichte der Stadt Wien 66, pp. 223-255.

Sovacool, Benjamin K./Hess, David J. (2017): "Ordering theories: Typologies and conceptual frameworks for sociotechnical change." In: Social Studies of Science 47/5, pp. 703-750.

Spitzbart-Glasl, Christina (2014): Kraftwerke, Flussbäder und Hochwässer: Eine Umweltgeschichte des mittleren Kamp ab 1890. Master Thesis, Vienna: Alpen-Adria-Universität Klagenfurt.

Štanzel, Arnošt (2017): Wasserträume und Wasserräume im Staatssozialismus: Ein umwelthistorischer Vergleich anhand der tschechoslowakischen und rumänischen Wasserwirtschaft 1948-1989, Göttingen: Vandenhoeck & Ruprecht.

Steinberg, Ted (2002): Down to earth: Nature's role in American history, New York: Oxford University Press.

Storm, Anna (2014): Post-industrial landscape scars, New York: Palgrave.

Toyka-Seid, Michael (2017): "Sichtbares Wasser in Mainz und Wiesbaden: Vom städtischen Umgang mit einer umstrittenen Ressource im ökologischen Zeitalter, 1970-2000." In: Jens Ivo Engels/Nina Janich/Jochen Monstadt/Dieter Schott (eds.), Nachhaltige Stadtentwicklung: Infrastrukturen, Akteure, Diskurse, Frankfurt a.M.: Campus, pp. 75-97.

van Dam, Petra J. E. M (2016): "An amphibious culture: Coping with floods in the Netherlands." In: Peter Coates/David Moon/Paul Warde, (eds.), Local places, global processes: Histories of environmental change in Britain and beyond, Oxford: Windgather Press, pp. 78-93.

Veichtlbauer, Ortrun (2015): Natur als Politikum: Beiträge zu einer österreichischen Umweltgeschichte. PhD Thesis, Vienna: Alpen-Adria-Universität Klagenfurt.

von Elverfeldt, Kirsten/Egner, Heike (2015): "Systemtheorien und Mensch-Umwelt-Forschung: Eine geographische Perspektive." In: Pascal Goeke/Roland Lippuner/Johannes Wirths (eds.), Konstruktion und Kontrolle: Zur Raumordnung sozialer Systeme, Wiesbaden: Springer VS, pp. 319-342.

White, Richard (2011) [1991]: The middle ground: Indians, empires, and republics in the Great Lakes Region, 1650-1815. Twentieth Anniversary Edition, New York: Cambridge University Press.

White, Richard (1995): The Organic Machine: The remaking of the Columbia River, New York: Hill and Wang.

Winiwarter, Verena/Gross, Robert (2015): "Commodifying snow, taming the waters: Socio-ecological niche construction in an Alpine village." In: Water History 7/4, pp. 489-509.

Winiwarter, Verena/Haidvogl, Gertrud/Hohensinner, Severin/Hauer, Friedrich/Bürkner, Michael (2016): "The long-term evolution of urban waters and their nineteenth century transformation in European cities: A comparative environmental history." In: Water History 8/3, pp. 209-233.

Winiwarter, Verena/Knoll, Martin (2007): Umweltgeschichte: Eine Einführung, Cologne/Weimar/Vienna: Böhlau.

Winiwarter, Verena/Schmid, Martin (2018): "Archäologie der fossil-nuklearen Gesellschaft als Zukunftsaufgabe." In: Jörg Drauschke/Ewald Kislinger/Karin Kühtreiber/Thomas Kühtreiber/Gabriele Scharrer-Liška/Tivadar Vida (eds.), Lebenswelten zwischen Archäologie und Geschichte: Festschrift für Falko

Daim zu seinem 65. Geburtstag (= Monographien des Römisch-Germanischen Zentralmuseums 150), Mainz: Verlag des Römisch-Germanischen Zentralmuseums, pp. 581-592.

Winiwarter, Verena/Schmid, Martin (2008): "Umweltgeschichte als Untersuchung sozionaturaler Schauplätze? Ein Versuch, Johannes Colers 'Oeconomia' umwelthistorisch zu interpretieren." In: Thomas Knopf (ed.), Umweltverhalten in Geschichte und Gegenwart, Tübingen: Attempto, pp. 158-173.

Winiwarter, Verena/Schmid, Martin/Dressel, Gert (2013): "Looking at half a millennium of co-existence: The Danube in Vienna as a socio-natural site." In: Water History 5/2, pp. 101-119.

Zumbrägel, Christian (2018): 'Viele Wenige machen ein Viel': Eine Technik- und Umweltgeschichte der Kleinwasserkraft (1880-1930), Paderborn: Ferdinand Schöningh.

Materiality and Practice Theory

Sebastian Haumann

'Materiality' is a key term of current theoretical debates in the humanities and social sciences. However, 'materiality' refers to a whole array of diverse research questions and theoretical stances rather than to a clearly defined concept. In the broadest sense, it relates to how organisms, things and matter are deployed to shape social phenomena. The notion emphasises that these material entities might be configured by human actors, but that their properties have powers in and of themselves that unfold beyond human control. As such, materiality is central to urban-environmental history interested in issues such as the provision and consumption of resources, the construction and configuration of the built environment and infrastructural networks, or urban pollution and ecosystems. All of these clearly are the result of human activities but their effects and dynamics do not necessarily conform to human intentions. Therefore, the debate on materiality is of great importance for issues of urban-environmental history.

The impact of material factors on the development of cities and urbanisation is by no means a new topic in historical research. Prominently, Fernand Braudel (1972 [1949]) already stressed the importance of topography, ecosystems and climate for urban development. However, over the last two decades our understanding of materiality has become more complex as theoretical deliberations, inspired by such diverse approaches as Material Culture Studies, Actor-Network Theory, New Materialism or Praxeology, have been applied to urban-environmental history. Whereas material factors were traditionally understood as the preset framework of a more or less static world in which social development would unfold, the current debate emphasises the co-evolution of social and environmental change in both a cultural and material sense (Winiwarter/Knoll 2007: 131-143). The debate has moved from simple interactionist models, in which material objects and social phenomena were neatly demarcated, to concepts in which environmental and social dynamics are inextricably intertwined. Across the different theoretical contexts in which materiality is currently discussed, the term is used to delineate the complex reciprocal *relationships* between organisms, things, matter and social phenomena (Smith 2018; Knoll 2014).

In studies on urban-environmental history, the notion of materiality has been adopted to analyse the co-evolution of social and environmental development in regard to a multitude of objects of investigation. The first part of this chapter gives a brief overview over the field and places the different strands of research within their respective theoretical contexts. It will focus on the main points of contestation, in particular those related to the distribution of agency and power. While the breadth of research reflects the loose definition of materiality and the variety of theoretical perspectives, the second part of this chapter sets out to sketch in more detail a conceptual approach to materiality that has emerged from praxeology. I propose that making past practices the unit of research will facilitate the empirical analysis of those nexuses in which organisms, things and matter are concretely enmeshed with social phenomena. As the debate on materiality is still ongoing, the praxeological approach sketched here might prove useful for research in urban-environmental history, although it is evident that there remain many unresolved challenges in coming to terms with materiality.

The Powers of Materiality

As with many questions in the field of urban-environmental history, the challenge to overcome the dichotomy of the 'city' opposed to 'nature' has been the starting point for deliberations on materiality (Melosi 2010). In the 2000s, the term 'materiality' was first adopted to describe those forces that are holding the two spheres inseparably together. It was used to indicate that social, economic, cultural and political processes underlying urban development were always intertwined with factors deemed 'natural'. Even more, the remarkable ascendency of cities in the 19th and 20th centuries was not interpreted as a sign of emancipation form 'nature' but as the result of intensified relations between social and environmental dynamics (Soens et al. 2019; Pritchard/Zeller 2010). In this, the material world became "a dynamic, differentiated and interactive force, within processes from which it has sometimes been analytically expunged" (Otter 2010: 39).

As Matthew Gandy (2002) has shown for New York City, the overall stability that characterised urban life even in the face of accelerated growth became possible only because ever more complex infrastructures ensured a reliable provision of water, foodstuff and energy. Also, urban ecosystems and topographies were altered, sometimes with adverse consequences but more often improving living conditions, including attempts to reduce the vulnerability to diseases transmitted by bacteria. Finally, urban development involved the translocation of enormous amounts of construction material which accumulated in the built environment and generated strong path dependencies (Toyka-Seid 2011; cf. Bernhardt in this volume). All of these transformations produced new kinds of interdependencies with the "dynamic, differentiated and interactive force" exerted by the material world. Apart from the occasional crisis, these increasingly complex interdependencies formed the prerequisite for sustained urban growth. The impact of material forces can therefore not be reduced to disturbances or restraints, but has to be understood as essential to the creation and stabilisation of urbanity (Schott 2014: 14-15).

While stability is essential for sustained urban growth, materiality has been predominantly discussed as a force that perpetuated patterns of social inequality. Already in 1980, the philosopher of technology Langdon Winner analysed how material properties of infrastructures and the built environment "embody specific forms of power and authority" (Winner 1980: 121). He prominently referred to the example of the bridges across New York's parkways of the 1930s, which were deliberately built too low for buses to pass and thus excluded low income groups, in particular African-Americans, from accessing recreational facilities. Furthermore, the "systematic social inequality" these material structures "embodied" outlasted the social context in which they were created and the material legacies continued to shape social constraints (ibid: 124). In a similar vein, Gandy (2002) argues that social stratification in New York was solidified by the arrangement of water provision, the creation of parks and the distribution of environmental hazards. This echoes the current debate on environmental justice to which the material forces of pollutants, radioactive fallout and other substances are essential (Kirchhelle 2018). The uneven exposure to these hazards aggravates social inequalities and the long-term legacies of materiality helps explain their persistence (Flanagan 2000; Luckin 2005; Massard-Guilbaud/Rodger 2011; Pichler-Baumgartner 2015).

Materiality is also involved in organising social relations beyond the vital impact on environmental justice. Research has paid particular attention to the role that things have played in the emergence of the 'modern subject', which is often closely linked to urbanity as a way of life. Chris Otter (2008) has analysed how the provision of gas and the design of streets has entrenched liberal ideals of domesticity and the public in the urban culture of Victorian Britain. The argument follows the Foucauldian idea of governmentality which implies that material arrangements support the self-regulation of society. In a recent study, Stefan Höhne (2017) has similarly shown how the design and arrangement of New York's subway system has formed a passenger behaviour considered to epitomise 'modernity'. In a more abstract sense, Patrick Joyce claimed that "the social [...] is seen to be performed by material things just as much as by humans" (Joyce 2010: 227). This overlaps with Material Culture Studies, which also highlight the relevance of things in the construction of subjectivation and social order (Miller 2006; Gerritsen/Riello 2014).

However, in comparison with Material Culture Studies, urban-environmental history is much more concerned with how environmental dynamics effect social phenomena beyond human control. On the local scale, this becomes evident in Michael Rawson's (2014) discussion of the constant remaking of Boston Harbor since the 18th century. While successive plans for dredging and filling in the Harbor, interventions central to maintaining the economic and social structure of the city, were devised and executed, they frequently proved to be based on insufficient knowledge of the marine hydraulics. On the global scale, cities are increasingly interpreted as a driver behind the transition into the 'Anthropocene'. Much of the controversy over the 'Anthropocene' hinges on the question to what degree change induced by humans, as through urbanisation, has set into motion self-propelling geological and biological processes (Davies 2016). In contrast to studies on social order and subjectivation, materiality figures as a force that cannot be deliberately deployed. Instead, this strand of research moves the focus of attention towards the unintended, unpredicted or uncontrollable effects of humans' engagement with environmental dynamics.

Focusing on the co-evolution of social and environmental change does therefore complicate the question how potency and power is distributed between humans and non-human entities. This question has been prominently raised by Actor-Network Theory (ANT). From an ANT-perspective, things, organisms and matter acquire agency that matches the agency of humans. Protagonists of ANT such as Bruno Latour and Michel Callon have therefore called for a symmetrical analysis of human and non-human entities involved in the creation of social phenomena (Callon 1986; Latour 2005). While Latour and others developed their ideas in the context of science studies, their approach has also been taken up in urban history. Bert de Munck (2012) has explicitly linked his research on urban commodity markets to ANT. De Munck argued that the market was never only organised through highly abstracted consumer and producer choices, but hinged on the material qualities inscribed in the commodities with which they formed a network. In a further step, de Munck (2017) developed his considerations on urban markets into a more general concept of 'Urban Agency'. In this conceptualisation, the city is considered a network made up of human and non-human entities, which are both endowed with agency to (re-)produce social phenomena.

The problem with the distribution of agency that ANT has highlighted stems from its opposition to the long tradition in Western thought which "locates agency in the human mind, separating it from both the body and the non-human environment" (Nash 2005: 67). In this reasoning, organisms (including human bodies), let alone things and matter cannot have agency, while the human mind is de-materialised. Over the last decades, this core assumption of Western thought has been criticised from a perspective that has come to be referred to as New Materialism. On the one hand post-humanist critics argue that autonomous will and reflected motivation are not exclusively reserved to humans. In order to understand *why* organisms, things and matter exert force it has to be acknowledged that they are endowed with agency comparable to that allegedly directed by the human mind (Bennett 2010; Coole/Frost 2010). On the other hand, Tim LeCain (2017) has recently asked to what extent the human mind actually is autonomous from the material conditions of human life. He argues, pollutants, foodstuffs and interaction with other organisms and materials have decisively shaped the cognitive and epigenetic development of humans. Even more, organisms and materials make humans think and act, a force that is conventionally reserved to the unique capacity of the human mind.

At this point, it is worth turning to some limits of the current debate on materiality and its applicability to urban-environmental history. First, referring to materiality as a force in history subjects research to the allegation of reintroducing environmental determinism, especially when stressing the symmetrical distribution of agency. There is a fine line between asserting that organisms, things and matter have a formative impact on social dynamics and relegating responsibility for social phenomena, including inequalities, to these forces. As Otter put it, the crucial question for studies in urban-environmental history is, how "can materiality be apprehended as more than an effect but less than a determinant?" (Otter 2010: 45) Many of the studies cited above are careful in reflecting this challenge, and it is indeed advisable to make such considerations explicit when working with concepts of materiality.

Second, materiality is often presented as a necessary corrective to what is considered the exaggerations of the 'cultural turn' (LeCain 2017: 67-139). Discussing environment and cities purely in terms of ideas and perceptions appears to reproduce the ills of the nature-culture dichotomy. However, cultural constructions are essential to our understanding of the environment. This poses a true epistemic dilemma. How do we know about materiality if not through the lens of some construction of popular or scientific knowledge? How are we able to evaluate and judge changes to the environment and the role material forces play in it if not from a normative perspective (Sutter 2013)? This problem seems to be particularly burdensome for historians who are to a large degree reliant on source material that represents the perceptions of past societies. Resorting to the findings of natural science and interdisciplinary research, as frequently suggested (McNeill 2003: 39-41), might be an alternative. But ultimately, scientific knowledge about nature also has to be considered a construction that changes over time (Brüggemeier 2014: 363). Nonetheless, many of the studies on urban-environmental history cited above have shown that if cultural constructivism is not dismissed outright but incorporated into the analysis of materiality, this can yield valuable insights into the co-evolution of environmental and social change.

Materiality in Practice

Practice theory provides a promising approach for a systematic engagement with the limits pertaining to the current debate on materiality, even though it does not ultimately solve the problems discussed above. Regarding the issue of agency, the leading theorist of praxeology, Theodore Schatzki, has recommended to moderate the tone of the controversy. Even though he shares the belief that the separation of the human mind from the material world is an illusion that needs to be transcended, he argues that it is legitimate to focus on the social as a subject in and of itself (Schatzki 2010: 124-125). On an empirical level, practice theory also allows for a specific interpretation of primary sources. Making practices the unit of research, offers a framework for a systematically reflected analysis of sources, which are at the same time the outcome of cultural construction and references to forces of materiality.

Conventionally, practice theory in historical research has been applied to social phenomena. This research is primarily concerned with the routinised interaction between humans and the formation of social structure, as in rituals, customs or knowledge formation (Haasis/Rieske 2015; Füssel 2015; Pickering 1992; Bourdieu 1977). However, practice theory does reserve a specific place for things, matter and organisms. These are highly relevant and essential to the constitution of practices, as Andreas Reckwitz' definition of practices indicates:

> A 'practice' [...] is a routinized type of behaviour which consists of several elements, interconnected to one another: forms of bodily activities, forms of mental activities, 'things' and their use, a background knowledge in the form of understanding, know-how, states of emotion and motivational knowledge. A practice [...] forms so to speak a 'block' whose existence necessarily depends on the existence and specific interconnectedness of those elements and which cannot be reduced to any one of these single elements. (Reckwitz 2002: 249-250)

While Reckwitz writes of practices as a 'block' in which activities and things are integrated, Schatzki locates things outside of practices but similarly emphasises that these are inseparably intertwined in practice-arrangement nexuses: "social life inherently transpires as part of nexuses of practice and materiality" (Schatzki 2003: 84). Significantly, Schatzki has explicitly pointed to examples taken from environmental history to illustrate the potential of practice theory to analytically incorporate the forces of materiality. One of the most prominent examples he refers to, horse farming in the Kentucky Bluegrass region, is essentially presented as a piece of environmental history (Schatzki 2010).

The notion of practices consisting of a 'block' in which elements—among them things which might also include matter and organisms more generally—are integrated, has been first taken up in urban-environmental history by Verena Winiwarter and Martin Schmid in their concept of Socio-Natural Sites (Winiwarter/Schmid 2008; Winiwarter/Schmid in this volume). They claim:

> Practices are impossible without material objects and human beings create, via their practices, arrangements from the material world. The arrangements are shaped by practices, being the material precipitates of these. Even a tree may be an arrangement, if its existence and shape owes anything to human intervention, but more commonly the term refers to e.g., dams, reservoirs

and so on (Winiwarter/Schmid/Dressel 2013: 109). It is coherent with the claim to overcome the nature-culture dichotomy insofar as the spheres of 'nature' and 'culture' are inextricably intertwined in practices. And it accounts for the co-evolution of environmental and social change as material and social elements constitute and constantly modulate each-other.

Even though practices are defined as a "routinized type of behaviour" (Reckwitz 2002: 249), practice theory does provide for change. The actual performance of a practice is never entirely identical with past instances, and at times it shifts significantly, involving other forms of activities, knowledge or things. Elizabeth Shove, Mika Pantzar and Matt Watson (2012) have systematically elaborated on the mechanisms involved in the dynamics of social practice. In their concept, practices are characterised by the dynamic interdependence of elements, such as human activities, knowledge, things and so on. Over time, some of these elements may be dissolved from a certain practice, while others may be newly integrated. Furthermore, as an interdependent system, the dissolution or integration of one element will have repercussions with other elements involved—hence these modulate each-other. Schatzki has explicitly referred to practices as an "evolving domain" (Schatzki 2010: 129) to indicate the dynamic integration of varying elements into a practice over time.

While Shove and her collaborators refer to change within a the span of lived experience, environmental history is more interested in legacies that on a whole transgress the human lifespan (Winiwarter/Schmid/Hohensinner/Haidvogl 2013). Cultivated plants and fluvial regulation are just a few examples of the kind of phenomena that are bound up in practices. Generally, issues of resource provision and consumption, the construction and configuration of the built environment and infrastructure networks, urban pollution and ecosystems all hinge on practices in which things, matter and organisms form a 'block' with human activities and knowledge. More specifically, practices are at the centre of urban metabolism (Schott 2014; Barles in this volume). For example, the throughput of wood as a source of energy was highly dependent on specific practices of heating, cooking, and so on. The subsequent shift to oil, gas and other energy sources then depended on the alteration of these practices (Hård/Oldenziel 2013: 212). Practices also constituted systems of provision. Networks and infrastructures that were built around urban metabolism had to be operated and maintained. The necessary practices could differ widely depending on whether wood or oil was to be provided to urban consumers (Hein 2018; Zumbrägel 2014).

Consumption in particular has become a hot topic of research on practices, within and beyond the field of urban-environmental history. In his work on the history of consumption, Frank Trentmann (2009: 297) has pointed out that practices "are entangled in a creative interplay with materiality". They "leave their mark on the world of things, how things work (or fail to work), and how material is organized and distributed" (ibid: 305). From this observation, Trentmann has extended his argument onto environmental questions. In a joint article with Anna Carlsson-Hyslop (2018) he has recently demonstrated how practices of consumption have left a mark on the (unsustainable) use of energy sources in the 20th century.

Analysing such seemingly small-scale every-day activities such as heating, cooking or car-driving ultimately leads to the large-scale and long-term transitions of climate change and resource exploitation. Together with not-so-everyday activities, such as iron melting, and the operation of steam engines, this multitude of practices underpinned the epochal shift from solar to fossil energy systems (Sieferle/Winiwarter/Krausmann/Schandl 2006: 131-139). In this picture, the individual practices and their routinised execution appear as pieces in a huge jigsaw puzzle of what Schatzki has called an "immense transmogrifying web of practices and arrangements" (Schatzki 2010: 130). Understanding large-scale environmental transitions through analysing every-day practices is particularly attractive because it implies that conscious efforts to alter these practices will have an effect on environmental change. Aims such as sustainable development might be achieved if humans reconsider and modify those practices to which certain resources and energy systems are tied, as Inge Røpke (2009) has argued. While for the most part "many routine practices are based on practical consciousness, implying that much consumption occurs without prior calculations" (ibid: 2496), it also becomes possible that these practices "upon reflection become open to change" (ibid: 2491).

With the high expectations in humans' ability to reflect their activities, praxeologically inspired research diverges sharply from the principles of post-humanist New Materialism. However, conscious reflection appears as an ambivalent aspect of practice theory, in particular with regard to the interconnectedness of activities and material elements (Soens et al. 2019: 19). The point is that even while routinised behaviour remains potentially reflectable and discourse may be incorporated into the praxeological approach as a "transformative instance of reflection" (Welskopp 2001: 105), material forces may transgress this logic. Fluvial regulation, one of the key examples analysed by Winiwarter and others (Winiwarter/

Schmid/Hohensinner/Haidvogl 2013), provides an illuminating case. While dam construction and other means of regulation clearly built on the reflection of previous practices, riverine forces tended to destruct these arrangements and dry periods or flooding thwarted the attempts to optimise flow conditions. Similarly, Schatzki (2003: 86) argues: "Although a house, for instance, is both a human artefact and a social phenomenon, the physical properties of its construction materials [...] are facts of nature". Human reflection, therefore, can make a difference— to a degree that is delimited by materiality.

The potential, albeit limited, reflexibility of practices thus is key to the analysis of primary sources interested in the forces of materiality. As outlined above, practices are composed of interdependent elements that include such divers types as "forms of bodily activities, forms of mental activities, 'things' and their use, a background knowledge in the form of understanding, know-how, states of emotion and motivational knowledge" (Reckwitz 2002: 249). Because they form an interdependent system, alterations in one element will have ripple effects through the entire system and cause alterations in other elements. The theoretical assumption here is that elements which carry with them material forces, such as things, organisms or matter, leave an imprint on those social elements, such as knowledge, economic interests or scientific reflection, that did go recorded in sources to which historians have access. Consequently, sources may be read as reflecting alterations to material elements of a practice and at the same time as documenting changes in knowledge, motivation, and so on, which were directed at altering material elements.

Primary sources include written documents but also graphic representations to which methods of historical-critical analysis can be applied (Knoll 2013). They have to be treated as elements integrated into the practices under scrutiny. Nonetheless, source analysis will remain an observation of the second order (Winiwarter/Schmid 2008: 162). As reflection is in most cases a purposeful effort, sources will usually be produced in instances when—observed or intended—alterations to certain practices are perceived as significant and challenging. Typically this is found in reports aimed at optimising routines, but also in investigations on failures, interruptions and accidents. From the perspective of the praxeological approach proposed here, materiality then appears as an imprint of the forces of things, organisms or matter on social elements like knowledge or motivation with which they are enmeshed in the 'block' of a practice. This provides a useful framework for the interpretation of sources in order to delineate the forces of materiality within practices.

Conclusions

'Materiality' is a loosely defined catchword used within diverse theoretical contexts. Beyond the shared focus on the complex reciprocal relationships between organisms, things and matter on the one hand and social phenomena on the other, it is hard to integrate the different approaches into a coherent concept. Most clearly, these approaches diverge over the hotly debated issue of power and agency. For urban-environmental history, the notion of materiality is crucial, however, because it appears to provide a key to our understanding of phenomena that are at the same time social and natural. In fact, studies in urban-environmental history have fruitfully applied different approaches to materiality in their analysis of social order and environmental justice, infrastructures and resource provision, or changes to urban hydrology and ecosystems.

The limits of all approaches to incorporate materiality as a force in the co-evolution of social and environmental change lie primarily in the epistemic dilemma of the nature-culture dichotomy. On the one hand, everything we know about nature is the outcome of some sort of cultural construction—a limitation that is significantly not resolved by resorting to natural sciences. What might be considered as the forces of materiality, therefore, is only accessible via constructions. On the other hand, explaining the origins of those forces which are observable leads to the assumption that things, matter and organisms are endowed with some kind of agency. While the distribution of agency is subject to debate, and environmental determinism hovers around the corner, the causation of historical change remains unaccountable. Practice theory allows to factor out these problems and interpret materiality from a human-centred perspective using established tools of historical-critical analysis, but only at the price of sidelining important theoretical questions. In particular, it does not explain what drives the co-evolution of social and environmental change except human reflection. Thus, practice theory as an approach to account for materiality in urban-environmental history may prove useful but preliminary.

References

Bennett, Jane (2010): Vibrant matter: A political ecology of things, Durham: Duke University Press.

Bourdieu, Pierre (1977): Outline of a theory of practice, Cambridge/New York: Cambridge University Press.

Braudel, Fernand (1972): The Mediterranean and the Mediterranean World in the age of Philip II, New York: Harper & Row.

Brüggemeier, Franz-Josef (2014): Schranken der Natur: Umwelt, Gesellschaft, Experimente 1750 bis heute, Essen: Klartext.

Callon, Michel (1986): "Some elements of a sociology of translation: Domestication of the scallops and the fishermen of St Brieuc Bay." In: John Law (ed.), Power, action and belief: A new sociology of knowledge? London: Routledge&Kegan Paul, pp. 196-223.

Coole, Diana H./Frost, Samantha (eds.) (2010): New materialisms: Ontology, agency, and politics, Durham: Duke University Press.

Davies, Jeremy (2016): The birth of the anthropocene, Oakland: University of California Press.

de Munck, Bert (2017): "Disassembling the city: A historical and an epistemological view on the agency of cities." In: Journal of Urban History 43, pp. 811-829.

de Munck, Bert (2012): "Conventions, the great transformation and actor network theory." In: Historical Social Research/Historische Sozialforschung 37/4, pp. 44-54.

Flanagan, Maureen A. (2000): "Environmental justice in the city: A theme for urban environmental history." In: Environmental History 5, pp. 159-164.

Füssel, Marian (2015): "Praktiken historisieren: Geschichtswissenschaft und Praxistheorie im Dialog." In: Franka Schäfer/Anna Daniel/Frank Hillebrandt (eds.), Methoden einer Soziologie der Praxis, Bielefeld: transcript, pp. 267-287.

Gandy, Matthew (2002): Concrete and clay: Reworking nature in New York City, Cambridge, Mass.: MIT Press.

Gerritsen, Anne/Riello, Giorgio (eds.) (2014): Writing material culture history, London: Bloomsbury.

Haasis, Lucas/Rieske, Constantin (eds.) (2015): Historische Praxeologie: Dimensionen vergangenen Handelns, Paderborn: Schöningh.

Hård, Mikael/Oldenziel, Ruth (2013): Consumers, tinkerers, rebels: The people who shaped Europe, Basingstoke: Palgrave Macmillan.

Hein, Carola (2018): "Oil spaces: The global petroleumscape in the Rotterdam/The Hague area." In: Journal of Urban History 44, pp. 887-929.

Höhne, Stefan (2017): New York City Subway: Die Erfindung des urbanen Passagiers, Cologne: Böhlau.

Joyce, Patrick (2010): "What is the social in social history?" In: Past & Present 206/1, pp. 213-248.

Kirchhelle, Claas (2018): "Toxic tales: Recent histories of pollution, poisoning, and pesticides (ca. 1800-2010)." In: NTM Zeitschrift für Geschichte der Wissenschaften, Technik und Medizin 26, pp. 213-229.

Knoll, Martin (2014): "Nil sub sole novum oder neue Bodenhaftung? Der material turn und die Geschichtswissenschaft." In: Neue Politische Literatur 59, pp. 191-207.

Knoll, Martin (2013): Die Natur der menschlichen Welt: Siedlung, Territorium und Umwelt in der historisch-topografischen Literatur der Frühen Neuzeit, Bielefeld: transcript.

Latour, Bruno (2005): Reassembling the social: An introduction to Actor-Network-Theory, Oxford/New York: Oxford University Press.

LeCain, Timothy J. (2017): The matter of history: How things create the past, Cambridge, Mass.: Cambridge University Press.

Luckin, Bill (2005): "Environmental justice, history and the city: The United States and Britain, 1970-2000." In: Bill Luckin/Geneviève Massard-Guilbaud/Dieter Schott (eds.), Resources of the city: Contributions to an environmental history of modern Europe, Aldershot: Routledge, pp. 230-245.

Massard-Guilbaud, Geneviève/Rodger, Richard (eds.) (2011): Environmental and social justice in the city: Historical perspectives, Cambridge: White Horse.

McNeill, John R. (2003): "Observations on the nature and culture of environmental history." In: History and Theory 42, pp. 5-43.

Melosi, Martin (2010): "Humans, cities, and nature: How do cities fit in the material world?" In: Journal of Urban History 36, pp. 3-21.

Miller, Daniel (2006): Materiality, Durham: Duke University Press.

Nash, Linda (2005): "The agency of nature and the nature of agency." In: Environmental History 10/1, pp. 67-69.

Otter, Chris (2010): "Locating matter: The place of materiality in urban history." In: Tony Bennett/Patrick Joyce (eds.), Material powers: Cultural studies, history and the material turn, Milton Park: Routledge, pp. 38-59.

Otter, Chris (2008): The Victorian eye: A political history of light and vision in Britain, 1800-1910, Chicago: University of Chicago Press.

Pichler-Baumgartner, Luisa (2015): "'Environmental justice' als analytische Kategorie der Wirtschafts-, Sozial- und Umweltgeschichte? Schwierigkeiten und Potenziale einer Anwendung." In: Vierteljahrschrift für Sozial- und Wirtschaftsgeschichte 102, pp. 472-491.

Pickering, Andrew (ed.) (1992): Science as practice and culture, Chicago: University of Chicago Press.

Pritchard, Sara B./Zeller, Thomas (2010): "The nature of industrialization." In: Martin Reuss/Stephen H. Cutcliffe (eds.), The illusory boundary: Environment and technology in history, Charlottesville: University of Virginia Press, pp. 69-100.

Rawson, Michael (2014): Eden on the Charles: The making of Boston, Cambridge, Mass.: Harvard University Press.

Reckwitz, Andreas (2002): "Toward a theory of social practices: A development in culturalist theorizing." In: European Journal of Social Theory 5, pp. 243-263.

Schatzki, Theodore (2010): "Materiality and social life." In: Nature and Culture 5, pp. 123-149.

Schatzki, Theodore (2003): "Nature and technology in history." In: History and Theory 42, pp. 82-93.

Schott, Dieter (2014): Europäische Urbanisierung (1000-2000): Eine umwelthistorische Einführung, Cologne/Weimar/Vienna: Böhlau.

Shove, Elizabeth/Pantzar, Mika/Watson, Matt (2012): The dynamics of social practice: Everyday life and how it changes, London: Sage.

Sieferle, Rolf Peter/Winiwarter, Verena/Krausmann, Fridolin/Schandl, Heinz (2006): Das Ende der Fläche: Zum gesellschaftlichen Stoffwechsel der Industrialisierung, Cologne: Böhlau.

Smith, Kate (2018): "Amidst things: New histories of commodities, capital and consumption." In: The Historical Journal 61, pp. 841-861.

Soens, Tim/Schott, Dieter/Toyka-Seid, Michael/de Munck, Bert (eds.) (2019): Urbanizing nature: Actors and agency (dis)connecting cities and nature since 1500, New York: Routledge.

Sutter, Paul S. (2013): "The world with us: The state of American environmental history." In: Journal of American History 100, pp. 94-119.

Toyka-Seid, Michael (2011): "Städtische Materialität" In: Martina Löw/Georgios Terizakis (eds.), Städte und Eigenlogik: Ein Handbuch für Stadtplanung und Stadtentwicklung, Frankfurt a.M.: Campus, pp. 127-131.

Trentmann, Frank (2009): "Materiality in the future of history: Things, practices and politics." In: Journal of British Studies 48, pp. 283-307.

Trentmann, Frank/Carlsson-Hyslop, Anna (2018): "The evolution of energy demand in Britain: Politics, daily life, and public housing, 1920s-1970s." In: The Historical Journal 61, pp. 807-839.

Welskopp, Thomas (2001): "Die Dualität von Struktur und Handeln: Anthony Giddens' Strukturierungstheorie als 'praxeologischer' Ansatz in der Geschichtswissenschaft." In: Andreas Suter/Manfred Hettling (eds.), Struktur und Ereignis, Göttingen: Vandenhoek&Ruprecht, pp. 99-119.

Winner, Langdon (1980): "Do artefacts have politics?" In: Daedalus 109, pp. 221-136.

Winiwarter, Verena/Knoll, Martin (2007): Umweltgeschichte: Eine Einführung, Cologne: Böhlau.

Winiwarter, Verena/Schmid, Martin (2008): "Umweltgeschichte als Untersuchung sozionaturaler Schauplätze? Ein Versuch, Johannes Colers 'Oeconomia' umwelthistorisch zu interpretieren." In: Thomas Knopf (ed.), Umweltverhalten in Geschichte und Gegenwart: Vergleichende Ansätze, Tübingen: Attempto, pp. 158-173.

Winiwarter, Verena/Schmid, Martin/Dressel, Gert (2013): "Looking at half a millennium of co-existence: The Danube in Vienna as a socio-natural site." In: Water History 5, pp. 101-119.

Winiwarter, Verena/Schmid, Martin/Hohensinner, Severin/Haidvogl, Gertrud (2013): "The environmental history of the Danube river basin as an issue of long-term socio-ecological research." In: Simron Jit Singh/Helmut Haberl/ Marian Chertow/Michael Mirtl/Martin Schmid (eds.), Long term socio-ecological research: Studies in society-nature interactions across spatial and temporal scales, Dordrecht/New York: Springer, pp. 103-122.

Zumbrägel, Christian (2014): "Die vorindustriellen Holzströme Wiens: Ein sozionaturales großtechnisches System?" In: Technikgeschichte 81, pp. 335-362.

Path-Dependency and Trajectories

Christoph Bernhardt

Most urban scholars will agree that cities develop along certain patterns and logics of change in which new trends emerge while other material, infrastructural, economic and social structures persist. Such persistence against change can be observed in the industrial profile of cities, in urban milieus and infrastructures, in the role of environmental or geographical conditions and in many other fields of urban history. The concepts of Path-Dependency (PD) and Trajectories claim to provide a theoretical framework and a vocabulary for the systematic analysis of the limits of and the obstacles against change (= PD) as well as of the logics of urban development (= Trajectories). Both concepts were originally presented by economic historians and have become of interest amongst urban historians in the last two decades.

This chapter presents a critical introduction to these concepts, discusses their value and some of their weaknesses and gives a report on some areas of research and studies in which the concepts were applied. The chapter will do this in three steps: 1. Retracing the emergence and some of the key components of the concepts, 2. Discussing their use in the fields of urban infrastructures, trajectories of cities and urban politics, and 3. Contextualising them against the background of related concepts and critically reflecting the challenges they imply.

Approaching Path-Dependency and Trajectories

The concept of Path-Dependency was first developed by economic historian Paul David and economic mathematician Brian Arthur in the 1980s. Initially the approach intended to critically revise some assumptions of neoclassical economists on questions of efficiency in economic change. From the pioneering study of David on the rise and durability of the 'QWERTY'-keyboard of the American typewriter (David 1985) and from Arthur's early contributions on the logic of urban development (Arthur 1988, see also below), the concept was imported to the social sciences. In the 1990s, it became a key element in Noble prize winner Douglas North's theory of institutional change (North 1990). In the 2000s, Paul Pierson and

James Mahony transferred the institutional perspective to the political sciences and discussed PD phenomena with regard to political power and institutions (Mahony 2000; Pierson 2000; Werle 2007).

Theories of PD assume that in the initial phase of a new development—like the invention of a technology or the creation of a new institutional setup of urban administration, such as municipal legislation on housing—choices and arrangements are made which exclude alternative options and can only be corrected in the future with high costs. Sometimes the decisions prove to be inefficient and may act as obstacles for further innovation. In these cases the initial configuration becomes 'locked-in' and persistent, so that for example in industrial cities certain mental patterns or institutional arrangements may block reforms. Path-dependency in this perspective implies a negatively connotated impediment for 'optimal' institutional solutions and dynamic change. Consequently the approach has been criticised as having an implicit 'conservative bias' (Beyer 2006).

As protagonists of PD theory have argued, a new path normally starts with a "critical juncture" in which a traditional logic is broken and the new arrangement has to be stabilised by "positive feed-back mechanisms" or "increasing returns", like growing demands for a product, support for a political intervention or effects of learning or social coordination. Every path is characterised by a specific set of joint orientations of actors, routinised acts and rules of decision (Werle 2007: 119-121).

As soon as the internal logics, diachronic and long-term dynamics of 'pathways' or 'trajectories' are discussed, 'sequences of events' and causal explanations become of interest. This perspective of 'trajectories' clearly transcends the implicitly normative PD concept and claims a diversity of different logics of development which cannot necessarily be assessed as 'better' or 'worse', dynamic or 'locked in' etc. On the contrary, local or regional characteristics which differ from dominating global patterns of change, like floodplains which were protected against industrial transformation, can be regarded as potential starting points for future developments or qualified as 'sustainable' instead of merely 'persistent' against change (Bernhardt 2003). This argument can be generalised in the sense that natural resources and rich urban habitats which were protected against commodification and exploitation in earlier historical periods can be regarded as precious natural capital instead of outdated leftovers of modern urban development.

As a result of these reflections and as a starting point for the following arguments this article calls for a clear distinction between PD approaches on the one hand and concepts of 'Trajectories' on the other—a distinction so far not made in scholarly debate. In this perspective, path dependency represents a specific mechanism within the more general dynamics of societal change. But it is only one key mechanism amongst others which work together in shaping the trajectories/pathways of cities or partial systems of cities (like infrastructures, housing policies etc.).

Path Dependency and Urban Infrastructures

Scholars working on urban technologies were amongst the first to take up the strand of research that the founding father of PD theory, Paul A. David, had laid out in his classical study on the 'QWERTY'-keyboard. Andrew Sorensen has summed up the key argument of a close relationship between path dependency and urban infrastructure, arguing that the large capital costs of investment in water supply, sewers, subways, and roads—the so-called 'sunk costs'—strongly determine "the most obviously enduring characteristic of urban infrastructure" (Sorensen 2017: 28). I have myself sketched the famous case of a controversy in Berlin after the Second World War. Here a strong political initiative to re-direct the city's development towards a modern, decentralised open urban landscape had to be abandoned because of the large 'sunk costs' of technical infrastructure in the Berlin underground (Bernhardt 2018: 16).

It were especially the technologies of modern water infrastructures and "the rise of the networked city" (Tarr/Dupuy 1988; Schott 1999) in the late 19th century, that were repeatedly discussed with regard to path dependency. Martin Melosi in his pioneering book *The sanitary city* was one of the first researchers who explicitly referred to PD-theory with regard to urban water networks in order "to assess the impact of policy choices made in selection and implementation of the services" (Melosi 2000: 2, 10-12; Melosi 2005). Melosi was primarily interested in more general questions, like that of "the constraint of choices available to later generations of decision makers" and did not explicitly connect his empirical analysis of the role of 'sunk costs' as financial and material constraints in historical situations to the concept of path dependency (Melosi 2000: 12-13). Matthew Gandy, one of the leading scholars in the study of postcolonial water management and urban regimes in the Global South, also underlined the role of "path dependencies from previous waves of development", highlighting the dominance of the "technocratic paradigm of large-scale infrastructure development" over "long-term planning" in cities (Gandy 2014: 16, 123-124). In a more general sense the infrastructural, institutional and cultural heritage from the colonial period and its impact on postcolonial urban history in countries like India can be regarded as striking cases of path dependency across the critical junction of political de-colonisation.

The persistence of infrastructures across political caesuras can also be seen in cases of territorial or political regime shifts. In the French city of Strasbourg during German rule between 1871 and 1918, traditional systems of water management were path-dependent in the sense that they were stabilised by established technologies (canals and wells), local economy (discharge by private entrepreneurs), institutions (rules for financial contributions of house-owners) and collective routines of behaviour (like local practices of water consumption). The lock-in of the pre-industrial system of water management was only broken up from the 1880s onwards by the newly established German administration, which applied massive cuts in finance, a stop of maintenance of the old system and huge investments in a new modern water infrastructure. In terms of path dependency, a 'critical juncture' was initiated by political decision-making which broke up the lock-in of the old system and replaced it by a modern water management which consisted of new large-scale technologies and institutional reform (Bernhardt 2018: 20-25).

A different type of political 'lock in' against modern sanitary concepts was analysed by Carsten Benke in the case of Leipzig. In this major Saxon city, urban liberal elites in the 19th century favoured a 'bounded innovation' of the old system. This meant modernising traditional cesspools and carriage systems and indeed helped to keep up with the challenges of a growing urban population and water consumption for some time. As a result, Leipzig introduced modern urban water infrastructure only as a late-comer in 1935 (Benke 2007). In contrast, Goddard/Sheail (2001) identified British small towns as forerunners of sanitary reform in the water sector.

Path dependencies of urban technical networks are mostly perceived as constraints to innovation but can also be interpreted as sources of resilience and adaptability in times of crisis. Timothy Moss discussed such questions of durability and adaptability of urban infrastructures along the case of Berlin between 1948 and 1989 "in the face of the major upheaval" of the division of the city. He found a remarkable resilience of the technical networks and a considerable capacity of the network managers to keep them running even after the shock of the blockade of 1948/49 (Moss 2009).

Trajectories of Cities

Path dependencies in the general development of cities are mostly discussed under the term of 'trajectories'. Surprisingly, urban historians and sociologists have not explicitly taken up an early intervention of W. Brian Arthur, one of the founding fathers of PD-theory, who discussed the relation of "Urban Systems and Historical Path-Dependence" in a 1988 paper. It were probably Arthur´s rigid and highly abstract theoretical vocabulary and his seemingly simple juxtaposition of the "two viewpoints" of "determinism"/"necessity" vs. "history-dependence"/"chance" (Arthur 1988: 2-5) as major rules of urban evolution that were not very inspiring for urban historians as a theoretical concept. But his basic argument of the determining role of clusters of industries for the trajectories of cities was in fact taken up as a point of departure for empirical analysis by a growing number of urban historians.

Studies on 'trajectories' of cities often pick up some elements of PD analysis and develop them in various directions. Of particular value were comparative studies which explain the rise and fall of cities beyond the individual case and identified convergences and divergences of urban trajectories. In most cases, these trajectories were reconstructed along population numbers, as did Turok/Mykhnenko (2007) in their analysis of the trajectories of 310 European cities with more than 200.000 inhabitants each between 1960 and 2005. They critically assessed the argument of a long-term decline in this period and found certain forms of 'revival' and growth of most cities after the year 2000 (ibid: 179-181).

In a similar way, other scholars tried to identify patterns of evolution of industrial cities along population growth and decline. By examining the development of Scottish cities between 1891 und 1981, Rodger showed that the specific industrial profile—textile, heavy industries etc.—strongly shaped the growth and decline of individual towns as well as of groups of cities. It was clearly the logics of economic agglomeration, as already discussed by Arthur, that shaped these trajectories. Rodger identified different types and time patterns of development, like long-term decline or stagnation, short-term cycles of decline and growth (Rodger 2013: 85-94).

In a study of the 'careers' of about 100 industrial cities in the GDR, Benke/Wolfes included the different size and age of cities beside their industrial profiles (Benke/Wolfes 2005). Amongst other results, they found that newly industrialised cities in the GDR grew much stronger than old industrial cities and that small towns had started to shrink long before the collapse of socialism and socialist industries around 1989. Studies of this type tend to analyse trajectories of decline and prosperity with a specific terminology in which descriptions like "continuously shrinking" or "growth after shrinkage" are common, resting primarily on quantitative data (inhabitants, economic statistics etc.) (Turok/Mykhnenko 2007: 170; Rodger 2013: 82-83).

For the Netherlands, Deinema/Kloosterman (2013) analysed the role of cultural industries for the trajectories of the cities of Utrecht, The Hague, Rotterdam and Amsterdam in the 20th century. By examining the economic profile of the four cities and the development of different sectors of cultural industries during the 20th century, they observed a relatively stable hierarchy between the cities and "fairly strong historical continuities", with Amsterdam holding the top rank (ibid: 15, 37). On the micro-level of the Cirque du Soleil in Montreal/Canada, Leslie and Rantisi (2011) discussed the place-specific and path-dependent trajectory of that cultural enterprise since the early 1980s.

Another strand of studies on urban trajectories has focussed on port cities. This type of cities shows specific path-dependencies which are determined by large-scale naval infrastructures and characteristic trajectories, as Dirk Schubert (2018) demonstrated in several studies. Christoph Strupp (2018) identified mental lock-ins among Hamburg urban elites who consequently followed the port city vision instead of diversifying the commercial profile of the city. In the case of Wilhelmshaven, Jörn Eiben retraced an attempt of the urban elites to expand this port city and shift to a new path of industrial production but the initiative failed so that the city remained in an economic lock-in (Eiben 2018; see also Borsay/Walton 2011).

While studies which use large numbers of highly aggregated data are often rather descriptive, other analyses on the trajectories of a limited number of cities, as published by Kress (2008) or Betker (2008), were able to give causal explanations for the cycles and logics of decline and prosperity. Sommer/Liebmann took the case of East-German cities and their trajectories before and after the collapse of the socialist system in 1989 and studied the path-breaking effects of this event. But they also found some path-dependencies in policies and collective mentalities which continued the industrial trajectory even beyond the turning point of 1989 (Sommer/Liebmann 2013). In a similar way, Dieter Schott (2018) recently showed how the southern German city of Darmstadt changed its trajectory as a result of the 'external shock' of World War I from a regional capital city to a slowly developing industrial city.

Institutional Change and Urban Policies

Besides path dependencies in the field of urban infrastructures and trajectories of general urban development, scholars have analysed the logics of institutional change and path dependencies in certain fields of urban policies. At least implicitly, these studies took up the approaches of institutional theory as developed by Douglas North and Paul Pierson (North 1990; Pierson/Werle 2007: 122-123). In an early paper, Woodlief discussed the role of path dependencies in the urban fiscal policies of Chicago and New York, 1944-89, and identified 'political lock-ins' caused by urban bureaucracies and resistances of interest-groups against reforms (Woodlief 1998: 418-429). Rast (2012) explored the basic dimensions of 'timing and sequence' and 'continuity and change' in path dependence explanations of urban policies and institutional development from a more theoretical perspective.

Beyond the sectors of infrastructural planning and industrial policies that have already been mentioned above, other areas of urban politics have also been explored with the concepts discussed here. Redfearn (2007) contributed a case study on path dependencies in the spatial distribution of employment in the Los Angeles metropolitan area which was strongly influenced by the regional freeway system, and Ghitter/Smart (2009) discussed path dependencies and unintended consequences of critical political decisions in the governance of the Calgary region in Canada. Schott reconstructed the logics of urban industrial and infrastructural policies in South-Western German cities (Schott 2002).

A relatively large number of studies has discussed the role of path dependencies in the policies of urban planning and urban renewal. Sorensen used an historical institutionalist approach to explore patterns of local governance and planning with regard to land, infrastructure and property (Sorensen 2017). Joel Rast (2009) studied path dependencies in the policies of urban redevelopment in Chicago and Milwaukee after World War II, Henderson/Bowlby and Raco (2009) the local policies of inner-city regeneration in the British city of Salford. Hommels (2000) applied the concept with special attention to problems of endurance and socio-technical scales on the planning history for the 'Hoog Catharijne' area in the Dutch city of Utrecht since the 1960s.

The relatively new field of urban-environmental history has not yet become a frequent object of studies based on an explicit use of PD concepts. Important exceptions are the environmental aspects of urban infrastructures and various aspects of water policies. Within this thematic subfield, Sundaresan, Allen and Johnson (2017) studied trajectories of regional 'blue infrastructures' in the case of the 'wetland networks' of the Indian cities of Bangalore and Madurai. Water historians have also embedded the trajectory concept into the larger framework of regime theory and found different institutional and metabolic systems in the water sector in a long term perspective. Disco (2017) identified four large regimes of water management in the history of the Dutch city of Amsterdam between 1100 and 2000, and Barles (2018) studied the metabolic trajectory of Paris since the early 19th century.

Related Concepts and Challenges

Parallel to the first discussions of the PD concept in the 1980s, the approach of 'Large Technological Systems' (LTS) was adopted by scholars of (urban) infrastructure. This approach was only one out of a number of related concepts which share a common interest in the key question of logics, patterns and persistence in urban and spatial development. The LTS approach as initially launched by Thomas Hughes (1983) developed key terms like 'reverse salient' or 'momentum' which in fact reflect problems of path dependency in the course of the expansion of technical networks (Schott 1999: 20-26). Following Hughes, this strand of research on the dynamics of urban technical infrastructures was strongly developed by Graham (2001), Coutard (1999) and others. Under the key term of 'splintering urbanism', they were discussing problems of destruction, failure and persistence of urban infrastructures and related questions of the governance of large technical systems.

Similar to PD theory, the concept of 'Urban Machinery' (Hård and Misa 2008) refers to the interdependencies of technological systems with multiple aspects and levels of everyday practices, institutions and discourses and is interested in the logics of urban development that emerge from these interdependencies. Recently Antoine Picon (2018) expanded this perspective by highlighting the role of social imaginations of key actors for the development of urban technical networks.

In the last two decades, concepts of 'Actor-Network Theory' as developed by Bruno Latour (1991) and others gained interest and can be regarded as competing with PD theory. In an 'anthropologie symétrique' (Latour), material artefacts are regarded as 'actants' who in networks and collectivities of material, social and discursive arrangements correspond with other human and non-human actants. Farias (2010) tried to adopt the ANT as a "toolbox for Urban Studies" (Farias 2010: 2-4). Up to now, studies using ANT have mainly focused on more recent urban development but the approach is favoured by some urban historians as a concept which reflects historical change in a more complex way than PD theory (Janssens/Soens 2019).

This shows that PD approaches are critically discussed and contested in the field of urban studies. However, most historians will be less interested in problems of modelling and theorising than many social scientists but primarily want to use the concepts as tools for qualitative empirical analysis. Yet I hope to have shown that a number of such studies is available in the field of urban sociology and planning, and some for urban history. Besides studies which follow a strongly reflected methodology and terminology, a relatively large number of articles uses key terms like 'path dependency', 'lock-in', or 'increasing returns' in a more metaphorical sense with no or little reference to the theoretical concepts. This might cause some confusion but in the conclusion of this article I discuss some strategies to overcome this problem.

Furthermore, two other objections which are often raised against concepts of PD in urban history, have lost relevance in the course of recent debates: While in the classical approach of Arthur and Davids human agency was not sufficiently conceptualised—as criticised by Melosi (2005), Eiben (2018b) and others—, the political sciences strand of research and a growing number of studies in urban history have closed this gap. The same is true for another, even more fundamental objection which reduced PD theory to the early and simplified slogan of 'history matters' which for historians makes little sense. This objection might be true for some early concepts of economic PD-theory but recent institutional analysis as followed by Sorensen (2017) and others shows that PD-analyses in the framework of complex approaches of historical and institutional change are innovative and helpful for urban historians.

Conclusions

Without denying the blind spots of the concepts and the challenges they imply it should have become clear that PD and Trajectories analysis provide useful tools for studies in urban(-environmental) history and stimulate cross-disciplinary debate. Some insights drawn from theoretical and empirical works discussed here might be helpful for future research. When working with concepts of PD and trajectories in an empirical study, the theoretical basis should be made clear to avoid a mere 'metaphorical' use of the concepts as is evident in a considerable number of studies. At the same time, the added value of the concept in comparison to a 'traditional narrative' perspective should be critically reflected. Re-directing the attention of scholars to formerly neglected processes is often a clear benefit. But, on the other hand, there is a pitfall of merely interpreting historical events along PD terminology with little added value.

Obviously the concept works better in some fields of urban history research than in others. This is clearly the case for the field of urban infrastructure and for studies at the crossroads of the built environment, urban social and institutional history, because they need to factor in material, economic, social and political persistence. The same is true for environmental history but this field is still to be explored through PD analysis. For quite complex systems and processes, like the trajectories of cities, the situation is more challenging. Here a clear focus on selected sections and/or indicators is crucial as it helps to avoid the discovery of a multitude of random path dependencies of any kind. Finally this article strongly argues for a clear-cut distinction between the concepts of path dependency on the one hand and trajectories on the other in the study of urban(-environmental) history and beyond.

References

Arthur, William Brian (1989): "Competing technologies, increasing returns, and lock-in by historical events." In: Economic Journal 99, pp. 116-131.

Arthur, William Brian (1988): Urban systems and historical path-dependence, Stanford, California, Stanford University, Stanford Institute for Population and Resource Studies, (Working Paper Series: Paper No. 0012).

Barles, Sabine (2018): Urban socio-ecological trajectories—conceptual framework, use and limits: Some insights form Paris, end 18th- beginning 20th century. Unpublished paper for the European Association for Urban History, 14th International Conference Rome 2018.

Benke, Carsten (2007): The emergence of modern water infrastructure in German cities—historical pathways and options: The case of Leipzig. Unpublished manuscript, Erkner: IRS, 2007.

Benke, Carsten/Wolfes, Thomas (2005): "Stadtkarrieren: Typologie und Entwicklungsverläufe von Industriestädten in der DDR." In: Christoph Bernhardt/Thomas Wolfes (eds.), Schönheit und Typenprojektierung: Der DDR-Städtebau im internationalen Kontext, Erkner 2005: IRS, pp. 127-164.

Bernhardt, Christoph (2018): "'Pfadabhängigkeiten' und 'Entwicklungspfade': Zwei Konzepte stadtgeschichtlicher Forschung." In: Moderne Stadtgeschichte 2, pp. 16-30.

Bernhardt, Christoph (2003): "Regionaler Institutionenwandel im Wassermanagement in historischer Perspektive: Das Beispiel des Oderraums in der DDR-Zeit." In: Timothy Moss (ed.), Das Flussgebiet als Handlungsraum: Institutionenwandel durch die EU-Wasserrahmenrichtlinie aus raumwissenschaftlichen Perspektiven, Münster: LIT, pp. 89-126.

Betker, Frank (2008): "Rostock und Halle: Paradoxien von Wachstum und Schrumpfung in der DDR." In: Axel Schildt/Dirk Schubert (eds.), Städte zwischen Wachstum und Schrumpfung: Wahrnehmungs- und Umgangsformen in Geschichte und Gegenwart, Dortmund: Rohn, pp. 131-144.

Beyer, Jürgen (2006): Pfadabhängigkeit: Über institutionelle Kontinuität, anfällige Stabilität und fundamentalen Wandel, Frankfurt a.M./New York: Campus.

Borsay, Peter/Walton, John K. (eds.) (2011): Resorts and ports: European seaside towns since 1700, Bristol: Channel View Publications.

Coutard Olivier (ed.) (1999): The governance of large technical systems, London/New York: Routledge.

David, Paul A. (1988): Path dependence: Putting the past into the future of economics, technical report No. 533, University of Stanford: Stanford, CA.

David, Paul A (1985): "Clio and the economics of QWERTY." In: American Economic Review 75, pp. 332-337.

Deeg, Richard (2001): Institutional change and the uses and limits of path dependency: The case of German finance. Max-Planck-Institut für Gesellschaftsforschung, Discussion Paper 01/6.

Deinema, Michael/Kloosterman, Robert (2013): "Polycentric urban trajectories and urban cultural economy." In: Johan Klaesson/Borje Johansson/Charlie Karlsson (eds.), Metropolitan regions: Knowledge infrastructures of the global economy, Berlin/Heidelberg: Springer, pp. 339-373.

Disco, Cornelis (2017): "Dividing the waters: Urban growth, city life and water management in Amsterdam 100-2000." In: Sarah Bell/Adriana Allen/Pascale Hofmann/Tse-Hui Teh (eds.), Urban water trajectories, Heidelberg: Springer, pp. 5-20.

Eiben, Jörn (2018a): "'Wilhelmshaven blickt seewärts' – Beginn und Ende eines wirtschaftspolitischen Pfades." In: Moderne Stadtgeschichte 2, pp. 86-98.

Eiben, Jörn (2018b): "History matters ... so what? Das Pfadkonzept und die Stadtgeschichte." In: Moderne Stadtgeschichte 2, pp. 5-15.

Farias, Ignacio/T. Bender (eds.) (2010): Urban assemblages, New York: Routledge.

Gandy, Matthew (2014): The fabric of space: Water, modernity, and the urban imagination, Cambrigde, Mass./London: MIT Press.

Ghitter, Geoff/Smart, Alan (2009): "Mad cows, regional governance and urban sprawl: Path dependence and unintended consequences in the Calgary region." In: Urban Affairs Review 5/44, pp. 617-644.

Goddard, Nicolas/John, Sheail (2001): "Victorian sanitary movement: Where were the innovators?" In: Bernhardt, Christoph (ed.), Environmental problems in European cities in the 19th and 20th century, Münster: Waxmann, pp. 87-105.

Graham, Stephen (2001): Splintering urbanism: Networked infrastructures, technological mobilities and the urban condition, London/New York: Routledge.

Hård, Mikael/Misa, Thomas J. (eds.) (2008): Urban machinery: Inside modern European cities, Cambrigde/Mass./London: MIT Press.

Henderson, Steven/Bowlby, Sophie/Rast, Mike (2009): "Refashioning local government and inner-city regeneration: The Salford experience." In: Urban Studies 8/44, pp. 1441-1463.

Hommels, Anique (2000): "Obduracy and urban sociotechnical change: Changing plan Hoog Catharijne." In: Urban Affairs Review 5/35, pp. 649-676.

Hughes, Thomas (1983): Networks of power: Electrification in western society 1880-1930, Baltimore/London: John Hopkins University Press.

Janssens, Ric/Soens, Tim (2019): "Looking beyond the transition to water modernity in the cities of the southern Low Countries, thirteen to nineteenth centuries." In: Tim Soens/Dieter Schott/Michael Toyka-Seid/Bert de Munck (eds.), Urbanizing nature: Actors and agency (dis)connecting cities and nature since 1500, London: Routledge, pp. 89-111.

Kress, Celina (2008): "Wachstum und Schrumpfung in der Region Merseburg." In: Axel Schildt/Dirk Schubert (eds.), Städte zwischen Wachstum und Schrumpfung: Wahrnehmungs- und Umgangsformen in Geschichte und Gegenwart, Dortmund: Rohn, pp. 115-130.

Latour, Bruno (1991): Nous n'avons jamais été modernes: Essai d'antropologie symétrique, Paris: Èditions La Découverte.

Leslie, Deborah/Rantisi, Norma M. (2011): "Creativity and Place in the evolution of a cultural industry: The case of Cirque du Soleil." In: Urban Studies 9/48, pp. 1771-1787.

Mahony, James (2000): "Path dependence in historical sociology." In: Theory and Society 29, pp. 507-548.

Melosi, Martin (2005): "Path dependence and urban history: Is a marriage possible?" In: Dieter Schott/Bill Luckin/Geneviève Massard-Guilbaud (eds.), Resources of the city: Contributions to an environmental history of modern Europe, Aldershot: Ashgate, pp. 262-275.

Melosi, Martin (2000): The sanitary city: Urban infrastructure in America from colonial times to the present, Baltimore/London: Johns Hopkins University Press.

Moss, Timothy (2009): "Divided city, divided infrastructures: Securing energy and water services in postwar Berlin." In: Journal of Urban History 7/35, pp. 923-942.

North, Douglas (1990): Institutions, institutional change and economic performance, Cambridge: Cambridge University Press.

Picon, Antoine (2018): "Urban infrastructure, imagination and politics: From the networked metropolis to the smart city." In: International Journal of Urban and Regional Research, 2/42, pp. 263-275.

Pierson, Paul (2000): "Increasing returns, path dependence, and the study of politics." In: American Political Science Review 94, pp. 251-268.

Rast, Joel (2012): "Why history (still) matters: Time and temporality in urban political analysis." In: Urban Affairs Review 1/48, pp. 3-36.

Rast, Joel (2009): "Critical junctures, long-term processes: Urban redevelopment in Chicago and Milwaukee, 1946-1980." In: Social Science History 4/33, pp. 393-426.

Redfearn, Christian L. (2007): Determinacy in urban form: Fixed investment & path dependence in urban areas, Working Paper No. 8559 from USC Lusk Center for Real Estate.

Rodger, Richard (2013): "Echoes of industrialization: Cities and trajectories of development." In: Clemens Zimmermann (ed.), Industrial cities: History and future, Frankfurt a.M.: Campus, pp. 66-88.

Schott, Dieter (2018): "Krieg als externer Schock oder Katalysator für neue Pfade: Zum Verhältnis von Krieg und Pfadabhängigkeite in deutschen Städten des 20. Jahrhunderts." In: Moderne Stadtgeschichte 2, pp. 44-58.

Schott, Dieter (2002): "The formation of an urban industrial policy." In: Christoph Bernhardt/Geneviève Massard-Guilbaud (eds.), Le demon modern, Clermont Ferrand: University Press, pp. 311-333.

Schott, Dieter (1999): Die Vernetzung der Stadt: Kommunale Energiepolitik, öffentlicher Nahverkehr und die 'Produktion' der modernen Stadt. Darmstadt-Mannheim-Mainz 1880-1918, Darmstadt: Wissenschaftliche Buchgesellschaft.

Schubert, Dirk (2018): "London und Hamburg um 1900." In: Stephan Sander-Faes/Clemens Zimmermann (eds.), Weltstädte, Metropolen, Megastädte: Dynamiken von Stadt und Raum von der Antike bis zur Gegenwart, Ostfildern: Jan Thorbecke, pp. 165-188.

Sommer, Hanna/Liebmann, Heike (2013): "Städtische Karrieren zwischen Pfadabhängigkeit und Zukunftsorientierung." In: Matthias Bernt/Heike Liebmann (eds.), Peripherisierung, Stigmatisierung, Abhängigkeit? Deutsche Mittelstädte und ihr Umgang mit Peripherisierungsprozessen, Wiesbaden: Verlag für Sozialwissenschaften, pp. 107-124.

Sorensen, André (2017): "Institutions and urban space: Land, infrastructure, and governance in the production of urban property." In: Planning Theory and Practice 1/19, pp. 21-38.

Strupp, Christoph (2018): "Freie und Hafenstadt Hamburg? Maritime Pfadabhängigkeiten in Hamburg seit den 1950er Jahren." In: Moderne Stadtgeschichte 2, pp. 59-72.

Sundaresan, Jayaraj/Allen, Adriana/Johnson, Cassidy (2017): "Reading urban futures through their blue infrastructure: Wetland networks in Bangalore and Madurai, India." In: Sarah Bell/Adriana Allen/Pascale Hofmann/Tse-Hui Teh (eds.), Urban water trajectories, Heidelberg: Springer, pp. 35-52.

Tarr, Joel/Dupuy, Gabriel (eds.) (1988): Technology and the rise of the networked city in America and Europe, Philadelphia: Temple University Press.

Turok, Ivan/Mykhnenk, Vlad (2007): "The trajectories of European cities, 1960-2005." In: Cities 3/24, pp. 165-182.

Werle, Raymund (2007): "Pfadabhängigkeit." In: Arthur Benz/Suanne Lütz/Uwe Schimank/Georg Simonis (eds.), Handbuch Governance: Theoretische Grundlagen und empirische Anwendungsfelder, Wiesbaden: Verlag für Sozialwissenschaften, pp.119-131.

Woodlief, Anthony (1998): "The path-dependent city." In: Urban Affairs Review 33, pp. 407-437.

Risk and Resilience

Dominik Collet

Urban Fragility and Persistence

Cities have always been identified as volatile environments. The urban concentration of people and materials that created so many opportunities also generated new risks of its own: from fast-spreading fires and epidemics to pollution and the dependence on imports and exports. At the same time, cities have proven to be extraordinarily resilient. Between 1100 and 1800 only 42 cities worldwide were *not* rebuilt after catastrophes or destruction. After 1800 this striking resilience of urban life has become a near universal fact (Vale/Campanella 2005: 3). Consequently, urban-environmental historians have investigated the dualism of risk and resilience extensively.

In recent years the field has benefited from the boom in research on urban fragility and persistence after 9/11 and the later terrorist attacks. However, with the increased threat of global climate change to urban infrastructures—from flooding and storms to disruptions in the energy supply—an environmental perspective on the city is now becoming the focus of debate. The growing challenges have sparked a fresh interest in the ways in which earlier societies dealt with similar hazards successfully or unsuccessfully. As a result, the pathways to robust and resourceful cities are as much a topic for historians as they are for urban planners and engineers.

Initially, the concepts of *risk* and *resilience* had to be lifted by historians from neighbouring disciplines, such as ecology, economy and psychology. Some have chosen to use these terms only descriptively, dropping much of the methodological and epistemological baggage. Others have creatively engaged with the normative, systems-oriented origins of these concepts or adapted them to fit a historical approach to the study of the urban past. This chapter will provide a short overview over these methodological engagements of the last decade. It will sketch the results of looking at cities as historical centres of both risk and resilience and highlight some areas of future research in this vibrant cross-disciplinary sub-field.

Risk

Urban settings have been formative to the study of risk from the very beginning. In the city, the confluence of volatile social structures and abundant environmental hazards coupled with a low degree of self-sufficiency creates particularly prominent and readily observable 'riskscapes' (Müller-Mahn 2013). As a result, the city formed—implicitly or explicitly—the backdrop to much of the pioneering research on the creation and mitigation of risk (cf. Beck 2009). These initial studies posited a sharp break between modern and pre-modern practices of risk, ranging from perception to prevention. The seminal works of Ulrich Beck and Niklas Luhmann on the formation of modern 'risk societies' assumed that earlier societies framed hazards primarily in religious terms, suffering rather than combatting what they identified as God's Will (Beck 1986; Luhmann 1991). Only the disenchanted 19th century witnessed the emergence of an understanding of hazards as threats open to mitigation through human action. In Beck's and Luhmann's view it was this new, calculating grasp that transformed contingent hazards into 'risks' that could be mathematised, contained and governed. It eventually paved the way for the proliferation of self-inflicted uncertainties and 'new risks'—ranging from nuclear pollution to climate change—that characterise modern societies. Beck, Luhmann, but also other intellectuals, such as Anthony Giddens, all considered the conceptualisation of 'risk' as a fundamental feature of modernity and a "prerequisite for modern innovation" (Itzen/Müller 2016: 11).

The initial sociological framings have met with a lively and generally positive response from urban and environmental historians in recent years. Particularly the notion that the exposure to risk is not a straightforward result of natural variables or determined by the physical environment has met with general approval. In-depth case-studies of urban disasters or individual cityscapes have illustrated that risks are in fact socially constructed and embedded into the cultural fabric of city life. The impact of classic urban disasters such as the Great Fire of Tokyo in 1923 (Schencking 2008; Clancey 2006), the destruction of San Francisco after the 1906 earthquake (Dyl 2017) or the catastrophic floods in Paris, Hamburg, New Orleans or the cities along the Ohio river (Jackson 2010; Heßler/Kehrt 2014; Rohland 2018; Lübken 2014) have all been attributed to the fatal combination of natural and social factors. These studies show that the biophysical impacts were matched, magnified or facilitated by various societal arrangements such as rampant social inequality, poor urban planning, casual racism, over-reliance on technological fixes as well as self-fashioned ecological or industrial hazards (Bankoff/Luebken/Sand 2012). As a result, the historical prevalence of urban risks has been accredited as much to human action, societal choices and infrastructural pathways as to natural triggers. The observed practices of urban 'cultures of disaster' situate risk-awareness and risk-management deep within the entangled socio-ecological realities of city life (Bankoff 2003; Rozario 2007). They suggest framing towns as Socio-Natural Sites (Winiwarter/Schmid in this volume) rather than as mere physical, legal or social assemblages.

In contrast, the notion that the concept of risk is a recent phenomenon has met with some reluctance. Many urban historians have traced the conceptualisation of risk as well as practices of managing it much further back in time (Schenk 2019; Scheller 2017). For example, major studies have looked at the early modern roots of insurance policies that reacted to urban risks such as fires and floods (Zwierlein 2011; Zwierlein 2017; Rohland 2011). Others have looked at the development of infrastructural mechanisms to cope with urban hazards, such as flood protection, water supply systems, sanitation, disease prevention, granaries or building regulations to reduce the risk of urban fires. Most of these arrangements have been traced back to medieval times or indeed the very beginning of urban life. The debates surrounding the construction, maintenance and adaptation of these early forms of 'critical infrastructures' of urban life do not only reveal a broad array of risk-management strategies, but also a rich cultural repertoire of urban risk awareness, perception and commemoration (Gerrard/Petley 2013; Pfister 2011; Wagner 2012). Case studies have looked at flood protection measures in the early modern and medieval cities in Switzerland (Rohr 2007), Italy and Southern Germany (Schenk 2012; Rüther 2013). Others have studied the early development of urban fire prevention (Zwierlein 2011; Allemeyer 2007b), food storage (Collet 2010; Pindl 2018), state-city-community interactions (Oliver-Smith 1986) or building techniques that adapted to increased risks of earthquakes (Bankoff 2003; Villanueva Muñoz 1986). These studies highlight that practices of negotiating and combatting risk were present long before the term itself gained wider prominence. They also question linear narratives of a long-term decrease or increase in urban risks by showcasing early manifestations of the 'security paradox'—the tendency of increased security measures to provoke more risky behaviour. This is illustrated by the observation that flood protection initiated more exposed settlement patterns or that public granaries encouraged reductions in private food stocks (Allemeyer 2006; Collet 2010). Instead of linear trends, 'the security paradox' establishes dynamic trade-offs between (individual) risk and (collective) security that were openly debated and negotiated in urban settings long before the 19th century (Allemeyer 2007a; Schenk 2012; Collet 2019).

All these studies either allow for a much longer gestation period of the modern concepts of risk or discard its chronology altogether. In general, they argue that while the current acceleration and proliferation of (urban) hazards is certainly notable and unprecedented in scope, the concepts of risk and probability cannot be tied exclusively to the emergence of the nation state or (Western) modernity per se (Mauelshagen 2018: 304; Rohr et al. 2018). The development and expansion of cities was driven from the very beginning by attempts to reduce environmental uncertainty. When the success of these measures created new forms of self-inflicted risks, from increased fire, pollution and epidemic hazards, to import dependency and vulnerable settlement patterns, it did so long before the advent of the modern, technological risk society (Mohun 2013).

Taken together, these studies of urban risk have unearthed the sedimented 'cultures of uncertainty' that existed in all historical societies, but often stand out most in an urbanised context (Bankoff 2003; Collet 2013). In the context of current challenges, this surprisingly rich repertoire of dealing with risk is attracting renewed interest. In many ways, the historical plurality of social, natural and religious perceptions and responses to risk seems to mirror contemporary heterogeneities, where different groups attribute risk to a variety of technological, economic or environmental drivers. In response to the pluralisation of risks, the field of security studies has increasingly moved away from its traditional focus on state security and embraced the concept of 'securitisation' that includes environmental, technological and social hazards. Indeed, many contemporary urban planners feel reminded of earlier constellations, not just in the observed 'return of nature', but also in view of broader groups of actors, more plural forms of action and the overlapping responsibilities of municipal, entrepreneurial, non-governmental and civilian bodies (Zwierlein 2015). Historical research into urban hazards and environmental justice has highlighted the stark asymmetries in the distribution of risk according to age, gender, class and status. It has illustrated that the conflicting interests of freedom and security, of economy and ecology resulted in specific 'built environments' that already embodied and pre-figured certain risks long before a flood or famine hit the cityscape. These studies draw attention to the way in which security and risk have not just been historically produced through technologies and bio-physical stressors but also shaped by social action or inaction. In this sense, the environmental perspective has questioned rather than reaffirmed the modern techno-centred narrative of the risk-society. It has highlighted the extent to which exposure to risks is both a matter of material protection as of social participation (Oliver-Smith 1986).

Resilience

In recent years, research on risk has increasingly moved on to what Luhmann termed 'second-order observations'. Instead of studying hazards per se, attention has turned towards their socio-ecological processing. In this context the study of 'resilience' has soared to prominence (Bonß 2015). For urban settings, resilience-studies gained popularity in response to 9/11 and the boom in urban rebuilding and rejuvenation projects. This also resonates with current concerns about sustainability, climate change and conservation. As a result, resilience has emerged as a key term in urban studies and city planning (Chelleri 2012).

Historians have been eager to capitalise on this trend. Resilience has become a trendy topic for panel presentations, with the 2018 International Conference on Urban History taking *Renewal and Resilience* as its motto. For some urban historians, the term simply offers a welcome way to connect their observations on past societies to current debates. But for many it also resonates with the double-edged nature of urban life they study, with cities creating their own set of risks on the one hand, while clearly belonging to the most persistent human endeavours on the other. Many cities are now over a thousand years old and have seen empires, ecologies and ideas come and go. They are clearly 'resilient' in the sense that they have withstood wars, epidemics, transformative technological change and political revolutions. Additionally, studies on resilience and the lack thereof also manage to tap into the long held fascination of abandoned and destroyed cities, such as Atlantis, Babylon, Persepolis, Tikal or Macchu Pichu (Vale/Campanella 2005: 5).

However, resilience denotes not just an evocative term but refers to a complex scientific concept. It comes with significant conceptual baggage that is often at odds with established historical methodology. So far, most historians simply refer to the term 'resilience' in its colloquial sense of persistence, toughness or ability to recover. They often treat it as antonym to 'vulnerability', irrespective of their very different scientific genealogies and diverging perspectives from 'above' and 'below'. Whereas vulnerability studies emerged as a critique to developmentalism and its victims, aimed at bottom-up social change and challenged the status quo, resilience thinking has often been associated with a more conciliatory tone that integrated well into a liberal economic agenda, and addressed the consequences rather than the causes of urban risks (Bankoff 2019; Miller et al. 2010). While current urban studies use the term normatively—cities should be resilient—, historians treat resilience as a descriptive term—cities can be more or less resilient (Imbusch 2015; Brand/Jax 2007). Engagement with the scientific concept of resilience, its far-reaching premises and challenging assumptions to urban-environmental history has been limited. This not only leads to misunderstandings and factual misappropriations, it has also cut historians off from the vibrant and productive criticism of the field.

As an academic concept, resilience began its life in various scientific fields such as psychology, medicine or engineering (Walker/Cooper 2011). However, urban studies have generally adopted its use in ecology. Following C. S. Holling, resilience is understood as the ability of a system to absorb disturbance and return to its original state (Holling 1973: 14; Slootweg/Jones 2001: 264). While this framing dominates current debates in urban studies, it sits uneasily with some core beliefs of historians and has sparked various reactions from pragmatic criticism to outright rejection.

The ecological orientation towards 'systems' has the obvious potential to veil historical contingency and obscure agency. The systemic perspective directs scrutiny not to the individual citizen but to the city itself, with the potential to mask internal division, asymmetries and conflict. Its totalising discourse has been blamed for obscuring the messiness of the socio-ecological arrangements that urban-environmental history studies (Vardy/Smith 2017). Additionally, the suggestion of a rebound to a 'normal' state has been identified as a fundamentally ahistorical assumption. Historical research in general neither recognises a supposedly 'normal' form of societal arrangements, nor does it accept that once an event has occurred, a return to a previous setting is even possible. It suggests that even if all political, economic and ecological parameters should revert to previous values, the very fact that people have experienced change will guarantee different future outcomes. Instead, historical research calls attention to the fact that the fragile identification of a 'normal' urban or societal state transports a range of value judgements and emplotments. Any selection of a supposed baseline supported by invariably biased premises would run the risk of pre-determining research outcomes to a large degree (Kirchhoff et al. 2010). Finally, the silent assumption that resilience is per se a good thing is alien to historical research. The fetish of stability is obviously anathema to historians who investigate the dynamics of change in constantly shifting environments. As history is generally understood as contingent and linear rather than as systemic and reversible, substantial challenges remain to transferring the concept of resilience (rather than the descriptive term) to historical research. Attempts to adapt resilience-thinking to social pathways rather than ecological models are therefore just beginning (cf. Endres/Maurer 2015).

Such concerns have also been voiced by a range of urban historians and researchers themselves. Some have drawn attention to the fact that the momentous transfer of the resilience concept from non-human systems to human societies is based purely on analogy rather than empirical research and entails naturalising societal ills (Olsson et al. 2015; Gleeson 2013). In this respect, resilience approaches to cityscapes have often been linked to a neo-liberal agenda. They are seen as an instrument to devolve public safety to civil society and the 'resilient citizen', prioritise economic recovery above social change and preserve the status quo through adaptation rather than addressing underlying conflicts (Bankoff 2019; McGuirk 2014; Joseph 2013). The focus on 'systemic' survival is criticised for obscuring the uneven distribution of costs and benefits according to class, gender, ethnicity and age. It is blamed for disguising power asymmetries, social stratification and uneven access to resources—imbalances that are particularly prevalent in urban settings (Vardy/Smith 2017). In fact, it risks masking one of the core discoveries of urban-environmental history: that even highly destructive events are socially patterned and affect the isolated, poor and weak much more severely (Matthewman 2015: 20).

Other observers have taken issue with the fact that the naturalism and scientism of the concept suggest a false neutrality that can naturalise precarity. Some warn that in such biased contexts even purely descriptive studies by historians can support quick technofixes that undermine the democratic process and legitimise the securitisation of social problems (Imbusch 2015). As a result, critics see research into resilience as a mainstreaming of urban-environmental studies that supports current dogma rather than encouraging open, exploratory research (Chelleri 2012).

Others strands of the debate have been less dismissive. Resilience studies are credited for encouraging new imaginaries of urban history that go beyond the defensive and authoritarian to include Promethean trajectories of resurgence and rebirth (Gleeson 2013). Environmental historians in particular value that the resilience approach inspires researchers to turn from political histories of the urban past to a more metabolic perspective. They see resilience-thinking as an encouragement to situate cities in larger ecological frameworks that include the constant flow of material and immaterial resources. It could also re-tune attention to the crucial infrastructures that organise these flows of food, material, fuel, or information. In fact, the persistence of the patterns of these flows is often considered the reason why cities are rebuilt rather than removed. Such integrated, metabolic approaches have also been credited for raising the awareness that social as well as physical efforts are needed to sustain urban life in the long run (Imbusch 2015). Resilience studies might draw more attention to the fact that safeguarding precarious city environments requires a broad set of actors that goes far beyond the narrow elites of experts and administrators often studied in more conventional urban histories. Universal concepts such as resilience require universal participation. In this sense, studying resilience-building can also unveil bottom-up processes of managing survival that are often overlooked by the histories of technology and security.

Many researchers have also suggested tackling the larger issues of transferring an ecological concept to the humanities. They recommend reconfiguring the systemic perspective by re-scaling resilience to various levels and/or fields—investigating emotional and cultural as well as physical resilience (Pillatt 2012; Kirschbaum/Sideroff 2005; Adger 2000). Some suggest that such a move could capture the important resilience trade-offs between various temporal and spatial levels (Chelleri et al. 2015). However, such attempts at a multi-level resilience analysis in tune with methods of the humanities have occasionally been rebuffed by scientists. They have voiced concern that such an approach might render a simple systemic model too complex and politically charged to be handled efficiently (Kirchhoff et al. 2010). Some scholars of risk and resilience encourage researchers to embrace the creative potential that the irritating transfer of disciplinary concepts provides. Historians could unpick the paradoxical fault line that long-term resilience often requires short-term change—a conceptual disjuncture that invites historical empiricism and scrutiny (Bonß 2015). The long range of historical observation could also reveal the substantial latitude of past societies at negotiating resilience—an agenda particularly suited for urban-environmental histories (Schott 2012). Empirical studies of the individual leeway and agency of the historical actors might not only enhance the current debate but and also complement the concept's systemic and presentist focus.

So far, the most fruitful contributions in urban-environmental history have taken the resilience concept as a mere starting-point for studies that offer a more pluralistic, process-oriented and empirically saturated perspective. Instead of establishing models, they tap into the rich historical tapestry of city life to establish factors that sustain the astonishing perseverance of urban environments. Several edited volumes have taken a comparative rather than a systemic perspective toward urban resilience and persistence (Wagner 2012; Vale/Campanella 2005; Ranft/Selzer 2004; Massard-Guilbaud et al. 2002; Körner 1999-2000). They bring together case-studies of individual cities ranging from medieval Bagdad and Basel to modern Beirut and Berlin. Most focus on sudden disruptive events, such as floods, fires and war, to reveal historical turning points, pathways and divergences. These analyses demonstrate not just the robustness of cities in the face of disaster, the resourcefulness of their populace in response to threats and their surprising potential for recouperance, with many cities emerging even more vibrant from a period of disaster. They also identify the plurality of urban responses, highlighting the fundamental significance of municipal infrastructure arrangements, frameworks for political participation within and beyond the city, and the uneven burden-sharing across the population.

The observed pluralities of urban 'resiliencing' are highlighted in a seminal study by Dieter Schott (2012). His research takes the ambivalence of cities as both a concentration of risks and a promise of security as point of departure. Drawing on the strikingly different results of the 1783 and the 1908 earthquakes in Messina, Schott argues for an approach to resilience studies that accounts for historical contingency and incorporates the wider framework of socio-ecological constellations. The study contrasts the piecemeal reconstruction after the Great Fire of London in 1666 with the fundamental redesign in response to the Lisbon Earthquake of 1755 and the technology-centred reaction to the 1962 flooding of Hamburg. A close reading of these events reveals the subtle but potent improvements made in London, the bitter conflict between ecclesiastical, noble and merchant interests in Lisbon and the way in which experts appropriated the Hamburg flood to disempower parliament and realise long-standing plans for harbour extensions. Underneath the citywide persistence Schott unveils not just agglomerations of capital, memory and motivation that keep cities alive, but also dynamic power struggles, momentous social stratification and highly diverse frameworks of legitimisation.

Similar studies have explored the difficult ideological framing of early resilience and prevention-thinking (Hannig 2016) or recalled the contribution of inert urban infrastructures and historical investments in the built environment—from postal networks to shipping lines and trading routes—to stabilising urban environments (Van Laak 2018). Some have used historical cases in the Ottoman and Japanese Empires to highlight forms of negative resilience, referring to the social costs of resilience lock-ins that do not just cement social inequality but also limit the potential for progressive development (Izdebski et al. 2018; Hein 2005).

These studies illustrate that beneath the level of systemic survival and physical resilience that most cities share, there is a rich reservoir of historical contingency, diverging pathways and socio-ecological heterogeneity ready for historical studies to explore. While 'resilience' has become a popular point of departure for many current research projects, their empirical findings of plurality, conflict and asymmetry remain somewhat at odds with the normative resilience concept used in contemporary urban studies. These studies of the historical urban environment portray the process of resiliencing as negotiation rather than structure and focus on constellations rather than systems. In this sense, observing the cultural embeddedness of urban resilience, the conflicted nature of its implementation and the trade-offs between resilience and historical change might become an important corrective to the conceptual overshoots of contemporary debates.

Future Challenges

Concepts of risk and resilience have certainly encouraged urban-environmental history to explore the vital entanglements between the registers of nature and culture. They have also become important boundary objects to facilitate interdisciplinary cooperation, debate and borrowing. However, some notable gaps and imbalances in current research designs remain.

Most studies focus on the 19th to 21st centuries, with earlier developments receiving far less attention. This skewed distribution not only misses out on the unique opportunities that cities provide in terms of their exceptional persistence and longevity. These preferences also risk implying (though often unintentionally) that urbanity and modernity are concurrent phenomena, or that premodern risks and resilience patterns followed fundamentally different pathways—a suggestion that should certainly be based on empirical research rather than negative evidence. In order to substantiate the implicit periodisation and to escape the lure of presentism, studies with a deeper chronological reach or diachronic designs are highly desirable.

Spatial imbalances are similarly notable. Almost all recent research is devoted to European and North-American cases. In-depth studies of non-Western cityscapes and urban pathways are rare and patchy. Again, this imbalance runs the risk of suggesting contrast where there is none. At the same time it deprives the current debate of exploring alternative urban pathways and arrangements of dealing with risk. This deficit has become so potent that it extends to the conceptual level, with 'resilience' largely remaining a Western approach that is geared towards the environmental and social patterns of the global North. As a result, current research and conceptual framings largely ignore settings, such as historical Japan or the contemporary Philippines, where urban disasters formed part of city life and have been accommodated rather than prevented (Bankoff 2019). Most existing research designs also disregard non-Western examples, such as contemporary Basra, Kabul or former Soviet urbanities, where the Phoenix effect might not be similarly ubiquitous and uniform (Herscher 2005). Extending urban-environmental history globally therefore remains an important priority with the potential to challenge established conventions and boundaries.

Even more pronounced is the fixation of current research on disaster events. Catastrophe-centred research has certainly proven to reveal socio-ecological arrangements as well as mental, political and material repertoires that would otherwise have remained hidden. It has been instrumental in criticising the naturalisation of risk and disaster and in establishing the constitutive socio-natural entanglements of urban metabolisms—important contributions in a world shaped by global warming and escalating self-fashioned risk. However, this emphasis has discouraged research into the many forms of non-disaster related resilience and long-term risks. It has again left its mark on the conceptual level, with resilience now being largely equated with post-disaster recovery. Forms of resilience that are non-cataclysmic, or types of risk that are slow, long-term and persistent, such as disease, pollution, dearth, environmental degradation, have attracted much less attention. Those studies that exist (e. g. Mosley 2001; Brüggemeier 1996; Evans 1985) have often been considered as external rather than complementary to risk research. The same applies to cases of long-term decline rather than abrupt collapse. Research on 'shrinking cities', such as 20th-century Detroit, Leipzig or New Orleans, attributed these contractions to teleconnections between long-term and abrupt shocks in macro-economic and ecological environments (Pallagst/Wiechmann/Martinez-Fernandez 2014). The exclusion of slow and long-term hazards runs the risk of encouraging circular and self-referential reasoning. Closing this gap may unlock alternative, more plural pathways, promote comparisons and become an important inspiration for future research. It might also reveal the extent to which resilience itself might turn into a disaster for some parts of the population.

A final desideratum is the reluctance of historians to engage with risk and resilience studies based in the natural sciences at the conceptual level. Resilience studies in particular are characterised by a complex scientific genealogy that transports many silent references and challenging assumptions. So far, historians often ignore the wider conceptual framing of resilience approaches in ecology and urban studies, turning a blind eye to their social construction in highly conflicted contexts. This risks stabilizing narratives that naturalise social facts or reproduce systemic presentism. It will be both laborious and rewarding to enrich the current ahistorical, cyclical and systems-oriented approach of (urban) resilience studies with a genuinely historical perspective on multiple scales that allows for plurality, contingency and agency. However, such delimiting boundary work is certainly necessary to progress from the simple overlap in content to genuine cooperation and empirical transfer. It will not just ensure that risk and resilience stay at the heart of the research field. It can also unlock the vast reservoir of urban histories for a contemporary debate, motivated by an environment increasingly perceived as risky and fragile.

References

Adger, Neil (2000): "Social and ecological resilience: Are they related?" In: Progress in Human Geography 24, pp. 347-64.
Allemeyer, Marie Luisa (2007a): "Profane hazard or divine judgement? Coping with urban fire in the 17th century." In: Historical Social Research 32, pp. 145-168.
Allemeyer, Marie Luisa (2007b): Fewersnot und Flammenschwert: Stadtbrände in der Frühen Neuzeit, Göttingen: Vandenhoeck & Ruprecht.
Allemeyer, Marie Luisa (2006): 'Kein Land ohne Deich...!' Lebenswelten einer Küstengesellschaft in der Frühen Neuzeit, Göttingen: Vandenhoeck & Ruprecht.
Bankoff, Greg (2019): Remaking the world in our own image: Vulnerability, resilience and adaptation as historical discourses." In: Disasters 43, pp. 221-239.
Bankoff, Greg (2003): Cultures of disaster: Society and natural hazards in the Philippines, London: Routledge.
Bankoff, Greg/Luebken, Uwe/Sand, Jordan (eds.) (2012): Flammable cities: Urban conflagration and the making of the modern world, Madison: University of Wisconsin Press.
Beck, Ulrich (2009): World at Risk, Cambridge: Polity Press.
Beck, Ulrich (1986): Risikogesellschaft: Auf dem Weg in eine andere Moderne, Frankfurt a. M.: Suhrkamp.
Bonß, Wolfgang (2015): "Karriere und sozialwissenschaftliche Potenziale des Resilienzbegriffs." In: Martin Endreß/Andrea Maurer (eds.), Resilienz im Sozialen, Wiesbaden: Springer, pp. 15-33.

Brand, Fridolin/Jax, Kurt (2007): "Focusing the meaning(s) of resilience: Resilience as a descriptive concept and a boundary object." In: Ecology and Society 12. (http://www.ecologyandsociety.org/vol12/iss1/art23).

Brüggemeier, Franz-Josef (1996): Das unendliche Meer der Lüfte: Luftverschmutzung, Industrialisierung und Risikodebatten im 19. Jahrhundert, Essen: Klartext.

Chelleri, Lorenzo (2012): "From the 'resilient city' to urban resilience: A review essay on understanding and integrating the resilience perspective for urban systems." In: Documents d'Anàlisi Geogràfica 58, pp. 287-306.

Chelleri, Lorenzo/Waters, James J./Olazabal, Marta/Minucci, Guido (2015): "Resilience trade-offs: Addressing multiple scales and temporal aspects of urban resilience." In: Environment and Urbanization 27, pp. 181-198.

Clancey, Gregory (2006): Earthquake nation: the cultural politics of Japanese Seismicity, Berkeley: University of California Press.

Collet, Dominik (2019): Die doppelte Katastrophe: Klima und Kultur in der europäischen Hungerkrise 1770-1772, Göttingen: Vandenhoeck & Ruprecht.

Collet, Dominik (2013): "Eine Kultur der Unsicherheit? Empowering Interactions während der Hungerkrise 1770-72." In: Christoph Kampmann/Ulrich Niggemann (eds.), Sicherheit in der Frühen Neuzeit: Norm, Praxis, Repräsentation, Cologne/Weimar/Vienna: Böhlau, pp. 367-380.

Collet, Dominik (2010): "Storage and starvation: Public granaries as agents of 'food security' in early modern Europe." In: Historical Social Research 35/4, pp. 234-252.

Dyl, Joanna L. (2017): Seismic City: An environmental history of San Francisco's 1906 earthquake, Washington: University of Washington Press.

Endreß, Martin/Maurer, Andrea (eds.) (2015): Resilienz im Sozialen, Wiesbaden: Springer.

Evans, Richard J. (1985): Death in Hamburg: Society and politics in the cholera years, 1830-1910, Oxford: Clarendon Press.

Gerrard Christopher/Petley, Davis (2013): "A risk society? Environmental hazards, risk and resilience in the later middle ages in Europe." In: Natural Hazards: Journal of the International Society for the Prevention and Mitigation of Natural Hazards 69/1, pp. 1051-1079.

Gleeson, Brendan (2013): "Resilience and its discontents." In: Research Paper No. 1, Melbourne Sustainable Society Institute (https://sustainable.unimelb.edu.au/__data/assets/pdf_file/0006/2763492/MSSI-ResearchPaper-01_Gleeson_Resilience_2013.pdf).

Hannig, Nicolai (2016): "The checkered rise of resilience: Anticipating risks of nature in Switzerland and Germany since 1800." In: Historical Social Research 41, pp. 240-262.

Hein, Carola (2005): "Resilient Tokyo: Disaster and transformation in the Japanese city." In: Lawrence Vale/Thomas Campanella (eds.), The resilient city, New York: Oxford University Press, pp. 213-234.

Heßler, Martina/Kehrt, Christian (eds.) (2014): Die Hamburger Sturmflut von 1962: Risikobewusstsein und Katastrophenschutz aus zeit-, technik- und umweltgeschichtlicher Perspektive, Göttingen: Vandenhoeck & Ruprecht.

Herscher, Andrew (2005): Review of Lawrence Vale/Thomas Campanella, The resilient city: How modern cities recover from disaster." In: H-Urban (http://www.h-net.org/reviews/showrev.php?id=10609).

Holling, Crawford Stanley (1973): "Resilience and stability of ecological systems." In: Annual Review of Ecology and Systematics 4, pp. 1-23.

Imbusch, Peter (2015): "Urbane Resilienz und endemische Gewalt." In: Martin Endreß/Andrea Maurer (eds.), Resilienz im Sozialen, Wiesbaden: Springer, pp. 245-264.

Izdebski, Adam/Mordechai, Lee/White, Sam (2018): "The social burden of resilience: A historical perspective." In: Human Ecology 46, pp. 291-303.

Jackson, Jeffrey H. (2010): Paris under water: How the city of light survived the Great Flood of 1910, New York: Palgrave MacMillan.

Joseph, Jonathan (2013): "Resilience as embedded neoliberalism: A governmentality approach." In: Resilience 1, pp. 38-52.

Kirchhoff, Tohmas/Fridolin Brand/Deborah Hoheisel/Volker Grimm (2010): "The one-sidedness and cultural bias of the resilience approach." In: Gaia 19, pp. 25-32.

Kirschbaum, Julie/Sideroff, Desirée (2005): "A delayed healing: Understanding the fragmented resilience of Gernika." In: Lawrence J. Vale/Thomas J. Campanella (eds.), The resilient city: How modern cities recover from disaster, Oxford: Oxford University Press, pp. 159-180.

Körner, Martin (ed.) (1999-2000): Stadtzerstörung und Wiederaufbau, Bern/Stuttgart/Vienna: Haupt.

Lübken, Uwe (2014): Die Natur der Gefahr: Überschwemmungen am Ohio River im neunzehnten und zwanzigsten Jahrhundert, Göttingen: Vandenhoeck & Ruprecht.

Luhmann, Niklas (1991): Risk: A sociological theory, Berlin: de Gruyter.

Massard-Guilbaud, Geneviève/Platt, Harold/Schott, Dieter (eds.) (2002): Cities and catastrophes/Villes et catastrophes: Coping with emergency in European history/Réactions à l'urgence dans l'histoire européenne, Frankfurt a. M./Berlin/Bern: Peter Lang.

Matthewman, Steve (2015): Disasters, risks and revelation: Making sense of our times, Houndmills: Springer.

Mauelshagen, Franz (2018): "The age of uncertainty: The challenges of climate change for the insurance business." In: Franz Mauelshagen/Claus Leggewie (eds.), Climate change and cultural transition in Europe, Leiden/Boston: Brill, pp. 301-319.

McGuirk, Justin (2014): Radical Cities: Across Latin Amerika in search of a new architecture, New York: Verso.

Miller, Fiona/Osbahr, Henny/Boyd, Emily/Thomalla, Frank/Bharawani, Sukaina/Ziervogel, Gina/Walker, Brian/Birkmann, Jörn/van der Leeuw, Sander/ Rockström, Johan/Hinkel, Jochen/Downing, Tom/Folke, Carl/Nelson, Donald (2010): "Resilience and vulnerability: Complementary or conflicting concepts?" In: Ecology and Society 15, pp. 1-25.

Mohun, Arwen P. (2013): Risk: Negotiating safety in American Society, Baltimore: Johns Hopkins University Press.

Mosley, Stephen (2001): The chimney of the world: A history of smoke pollution in Victorian and Edwardian Manchester, Cambridge: White Horse Press.

Müller-Mahn, Detlef (2013): "Riskscapes: The spatial dimensions of risk." In: Detlef Müller-Mahn (ed.), The spatial dimension of risk: How geography shapes the emergence of riskscapes, London/New York: Routledge, pp. 22-36.

Oliver-Smith, Antony (1986): The martyred city: Death and rebirth in the Andes, Mexico City: University of New Mexico Press.

Olsson, Lennart/Jerneck, Anne/Thoren, Henrik/Persson, Johannes/O'Byrne, David (2015): "Why resilience is unappealing to social science: Theoretical and empirical investigations of the scientific use of resilience." In: Science Advances 1 (doi:10.1126/sciadv.1400217).

Pallagst, Karina/Wiechmann, Thorsten/Martinez-Fernandez Cristina (2014): Shrinking cities: International perspectives and policy implications, New York: Routledge.

Pfister, Christian (2011): "'The monster swallows you': Disaster memory and risk culture in Western Europe, 1500-2000." In: Rachel Carson Center Perspectives 1, pp. 1-23.

Pillatt, Toby (2012): "Resilience theory and social memory: Avoiding abstraction." In: Archaeological Dialogues 19, pp. 62-74.

Pindl, Kathrin (2018): "Grain policies and storage in southern Germany: The Regensburg hospital (17th-19th centuries)." In: Jahrbuch für Wirtschaftsgeschichte 59/2, pp. 415-445.

Ranft, Andreas/Selzer, Stephan (eds.) (2004): Städte aus Trümmern: Katastrophenbewältigung zwischen Antike und Moderne, Göttingen: Vandenhoeck & Ruprecht 2004.

Rohland, Eleonora (2018): Changes in the air: Hurricanes in New Orleans from 1718 to the Present, New York/Oxford: Berghahn.

Rohland, Eleonora (2011): Sharing the risk: Fire, climate and disaster, Swiss Re 1864-1906, Lancaster: Carnegie Publishing.

Rohr, Christian (2007): Extreme Naturereignisse im Ostalpenraum: Naturerfahrung im Spätmittelalter und am Beginn der Neuzeit, Cologne/Weimar/Vienna: Böhlau.

Rohr, Christian/Bieber, Ursula/Zeppezauer-Wachauer, Katharina (eds.) (2018): Krisen, Kriege, Katastrophen: Zum Umgang mit Angst und Bedrohung im Mittelalter, Heidelberg: Springer.

Rozario, Kevin (2007): The culture of calamity: Disaster and the making of modern America, Chicago: The University of Chicago Press.

Rüther, Stefanie (2013): "Zwischen göttlicher Fügung und herrschaftlicher Verfügung: Katastrophen als Gegenstand spätmittelalterlicher Sicherheitspolitik." In: Christoph Kampmann/Ulrich Niggemann (eds.), Sicherheit in der Frühen Neuzeit: Norm, Praxis, Repräsentation, Cologne/Weimar/Vienna: Böhlau, pp. 335-350.

Scheller, Benjamin (2017): "Die Geburt des Risikos: Kontingenz und kaufmännische Praxis im mediterranen Seehandel des Hoch- und Spätmittelalters." In: Historische Zeitschrift 304, pp. 305-333.

Schenk, Gerrit Jasper (2019): "Die Zukunft zähmen? Die Entstehung eines Risikobegriffs in der Sicherheitskultur spätmittelalterlicher Städte." In: Benjamin Scheller (ed.), Kulturen des Risikos im Europa des Mittelalters und der Frühen Neuzeit, Munich: Oldenbourg [in print].

Schenk, Gerrit Jasper (2012): "Managing natural hazards: Environment, society, and politics in Tuscany and the Upper Rhine Valley in the Renaissance (1270-1570)." In: Andrea Janku/Gerrit Jasper Schenk/Franz Mauelshagen (eds.), Historical disasters in context: Science, religion, and politics, New York/London: Routledge, pp. 31-53.

Schencking, J. Charles (2008): "The great Kantō earthquake and the culture of catastrophe and reconstruction in 1920s Japan." In: Journal of Japanese Studies 34/2, pp. 295-331.

Schott, Dieter (2012): "Resilienz oder Niedergang? Zur Bedeutung von Naturkatastrophen für Städte in der Neuzeit." In: Ulrich Wagner (ed.), Stadt und Stadtverderben, Ostfildern: Jan Thorbecke, pp. 11-32.

Slootweg, Roel/Jones, Mike (2011): "Resilience thinking improves SEA: A discussion paper." In: Impact Assessment and Project Appraisal 29, pp. 263-276.

Vale, Lawrence J./Campanella, Thomas J. (eds.) (2005): The resilient city: How modern cities recover from disaster, Oxford: Oxford University Press.

Van Laak, Dirk (2018): Alles im Fluss: Die Lebensadern unserer Gesellschaft. Geschichte und Zukunft der Infrastruktur, Frankfurt a.M.: S. Fischer.

Vardy, Mark/Smith, Mick (2017): "Resilience." In: Environmental Humanities 9, pp. 175-179.

Villanueva Muñoz, EA (1986): "La planificacion urbana de Vera tras el terremoto de 1518: Forma y significado." In: Roel. Cuadernos de civilizacion de la cuenca del Almanzora 7/8, pp. 127-143.

Wagner, Ulrich (ed.) (2012): Stadt und Stadtverderben, Ostfildern: Jan Thorbecke.

Walker, Jeremy/Cooper, Melinda (2011): "Genealogies of resilience: From systems ecology to the political economy of crisis adaptation." In: Security Dialogue 42, pp. 143-160.

Winiwarter, Verena/Schmid, Martin/Dressel, Gert (2013): "Looking at half a millennium of co-existence: The Danube in Vienna as a socio-natural site." In: Water History 5/2, pp. 101-119.

Zwierlein, Cornel (2017): "Perceiving urban fire regimes in Europe and China, 1830s to 1870s: British fire insurance businesses and the sudden challenge of globalisation." In: Gerrit J. Schenk (ed.), Historical disaster experiences, Heidelberg: Springer, pp. 327-352

Zwierlein, Cornel (2015): "Return to premodern times? Contemporary security studies, the early modern Holy Roman Empire, and coping with achronies." In: German Studies Review 38/2, pp. 373-392.

Zwierlein, Cornel (2011): Der gezähmte Prometheus: Feuer und Sicherheit zwischen Früher Neuzeit und Moderne, Göttingen: Vandenhoeck & Ruprecht.

Sustainability

Ansgar Schanbacher

Widely used as an argument in current public debates, the term and concept of sustainability has an intricate history of its own and accordingly plays an important role in historical research, especially in the fields of environmental and economic history. The concept is ambiguous, though, and it is necessary to distinguish between the development of the term—originating in the early modern management of forest resources and still a paradigm of scientific forestry—, its analytical use as a research tool, and finally its normative use in political debates. This article presents an overview of the concept of sustainability and its development since the 18th century and also reviews the historical scholarship in the field.

The term 'sustainability' has been a standard feature of public, political and economic discourse since the 1980s, at least in the Western world (Caradonna 2018: 9). In a general understanding sustainability seems to be a rather positive term which is associated with durability and an ecologically sound development but at the same time it is abstract and vague (Pufé 2017: 23).

There are various definitions and models of sustainability in different fields of research. At the general level sustainability can be defined as a "capacity to maintain some entity, outcome, or process over time." (Jenkins 2010: 380) Different notions of sustainability can be grouped around economic, ecological and political models which emphasise different views of the concept (ibid: 383). While economic models focus on sustainability as an investment problem whereby opportunity (capital) should be sustained, ecological models stress the importance of biological diversity and ecological integrity, and Social Ecology conceives sustainability as the capacity to maintain "vital physical exchange processes between societies and their natural environment" (Haberl et al. 2004a: 194). Moreover, political models propose to support social systems which defend human dignity and reduce social inequalities toward achieving political stability in society.

A popular—albeit not uncontested—scheme is the three-sector model of sustainability which aims to balance the interests of environmental, economic and social domains in pursuit of sustainable development (Fig. 1).[1]

Figure 1: Triad Model of sustainability[2]

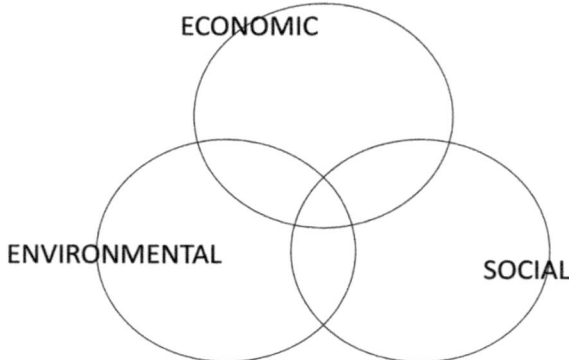

These current discussions about sustainability are reflected in historical research. First, there is the history of the term sustainability itself, which in its German equivalent reaches back to the 18th century and has been scrutinised from the perspective of the history of knowledge and science. Second, the concept of sustainability helps historians think about past societies, both in a normative and an analytical way.

The History of a Concept

The origins of the concept of sustainability date back to the 18th century, although practices of sustainable land and resource use were much older. One strand of research has focused on how the concept developed from its origins in forestry to become a now ubiquitous buzzword (Fig. 2).

---

[1] Mulligan 2018: pp. 89-93. Another approach differentiates between 'weak sustainability', according to which natural resources and man-made capital are mutually substitutable, and 'strong sustainability' which denies this possibility; Muraca/Döring 2018: pp. 345-347.

[2] See Pufé 2017: 112. There is a huge number of similar and more developed models, see for example the spider model in Freitas 2012: p. 162.

Figure 2: Campaign of the German forestry lobby, pointing out the long-standing tradition and yet actuality of sustainability ('Nachhaltigkeit')[3]

For the historian Paul Warde (2018), who writes about discourses on sustainability as an aspect of European intellectual history from the 16th to the 19th centuries, sustainability was not 'discovered' at one specific time but first became evident as a concern in the work of individual historical actors, who were experts in fields such as state economy or agriculture. Their thoughts centred on "the idea that to endure, a society must not undermine the ecological underpinnings on which it is dependent. It must not degrade, to use a more archaic term, 'the Earth'" (ibid: 356-357). Warde points to the importance that early modern states ascribed to the efficacy of acquisition and distribution of resources such as food and wood, when populations were growing and rulers had to face expanding fiscal and military pressures. In this context, he analyses how attempts to raise agricultural productivity were promoted by a growing literature on husbandry (ibid: 145, 228-229, 235; see also Thomas 2018 who explores 19th and 20th century intellectual history of sustainability). The actual term sustainability was strongly influenced by Hans Carl von Carlowitz, a Saxon mining commissioner, who used the German adjec-

---

3 https://www.forstwirtschaft-in-deutschland.de/nachhaltigkeit/kampagne-300-jahre-nachhaltigkeit/ [accessed on 8 Jan. 2019].

tive 'nachhaltend' ('sustaining') in his work *Sylvicultura oeconomica* in 1713.[4] Born at a time of allegedly growing wood shortages, the term and concepts were further developed by German scientific forestry. The first mention of 'Nachhaltigkeit' ('sustainability') was made in 1760, and around 1850 the term 'nachhaltige Forstwirtschaft' was translated into English as 'sustained yield forestry'. From then on, the term found its way into the international vocabulary of forestry (Huss/Gadow 2013: 27; Grober 2013: 20).

The subsequent semantic changes caused the substance of the concept also to develop. While Carlowitz used the term as synonymous to words meaning durable, continuously etc. and did not put much emphasis on it, later authors, such as Wilhelm Gottfried Moser in the second half of the 18th century, highlighted the concept as being crucial toward securing the scarce resource of timber for the future. After 1800 the concept spread to other countries (Mosley 2010: 43) and also attracted attention in the field of agriculture.[5] Simultaneously, sustainable land usage, especially in regard to forests, became a question of power relations. At the end of the 18th century scientific foresters and public authorities in Germany reclaimed resources which had been used as commons by people living nearby for hundreds of years (Radkau 2013: 133-134; Hölzl 2010: 434-435). In scientific forestry the idea of maintaining tall forests gained momentum and suppressed other forest uses (Radkau 2007: 166-170). From the second half of the 19th century into the 20th century, forest scientists finally began to extend the concept of sustainability and also considered ecological developments (Röhrig et al. 2006: 26-29; Hölzl 2010: 439-441).

The social relevance of the concept declined during the 19th century, and later the United Nations reintroduced the concept of sustainable development in the 1970s. This renewed concern about sustainability drew on the older concepts but emerged within the context of growing environmental awareness in Western society. Conferences and committees such as the 1972 Stockholm Conference and the World Commission on Environment and Development (1983-1987) came into being (Caradonna 2018: 11). The latter published the famous *Brundtland Report*, which defined the goals of sustainable development as follows:

> Humanity has the ability to make development sustainable to ensure that it meets the needs of the present without compromising the ability of future generations to meet their own needs. It contains within it two key concepts: the concept of 'needs',

---

[4] A similar word ('Nachhalt') occurs two years earlier in a letter by the Saxon Timber Commission; Schmidt 2013: p. 32.

[5] Schmidt 2013: pp. 33-34; Reith 2008: pp. 1010-1011. A similar idea in French scientific forestry, équilibre agrosylvopastoral, symbolizes the optimal organization of human usage of land (forests, fields, grasslands); Nougarède 1994: p. 165.

in particular the essential needs of the world's poor, to which overriding priority should be given; and the idea of limitations imposed by the state of technology and social organization on the environment's ability to meet present and future needs. (Our Common Future 1987: I. § 27)[6]

Then, during the UN Conference on Environment and Development in Rio de Janeiro in June 1992, representatives from 172 countries signed Agenda 21, which transfers the responsibility for sustainable development to national states, municipalities and citizens (Pufé 2017: 52). The idea of intergenerational justice as a normative demand, outlined in the Rio conference, leads to the question of sustainability as an analytical tool in historical research.

Sustainability in Historical Research

For a long time, past sustainability research was closely linked with the history of forests and was widely neglected in main-stream historical research.[7] This has been changing over the last 20 years when the sustainability of past societies began to be addressed along with the appropriate methodology to deal with this topic.

There are several propositions on how to utilise the concept of sustainability in historical research. While "formulations of sustainability are frequently rather vague, […] they generally address the sense that humankind must ensure its material reproduction in a way that does not diminish the fortunes of future generations" (Warde 2011: 153). Jeremy Caradonna (2018) more generally suggested linking the history of sustainability with 'systems thinking', namely, "the ways in which human societies have conceptualised, dealt with, and responded to the relationship between the natural environment, human wellbeing, and economic systems." (ibid: 11)

In a more practical approach, historian Rolf Peter Sieferle in 2003 revised the concept to include four criteria: energy, material (resources and sinks), biodiversity and population dynamics. He rejected other criteria of the modern concept of sustainability such as social and political aspects as being results of democrat-

---

6 This approach comprised proposals in the areas of population, food security, the extinction of species and genetic resources, energy, industry, and human settlements, which were seen as interconnected; ibid: II. § 40.

7 For example there are only very brief mentions of sustainability in some American works on environmental history: Merchant 2007; Krech et al. 2004; Black/Lybecker 2008.

ic standards in recent societies that can not be projected onto past societies.[8] In Sieferle's (2003) opinion, even agrarian civilisations were not stable, insofar as over "the long term each political, social and economic dimension was exposed to permanent and often violent change" (ibid: 124) frequently because of environmental issues. Nevertheless, when looking at production modes and the duration of these societies, they were sustainable for several thousands of years (ibid)—an assumption which is challenged by the archaeologist Simone Riehl (2015: 291). Pertaining to the collapse of the Early Bronze Age civilisations in the Middle East, she proposed a more differentiated analysis of regional climate effects. Also, Ian G. Simmons (2008) rather sceptically assumed that sustainability understood as long-term equilibrium never has existed (ibid: 231-235).

Sieferle proposes in addition applying the concept of sustainability to physical relations between social and natural systems in the past and suggests research questions such as: "If and how far was a single society (or region, or community) sustainable in the sense that it was able to continue certain economic activities without destroying their physical foundations?" (Sieferle 2003: 124). In a similar way, the anthropologist Bernd Herrmann argues that sustainability understood as permanent existence is always inherent in the actions of a given population.[9] This means that there is always the constancy of change with "greater or lesser degrees of stability" (Friedel 2016: 220) which is challenged by human behaviour such as, for example, mobility and excessive resource use. Following from this, human actions can result in unsustainability which leads to the transformation or even collapse of civilisations (Caradonna 2018: 16-17).

The anthropologist Joseph A. Tainter (2018) criticised the short-term outlook of sustainability studies and pleaded for long-term observations, because "the processes that make a society sustainable or vulnerable to collapse develop over long time-periods, typically stretching to generations or centuries." (Tainter 2018: 40) The geographer Ian Douglas (2013) also emphasised the analysis of long-term developments when he scrutinised the thrifty use of resources by cities: "For centuries, the majority of the world's urban settlements were sustainable in that they supported their population with food and water from their immediate surroundings and used local materials for their buildings and streets." (ibid: 286) This did change, at least in the 20th century, and no city could sustain itself from nearby resources alone. The durable development of cities and their role as innovation

---

8 Sieferle 2003: pp. 123-125. For example, the "agrarian civilizations dominating the history of the last 5000 years had sharp class distinctions, often legally fixed, which set unsurmountable obstacles to individual freedom." ibid: p. 123.

9 Herrmann 2014: p. 112. Similarly Radkau (2013: p. 135) equates sustainability with durability which he decidedly relates with power and authority.

centres are areas of historical research that also offer solutions to present-day problems of cities (Schott/Toyka-Seid 2010: 14).

In an overview article on sustainability the medievalist Oliver Auge (2014: 50-51) emphasised the difference between understanding sustainability in an eco-political sense with a focus on ecological diversity, and historical analysis of resource management which can be divided further into the study of a single resource such as fire wood. Auge concluded, whatever definition is used, sustainability should recognise different temporal and spatial dimensions which could result in different sustainability levels that might be achieved by different societies. In the context of 20th century history, however, the environmental historian Donald Worster (2016: 217; Reith 2011: 136) questioned the possibility of sustainability.

Based on these controversies, attempts have been made to measure past sustainability. One such concept is Material and Energy Flow Accounting (MEFA) which deals with the socio-economic metabolism of a given system and the colonisation of natural processes, especially via land use (Haberl et al. 2004b). The model consists of at least three parts: Material Flow Accounting (MFA) which comprises material input and output, Energy Flow Accounting (EFA) which calculates energy inputs and emissions and the Human Appropriation of Net Primary Production (HANPP) which refers to human land use (ibid: 204-205; Haberl/Erb 2017: 284-285). Reductions of such flows and human land use can be interpreted as "progress towards sustainability" (Haberl et al. 2004b: 206-207). Although this concept can be applied to present and past societies, the vast amount of quantitative data needed sets clear constraints for historical analysis before 1800, while cooperation between natural and social scientists is impeded by their respective focuses on different spatial and temporal scales (ibid: 203).

Empirical Studies on Past Sustainability

Exploring examples of how historical sustainability is dealt with in empirical studies, one finds different approaches with more or less elaborate operationalisations of the concept.

To name but a few examples, Annika Schmitt (2015), adopting a strictly local focus, explored the sustainability of commons in the prince bishopric of Osnabrück around 1800. She describes sustainability as a category to analyse land use systems like the commons as a societal discourse about the proper management of natural resources. She concludes that the rural society discussed, established and used rules to maintain the fertility of the soil via constraints, especially regarding the number of people entitled to use the land. This successful system was challenged by population growth, rising taxes and the continuing restrictions for the rural population which prompted the agrarian reforms and the end of the commons.

With regard to climate change, Kunnas et al. (2014) used carbon dioxide emissions as an indicator of sustainability. Calculating the carbon emissions by Great Britain and the USA for the past two centuries, the authors showed how the emissions of past generations might diminish the well-being of future generations (ibid: 243-244). Placing the focus on the transformation of agrarian into industrial societies, Sieferle et al. (2006) showed that the former always were energetically sustainable, because of their limited access to energy. Given high transportation costs and fossil fuels being rarely accessible, there was no possibility to store energy in the long-run, with the exception of forests as an energy buffer. Moreover, agriculture could be self-sufficient using local sources of nitrogen and phosphorous such as manure. As a result of these constraints, there was no economic growth (ibid: 32-34, 44). Case studies on four villages in different climatic and geomorphological settings in Austria showed the importance of maintaining soil fertility in an agricultural production cycle, which only changed with the advent of fossil fuels and synthetic fertilisers, arriving in agrarian settlements particularly after World War II (ibid: 91-92, 138).

The above-mentioned MEFA framework is exemplified by Krausmann et al. (2004) for Austria in the second half of the 20th century, looking at materials and energy consumption, imports and exports and economic growth. The authors conclude that efficiency gains did not suffice to reduce material and energy flows, which resulted in a less sustainable development (ibid: 227).

On a larger geographical scale the sinologist Mark Elvin (2013) analysed Chinese history with respect to environmental impact and concluded that population growth and progress were generally unsustainable at least with regard to forests (which were mainly destroyed until 1900) and water management (where suitable places for new irrigation projects ceased to exist). He argues: "The Chinese economy survived these millennia [...] because it mastered new technological skills such as hydraulically sophisticated irrigated rice-farming, and because it was continually expanding into fresh resource areas." (ibid: 234-244) Simultaneously, Chinese philosophers developed environmental awareness and conservation policies almost two thousand years earlier than in Europe which resulted in agricultural practices that maintained fertile soils for hundreds of years (Miller 2017: 596-597; Winiwarter/Bork 2014: 34-35).

A European example of rather successful resource management was the case of Lake Constance fisheries between 1350 and 1900. Regulated by ordinances that were issued by the local authorities and treaties which restricted fishing, there was a sustainable supply of fish for the local population without any species going extinct (Zeheter 2015). Thus, both regulations and technical improvements could temporarily foster sustainability, while in the end the overall consumption of resources remained the decisive parameter for the long-term development.

Besides historical research on regions and territories, there are also approaches to applying the concept of sustainability to urban history. Following the call for long-term research, Ljungkvist et al. (2010: 369-370, 387) analysed the history of Constantinople regarding sustainability spanning more than 2000 years. The authors looked at the resilient production of ecosystem services and other resources for city dwellers using both archaeological data and historical documents. They drew the conclusion that particularly stretches of land reserved for food production within the city walls made possible the survival of the city. For the early modern period Schanbacher (2019) emphasised the permanence and growth of most Central European cities and described their attempts to secure resources for future use regardless of ecological aspects. In a more general way, Schott and Toyka-Seid (2010: 9-13) examined urban sustainability under the Brundtland definition and argued that at all times cities overused and polluted the resources of their environment and had to react to these challenges. Possible successful reactions were: a more efficient use of resources such as forests, an extension of the resource catchment area through economic power or political pressure and a substitution of resources.

The significance of resources such as clean air and open space increased since the 19th century. The study by Jeffrey C. Sanders (2010) on Seattle analysed on a micro level how the ideas of sustainability (including environment, economy and social equality) were tested and engendered novel solutions for urban and environmental problems between the 1960s and 1980s (ibid: 3, 10). Sustainability as a normative aim of urban policy in the late 20th century has been contrasted against local practices and citizen engagement with regard to the provision of water in Mainz and Wiesbaden (Engels et al. 2017: 9).

Apart from the question of whether individual settlements or territories were sustainable, there is also research concerning the sustainability of economic practices. One example is slash-and-burn cultivation in forest regions which has been analysed comparatively for Finland and Southeast Asia (Myllyntaus et al. 2002). Utilising a sustainability model consisting of ecological, social and economic aspects, the study concedes that ecological sustainability is difficult to prove, but maintains that "slash-and-burn cultivation has for centuries provided a basis for some fairly sustainable societies." (ibid: 267)

Similarly, Victoria Hightower (2013) analysed the practice of pearling and the pearl industry in the Persian Gulf since 1870. Implicitly following an understanding of sustainability which equates sustainability with durability, she stated that the pearl industry did not collapse because of over-exploitation but because of the introduction of Japanese cultured pearls and the discovery of oil in the northern Gulf after 1930 (ibid: 49-53).

In summary, there is a broad range of historical research dealing with sustainability. Besides sceptical remarks, historians analyse sustainability usually with a focus on the physical relations between humans and their environment, be it natural resource use or management, and the question of the permanence or collapse of past economic systems, practices and societies. Studies with a global view are increasingly complemented by regional, local and micro-level studies.

Conclusions—Potentials and Limits

For decades historical research mainly considered sustainability within the field of forest economy since Carlowitz (1713). Later, and particularly after the UN and other international organisations adopted and extended the concept from the 1980s onwards, historians began to use the concept in different forms and with different methods, operating with normative and analytical approaches. Research questions aimed to explain the origins of the present environmental crisis, the causes for the collapse or persistence of past social systems, by natural resource management. Because of the manifold possibilities to use the concept and its general ambiguity, it seems necessary to differentiate its meaning clearly before using it or else switch to other concepts such as resilience which possibly allow better handling of the historical phenomena concerned (Reith 2008: 1011; Winiwarter 2013: 16).

There are at least three feasible ways to utilise the concept. First, it is possible to project the current holistic definition of sustainability (including environment, economy, social equality) onto past societies. Probably, this works best for 20th and 21st century histories when all these concepts existed in the public debate. It also motivates new interpretations of the sources and novel methodological approaches to earlier times. Second, in a metabolic approach the focus lies on the management of and discourses about natural resources. In premodern societies it would be recommendable to concentrate on discourses and practices, since statistical data usually do not allow a detailed analysis of material and energy flows and estimates vary greatly. Such an approach focuses on the knowledge and practices of past societies in order to identify solutions to current problems. Third, there is the possibility to make use of the concept of sustainability to analyse human attitudes towards nature, especially with regard to the variety of species, pollution and aesthetic aspects.

References

Auge, Oliver (2014): "'Nachhaltigkeit' als historisches Thema: Eine Hinführung." In: Jahrbuch für Regionalgeschichte 32, pp. 45-53.

Black, Brian/Lybecker, Donna L. (2008): Great debates in American environmental history, Westport/Conn.: Greenwood Press.

Caradonna, Jeremy L. (2018): "Sustainability: A new historiography." In: Jeremy L. Caradonna (ed.), Routledge handbook of the history of sustainability, London/New York: Routledge, pp. 9-25.

Douglas, Ian (2013): Cities: An environmental history, London: Tauris.

Elvin, Mark (2013): "Three thousand years of unsustainable growth: China's environment from archaic times to the present." In: John R. McNeill/Alan Roe (eds.), Global environmental history, London: Routledge, pp. 231-282.

Engels, Jens Ivo/Janich, Nina/Schott, Dieter (2017): "Einleitung: Städte auf dem Weg zur nachhaltigen Entwicklung." In: Jens Ivo Engels/Nina Janich/Dieter Schott (eds.), Nachhaltige Stadtentwicklung: Infra-strukturen, Akteure, Diskurse, Frankfurt a.M./New York: Campus, pp. 7-24.

Freitas, Mário (2012): "Participation and the construction of sustainable societies." In: Angela Mendonca, Ana Cunha, Ranjan Chakrabarti (eds.), Natural resources, sustainability and humanity, Dordrecht: Springer, pp. 143-166.

Friedel, Robert (2016): "History, sustainability, and choice." In: Ruth Oldenziel/Helmuth Trischler (eds.), Cycling and recycling, New York/Oxford: Berghahn, pp. 219-225.

Grober, Ulrich (2013): Die Entdeckung der Nachhaltigkeit, Munich: Kunstmann.

Haberl, Helmut/Erb, Karl-Heinz (2017): "Land as planetary boundary: a socio-ecological perspective." In: Peter A. Victor/Brett Dolter (eds.), Handbook on growth and sustainability, Cheltenham/Northampton, MA: Edward Elgar, pp. 277-300.

Haberl, Helmut/Wackernagel, Mathis/Wrbka, Thomas (2004a): "Land use and sustainability indicators: An introduction." In: Land Use Policy 21/3, pp. 193-198.

Haberl, Helmut/Fischer-Kowalski, Marina/Krausmann, Fridolin/Weisz, Helga/Winiwarter, Verena (2004b): "Progress towards sustainability? What the conceptual framework of material and energy flow accounting (MEFA) can offer." In: Land Use Policy 21/3, pp. 199-213.

Herrmann, Bernd (2014): "Kritisches Nachwort eines Umwelthistorikers." In: Jahrbuch für Regionalgeschichte 32, pp. 109-120.

Hightower, Victoria Penziner (2013): "Pearls and the Southern Persian/Arabian Gulf: A lesson in sustainability." In: Environmental History 18, pp. 44-59.

Hölzl, Richard (2010): "Historicizing sustainability: German scientific forestry in the eighteenth and nineteenth centuries." In: Science and Culture 19/4, pp. 431-460.

Huss, Jürgen/Gadow, Friederike von (2013): "Einführung." In: Hannß Carl von Carlowitz, Sylvicultura oeconomica, Remagen: Kessel, pp. 3-53.

Jenkins, Willis (2010): "Sustainability theory." In: Willis Jenkins (ed.), Berkshire Encyclopedia of Sustainability. Vol. 1. The Spirit of Sustainability, Great Barrington: Berkshire, pp. 380-384.

Krausmann, Fridolin/Haberl, Helmut/Erb, Karl-Heinz, Wackernagel, Mathis (2004): "Resource flows and land use in Austria 1950-2000: Using the MEFA framework to monitor society-nature interaction for sustainability." In: Land Use Policy 21/3, pp. 215-230.

Kunnas, Jan/Mclaughlin, Eoin/Hanley, Nick (2014): "Counting carbon: Historic emissions from fossil fuels, long-run measures of sustainable development and carbon debt." In: Scandinavian Economic History Review 62/3, pp. 243-265.

Ljungkvist, John/Barthel, Stephan/Finnveden, Göran/Sörlin, Sverker (2010): "The urban anthropocene: Lessons for sustainability from the environmental history of Constantinople." In: Paul Sinclair/Gullög Nordquist/Frands Herschend/Christian Isendahl (eds.), The Urban Mind: Cultural and environmental dynamics, Uppsala: Uppsala University, pp. 367-390.

Merchant, Carolyn (2007): American environmental history: An introduction, New York: Columbia University Press.

Miller, Ian Matthew (2017): "Forestry and the politics of sustainability in Early China." In: Environmental History 22, pp. 594-617.

Mosley, Stephen (2010): The environment in world history, New York: Routledge.

Mulligan, Martin (2018): An introduction to sustainability, London/New York: Routledge.

Muraca, Barbara/Döring, Ralf (2018): "From (strong) sustainability to degrowth: A philosophical and historical reconstruction." In: Jeremy L. Caradonna (ed.), Routledge handbook of the history of sustainability, London/New York: Routledge, pp. 339-362.

Myllyntaus, Timo/Hares, Minna/Kunnas, Jan (2002): "Sustainability in danger? Slash-and-burn cultivation in 19th Century Finland and 20th century Southeast Asia." In: Environmental History 7/2, pp. 267-302.

Nougarède, Olivier (1994): "L'équilibre agrosylvopastoral, premier essai de réconciliation entre l'agriculture et la forêt." In: Revue forestière française 46, pp. 165-178.

Pufé, Iris (2017): Nachhaltigkeit, Konstanz: UVK.

Radkau, Joachim (2013): "'Nachhaltigkeit' als Wort der Macht." In: François Duceppe-Lamarre/Jens Ivo Engels (eds.), Umwelt und Herrschaft in der Geschichte, Munich: Oldenbourg, pp. 131-136.

Radkau, Joachim (2007): Holz: Wie ein Naturstoff Geschichte schreibt, Munich: oekom.

Reith, Reinhold (2008): "Nachhaltigkeit." In: Friedrich Jaeger (ed.), Enzyklopädie der Neuzeit, Vol. 8, Stuttgart: Metzler, pp. 1009-1012.

Reith, Reinhold (2011): Umweltgeschichte der Frühen Neuzeit, Berlin/Boston: Oldenbourg.

Riehl, Simone (2015): "Understanding the reasons for non-sustainability in past agricultural systems." In: Susanne Kerner/Rachael Dann/Pernille Bangsgaard (eds.), Climate and ancient societies, Copenhagen: Museum Tusculanum Press, pp. 291-311.

Röhrig, Ernst/Bartsch, Norbert/von Lüpke, Burghard (2006): Waldbau auf ökologischer Grundlage, Stuttgart: UTB.

Sanders, Jeffrey Craig (2010): Seattle and the roots of urban sustainability: Inventing ecotopia, Pittsburgh: University of Pittsburgh Press.

Schanbacher, Ansgar (2019): "Umwelt und Ressourcen in der frühneuzeitlichen Stadt Mitteleuropas." In: Arnd Reitemeier/Ansgar Schanbacher/Tanja S. Scheer (eds.), Nachhaltigkeit als Argument, Göttingen: Universitätsverlag, pp. 98-122.

Schmitt, Annika (2015): Naturnutzung und Nachhaltigkeit: Osnabrücker Markenwirtschaft im Wandel (1765-1820), Münster: Aschendorff.

Schmidt, Uwe E. (2013): "Nachhaltigkeit im Wandel: Eine historisch-kritische Begriffsanalyse." In: Uwe E. Schmidt (ed.), Nachhaltigkeit im Wandel, Remagen: Kessel, pp. 30-45.

Schott, Dieter/Toyka-Seid, Michael (2010): "Stadt und Nachhaltigkeit." In: Informationen zur modernen Stadtgeschichte 2, pp. 7-21.

Sieferle, Rolf Peter (2003): "Sustainability in a world history perspective." In: Brigitta Benzing/Bernd Herrmann (eds.), Exploitation and overexploitation in societies past and present, Münster: Lit, pp. 123-141.

Sieferle, Rolf Peter/Krausmann, Fridolin, Schandl, Heinz/Winiwarter, Verena (2006): Das Ende der Fläche: Zum gesellschaftlichen Stoffwechsel der Industrialisierung, Cologne/Weimar/Vienna: Böhlau.

Simmons, Ian G. (2008): Global environmental history, Edinburgh: Edinburgh University Press.

Tainter, Joseph A. (2018): "Understanding sustainability through history: Resources and complexity." In: Jeremy L. Caradonna (ed.), Routledge handbook of the history of sustainability, London/New York: Routledge, pp. 40-56.

Thomas, Craig (2018): Sustainability and the American naturalist tradition: Revisiting Henry David Thoreau, Aldo Leopold, Rachel Carson, and Edward O. Wilson, Bielefeld: transcript.

Warde, Paul (2018): The invention of sustainability: Nature and destiny, c. 1500-1870, Cambridge: Cambridge University Press.

Warde, Paul (2011): "The invention of sustainability." In: Modern Intellectual History 8/1, pp. 153-170.

Winiwarter, Verena (2013): "Zur Krise und Bedeutung der Nachhaltigkeit: Eine diagnostische Skizze." In: Uwe E. Schmidt (ed.), Nachhaltigkeit im Wandel, Remagen: Kessel, pp. 9-20.

Winiwarter, Verena/Bork, Hans-Rudolf (2014): Geschichte unserer Umwelt, Darmstadt: primus.

Worster, Donald (2016): "Can history offer pathways to sustainability?" In: Ruth Oldenziel/Helmuth Trischler (eds.), Cycling and recycling, New York/Oxford: Berghahn, pp. 215-218.

Zeheter, Michael (2015): "Order in the lake: Managing the sustainability of the Lake Constance Fisheries, 1350-1900." In: Environment and History 21/4, pp. 597-629.

Urban Metabolism

Sabine Barles

Urban-environmental history concerns *inter alia* the many and varied interactions between societies and the biosphere. The most concrete part of these interactions consists of exchanges of energy and materials: what some scholars call 'urban metabolism'. Societies and cities in particular are major consumers of materials and energy, either directly within their territory, or indirectly via the materials, goods and services that they import or export. Thence, the urban metabolism has both upstream and downstream consequences in terms of the depletion/use/indraw of resources and the disposal of waste (into the atmosphere, water and soil, in liquid, solid or gas form) with multiple impacts on ecosystems and the biosphere in general, and, in turn, on human societies.

From a historical point of view, the question of urban metabolism can be addressed in (at least) two ways. The first concerns the history of the notion of 'metabolism': when and in which context did it appear as a way to analyse the city? How did it change through time? The second concerns the way the notion can be used and applied in a historical research: what can we learn from a metabolic approach to the history of the city? How can a city's metabolism be operationalised and quantified?

The History of a Notion

Urban Chemistry

Research on urban metabolism is older than the notion of 'urban metabolism'. It dates back to the 19th century, and was carried out mostly by chemists interested in food production and agricultural fertilisation (Barles 2005, 2010). Among European scientists and intellectuals, demographic growth coupled with limited stocks of rural organic fertilisers (farm manure and various plant and animal residues) led to fears of soil exhaustion and recurring or even permanent food shortages. As they were home to constantly larger numbers of people, cities were considered not only as hubs of consumption but as new sources of fertiliser via their myriad *excreta*: human and animal excrement, organic mud, household and workshop waste, and unused waste from butchers and slaughterhouses etc. This research resulted in the emergence of urban chemistry (Hamlin 2007)—predating biochemistry and the work of Pasteur—that sought to get to grips with flows of organic materials and nutrients, notably nitrogen, then phosphorus and potassium. Chemistry came to hold the key to "the mysterious circle of organic life at the surface of the globe" (Dumas 1842: 7). There was general agreement that "all places that have had large populations but have not given back to the earth what the action of man has taken in order to produce harvests have faced sterility and ruin" (Liebig quoted by Moll 1863: 342). This made it essential to quantify and gather this "material for which cities owe a debt to the earth" (Dumas 1866: xxxi). Jean-Baptiste Dumas, Jean-Baptiste Boussingault and Justus von Liebig were among the most renowned European urban chemists and largely contributed to the first urban material flow accounts (see table 1).

In life sciences, the term 'metabolism' emerged parallel to the development of urban material balances: it was first defined in 1858 in the eleventh edition of Pierre-Hubert Nysten's *Dictionnaire de médecine* as a "changement de nature moléculaire des corps" [change in the molecular nature of bodies], this change—a set of chemical reactions—being seen as necessary for life. The term 'metabolism' was used by Karl Marx, who, as many thinkers of his time, was aware of the advances in natural sciences. In *The Capital*, Marx referred to the term in order to depict the way human societies use natural resources and transform them through work (Fischer Kowalski 1998: 64), while suggesting that their overexploitation would cause a 'metabolic rift' (Foster 1999). Later on, Patrick Geddes, who was trained as a biologist, explored society's metabolism through physical accounting (Geddes 1885; Deléage 1992: 69). He made a significant contribution to urban planning, and emphasised the role of energy and material flows, together with the need for connecting the city to its hinterland and catchment area (Geddes 1915).

Despite Marx's emphasis on the 'metabolic rift' and Geddes' attention to energy and material flows, urban chemistry as it existed during the 19th century more or less disappeared during the first half of the 20th century. Chemists abandoned the city and focused on agriculture (and became agronomists) or on industry (through chemical engineering). Urban planners and urban theorists concentrated their efforts on the socio-spatial organisation of cities. Meanwhile urban engineers, despite their concern with flows (itself due to the mechanical and hydraulic basis of their training), were more interested in scaling up urban infrastructure than in the metabolic implications for cities that came with it.

Table 1: "Fertility statistics" ("Statistique des principes de la fertilité agricole"), Paris, 1895, kilograms

	Nitrogen	Phosphoric acid	Potash
Food supply			
Animal	6.828.516	2.182.839	3.655.609
Human	16.626.460	6.078.457	5.596.455
Removal			
Street sludge	2.166.129	1.767.105	1.197.071
Manure	3.917.631	2.508.491	1.197.321
Night soil	3.981.204	452.409	193.889
Sewer water	13.174.179	3.445.576	5.934.047

Source: Vincey, 1901

Urban Ecology

Several decades would elapse before there was any renewed interest in urban metabolism. Urban ecology[1] emerged in the 1960s alongside scientific ecology, particularly the theory of ecosystems. By the 1950s, ecology had developed the bulk of its concepts and methods which were summarised in the seminal work *Fundamentals of Ecology*, written in 1953 by the ornithologist and ecologist Eugene Odum with the help of his brother Howard (Odum 1953).

In this context the dual concern about the capacity of the planet to feed and support a rapidly growing population on the one hand, and the destructive power of humans given the finite, limited and singular nature of the earth on the other hand emerged. This was highlighted at the Intergovernmental Conference of Experts on the Scientific Basis for Rational Use and Conservation of the Resources of the Biosphere, sometimes referred to simply as the Conference on the Biosphere, held in Paris in 1968 where "the problems of the environment were stated for the first time at the UN in their modern form" (Acot 1988: 229). These planetary concerns were coupled with severe criticisms of the industrial city. *The City in History*, to mention just one work, was published by Lewis Mumford in 1961. The author was fully aware of the development in scientific ecology which led him to denounce the "myth of megalopolis" (ibid: 654). Like many of his contemporaries,

---

[1] Understood here in the sense of ecology of the city rather than ecology in the city (cf. Grimm et al. 2000).

he predicted the decline of the industrial city as the result of its expansion, of its power, and of its resource consumption.

These scientific and popular debates were the backdrop to a number of works on urban ecology when, in 1965, the engineer Abel Wolman introduced the notion of 'urban metabolism' for the first time. Wolman defined metabolic processes as encompassing "all the materials and commodities needed to sustain the city's inhabitants at home, at work and at play" (Wolman 1965: 156) over the entire metabolic cycle, in particular food, clean water and fuels as inputs to the city, and waste water, solid waste and atmospheric pollution as outputs. Some years later Eugene Odum showed how the city "is a heterotrophic ecosystem dependent on large inflows of energy from outside sources" (Odum 1975: 39; see table 2) which he would subsequently compare to a parasitic ecosystem (Odum 1989: 17). The Belgian ecologist, Paul Duvigneaud, who was a central figure in setting up many international environmental research programmes, assigned a key role to the *"urbs* ecosystem" in his hugely popular *Synthèse écologique* (1974: 229).[2] This ecosystem "must be recognised scientifically in order to ensure appropriate development of the territory in which most people live" (ibid: 245).

Table 2: *"Ecosystems classified according to source and level of energy [...] Numbers in parentheses are estimated round-figure averages, actually little more than guesses since the earth's ecosystems have yet to be inventoried in sufficient depth to calculate average"*

Category	Example	Annual energy flow (Power level) (kCal/m^2)
1. Unsubsidised natural solar-powered ecosystems	Open oceans, upland forests, grasslands	1000-10.000 (2000)
2. Naturally subsidised solar-powered ecosystems	Tidal estuaries, some rain forests	10.000-40.000 (20.000)
3. Human-subsidised solar-powered ecosystems	Agriculture, aquaculture	10.000-40.000 (20.000)
4. Fuel-powered urban-industrial systems	Cities, suburbs, industrial parks	100.000-3.000.000 (2.000.000)

Source: Odum 1975: 16

The early publications on urban ecology based in the natural sciences received quite a lot of international attention. They were particularly influential within the scope of the UNESCO *Man and Biosphere* programme set up in 1971, in which (among others) Rome, Barcelona and Hong Kong were subjected to a detailed analysis. The

---

2 A second edition ascribing an even more important role to the urbs ecosystem was published in 1980 and was in its third reprint by 1984.

ecology of a city and its people: the case of Hong Kong, published in 1981 by a group of Australian researchers, can be viewed as very representative and perhaps the apogee of these works about urban metabolism, bringing together material flow accounting and sociological surveys on the basis of a strong hypothesis: human health and well-being, as well as the state of the environment, are the result of urban metabolism and energy consumption (Boyden et al. 1981).

These theses were heavily criticised in the 1980s (Theys and Emelianoff 2001; Gandy 2002) for their 'totalitarian temptation' of ecology (Lévêque 2003). Moreover, the authors ended in an energetic determinism and an anti-urban stance—the city as parasite—that precluded them from considering what initiatives could be taken to control the environmental impact of cities. However, while the theses were controversial, the methods for analysing urban metabolism remained rather underdeveloped.

Industrial Ecology, Social Ecology, Territorial Ecology

In parallel to urban ecology based in the natural sciences, another field of research and action evolved since the 1960s: industrial ecology. The disciplinary background of the protagonists of industrial ecology differed from that of the first urban ecologists: while the latter were zoologists or botanists, the early industrial ecologists were physicists, chemists, chemical engineers or biogeochemists, most prominently Allen V. Kneese et al. (1970), Robert U. Ayres (1978), or Gilles Billen et al. (1983). They have contributed to numerous methodological enhancements for energy and material flow accounting.

As Suren Erkman stresses:

> From the beginnings of scientific ecology, researchers recognised that the biophysical substratum of human activities obeyed the same laws as natural ecosystems and, consequently, the industrial system may be considered a subsystem of the Biosphere. So the industrial ecosystem concept is clearly present even though it is not explicitly referred to by name (Erkman 2004: 49).

However, until the late 1980s, research initiatives in this field remained fairly isolated, focusing on either industrial material and energy flows or on industrial ensembles as ecosystems. One of the main features of these approaches is the combination of economic analyses, in particular monetary flows, and ecological analyses of the flow of energy and materials. This even led to the inclusion of certain principles from ecology and physics (e.g., law of conservation of matter and energy) in economic theory.

Erkman traces the current boom in industrial ecology back to 1989 when an issue of the *Scientific American* journal, "Managing Planet Earth", featured an article by Robert Frosch and Nicholas Gallopoulos entitled "Strategies for manufacturing". Apart from the prestige and readership of the review, the scientific recognition of the two authors, their senior position within the hierarchy of General Motors (being part of the system they proposed to improve) and the favourable context that followed with the Brundtland Report all help to explain the article's impact and the dissemination of industrial ecology (Erkman 2004: 63-64). A number of seminal publications appeared around the same time (Ausubel/Sladovich 1989; Reconciling 1989) and the following decade witnessed a boom in research, experiments and publications in this area (Baccini/Brunner 1991; Ayres/Simonis 1994). The creation of the Journal of Industrial Ecology in 1997 and the International Society for Industrial Ecology (ISIE, http://www.is4ie.org/) in 2000 helped structure the field.

At the turn of the century, some scholars stressed the fact that, by concentrating on the production sector, industrial ecology was missing a great part of society-nature interactions. They proposed to extend the focus to industrial society as a whole, including cities, agricultural areas, etc. This approach is characteristic of social ecology (Haberl et al. 2016). Moreover, a discussion emerged on the need for taking into account the socio-spatial dimension of social or industrial metabolism that gave birth to territorial ecology. Territorial ecology considers society's metabolism as the result of both natural and social processes and takes into account the political, technical, spatial and social dimensions of material and energy flows (Buclet 2015). Some scholars still prefer to use the first appellation (industrial ecology) although they advocate an extended perspective on metabolism (Barles 2010).

Urban Metabolism in Historical Research

In connection with the debates that emerged at the turn of the century on industrial, social and territorial ecology, urban metabolism has been introduced as a concept first to solve historical questions within urban ecology and then into environmental history. This happened in a wider context in which the role of cities in global environmental change, the idea of a circular economy and of an ecological transition came to the fore of the political agenda. These political debates encouraged new research that allowed to better characterise city-nature interactions through material, energy and substance flow analyses, or urban-environmental imprints (like the 'ecological footprint', 'water footprint', 'carbon and nitrogen imprints', and so on). Even if most of these works deal with the current or future situation, historical or long-term approaches developed into at least three interconnected strands of research.

Environmental Sciences Approaches

The first strand of research builds on a retrospective evaluation of environmental dynamics making use of energy and material flow analyses. It considers past social or, more specifically, urban impacts on the natural ecosystems by accounting for urban resource consumption and flows. The study of the flow of phosphorus in food through the town of Linköping, located in the southeast of Sweden, from 1870 to 2000 is quite representative of these approaches (Schmid Neset et al. 2008). It shows the complex and cumulative effects of agriculture, human diet, and urban waste and wastewater management on phosphorus flows—a resource that could be exhausted in the next decades (Cordell 2009). To summarise, between 1870 and 2000, the fertiliser revolution and the use of fossil phosphates, together with the increasing amount of meat consumed in Linköping, resulted in an increasing mobilisation of phosphorus. At the same time, abandoning local recycling of human manure and the installation of a sewage system led to increased water pollution due to eutrophication. The phosphorus recycling rate peaked round 1880 (90 per cent) then decreased to nearly 0 per cent in the 1950s (Schmid Neset et al. 2008).

Similar studies have been conducted on water, nitrogen or energy, helping to characterise the changing biogeochemical role of cities and the impact on their hinterlands through the quantification of urban environmental imprints. A special issue of *Regional environmental change* published in 2012 gives a good overview of this approach for cities like Paris, London, Athens, Barcelona or New York (Billen et al. 2012). One of the results of these studies is that the impact is often more incisive outside than within the city, especially since the 20th century, in connection with resource extraction and transformation, and due to increasing globalisation.

Another ambition of such approaches is to better understand the current state of the environment in order to support environmental policy-making and management by assessing the inherited pollution due to urban activities. For instance, on the basis of a present-day concern, the research on mercury in Stockholm's environment made necessary a historical analysis of the urban consumption of this metal in the past two centuries (Svidén, Jonsson 2001). The study showed that the main use of mercury was medical, especially for the cure of syphilis, then dental, through dental fillings from 1900s onwards. It was applied in the production of batteries from the 1950s onwards, in paper and cardboard (1940-1968), mirror foliation (1795-1890s), and electronics from 1900 onwards. Other minor uses existed like felt hat making, thermometers, biocides and fouling, etc. The result of this research showed that the present problem with mercury rested not in its present use, which had declined since the 1960s, but in the past discharge to the environment, especially to water and sediments.

Even without a clear historical interest, these works prove very useful for urban-environmental history. In other words they address questions that need historical methods and data, while they contribute to historical research by revealing and quantifying the changing environmental impact of urban life. One of the challenges in this strand of research is to combine historical approaches and sources with physical modelling.

Urban-Environmental History

Some researchers have explicitly addressed the historicity of urban metabolism by analysing the way cities, understood as a social entity of diverse actors, have considered, perceived, managed and transformed their metabolism. Such approaches do not necessarily require quantification, but are characterised by their environmental and material concern through the study of urban flows. They offer another perspective on processes of industrialisation, draw to attention the negative effects of progress, and connect city to nature and urban history to rural and global history.

William Cronon's *Nature's Metropolis* (1991) could be considered as belonging to this strand of research even if it does not emphasise the metabolic terminology. It shows the intertwined and inter-dependant histories of Chicago and its hinterland during the 19th century, materialised in the flow grain, wood and meat, and the development of infrastructures like railways and telegraphs. Indeed, the metabolic perspective has reactivated the topics of urban-rural relationships and of urban hinterlands: location of supply and discharge areas, characterisation of the power relations between these and the cities they serve. It has revived the notion of hinterland in order to take into account a wide range of the extra-urban manifestations of cities (Barles/Knoll 2019, see also the session *Cities—Regions—Hinterlands* that took place during the 2018 European Association of Urban History Conference).

Joel Tarr's (2002) article on "The metabolism of the industrial city" is another example, even if it looks at a limited set of flows and concentrates on the relationship between the city of Pittsburgh and its immediate surroundings. The focus on land consumption is worthy to note in Tarr's paper, as it is too rarely considered in urban metabolic studies. Indeed, being a non-renewable resource, land is a major socio-ecological issue. Tarr analyses the way in which these resources "were used, misused, and remediated" (ibid: 512). He stresses the sometimes counterproductive effects of technological choices in terms of sanitation. In Pittsburgh as in other cities during the 19th century, the development of water supply and sewerage systems provoked an increase in typhoid death rate, some wastewater being discharged above the water supply pumping stations. Tarr also addresses the scientific and political controversies around these environmentally damaging technological choices. In a similar way, Dieter Schott (2014) analyses the history of the relation between urban development and the environment since the High Middle Ages through the prism of metabolism.

Focusing on a single type of flow—urban excreta—, Barles (2005) shows the relevance of a material approach to the city. Following the material flows rather than following the actors revealed the metabolic links that existed between Paris and its hinterland. It also showed the value that was placed on urban excreta, such as human manure, garbage and so on—a phenomenon that is strongly connected to the development of urban chemistry described at the beginning of this chapter. The present quantification of flows (Barles 2007; Esculier/Barles, in press) showed the growing efficiency of recycling technologies, especially in the case of fertiliser production up to the beginning of the 20th century. Thereafter, the decline in the value of urban excreta was responsible for environmental degradation as urban excreta were disposed of in nature. This was, for instance, one of the major reasons for the biological death of the river Seine downstream from Paris up to the end of the 1980s. More recently, the work by Roberto D'Arienzo (2017) on Naples in Italy showed that similar processes characterise the built environment: recycling of construction materials, buildings and land was common up to the 20th century, before the systematic use of new materials, new constructions and new land for urban development set in. This led to increasing amounts of rubble being disposed of and to the growth of brownfields and wastelands.

Figure 1: Dietary nitrogen circulation, Paris, 1913, tN/yr (gN/cap/day) (Barles 2007). At the beginning of the 20th century, nitrogen recycling rate peaked as a result of agricultural demand

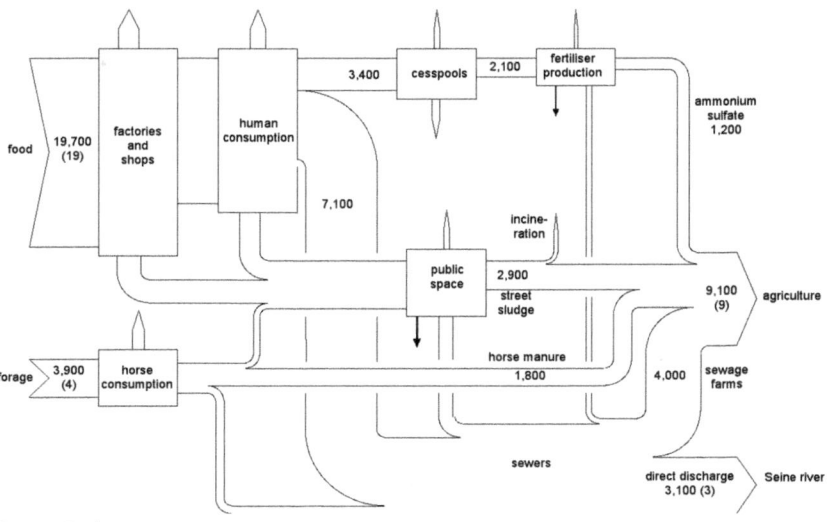

Source: Barles 2007

Socio-Ecological Studies

Another strand of research belongs to the field of socio-ecological studies which "utilizes interdisciplinary and transdisciplinary methods to examine complex cause-effect relationships and feedback cycles occurring between natural and human ecosystems and, intentionally, treating them as an integrated coupled (socioecological) system" (Dick et al. 2018: 1227).

Some of these works apply a long-term approach, looking at socio-ecological regimes, trajectories and transitions. They are based on a macroscopic periodisation of human history into three socio-ecological regimes: 'fire regime', 'agrarian regime' and 'industrial regime' (De Vries/Goudsblom 2002), the first one being referred to as 'hunter-gatherers regime' in other works (Haberl et al. 2016). Studies from this strand of research use overall indicators in order to characterise society-nature relations. Energy is one of them, and probably the most used. Table 3 gives an overview over the metabolic profiles of the three main socio-ecological regimes. Even if the urban dimension is not addressed, it has to be noted that the last regime, generally called industrial, is also an urban one.

Table 3: Metabolic profiles of socio-metabolic regimes
(adapted from Krausmann et al. in Haberl, 2016)

		Hunter-gatherers	Agrarian[a]	Industrial[b]
Energy use per capita (DEC)	GJ/cap/year	10-20	40-70	150-400
Material use per capita (DMC)	t/cap/year	0.5-1	3-6	15-25
Population density	Cap/km²	<0.1	<40	<400
Agricultural population	%	-	>80	<10
Biomass (share of DEC)	%	>99	>95	20-30

DMC: domestic material consumption; DEC: direct energy consumption
[a] typical values for an advanced European agrarian regime (18th century)
[b] typical values for fully industrialised economies

In addition to such generalising typologies, place-based studies help to better understand the way in which a particular socio-ecological trajectory is shaped and to tease out the local characteristics of a regime. The Viennese Institute of Social Ecology has produced several seminal studies of this kind, such as Fridolin Krausmann's (2013) analysis of Vienna's energy metabolism. It shows the gradual transition from biomass-based energy provision to industrial metabolism, characterised by a high and stabilised level of fossil energy consumption, between 1865 and 1973. During this 100 years transition Krausmann identifies the coal phase (1865-1928) and the oil-driven growth phase (1934-1973). Another result of Vienna's energy accounting is the remarkable per capita stability of energy consumption during the 19th century swinging between 20 and 35 GJ/cap/year, as compared to the period since 1973, when energy consumption had risen to about 100 GJ/cap/year. Similar results were obtained for Paris (Kim and Barles 2012, see also table 4). This questions the intuitive assumption that per capita urban energy consumption should have increased during the 19th century in connection with the development of industry, of energy devices at home, of mechanised transportation systems, etc. The hypothesis of increased energy savings thanks to growing technological efficiency could be considered here. This example highlights the need for historicising socio-ecological studies in order "to develop a natural history of cities" (Weisz 2013: 330).

Table 4: Changing metabolism: some indicators about Paris urban area*, 19th-20th century

	1801	1906	2015
Population	547.756	4.370.000	10.706.072
Urban area (km2)	37	293	2845
m2/cap	68	67	266
Land consumption between the two years (m2/yr)	-	2	23
m2/new inhabitant	-	67	403
Water consumption (Mm3/yr)	3	328	1172
l/cap/day	14	206	300
Primary energy consumption /PJ/yr)	14	109	1338
GJ/cap/yr	25	25	125
Final energy consumption (PJ/yr)	13	105	749
GJ/cap/yr	24	24	70
Fossil fuels (% of primary consumption)	0	84	93
C emission (ktC/yr)	0.2	-	9557
kgC/cap/yr	0.4	-	893

* Paris urban area is defined according to the continuity of the urban fabric. In 1800, it is limited to Paris within its administrative limits and includes surrounding muncipalities thereafter.

Conclusions

Whereas 'urban metabolism' as a notion has quite a long history, historical research into urban metabolism remains relatively scarce: even if the references given here are not exhaustive, they cover a great part of the field. This situation has a number of reasons. The first one is probably epistemological. Looking at the city through the prism of ecology poses several problems: can a city be considered as, compared to, likened to an ecosystem? Isn't there a risk of biological determinism in applying ecosystem theory to (urban) historical questions? More than that, isn't there an epistemological contradiction in such a scientific choice? The second challenge relates to the possibilities for interdisciplinary collaboration, both in theory and in practice, considering the existing organisation of scientific research, as the debate around 'environmental history' vs. 'history of the environment' indicates. The third problem is the lack of data: studying nitrogen during the 19th century in France is 'quite' easy, as nitrogen was a matter of concern, and statistics are numerous. But what about, for example, energy in the Middle Ages, when this notion even did not exist?

Despite these limitations, a typical urban metabolic profile can be established on the basis of existing research. Its main feature is externalisation: cities depended on other areas that supply them with food and other resources; their development is strongly connected to the metabolic performance of rural areas and to the ability of the latter to export food. The industrial revolution has led to the (quasi) total externalisation of urban metabolism in terms of supply and discharge, increasing the cities' material dependence. At the same time, and similar to human society as a whole, cities experienced the linearisation and the intensification of their metabolism: the growing and continuous extraction of new materials and the disposal of useless ones. The major material flows involved in urban metabolism are water, construction materials, food and energy carriers. Beyond these, a growing array of biogeochemical cycles has been or is now significantly influenced by urban metabolism.

This is reason enough to take up the challenges to historical research on urban metabolism. It is a question of scientific knowledge: we know too little about the history of city-nature interactions in their material, social, human and non-human dimensions. This is also and obviously a question of commitment to current issues dealing with global environmental change.

References

Acot, Pascal (1988): Histoire de l'écologie, Paris: PUF.
Ausubel, Jesse H./Sladovich, Hedy E. (1989): Technology and environment, Washington DC: National Academic Press.
Ayres, Robert U. (1978): Ressources, environment and economics: Application of the materials/energy balance principle, New York: John Wiley and sons.
Ayres, Robert U./Simonis, Udo E. (eds.) (1994): Industrial metabolism, Tokyo: United Nations University Press.
Baccini, Peter/Brunner, Paul H. (1991): Metabolism of the anthroposphere, Berlin: Springer.
Barles, Sabine (2010): "Society, energy and materials: What are the contributions of industrial ecology, territorial ecology and urban metabolism to sustainable urban development issues?" In: Journal of Environmental Planning and Management 53/4, pp. 439-455.
Barles, Sabine (2007): "Feeding the city: Food consumption and circulation of nitrogen, Paris, 1801-1914." In: The Science of the Total Environment 375, pp. 48-58.
Barles, Sabine (2005): L'invention des déchets urbains, France, 1790-1970, Seyssel: Champ Vallon.
Barles, Sabine/Knoll, Martin (2019): "Long-term transitions, urban imprint and the construction of hinterlands." In: Tim Soens/Dieter Schott/Michael Toyka-Seid/Bert De Munck (eds.), Urbanizing nature: Actors and agency (dis)connecting cities and nature since 1500, Abingdon/New York: Routledge, pp. 29-49.
Billen, Gilles/Garnier, Josette/Barles, Sabine (eds.) (2012): Special issue "History of the urban environmental imprint." Regional Environmental Change 12/2.
Billen, Gilles/Toussaint, Francine/Peeters, Philippe/Sapir, Marc (1983): L'écosystème Belgique: Essai d'écologie industrielle, Bruxelles, Centre de recherche et d'information socio-politique.
Boyden, Stephen/Millar, Sheelagh/Newcombe, Ken/O'Neill, Beverley (1981): The ecology of a city and its people: The case of Hong Kong, Canberra: Australian National University Press.
Buclet, Nicolas (ed.) (2015): Essai d'écologie territorial: L'exemple d'Aussois en Savoie, Paris: CNRS Editions.
Cordell, Dana/Drangert, Jan-Olof/White, Stuart (2009): "The story of phosphorus: Global food security and food for thought." In: Global Environmental Change 19, pp. 292-305.
Cronon, William (1991): Nature's Metropolis: Chicago and the Great West, New York: W. W. Norton & Company.

D'Arienzo Roberto (2017): Métabolismes urbains: De l'hygiénisme à la ville durable, Naples, 1884-2004, Genève: Métis Presses.

De Vries, Bert/Goudsblom, Johan (eds.) (2002): Mappae Mundi: Humans and their habitats in a long-term socio-ecological perspective, Amsterdam: Amsterdam University Press.

Deléage, Jean-Paul (1992): Histoire de l'écologie: Une science de l'homme et de la nature, Paris: La Découverte.

Dick, Jan et al. (2018): What is socio-ecological research delivering? A literature survey across 25 international LTSER platforms, Science of the Total Environment 622-623, pp. 1225-1240.

Dumas, Jean-Baptiste (1866): Enquête sur les engrais industriels, Paris: Imprimerie impériale, vol. 2.

Dumas, Jean-Baptiste (1842): Essai de statique chimique des êtres organises, Paris: Fortin, Masson & Cie.

Duvigneaud, Paul (1974): La synthèse écologique: Populations, communautés, écosystèmes, biosphère, noosphère, Paris: Doin.

Erkman, Suren (2004 [1998]): Vers une écologie industrielle, Paris: Charles Léopold Mayer & la librairie FPH.

Esculier, Fabien/Barles, Sabine (in press): "Past and future trajectories of human excreta management systems: The case of Paris 19th-21st centuries." In: Nicolas Flipo/Pierre Labadie/Laurence Lestel (eds.), The Seine River Basin, Heidelberg: Springer Nature.

Fischer Kowalski, Marina (1998): "Society's metabolism: The intellectual history of material flow analysis, part I, 1860-1970." In: Journal of Industrial Ecology 2/1, pp. 61-78.

Foster, John Bellamy (1999): "Marx's theory of metabolic rift: Classical foundations for environmental sociology." In: American Journal of Sociology 105/2, pp. 366-405.

Gandy, Matthew (2002): Concrete and clay: Reworking nature in New York City, Cambridge: MIT Press.

Geddes, Patrick (1915): Cities in evolution: An introduction to the town planning movement and to the study of civics, London: Williams & Norgate.

Geddes, Patrick (1885): An analysis of the principles of economics, London: Williams & Norgate.

Grimm, Nancy B. et al. (2000): "Integrated approaches to long-term studies of urban ecological systems." In: Bioscience 50/7, pp. 573-584.

Haberl, Helmut/Fischer-Kowalski, Marina/Krausmann, Fridolin/Winiwarter, Verena (eds.) (2016): Social ecology: Society-nature relations across time and space, Heidelberg: Springer Nature.

Hamlin, Christopher (2007): "The city as chemical system? The chemist as urban environmental professional in France and Britain, 1780-1880." In: Journal of Urban History 33/5, pp. 702-728.

Kim, Eunhye/Barles, Sabine (2012): "The energy consumption of Paris and its supply areas from 18th century to present." In: Regional Environmental Change 12/2, pp. 295-310.

Kneese, Allen V./Ayres, Robert U./D'Arge, Ralph C.(1970): Economics and the environment: A material balance approach, Washington: Resources for the Future.

Krausmann, Fridolin (2013): "A City and its hinterland: Vienna's energy metabolism 1800-2006." In: Simon J. Singh/Helmut Haberl/Marian Chertow/Michael Mirtl/Martin Schmid (eds.), Long term socio-ecological research: Studies in society-nature interactions across spatial and temporal scales, New York: Springer, pp. 247-268.

Moll, Louis (1863): "L'assainissement des villes par la fertilisation des campagnes." In: Annales du conservatoire des arts et métiers 4, pp. 337-376.

Mumford, Lewis (1961): The city in history: Its origins, its transformations, and its prospects, New York: Harcourt, Brace & World.

Odum, Eugene P. (1989): Ecology and our endangered life-support systems, Sunderland: Sinauer Associated Inc. Pub.

Odum, Eugene P. (1975 [1963]): Ecology: The link between natural and social sciences, New York: Holt, Rinehart and Winston.

Odum, Eugene P. (1953): Fundamentals of ecology, Philadelphia: Saunders.

Reconciling (1989): Special issue "Reconciling the sociosphere and the biosphere." In: International Social Science Journal XLI/3.

Schmid Neset, Tina-Simone/Bader, Hans-Peter/Sheidegger, Ruth/Lohm, Ulrik (2008): "The flow of phosphorus in food production and consumption: Linköping, Sweden, 1870-2000." In: The Science of the Total Environment 396, pp. 111-120.

Schott, Dieter (2014): "Urban development and environment." In: Mauro Agnoletti/Simone Neri Serneri (eds.), The basic environmental history, Heidelberg: Springer, pp. 171-198.

Svidén, J./Jonsson A. (2001): "Metabolism of mercury turnover, emissions and stock in Stockholm, 1795-1995." In: Water, air and soil pollution focus 1/3-4, pp. 179-196.

Tarr, Joel A. (2002): "The metabolism of the industrial city: The case of Pittsburgh." In: Journal of Urban History 28/5, pp. 511-545.

Theys, Jacques/Emelianoff, Cyria (2001): "Les contradictions de la ville durable." In: Le Débat 113, pp. 122-135.

Vincey, Paul (1901): Projet de régime nouveau pour les ordures ménagères de Paris, Paris: Imprimerie Chaix.

Weisz, Helga (2013): "Towards a socio-metabolic history of cities." In: Harald A. Mieg/Klaus Töpfer (eds.), Social urban transformations: Social innovations for local and global sustainability change, Abingdon/New York: Routledge, pp. 323-334.

Wolman, Abel (1965): "The metabolism of cities." In: Scientific American 213/3, pp. 179-190.

Material Flows and Circular Thinking

Heike Weber

For centuries, natural philosophers, scientists and engineers have referred to certain natural and technical processes as 'circulation'. Today, we speak of biogeochemical cycles of nutrients, nitrogen and phosphorus, of the circulation of blood in our bodies and of water in the wider ecosystem—to name but a few examples. Alchemists, physiologists and economic thinkers of the early modern period used the Latin term 'circulatio', or the French and English term 'circulation', to describe the transmutations and movements of materials, of bodily substances and fresh air, of commodities, traffic, wealth and money through entities such as nature, the body and the economy (Schramm 1997). In the 19th century, the borrowed term 'Zirkulation' entered the German language (Kilcher 2011), and circulation turned into the leading metaphor used to describe urban sanitation schemes. Since then, diverse fields of science and engineering have appropriated circulatory thinking in one way or another. The metaphor guides quantifying methods within bio-economics, ecosystem analysis and lifecycle analysis as well as geophysical thinking about longterm rock cycles and the 'uranium fuel cycle' of nuclear engineering (cf. Garcier 2012). More recently, the vision of a 'circular economy' has entered politics, industry and environmental activism in the context of a critique of consumer societies' wastefulness, and as a means of creating a sustainable society. Meanwhile the Anthropocene thesis claims that humans have irreversibly interrupted basic biogeochemical cycles and according to the geologist Peter Haff, the earth has turned into a self-operating 'technosphere' (Otter in this volume).

As this list demonstrates, the circulation trope is a common way to frame, but also to criticise the status quo of the socio-natural sphere as well as its ongoing transformations. It has a long intellectual tradition in the humanities, the sciences and engineering. It was and is used as a scientific model, as a depiction of an ideal and as a theoretical framework for analysis, e.g. in political ecology or history. To narrow down the field, this chapter will concentrate on circulatory thinking in the context of urban hygiene, urban studies and urban-environmental history.

On the one hand, it will provide an overview of the historical use of the trope of 'circulating' matter and 'circulation', and of its appropriation as a paradigm in urban as well as historical research. On the other hand, it will argue that circulatory thinking has epistemic limitations and blind spots. In an age that has coined the term Anthropocene, and in which urban studies reason about a conflictual planetary urbanisation (Brenner 2014), environmental historians should problematise this century-old metaphor and set it in relation to contradictory paradigms such as entropy, dissipation and human-made sinks.

Circulatory Thinking within Urban-Environmental History

In the context of the city, circulation has become a widely used term, referring to diverse transformative processes—from water flows to urban networks, from migration to pollution and other changes in the urban environment. In a broad sense, urban studies apply it to mobility, fluidity and the interactions of people, things, and knowledge and data within the urban fabric. Boutros et al. (2010), for example, see circulation at work in nearly every urban process, be it the controlled infrastructures of traffic, transport and communication, or scattered, chaotic and ephemeral phenomena such as the wandering of urban people, hidden work, homelessness, the flow of data and urban decay.

In urban-environmental history, the concept of circulation is applied less widely and refers to flows of materials and energy. The initial major field of historical investigation was the sanitation of cities. Biological metaphors such as circulation, organism and lungs and arteries were common in 19th century discourse on sanitation and were used to describe urban life and functions, such as water provision or the airing and cooling effects of green spaces. Urban reconstruction measures that promoted the circulation of air and water within urban spaces through corridors for ventilation and water flows were seen as a means to promote urban health and vitality. In line with the contemporary miasma theory, these measures also involved combatting the stagnation of putrid matter and water, as well as foul odours that could bring on sickness, diseases or 'great stinks' as in London in 1858 (Corbin 1982; Hardy 2005). Moreover, hygienists and social reformers linked filth to bourgeois moral imaginations of poverty and crime.

Historians have explored 19th century sanitary engineering measures by identifying such past circulatory thinking and by appropriating the metaphor themselves. Urban-environmental historians such as Dieter Schott (e.g. 2006, 2014) have described a technical transformation of natural water circulation in modern urban water provision and removal. City planning and sanitary engineering substantially transformed the material exchanges between the city and the so called 'urban hinterland', in particular with regard to the flows of water, excrement and waste—a transformation that was highly controversial, as historians have shown, since it stood in opposition to the contemporary ideal of circulation. When rural areas became urbanised in the course of the 20th century, the hinterland became a global one and the accumulation, transformation and technological management of these flows generated global environmental problems (Barles/Knoll 2019).

Historical narratives that describe these transformations use circulation as a metaphor, and speak of an 'interruption' or 'breaking open' of once circulating flows, but they also use the partly contrasting, partly interlinked concepts of 'networks' and 'metabolism' (Schramm 2006). The 'network' or 'networked city' ('vernetzte Stadt') approach is less interested in circulation and flows and more in the technologies and structures behind them— technologies and structures necessary for the transportation and exchange of materials, people, goods and data. Infrastructures, for instance, were and are seen as 'life veins' for society's circulatory processes—from water provision to communication, traffic and waste disposal—and modernity has been associated with an expansion of these flows and exchanges on the basis of vital, expanding infrastructures (van Laak 2018: 12). Elisabeth Heidenreich (2004) has added to this the notion of 'technological spaces of flow' ('technische Fließräume'). She defines the provision of drinking water as involving a 'liquidised nature' created by and channelled through water infrastructures.

The circulation metaphor has been particularly meaningful for the emerging research fields of urban political ecology, industrial ecology and urban metabolism studies, all of which are guided by the metabolism paradigm (Barles in this volume). 'Metabolism' entered the German language as 'Stoffwechsel' ('exchange of matter') via 19th century biology and Karl Marx's political economy. Similar to 'circulation', the terms 'urban metabolism' and 'social metabolism' are often used metaphorically to describe the many flows, exchanges and material transformations in a socio-natural setting such as a city or a region.

Urban Political Ecology (UPE), which in its beginnings was spearheaded by a Marxist logic, refers to socio-natural metabolism, circulation and hybridisation in order to overcome the nature-society dualism, as well as to delineate the uneven relations of power and capital in urbanisation processes (Heynen et al. 2006; Heynen 2014). Erik Swyngedouw, for example, refers to the "production of the hydro-social cycle through metabolic circulation" as "a process of fusion", of "constructing longer or shorter networks" and of "the making of 'heterogeneous assemblages'" (2015: 35).

In industrial ecology and urban metabolism studies, the circulation trope contributes to realising an ideally comprehensive, holistic, quantifying survey of a city or region which, as an object of investigation, is equated with a kind of socio-natural 'organism'. Studies in the field of Material Flow Analysis (MFA) try to collate input flows (of resources such as water, nutrients, waste, etc.), output flows (emissions, sewage, waste) as well as storage in stocks for a certain time period in a defined geographical region. Social metabolisms are characterised by complex input and output flows, and, as in the biological archetype, these need not necessarily be circular but can involve excrescence, deposits, excretions, dissipation, and losses. The city organism, for instance, lives by metabolic internalisation from and externalisation to its hinterland (Barles/Knoll 2019). Current MFA visualisations accordingly use flow charts to indicate flows, stocks and loose ends rather than closed-circle diagrams.

The metaphor of a circle and that of a metabolism have shortcomings, as they do not incorporate the parameters of time and labour. Yet in the social setting of a city, a region or even the globe, temporal relations are critical to inhabitants, and every flow includes underlying work to channel it and move it around. Stocks of raw materials, for instance, have to be extracted, transported and transformed over time in order to be turned into usable resource flows. Moreover, material flows can stagnate for a certain time and form 'stocks' when materials become fixed in the form of infrastructures or buildings or even 'sinks' (waste depots). As UPE argues, urban metabolism studies and their quantifications on the macro-scale thus need to be complemented by qualitative analysis in order to understand the political forces and power relations, socio-economic hierarchies and cultural dynamics behind the flows and their reconfigurations.

History of Water and Faeces:
Sewage Infrastructure as a Disruptor of Natural Circulation

Water engineering served to modernise states, as detailed studies have shown—for example for 18th to early 20th Germany and 20th century Spain (Blackbourn 2006; Swyngedouw 2015). Water engineering included the drainage of land, the construction of canals for transportation and dams for water provision and hydropower, and the realisation of potable water supplies and sewage systems. Urban sewage systems were among the largest technological projects of the 19th and early 20th centuries, resulting in a substantial reconfiguration of the flows of water and faecal matter between the city and its hinterland.

Traditionally, excrement had been dumped into rivers or collected in tanks, privies and cesspools that had to be regularly emptied. In Asia, urban faeces were intensively used as night soil in the local agricultural system which emphasised plant cultivation rather than animal husbandry—in Hong Kong, for example, up to the 1950s, and even longer in mainland China (Boyden et al. 1981). But in American and European cities, too, haulers and farmers transported urban waste—faeces from humans and animals along with leftovers from urban markets and households—to the periphery where it then was often applied for cultivation or land reclamation (Tarr 1996,: 293-308; Barles 2005a, 2005b). When Edwin Chadwick (1800-1890) argued for draining away human waste and drain water, he had a circulatory water provision and removal system in mind, even if London's sewage system of 1865 ultimately channelled its waste water into the Thames (Schneider 2011).

In line with past observers, historians have interpreted the traditional recovery of excrement as a closing of the nutrient cycle. By contrast, Sabine Barles has shown that in Paris substantial amounts of the inflows of dietary nitrogen were lost in the cesspool drainage process: According to her calculations, only around 20 (1817) to 40 per cent (1913) made it back to the land as dung or by way of sewage farming (Barles 2007: 56). The circulatory ideal was eventually repressed when the scientific findings of Pasteur and Koch replaced miasma doctrines with bacteria theory during the late 19th century (Evans 1987). The new hygienic regime defined purity in bacteriological terms, and in the long run promoted disposal over unhygienic recovery procedures—first, for sewage and faeces, and later for other urban waste. In the course of the 20th century, sewer drainage ('tout-à-l'égout' in French or 'Schwemmkanalisation' in German), followed by urban waste collection and disposal services, became the dominant way to get rid of urban excrement and waste.

Up until the 19th century, the circulation idea was embedded in a larger belief in eternal motion and the cyclic structure of creation. In the field of agricultural chemistry, Christopher Hamlin (2007: 709) and Erland Mårald (2002) have described this belief as 'Chemico-Theology'. Justus von Liebig (1845-73), for example, developed a theory about plant nutrients that argued that for every sack of grain a farmer delivered to the city, he should recover a sack of urban waste to use as manure on his land. This would perpetuate balanced material flows between city and nature and ensure food production (Schramm 1997). The very same idea of returning extracted nutrients to the land guided Paris, Berlin and other cities to install irrigation systems for sewage farming in tandem with new sewage networks. Moreover, scientists began to analyse the material flows into cities (in the form of foodstuffs) and out of cities (via municipal waste disposal) in more detail, in ways similar to later MFA quantifications. Alfred Durand-Claye (1841-88) and Theodor Weyl (1851-1913), for example, calculated inflowing quantities of foodstuffs to Paris and Berlin, as well as the composition of these cities' urban waste, in order to evaluate the losses incurred in disposal and the potential value of the waste as an asset (Barles/Lestel 2007; Weyl 1894). For faeces and urine, studies determined the concentration of nutrients that might be regained by excrement recycling via sewage farming and the production of human fertiliser (Schneider 2011: 126). Through their focus on 'circulation', chemists at the time became important actors in the emerging field of urban planning (Hamlin 2007; Barles/Lestel 2007)—a function later on fulfilled by sanitary engineers who would become the 20th century experts on wastewater treatment. In addition, a separate synthetic fertiliser industry emerged which supplanted the limited amount of traditional fertiliser and promised to provide farmers with all the necessary nutrients for their crops.

Through sewage and synthetic fertiliser production and application, humans have massively altered the earth's flows of nutrients. From 1940 to 1990, the amount of industrially fixed nitrogen rose from 3 to 100 million metric tons. Today, human activity is responsible for around 60 per cent of the fixed nitrogen in the soil, an amount which exceeds the nitrogen released by bacterial activity and causes severe environmental problems (Gorman 2012; 2014). Likewise, the soil's phosphate content has risen, while phosphorus reservoirs have been depleted for artificial fertiliser production. As a consequence of these anthropogenic transformations of so-called nutrient cycles, the issues of faeces and sewage sludge have once again entered political and scientific debates, and the recycling of phosphates in waste water is currently being mandated by governments and municipalities.

Waste Histories: Scarcity, Abundance and the 'Ultimate Sink'

Industrialisation, urbanisation and 20th century mass consumption resulted in increasing amounts of urban waste; remnants which could not easily be channelled back to the spheres of nature, production or consumption accumulated and became a threat to urban hygiene. Environmental historians have identified the growing amount of urban solid waste and its disposal by municipal waste services as another disruptor of 'circular' flows. In Strasser's words, the "late-twentieth-century city takes in most of what it uses by truck and train and airplane, and flushes its waste into landfills, sewage treatment plants, and toxic dumps." (1999: 14-15) Sabine Barles sees an "opening of the bio-geochemical cycles" at work (Barles 2014: 223).

In the case of faeces, as the preceding section has shown, hygienic arguments quickly gained the upper hand and faeces were washed away rather than recycled, even more so as the methods to do so were limited and not economically profitable (Schneider 2011). In retrospect, more and more historians see the universal introduction of sewage systems as the first step toward Western throwaway societies. Municipal waste services, as they came into being in the late 19th century, completed the transition. Most of them opted for disposal rather than reuse as a treatment for urban waste, the quantities of which were steadily increasing. As will be shown in more detail in the following, the practices of disposal and reuse of urban waste— just as in the case of faeces—were influenced by circulatory thinking on the one hand and the wish to combat filth and nuisance for the sake of health and hygiene on the other. They were also determined by a complex relationship between scarcity, abundance and the costs of labour—a relation which was historically and regionally specific and which also differed for different kinds of waste.

Historians, in particular economic historians, often state that during the pre-modern era, materials and goods remained in 'circulation'. Metals, paper, wood, earthenware, stones and rubble were sorted and reused, while dogs, pigs or hens devoured kitchen waste. Used goods such as textiles or books were re-sold and traded as second-hand goods or passed down from user to user (Reith 2001, 2003; Stöger 2019; Fontaine 2008; Woodward 1995). Rags were the dominant raw material for paper mills before paper industry began to exploit wood fibres in the late 19th century. Next to the rag-and-bone trade, a lively scrap metal trade existed (Zimring 2005; Strasser 1999; Barles 2005; Weber 2014a).

In a makeshift economy, 'urban by-products', as Sabine Barles calls them—rags, bones, excrement, etc.—, were recovered and had economic value. By and large, pre- and early modern economies were characterised by goods which remained in use for a long time, by repair and recycling, and by natural processes of decay and ageing, while their solar energy base of the pre-industrial era set clear-cut limits on agriculture, production and consumption. The modern shift in price relations which accompanied the fossil energy regime made labour more expensive than resources and transport, with the result that the recovery of many waste materials gradually lost its economic justification (Reith 2003).

At the same time environmental history studies have also made clear that the 'circulation' analogy often is an idealisation: Pre-modern cities suffered from insufficient waste removal and unhealthy dirtiness and decay, and 19th century industrial cities, despite their many sanitary efforts, struggled with smoke emissions and the contamination of water. Pre-modern societies also left behind excess matter that was stockpiled in 'ultimate sinks'. Rome's Monte Testaccio illustrates this point: Rome's eighth hill dates from classical times and was created through the dumping of broken amphorae which had previously carried oil and other foodstuffs into the city.

Martin Melosi's pioneering work on urban waste removal (2000, 2005) and subsequent waste studies have emphasised the role of hygiene and urban sanitation as drivers for the establishment of municipal waste services in the decades around 1900. With these services, household waste and its removal became issues of public responsibility. Tellingly, at just this time the first general terms came in use to refer to city waste—for example the German term *Müll* and the French *ordures ménagères*. Previously terms specific to different materials had been used, such as rubble, scrap, rags, garbage (for kitchen waste) or sweepings. Joel Tarr (1996) pointed out that the waste problem translated into a "search for the ultimate sink": Societies were and are in need of final sinks into which they can dispose of pollutants and waste with minimal environmental degradation.

Sabine Barles' detailed *longue durée* study of waste recovery in Paris (2005) has shown that waste recovery efforts did not cease all at once. According to Barles, the "closing of materials' cycles" became an essential "urban management issue" in the 19th century not only because cities produced waste, but also because industry and agriculture needed certain fractions of it as resources (2014). In her analysis of material cycles in Paris, Barles (2005) showed in detail how faeces, sewage, bones and rags were used in farming and in diverse industrial branches. Depending on the availability of alternative resources such as wood pulp and artificial fertiliser, their recycling came to an end at different times. According to Barles, this gradual 'divorce' of city, land and industry resulted in a final break of circulatory flows during the interwar years.

In line with Barles' perspective, several other studies have pointed out the diverse recycling trades which arose in parallel to industrialisation, e.g. the exploitation of by-products from the coal and steel industries such as tar residues and slags (Desrochers 2007; Weber 2014b). Here again, contemporaries often operated within the framework of circulatory thinking, as has been shown of Peter Lund Simmonds (1814-1897) and his popularisation efforts for waste recycling, which took eternal material cycles for granted (Cooper 2011; Desrochers 2007). Meanwhile the term 'recycling' emerged in the 1920s oil industry, where it referred to the practice of returning residues back into the refinery process.

But even in the realm of household waste disposal, the circulatory idea never fully vanished. Four trenchant examples—from the fields of rag-picking, composting, landfilling, and recycling—might demonstrate this. Rag-picking was on its last legs in the 1920s. Still, the 'life of a rag' was not solely seen as a threat to hygiene, but it was also described as 'an eternal cycle'—in a German newspaper article, for instance, as one that at the time secured the existence of around 60.000 people in Germany (Windmüller 2004: 187).[1] Composting was emphatically promoted as a waste treatment alternative in the early 1960s, as it would close the 'nutrient loop' between urban and rural areas (Page 2019: 13; Weber 2020) (Fig. 1). Even landfilling was seen as operating within the circulatory framework of nature: The dumped waste was supposed to gradually transform by natural decay processes into 'waste earth'. Only from the late 1960s onwards, when landfilling was modernised and became the object of enhanced control, safety procedures and environmental engineering, were landfills conceptualised as human-made and potentially toxic sinks in need of aftercare (Weber 2014c). Today, the waste hills of 20th century consumer society are prominent urban and suburban landmarks and testify to the non-circularity of the 20th century urban metabolism and its search for an ultimate sink (Weber 2019). Recycling was and is promoted by the circular metaphor, even if 'downcycling' effects are unavoidable and refute the circular ideal.

---

1 Quote from Der Tag (Berlin, 14.01.1926, "60.0000 Lumpensammler in Deutschland").

Figure 1: Brochure by the German composting advocate Erhard Spohn with the title "Current questions about compost. The circulation of the living" The visualisation suggests that waste is composted (upper part) and re-used as soil in gardening. Below, we see a vegetable market and a woman peeling potatoes

Source: Spohn, Erhard: Aktuelle Fragen über Kompost. Der Kreislauf des Lebendigen. Heidelberg 1962 (Published by the *Heidelberger Portländer*, trade magazine of the Portland-Zementwerke Heidelberg AG). Sammlung Erhard, Umweltbundesamt, Dessau.

The recycling movement which emerged in Western mass consumer societies in the 1970s in the context of environmental politics and a growing ecological awareness, has by and large adopted this kind of circular thinking and as we will see in the last section, it has become the mainstay of current 'circular economy' concepts.

The circulatory idea thrived in wartime economies and under fascist and socialist regimes (Oldenziel/Weber 2013). By the late 1930s, the Nazi regime had put the idea centre stage in its exploitative, even murderous waste and recycling policies (Weber 2020; Berg 2015; Hauser 2010). Propaganda books on waste recovery such as Claus Ungewitter's 'Verwertung des Wertlosen' ('Exploitation of the Worthless') (1938) promoted a "total" utilisation of waste and a "rational materials economy" in which natural products would be inserted into cycles of goods just as would any material and rubbish. The Nazi regime had municipalities establish infrastructures to collect kitchen scraps as feed for swine, and forced the paper and textile industries to increase their quotas of wastepaper and used-fibre utilisation. Schools served as pillars for waste collection, and inmates of concentration camps were enrolled in a sometimes murderous waste exploitation process.

Socialist states such as the GDR and Hungary stipulated a closed-loop management of materials and wastes from production as well as consumption to make more efficient use of scarce resources (Möller 2014; Gille 2007). From the 1980s onwards, the GDR expanded its bring-back system for recyclable household waste under the header of 'SERO' (*Sekundär-Rohstofferfassung*—capture of secondary raw materials) (Hartard/Huhn 1992) (Fig. 2).

Figure 2: Enamel plate "VEB Sekundärrohstofferfassung" with the SERO logo (Sekundär-Rohstofferfassung—capture of secondary raw materials)

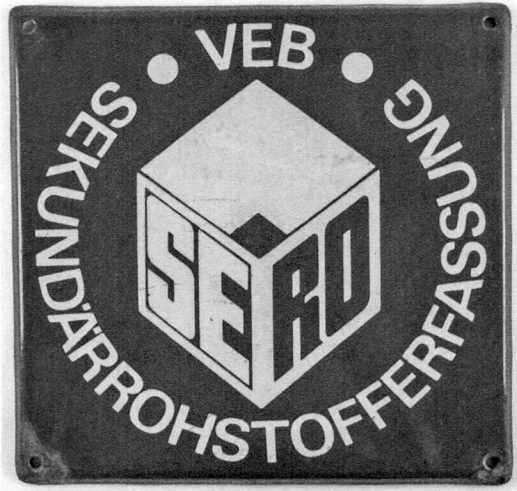

Source: © Sammlung DDR Museum, Berlin, Inventarnummer 1015767.

The ecological recycling movement hardly recognised or studied the socialist experiences and concepts, even if both shared the hope of closing material cycles. For instance, West Germany's most popular and successful 1980s recycling project, glass recycling, was promoted as closing the 'glass cycle' and its visual logo at that time represented two merging hands which exchanged an empty for a full bottle. While inside the GDR's economic framework, the disposable bottle was absent, in many Western countries, its introduction into the beverage market caused severe disputes among waste disposal services, the beverage and the glass industry, supermarkets, politics, and citizens around 1970. In the end, in West Germany, and in contrast to several Scandinavian countries, the non-returnable glass bottle was not prohibited, as the glass industry had agreed to build up a recycling infrastructure for glass containers as an act of voluntary commitment.

The recycling icons (see Fig. 2, 3) suggest an unproblematic process of circulation. Iconographically, they not only point to the circle, but also to the ancient

Ouroboros symbol: a serpent eating its own tail. By contrast, the actual ecological balance of recycling is hotly disputed (MacBride 2012). In the case of glass recycling, for instance, more and more glass has been recycled—but at the same time, the increasing consumption of bottled drinks in non-returnable containers has produced more and more waste. Since the 1970s, 'green' recycling has turned into a highly profitable business (Brownell 2011). Today, it is characterised by global corporations and high-tech recycling methods, but also by shadow economies, dubious waste exports and informal, even hazardous recycling processes being exported to poor regions of the globe.

Figure 3: Gary Anderson's Recycling Logo prototype, 1970. It was developed for a contest sponsored by the Container Corporation of America to honour the first Earth Day in 1970. The three arrows, in the form of a Möbius strip, visualise an infinite, timeless closed cycle

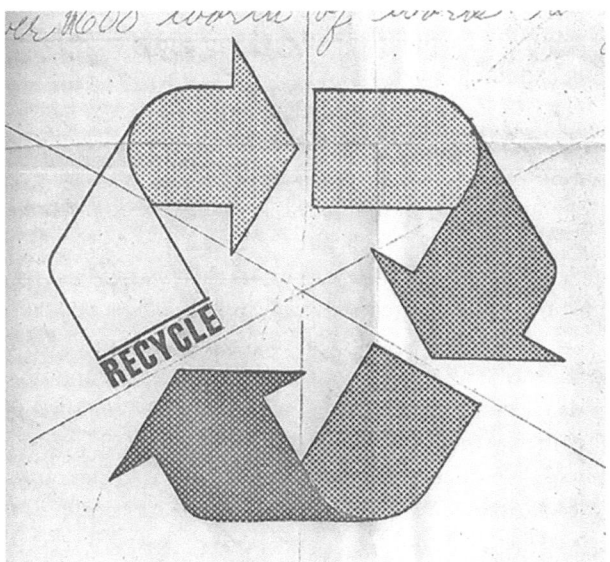

Source: Dunaway, Finis (2015): Seeing Green: The Use and Abuse of American Environmental Images. Chicago: University of Chicago Press, p. 99.

Future research might clarify whether, in Europe, the circulatory ideal affected municipal waste disposal in a more lasting way than in the U.S., a country characterised by a natural abundance of resources (Worster 2016). Moreover, we still lack comprehensive studies on waste streams besides those from households, even though further waste sub-categories emerged over the second half of the 20th century—such as industrial waste, agricultural waste, and nuclear and hazardous waste, most of which reach higher levels or are more toxic than household waste. Cities, for instance, have produced high quantities of construction waste in a perpetual continuum of construction, demolition and reuse of building material which has hardly been studied so far (Hommels 2008). Moreover, waste became an issue not only of hygiene, but also of toxicity. 20th century mass production and mass consumption have left behind manifold waste legacies, and from the 1980s onwards remediation of contaminated sites and aftercare for legacies have entered the field of waste management. Critical substances such as asbestos or PCBs (an organic chlorine compound widely used as a fluid in electrical appliances) which once had been fundamental materials in construction and electrification in the process of urban sprawl, have been identified as toxic. Remedial action is in course to remove them from infrastructural stocks and dispose of them in secure ultimate sinks.

Closing the Loop via Technology?—Recycling and the Current Idea of a 'Circular Economy'

The recycling movement is a reaction to the 'great acceleration' (Engelke/McNeill 2014) of the post-war decades. In parallel to booming resource extraction and production, quantities of waste multiplied, as did its material complexity and its potential toxicity (Köster 2016; Weber 2020). By the late 20th century, societies increasingly lacked sinks for the final disposal of their waste. This lack, along with the environmentalist push to preserve raw materials and reduce energy use have, once again, turned recycling and circular material flows into a leading paradigm for waste treatment. Similar to the 19th century debates about water, excrement and waste, this recent postulation of circularity can be found in different scientific fields. It criticises the fundamental disruption of the 'biogeochemical cycles' of the ecosystem, in particular for water, carbon, nitrogen and phosphorus. Promoting the idea of circulation here thus also functions as a critique of the current state of the social metabolism.

The scarcity of resources, increasing flows of pollutants and the limits of natural abundance have been widely discussed in economics, environmental politics and public discourse since the 1970s. Pioneering studies were the Paley report of 1952, Barry Commoner's *The Closing Circle* (1971), the Club of Rome's *Limits to Growth* (1972) and Kenneth Boulding's call for a 'spaceship economy' to replace the 'cowboy economy' (1966) (Höhler 2015; Fischer-Kowalski 1998). More recently, Johan Rockström and others have proposed the concept of planetary boundaries, warning global society against crossing major critical thresholds in the finite earth system, since doing so could cause irreversible, abrupt planetary changes (Steffen 2015).[2]

The seminal trope of the last decades is the so-called 'circular economy' in which recycling will close material loops and engender a 'zero-waste society'. Once again, pre-modern agricultural practices and natural processes are taken as models: Current resource strategies are popularised with reference to traditional subsistence farming's re-use of organic wastes (Gäth/Meißner 2013:107), and the authors of the 'cradle-to-cradle' approach claim—with the image of the wastefulness of a blossoming cherry tree—that technical cycles can emulate biological ones if only all waste is absorbed and production avoids toxic materials (McDonough/Braungart 2002: 72-73). Seen in the longer historical perspective, past and present circular thinking have similar aims, but see different actors and agency at work: It is neither nature as such nor the collecting, trading and transport activity of the rag-and-bone men that are now seen as eternal impulse and guarantors for the circular flows, but rather chemistry, recycling technology and diverse waste infrastructures.

The persistence of the circulation metaphor calls for explanation. By the late 19th century, the science of thermodynamics had demystified circular thinking as an unreachable ideal which, however, still ought to be pursued due to the finite availability of resources (Hellige 1994). Today's scientists and engineers are well aware that any *re*cycling represents a *down*cycling: it entails losses in material and quality, dissipation of materials, the need for energy input and waste labour, transport expenses and the generation of new waste. Nevertheless, there is a broad consensus that the metaphor will help to reach higher recycling quotas and to reduce the final disposal of sewage and waste in sinks. But at the same time, the metaphor has enabled politics, industry and consumers to 'greenwash' the surge of consumption in mass consumer societies that arose in parallel to an increase in environmental awareness (MacBride 2012; Weber 2020). 'Green' recycling has cast consumers as 'consumer-recycler-citizens' who see to it that waste flows enter recycling channels, and as a consequence can feel that they are contributing to the rescue of nature and her eternal cycles.

Conclusions

For centuries the idea of material cycles has functioned as a boundary object for actors within science, engineering and the larger society (Schramm 2006: 50; Weber 2020). The circulation metaphor has served as a scientific model and a depic-

---

2 According to Rockstrom et al., we have already crossed the thresholds in the cases of climate, biodiversity, and the nitrogen cycle.

tion of a wished-for or lost ideal, and has guided analytical research in the humanities. In urban development debates, actors such as urban planners, hygienists, chemists and waste experts have used it to criticise existing socio-metabolic waste regimes and to propose or disqualify novel socio-metabolic schemes. In addition, contemporaries saw and see circulation at work in diverse transformative processes such as the rag-and-bone men's waste-picking activity, sewage farming, the Nazi autarkic waste recovery project or the current recycling economy. As a conceptual approach in urban-environmental history, circulation has been very productive in initiating and guiding studies on the flows of water, excrement and waste and their change over time. Lately, research has also increasingly highlighted the limitations of the metaphor.

Social metabolism studies have demonstrated that past recycling efforts neither closed material cycles nor resulted in shrinking waste quantities or a decrease in resource extraction (Haas et al. 2015). The circulatory paradigm recognises neither the arrow of time nor distortions of its flows through the likes of stocks and sinks, accumulations and stagnations, refluxes and breakaways, losses and dissipation. It ignores waste and recycling labour and the diverse networks, nodes and infrastructures that operate to remove waste from its dispersed places of origin to hubs of waste elimination, disposal and recycling. It is blind to the environmental injustice involved in waste work, waste exports and waste disposal, to issues of toxic residues which should not be kept in circulation, and to waste legacies and pollution generated by the dumping, incineration and recycling of faeces, sewage and other waste.

In the age of the Anthropocene, we might thus wish to question or even abandon circular and flow metaphors which have nature and natural cycles as their model—analogies that imply a timeless biological archetype. Instead, it is time to turn to the entropic principle to assess how mass consumer societies have dispersed and continue to disperse pooled natural resource stocks into widespread remains that resist any simple circular transformation.

References

Barles, Sabine (2014): "History of waste management and the social and cultural representations of waste." In: Mauro Agnoletti/Simone Neri Serneri (eds.), The basic environmental history, London/New York: Springer, pp. 199-226.

Barles, Sabine (2007): "Feeding the city: Food consumption and flow of nitrogen, Paris, 1801-1914." In: Science of the Total Environment 375, pp. 48-58.

Barles, Sabine (2005a): L'invention des Déchets Urbains: France, 1790-1970, Seyssel: Champ Vallon.

Barles, Sabine (2005b): "A metabolic approach to the city: Nineteenth and twentieth century Paris." In: Bill Luckin/Geneviève Massard-Guilbaud/Dieter Schott (eds.), Resources of the city: Contributions to an environmental history of modern Europe, Aldershot: Ashgate, pp. 28-47.

Barles, Sabine/Knoll, Martin (2019): "Long-Term transitions, urban imprint and the construction of hinterlands." In: Tim Soens/Dieter Schott/Michael Toyka-Seid/Bert De Munck (eds.), Urbanizing nature: Actors and agency (dis)connecting cities and nature since 1500, New York: Routledge, pp. 29-49.

Barles, Sabine/Lestel, Laurence (2007): "The nitrogen question: Urbanization, industrialization, and river quality in Paris, 1830-1939." In: Journal of Urban History 33/5, pp. 794-812.

Berg, Anna (2015): "The nazi rag-pickers and their wine: The politics of waste and recycling in nazi Germany." In: Social History 40/4, pp. 446-472.

Blackbourn, David (2006): The conquest of nature: Water, landscape and the making of modern Germany, London: W. W. Norton.

Boutros, Alexandra/Straw, Will (eds.) (2010): Circulation and the city: Essays on urban Culture, Montreal: McGill-Queen's University Press.

Boyden, Stephen/Millar, Sheelagh/Newcombe, Ken/O'Neill, Beverley (1981): The ecology of a city and its people: The case of Hong Kong, Canberra/London/Miami: Australian National University Press.

Brenner, Neil (ed.) (2014): Implosions/explosions: Towards a study of planetary urbanization, Berlin: Jovis.

Brownell, Emily (2011): "Negotiating the new economic order of waste." In: Environmental History 16, pp. 262-289.

Cooper, Timothy (2011): "Peter Lund Simmonds and the political ecology of waste utilization in victorian Britain." In: Technology & Culture 52/1, pp. 21-44.

Corbin, Alain (1982): Le Miasme et la Jonquille: L'odorat et L'imaginaire Social 18e-19e siècles. Paris: Aubier Montaigne.

Desrochers, Pierre (2007): "How did the invisible hand handle industrial waste? By-product development before the modern environmental era." In: Enterprise and Society 8/2, pp. 348-374.

Engelke, Peter/McNeill, John (2014): The great acceleration: An environmental history of the anthropocene since 1945, Cambridge: Harvard University.

Evans, Richard J. (1987): Death in Hamburg: Society and politics in the cholera years, London: Penguin Books.

Fischer-Kowalski, Marina (1998): "Society's metabolism: The intellectual history of materials flow analysis. Part I, 1860-1970, Part II, 1970-1998." In: Journal of Industrial Ecology 2/1, pp. 61-78 and 2/4, pp. 107-137.

Fontaine, Laurence (ed.) (2008): Alternative exchanges: Second-hand circulations from the sixteenth century to the present, Oxford: Berghahn.

Garcier, Romain (2012): "One cycle to bind them all? Geographies of nuclearity in the uranium fuel cycle." In: Catherine Alexander/Joshua Reno (eds.), Economies of recycling: The global transformation of materials, values and social relations, London/New York: Zed, pp. 76-97.

Gäth, Stefan/Meißner, Simon (2013): "Ressourcenschonung durch innovative Recycling- und Kreislaufkonzepte." In: Luitgard Marschall/Simon Meißner/Armin Reller/Claudia Schmidt (eds.), Ressourcenstrategien: Eine Einführung in den nachhaltigen Umgang mit Rohstoffen, Darmstadt: WBG, pp. 105-122.

Gille, Zsuzsa (2007): From the cult of waste to the trash heap of history: The politics of waste in socialist and postsocialist Hungary, Bloomington: Indiana University Press.

Gorman, Hugh S. (2012): The story of N: A social history of the nitrogen cycle and the challenge of sustainability, New Brunswick/London: Rutgers University Press.

Gorman, Hugh S. (2014): "Thinking in cycles: Flows of nitrogen and sustainable uses of the environment." In: Uwe Lübken/Frank Uekötter (eds.), Managing the unknown: Essays on environmental ignorance, Oxford/New York: Berghahn, pp. 32-52.

Haas, Willi/Krausmann, Fridolin/Wiedenhofer, Dominik/Heinz, Markus (2015): "How circular is the global economy? An assessment of material flows, waste production, and recycling in the European Union and the world in 2005." In: Journal of Industrial Ecology 19/5, pp. 1-13.

Hamlin, Christopher (2007): "The city as a chemical system? The chemist as urban environmental professional in France and Britain, 1780-1880." In: Journal of Urban History 33, pp. 702-728.

Hartard, Susanne/Huhn, Michael (1992): Strukturanalyse des SERO-Systems der DDR im Hinblick auf Effizienz und Eignung unter marktwirtschaftlichen Bedingungen, Berlin: Umweltbundesamt.

Hauser, Susanne (2010): "Recycling: Ein Transformationsprozess." In: Anselm Wagner (ed.), Abfallmoderne: Zu den Schmutzrändern der Kultur, Vienna: LIT, pp. 45-62.

Hardy, Anne I. (2005): Ärzte, Ingenieure und städtische Gesundheit: Medizinische Theorien in der Hygienebewegung des 19. Jahrhunderts, Frankfurt a.M./New York: Campus.

Heidenreich, Elisabeth (2004): Fließräume: Die Vernetzung von Natur, Raum und Gesellschaft seit dem 19. Jahrhundert, Frankfurt a.M.: Campus.

Hellige, Hans Dieter (1994): "Wirtschafts-, Energie- und Stoffkreisläufe in säkularer Perspektive: Von der thermodynamischen Entzauberung der Welt zur recyclingorientierten Wachstumsgesellschaft." In: Gangolf Hübinger/Jürgen Osterhammel/Erich Peltzer (eds.), Universalgeschichte und Nationalgeschichten, Freiburg: Rombach, pp. 291-315.

Heynen, Nikolas (2014): "Urban political ecology I: The urban century." In: Progress in Human Geography 38/4, pp. 598-604.
Heynen, Nikolas/Swyngedouw, Erik/Kaika, Maria (eds.) (2006): In the nature of cities: Urban political ecology and the politics of urban metabolism, London/New York: Routledge.
Höhler, Sabine (2015): Spaceship earth in the environmental age 1960-1990, London: Pickering & Chatto.
Hommels, Anique (2008): Unbuilding cities: Obduracy in urban sociotechnical change, Cambridge/London: MIT Press.
Kilcher, Anderas B. (2011): "Assimilation und Zirkulation: Ein universalistisches Wissensmodell des 19. Jahrhunderts." In: Nach Feierabend. Zürcher Jahrbuch für Wissensgeschichte 7, pp. 15-36.
Köster, Roman (2016): Hausmüll: Abfall und Gesellschaft in Westdeutschland, 1945-1990, Göttingen: Vandenhoeck & Ruprecht.
Laak, Dirk van (2018): Alles im Fluss: Die Lebensadern unserer Gesellschaft – Geschichte und Zukunft der Infrastruktur, Frankfurt a.M.: Fischer.
MacBride, Samantha (2012): Recycling reconsidered: The present failure and future promise of environmental action in the united states, Cambridge/London: MIT Press.
Mårald, Erland (2002): "Everything circulates: Agricultural chemistry and recycling theories in the second half of the nineteenth century." In: Environment and History 8/1, pp. 65-84.
McDonough, William/Braungart, Michael (2002): Cradle to cradle: Remaking the way we make things, New York: North Point Press.
Melosi, Martin V. (2005): Garbage in the cities: Refuse, reform, and the environment, Pittsburgh: University of Pittsburgh Press.
Melosi, Martin V. (2000): The sanitary city: Urban infrastructure in America from colonial times to the present, Baltimore: Johns Hopkins University Press.
Möller, Christian (2014): "Der Traum vom ewigen Kreislauf: Abprodukte, Sekundärrohstoffe und Stoffkreisläufe im 'Abfall-Regime' der DDR, 1945-1990." In: Technikgeschichte 81/1, pp. 61-90.
Oldenziel, Ruth/Weber, Heike (eds.) (2013): Social history of recycling and re-use in the twentieth century. Special Issue, Contemporary European History 22/3.
Page, Arnaud (2019): 'Fertility from urban wastes? The case for composting in Great Britain, 1920s-1960s.' In: Environment and History 20/1, pp. 3-22.
Reith, Reinhold (2003): "Recycling im späten Mittelalter und der frühen Neuzeit: Eine Materialsammlung." In: Frühneuzeit-Info 14, pp. 47-65.
Reith, Reinhold (2001): "Recycling: Stoffströme in der Geschichte." In: Sylvia Hahn/Reinhold Reith (eds.), Querschnitte 8: Umwelt-Geschichte: Arbeitsfelder, Forschungsansätze, Perspektiven, Vienna/Munich: Oldenbourg, pp. 99-120.

Schneider, Daniel (2011): Hybrid nature: Sewage treatment and the contradictions of the industrial ecosystem, Cambridge: MIT Press.

Schott, Dieter (2014): Europäische Urbanisierung (1000-2000): Eine umwelthistorische Einführung. Cologne/Weimar/Vienna: Böhlau.

Schott, Dieter (2006): "Industrialisierung und städtische Umwelt in Deutschland." In: Franz Bosbach/Jens Ivo Engels/Fiona Watson (eds.), Umwelt und Geschichte in Deutschland und Großbritannien: Environment and History in Britain and Germany, Munich: Saur, pp. 91-104.

Schramm, Engelbert (2006): "Kreislauf, Metabolismus, Netz: Leitbilder für einen veränderten städtischen Umgang mit Wasser." In: Susanne Frank/Matthew Gandy (eds.), Hydropolis: Wasser und die Stadt der Moderne, Frankfurt a.M./New York: Campus, pp. 41-56.

Schramm, Engelbert (1997): Im Namen des Kreislaufes: Ideengeschichte der Modelle vom ökologischen Kreislauf, Darmstadt: Iko-Verlag.

Steffen W. et al. (2015): "Planetary boundaries: Guiding human development on a changing planet." In: Science 349, No. 6254, pp. 1286-1287 (doi:10.1126/science.aad0674).

Stöger, Georg (2019): "Re-use and recycling in western European cities." In: Tim Soens/Dieter Schott/Michael Toyka-Seid/Bert De Munck (eds.), Urbanizing nature: Actors and agency (dis)connecting cities and nature since 1500, New York: Routledge, pp. 157-176.

Strasser, Susan (1999): Waste and want: A social history of trash, New York: Metropolitan.

Swyngedouw, Erik (2015): Liquid power: Contested hydro-modernities in twentieth-century Spain, Cambridge: MIT Press.

Tarr, Joel A. (1996): The search for the ultimate sink: Urban pollution in historical perspective, Akron: University of Akron Press.

Weber, Heike (2020): Reste und Recycling bis zur 'grünen Wende': Eine Stoff- und Wissensgeschichte alltäglicher Abfälle, Göttingen: Vandenhoeck & Ruprecht.

Weber, Heike (2019): "20th century wastescapes: Cities, consumers, and their dumping grounds." In: Tim Soens/Dieter Schott/Michael Toyka-Seid/Bert De Munck (eds.), Urbanizing nature: Actors and agency (dis)connecting cities and nature since 1500, New York: Routledge, pp. 261-289.

Weber, Heike (2014a): "Den Stoffkreislauf am Laufen halten: Restearbeit und Resteökonomien des 20. Jahrhunderts." In: Kijan Espahangizi/Barbara Orland (eds.), Stoffe in Bewegung: Beiträge zu einer Wissensgeschichte der materiellen Welt, Zürich: Diaphanes, pp. 145-171.

Weber, Heike (2014b): "'Entschaffen': Reste und das Ausrangieren, Zerlegen und Beseitigen des Gemachten (Einleitung)." In: Technikgeschichte 81/1, pp. 1-32.

Weber, Heike (2014c): "Von wild zu geordnet? Konzeptionen, Wissensbestände und Techniken des Deponierens im 20. Jahrhundert." In: Technikgeschichte 81/2, pp. 1-29.

Weyl, Theodor (1894): Versuch über den Stoffwechsel Berlins: Eine hygienisch-statistische Untersuchung, Berlin: W. Baensch.

Woodward, Donald (1995): "'Swords into ploughshares': Recycling in pre-industrial England." In: The Economic History Review 38, pp. 175-191.

Worster, Donald (2016): Shrinking the earth: The rise and decline of American abundance, New York: Oxford University Press.

Zimring, Carl A. (2005): Cash for your trash: Scrap recycling in America, New Brunswick/London: Rutgers University Press.

Urban Infrastructure and the Cultural Turn

Martin V. Melosi

Cities not only share boundaries with the natural world, interact with nature and the countryside, but also are connected to it. Cities are only artificial in our eyes if humans themselves are excluded from the natural world. In many respects, cities are a form of cultivation like agriculture, and important examples of human priorities in ordering necessary life support services, such as food, water, heat, light, shelter, and waste disposal (Melosi 2010: 3-21). They are made cohesive through technical systems and infrastructure, such as roads, drains and sewerage, power lines, telegraphs and telephones, and are complemented by city services such as water supplies, mass transit, electrical grids, and heat and light systems.

Urban cultivation essentially takes the form of infrastructure, which has material, organisational, and cultural components. There was a time when infrastructure was recognised primarily for its materiality. A good deal of the older work on infrastructure was descriptive in nature or centrally focused on trying to understand how certain forms of technology met certain urban needs. In the 1980s, Joel Tarr and Gabriel Dupuy referred to urban infrastructure as the "technical sinews of the modern metropolitan area", but they also recognised that these infrastructures existed within systems and networks that were both public and private and were "constructed and operated, with variations not only from country to country but also from time period to time period within nations." (Tarr/Dupuy 1988: xiii) Such an observation added an important social history layer—social structures and the interaction of various groups in society—to our grasp of infrastructure. Such efforts to define infrastructure materially and organisationally have guided a generation or more of social scientists, but now face revisions or enhancements from an emerging group of new scholars. More recently, especially in the last ten or fifteen years, urban-environmental studies has been strongly influenced by the cultural turn in history and other disciplines; sometimes referred to as the linguistic turn, culturalism, or postmodernism. They have incorporated cultural perspectives into the study of urban infrastructure.

Urban Infrastructure as System

Cities are in a constant state of change, growing outward and upward, sprawling and contracting, being paved over and dug up. The transformation of the urban landscape influences water flow, mobility, climate and air quality (Melosi 2000: 119). Many things influence a city's metabolism, including technical systems and service networks, which are part of what Lewis Mumford called the "underground city" or the "invisible city" (1962: 478-80, 563-67). For Tarr and Dupuy (1988), urban infrastructures "guide and facilitate urban functioning and urban life in a multitude of ways. Some positive and others negative, some visible and others invisible." (1988: xiii).

Other elements have been added to more comprehensively define urban infrastructure. For example, geographer David Harvey (1973) viewed an urban system as "a giant man-made resource system", where growth of this resource system "involves the structuring and differentiation of space through the distribution of fixed capital investments." (1973: 309) Geographer Brian J. L. Berry (1964) was particularly interested in the systemic nature of cities: "It is clear that cities may be considered as systems—entities comprising interacting, interdependent parts. They may be studied at a variety of levels, structural, functional, and dynamic, and they may be partitioned into a variety of subsystems." He added, "Cities are systems susceptible of the same kinds of analysis as other systems and characterised by the same generalisations, constructs, and models." (1964: 147-63)

Historian Thomas P. Hughes (1989) argued that systems "involved far more than the so-called hardware, devices, machines and processes, and the transportation, communication, and information networks that interconnect them." "Some systems," he added, "consist also of people and organizations." (1989: 3) Taken as a whole, infrastructure as technical systems—no matter how large or consolidated they are—do not become autonomous, but exist within limits imposed by the available technology, the hand of their operators, and the function dictated by their users. Also, the implementation of new urban technologies are not automatic, coincidental, or inadvertent, but are intentional efforts by decision-makers to confront existing problems faced by cities as they grow. (Melosi 2001: 8).

The basic narrative[1] for city-building—in Western cultures at least—has been written in this way: European and North American cities, in particular, underwent dynamic system building in the late 19th century (Melosi 2013). Beginning in the major cities of the industrial era, the determination to utilise new technologies grew out of "struggles to surmount the limitations and failings of older urban

---

1 A good deal of this narrative was drawn from Martin V. Melosi (2013): "The Urban Environment." In: Peter Clark (ed.), The Oxford Handbook of Cities in World History, New York: Oxford University Press, pp. 705-707.

arrangements that became apparent as a consequence of big-city growth." (Peterson 1982: 344) Decision makers, therefore, acted on technical choices to alter the function of cities. A good example was the diversion of sewage from homes and businesses through a city-wide waste carriage system rather than by individual privy vaults or cesspools (Melosi 2001: 17-57).

Urban Infrastructure and the Cultural Turn

The rise of cultural history in the late 20th century provided substantially new wrinkles to understanding and assessing infrastructure beyond a certain process of development, construction, and use. A persuasive definition of cultural history suggests that it

> is not simply the study of high culture or alternatively of peoples' past rituals. It is best characterised as an approach which considers the domain of representation and the struggle over meaning as the most fruitful areas for the pursuit of historical understanding. (Making History 2008).

Cultural history's modern form grew out of several sources, including the 'new' social history of the 1960s, which sought to understand the lives and actions of non-elites, and also the 'linguistic turn', focusing on contested meanings and how they were expressed in language. The various perspectives of cultural history as applied to infrastructure broadened the dialogue over the context in which infrastructures exist and function. A cultural perspective on infrastructure focuses on questions about meaning, e.g. the intent of infrastructure and its influence on societal changes. In so doing, however, the materiality of infrastructures sometimes has been underplayed in the cultural discourse that is, form and function take a backseat to abstract implications.

However, modern cities are networked cities both materially and culturally. Materially, networked infrastructures are connected by a variety of technologies. An electric grid, for example, depends on wires, switches, transformers, and so forth. Organisationally, networked infrastructures depend on operational components—like a railroad dispatcher for trains—and are controlled by bodies with managerial and financial functions—like a municipal service. The cultural connection can be more complex. For example, traditional fire protection in the United States in the past focused on investment in fire-fighting capacity, whereas in Europe strict building codes had been utilised to reduce the risk of fire. Such divergences do not only mark a distinction between strategies but also reflect different views on such social configurations as private property. The American tradition placed high priority on the rights of the individual property owner, while the European model emphasised a more coercive public responsibility.

'Culture' is defined very broadly to suggest a variety of non-material elements and issues. Not all new urban scholars have embraced the most unbending elements of the cultural turn, but some have helped to shift the focus of the field away from the older orthodoxy. Keep in mind that the change was a 'turn' and not so much a 'redirection'. Several new studies fill gaps, reinterpret older works, and explore new topics while not fundamentally embracing a cultural orientation. There is a greater emphasis on the cultural implications of infrastructure as ever before. At the least, the field of infrastructure studies today is marked by more diversity and a wider conversation and orientation, which in several respects looks at infrastructure and related issues in very different ways.

Urban Infrastructure, Power and Resilience

The Call for Papers (and the subsequent panels) for "The Second Interdisciplinary Conference: Perspectives on Urban Infrastructure History and Social Science" held in Venice, Italy, in June 2018, demonstrates some very recent changes in emphasis on infrastructure studies.[2] The call emphasised that recent work "has explored the multiple social effects of infrastructure." Various studies has not only examined the

> provisions of the services to urban residents [...] but also distributions of political power, embodiments of ritual and religious practice in public space, the social dimensions of specific components of infrastructure, such as water, the organisation of capital, contentious claims by and about labour, environmental and distributional inequalities.

The tone and substance of the call suggests a focus on the various implications of infrastructural decision-making and social impacts, but also cultural changes including questions of how social—and environmental—justice can influence infrastructural development and control. It is particularly important to look at material questions from a different vantage point, and to raise hard questions about the functioning and impacts of infrastructural decisions (Easterling 2016;

---

2   The conference was co-sponsored by the Department of Technology, Culture, and Society, NYU Tandon School of Engineering; Universit`a Ca' Foscari, Venice; NYU Shanghai; and the Department of Urban Studies at the New School. In June 2017, the NYU Tandon School and NYU Paris sponsored 'Interdisciplinary Perspectives on Urban Infrastructure Conference Urban Infrastructure and The Environment', Paris, France.

Graham/Marvin 2001; Graham/McFarlane 2015; Marklund/Rudiger 2017; Coutard/Rutherford 2018).

Scholars are most curious about the implications of access to infrastructure, urban resilience, and the longer-range implications of infrastructural implementation. Infrastructure and various technical systems represented 'public goods' requiring municipal, regional, and national commitments to increased public spending. Traditions varied from place to place. In France, for example, two companies dominated water service in Paris: Generale des Eaux, established by Napoleon III in 1852, and Lyonnaise des Eaux, founded in 1880. Both established the tradition of private water delivery in France and benefited from years of government protectionism (Melosi 2011: 192-93). In some cases, the provision of urban services "switched back and forth between the public and private sectors as technology and markets changed." (Anderson 1977: 2)

Urban decision making was complex, but generally treated by earlier scholars from the perspective of contemporary political mores and existing public and private institutions. Political power was diffuse, of course, and no one group—city officials, planners, or engineers—operated independently. Civil engineers were key actors who conveyed technical and scientific expertise to city officials. While they regularly denied it, engineers often determined the choice of infrastructures. Engineers were receptors and disseminators of the prevailing environmental views of the day that helped shape the systems. They were also susceptible to the promotion of then-popular technologies or readily available solutions. In the short run, implementation of technologies often met expectations of city leaders to improve their municipalities, especially the desire for good economic well-being for the business community. Emphasis on the immediate design of a project rather than careful planning for the long-run tended to neglect the potential resilience of the system or its capacity to adapt to growth. Commitment to an assumption of infrastructural permanence or immediate needs of the community locked in specific technologies with few projections on how a variety of changes could impact the success or failure of what essentially was a short-term technical fix.

Problems could arise if systems were either too well built or too poorly constructed. In the former case, an existing system could prove resistant to change; in the latter, it might be in need of replacement or repair. As a consequence, decisions made about many technical systems in the 19th century had a profound impact on cities more than 100 years later. Such circumstances call for examining the contemporary justification for employing a particular technology and a deeper understanding of possible constraints to alternatives. These may include not only economic limitations but also particularities of governance, or the cultural appeal of a technology, and other broad issues not immediately obvious in the decision.

Another key question was service coverage. Until the late-19th century in Europe, for example, infrastructure systems were built in limited areas of cities. After 1880 or so, they might be adapted to entire urban areas. The new urban structures and spaces "were treated as if the social, economic, and technological conditions to which they corresponded were permanent and so could be fixed into permanent form." (Konvitz 1985: 156; see also 157-58, 164-66.) In addition, not building infrastructure at all in some areas disproportionately hurt the lower classes or those outside the business centres.

Urban Infrastructure and Modernisation

The modern networked cities most often came to be identified with major changes in their economic role. In the traditional historical framework, industrial cities in particular were understood as forerunners of physical urban transformation. Manchester, England, arguably the first true industrial city, was a critical exception as the city's development did not coincide with changes in new technical networks like water systems and electrical power until deeper in the 19th century (Hall 1998: 310-347).

In contrast to early Manchester, the new industrial cities were not only the palpable expression of the economic revolution, they were also the spatial manifestation of a complementary infrastructural revolution which transformed the physical city. In the mid-19th century, an array of sophisticated technical systems blanketed several large and medium-sized cities, altering city building practices and service delivery. Technological innovations in transportation, communications, energy, and environmental services were stimuli to economic growth as well as to the physical transformation of cities. Ironically, while industrialisation remained local or regional for many years, these new technological innovations were quickly diffused. This suggests that while cities did not uniformly benefit from the direct economic impact of industrialism, they were nonetheless physically modernised as a result of new technologies generated in the era.

Building technology and related infrastructural development underwent a second wave of extraordinary changes as skyscrapers dotted the skyline and newly paved streets radiated outward from central business districts in several large cities. Investment in and implementation of electrical power led to major changes in transportation, communications, and heating and lighting. Electric streetcars replaced horses; telegraph and telephone lines crisscrossed the skyline; arc lights and incandescent bulbs challenged gas lighting; central stations undercut home and industrial uses of wood and coal. The demand for more and better housing resulted in altering existing buildings or changing current land uses. Laying water mains or extending sewer lines improved neighbourhood health or created new neighbourhoods. In the U.S. model, the compact 'walking city' of the pre-industrial age was replaced by an upward rising, mechanised core city with expanding suburbs. However, industrial cities were paradoxes of progress—their role "as places to work seemed incompatible with their role as places to live." This proved particularly true as pollution problems intensified (Platt 2005: 11).

In parts of the world outside of Europe and North America, the coincidence of economic transformation and networked technologies most often came later, but with similar results. In China the shift from rural to urban-based industrialisation did not occur until the Maoist revolution in the 1950s. Industrial urbanisation in Japan was largely an early-20th century phenomenon concentrated in cities like Tokyo. During that same period Russia (and then the USSR) gave the appearances of a developing country, not nearly as urbanised as Japan, and lagging behind developed countries in scale of urbanisation and industrialisation. In the Third World—including Africa and Latin America— 'overurbanisation' was possible in some places, that is, rapid growth of cities in size, but lagging in jobs and housing, and in modern technical networks (Orum/Chen 2001: 100-101; Light 1983: 127-47, 155-176).

Conclusions

In focus and in texture, some recent books dealing with the history of the American urban environment in particular demonstrate a clear generational shift. It is not so much that newer works dismiss the earlier pioneering studies; it is just that they have different things to say from different points of view, or at least have different ways of saying them. The cultural turn that has influenced the fields of urban and environmental history in general, and many other fields of history, is well represented among the recent works of urban-environmental history (Melosi 2015). Not every new book is bound by allegiance to new approaches or methodologies, a paradigmatic shift, and in many respects the cultural turn has been more of a course correction than a paradigm shift. The vitality of the field requires avoiding the construction of walls or impenetrable membranes around it. New ideas and approaches should be welcome, for there is much yet to be done. At the very least, the cultural turn has put more humans and more vantage points into the narratives about city building, avoiding a mechanistic approach to history in the same way that our understanding of the impacts of technological change should not embrace the idea of an 'autonomous technology'.

Infrastructure studies have been dominated by the materiality of cities, and although this is an important dimension, more recent studies have infused them with new ideas, alternative discourses, cultural construction, and more which enhances what has come before. The traditional narrative about city building in the industrial era and its accompanying infrastructure, correlates well—in many cases—with the implications suggested by path dependence (Melosi 2005; Bernhardt in this volume). It has been an important approach for exploring the role of decision making on the development and impact of specific technologies or technical systems, but in a crucial way it complements the cultural turn by putting the materiality and impact of infrastructure in a broader context than traditional studies on city building. Key is the intention to consider alternatives to existing infrastructure and what other developmental paths might have meant for the future utility and sustainability of a variety of urban services.

The theory focuses attention on the means by which choices are made, the connection of those choices to future options and sequences of events, to outcomes, and the extent to which past decisions are locked in with no other options available. The use of path dependence reinforces the idea that a variety of externalities influence the adoption of technologies. It can help historians turn from concentrating so heavily on a singularly past-centred perspective to a present-centred perspective that devotes significant attention to results as well as constraints on outcomes. This is especially useful if historians are interested in the policy implications of their work in a much broader context than simply describing past practices.

Social scientists, especially economists, began exploring path-dependence theory in the mid-1980s. Although definitions vary, simply put, path dependence exists "when the present state of a system is constrained by its history." (Gorringe 2001) As a result, 'history matters' became a guiding principle in path dependence, especially for economists and other social scientists whose work has been dominated by a strong behaviourist philosophy built upon quantitative methodologies. This departure required a broad lens, one that takes into account a variety of factors, several of which are culturally based.

Rather than taking on the notion as to whether an inferior technology could succeed in a market economy, path dependence has been most useful in addressing questions from a slightly different vantage point. What are the constraints placed on a current generation because of choices made in the past? What are the limits of a chosen path, as opposed to what is or is not changeable? What are the implications of particular choices and potential lock-ins on practice and policy? What kinds of impacts are possible with path-dependent actions? In many respects, these are qualitative issues, but the kinds of issues that complement uses of historical causation in understanding technologies, institutions, and politics. Thus, it seems that a major virtue of path dependence is to determine how future choices are constrained or limited rather than how they are precluded. 'Lock-in' of a technology need not be a permanent condition, nor is it the best issue to track.

Utilising path dependence in a broad context that takes into account how we can understand the role of infrastructural networks in the historical development of a changing society and culture, and in terms of modern expectations, has more than rhetorical consequences. Indeed, the study of infrastructure, its materiality, its social consequences, and its cultural roots may provide useful insights concerning the contesting forces that produce (and reproduce) urban space.

References

Anderson, Alan D. (1977): The origin and resolution of the urban crisis, Baltimore: Johns Hopkins University Press.
Berry, Brian J. L. (1964): "Cities as systems within systems of cities." In: Regional Science Association Papers 13, pp. 147-63.
Coutard, Olivier/Rutherford, Jonathan (eds.) (2018): Beyond the networked city: Infrastructural reconfigurations and urban change in the north and south, London: Routledge.
Easterling, Keller (2016): Extrastatecraft: The power of infrastructure space, New York: Verso.
Gorringe, P. A. (2001): "Path dependence: causes, consequences and policy." In: Arthur Grimes/Alan Jones/Roger Procter/Grant Scobie (eds.), Economics for policy: Expanding the boundaries: Essays by Peter Gorringe, Wellington, NZ: Wellington Institute of Policy Studies.
Graham Stephen/McFarlane, Colin (eds.) (2015): Infrastructural lives: Urban infrastructure in context, London: Routledge.
Graham Stephen/Marvin, Simon (2001): Splintering urbanism: Networked infrastructures, technological mobilities, and the urban condition, London: Routledge.
Hall, Peter (1998): Cities in civilization, New York: Pantheon.
Harvey, David (1973): Social justice and the city, Baltimore: Johns Hopkins University Press.
Hughes, Thomas R. (1989): American genesis: A century of invention and technological enthusiasm, 1870-1970, New York: Viking.
Konvitz, Josef (1985): The urban millennium: The city building process from the early middle ages to the present, Carbondale/IL: Southern Illinois University Press.
Light, Ivan (1983): Cities in world perspective, New York: Macmillan Pub. Co.
"Making History: the changing face of the profession in Britain," (2008) (https:// www.history.ac.uk/makinghistory/themes/cultural_history.html)
Marklund, Andreas/Rudiger, Mogens (eds.) (2017): Historicizing infrastructure, Aalborg: Aalborg University Press.
Martin V. Melosi (2005): "Path dependence and urban history: Is a marriage possible?" In: Dieter Schott/Bill Luckin/Genevieve Massard-Guilbaud (eds.), Resources of the city: Contributions to an environmental history of modern Europe, Hampshire, UK: Ashgate, pp. 262-275.

Melosi, Martin V. (2015): "Rethinking the city-building process and infrastructure: The cultural turn in American urban environmental history" In: Informationen zur Modernen Stadtgeschichte 1, pp. 17-29.

Melosi, Martin V. (2013): "The urban environment." In: Peter Clark (ed.), The Oxford handbook of cities in world history, New York: Oxford University Press, pp. 705-707.

Melosi, Martin V. (2011): Precious commodity: Providing water for America's cities, Pittsburgh: University of Pittsburgh Press.

Melosi, Martin V. (2010): "Humans, cities, and nature: How do cities fit in the material world?" In: Journal of Urban History 36/January, pp. 3-21.

Melosi, Martin V. (2001): The sanitary city: Urban infrastructure in America form colonial times to the present, Baltimore: Johns Hopkins University Press.

Melosi, Martin V. (ed.) (2000): Effluent America: Cities, industry, energy and the environment, Pittsburgh: University of Pittsburgh Press.

Mumford, Lewis (1962): The city in history, New York: Harcourt, Brace & World.

Orum, Anthony M./Chen, Xiangming (2001): The world of cities, Malden, MA: Blackwell Pub.

Peterson, Jon (1982): "Environment and technology in the great city era of American history." In: Journal of Urban History 8/May, p. 344.

Platt, Harold L. (2005): Shock cities: The environmental transformation of Manchester and Chicago, Chicago: University of Chicago Press.

Tarr, Joel A./Dupuy, Gabriel (1988): Technology and the rise of the networked city in Europe and America, Philadelphia: Temple University Press.

Cities and Rivers

Uwe Lübken

River Histories

The relationship between cities and rivers is multi-faceted, shaped by local and regional environments and subject to change over time. It is also a mutual relationship. Rivers have been critical for the foundation and development of many cities, while urban development has had a profound impact on rivers—not only on their urban stretches, but often far beyond the city limits. Yet, the historical importance of city-river relations has, with a few exceptions such as André Guillerme's 1983 study *Les temps de l'eau* been overlooked until the end of the 20th century. While geographers and urban historians considered the creeks and streams flowing through cities mostly with regard to their spatial rather than environmental importance, environmental historians, including those who focused on rivers, disregarded the particular urban contexts almost completely up until the 1990s (Tvedt/Oestigaard 2014: 1-2; Melosi 1993).

In its beginnings, even the blossoming field of river histories has only scratched urban topics. Rivers have been analysed as the backbones of hydraulic societies, most prominently in Donald Worster's influential study *Rivers of Empire* (1985), an analysis of the relationship between irrigation policies and bureaucracy in the Western part of the United States that was based on the work of Karl August Wittfogel, most importantly his controversial study *Oriental Despotism* (1957). Rivers have also been interpreted as sites of memory. The Elbe and Odra rivers, for example, still represent the division of Europe during the Cold War, while the Ohio River is remembered by many African Americans as 'River Jordan'—the boundary between freedom and slavery (Hausmann 2009; Rada 2013; Trotter 1998; Bigham 1986). Furthermore, some rivers, predominantly big ones such as the Volga, Mississippi and Rhine River, have an intricate relationship with the construction of national and sometimes transnational identities (Zeisler-Vralsted 2014; Febvre 2006).

A different strand of research focuses on rivers' hybrid nature, emphasising the ambivalence of being both used, abused and heavily modified by society while at the same time constituting a part of a global water cycle that mostly operates according to its own rules (at least before having been influenced by anthropogenic climate change). Richard White's influential book *Organic Machine* (1995), for instance, describes the Columbia River as a powerful force in the history of the Pacific Northwest. The river has been literally at work by providing energy that has been harnessed by Native Americans in catching salmon and settler societies by producing water power. Marc Cioc (2002) has used the term 'eco-biography' to describe the Rhine River's historical trajectories, while Verena Winiwarter and Martin Schmid (2008) have suggested to look at rivers as unique 'socio-natural sites' (Winiwarter/Schmid in this volume). Based on their work on the Danube, Winiwarter and Schmid have demonstrated how societies and nature interact not just in space but also over time (Winiwarter/Schmid 2013). Furthermore, rivers represent spaces of opportunity and hazard, and have thus produced what can be described as 'risk societies' along their banks (Beck 1986).[1] Recent scholarship has interpreted rivers as enviro-technological systems since their natural flow regimes have in many ways been tampered with, for instance in the form of embankments, levees, dams, reservoirs, pumping stations, etc. (Pritchard 2011). From an ecological and environmental perspective, this story has quite often been framed as a declensionist narrative: a history of the loss of biodiversity and wildness.

This growth in river histories has certainly contributed to a deeper understanding of the relationship between cities and their waterways. More recently, several monographs, edited volumes and articles have addressed this relationship explicitly. The volume *Urban Rivers*, edited by Stéphane Castonguay and Matthew Evenden (2012), looks at case studies from Europe and North America to highlight the historical trajectories of city-river relations in the time of urbanisation and industrialisation. Another collection of essays, *Rivers Lost, Rivers Regained*, focuses on the experience of loss, on urban river cultures, on the importance of a city's riverine hinterland and on the restoration of urban rivers (Knoll/Lübken/Schott 2017). Several monographs deal with the importance of rivers from the perspective of a specific city (Kelman 2003; Colten 2005; Gumprecht 1999), while an interdisciplinary Viennese team has intricately studied the waterscape of the Austrian capital, leading to various publications (Water History 5/2 2013; Neundlinger et al. 2014).

Rivers as Sites of Opportunity

In addition to providing drinking water, rivers were used to transport goods and people, they provided routes of communication, served as a source of food and energy and as sinks for unwanted material, such as human waste and garbage.

---

[1] Beck, however, was much more interested in environmental rather than natural catastrophes when he coined the term.

Settlements were often founded where rivers could be crossed easily, at the confluence of two or more rivers, at places where they were difficult or impossible to navigate such as rapids or falls, and where potential settlers had easy access to the river, yet were more or less protected from flooding by bluffs or natural levees. The concrete relationship between a city and its river varies, however, and depends on the local climate and topography, on the technology employed to utilise the waterway and to protect citizens against flooding, on river imageries, and on social as well as economic conditions.

Urbanisation and industrialisation tremendously increased the importance of rivers, especially before the railroad created its own spatial logic of transportation and communication (Schott 2014). Rivers were conduits for a significant part of the vastly growing urban metabolism, i.e. the flow of resources and waste into and out of the city that made urban life possible in the first place (Barles in this volume). Moreover, specific sites such as warehouses and river ports highlighted the often tremendous geographical scale of economic interactions carried out along rivers while city governments tried to exert influence upstream and downstream of their location. In this regard, rivers remained important and often withstood the increasing competition by the railroad and other means of transportation during the 19th and 20th centuries.

As Stéphane Castonguay and Matthew Evenden (2012: 1-2) have pointed out,

> rivers were subjected to a new era of modern engineering and rationalization; new modes of transportation and power generation affected river courses; and the water supply and sewage needs of urban centers altered the flow and ecology of urban rivers as well as distant sources.

Through this massive transformation rivers acquired several new functions over the course of the 19th century: they now had to guarantee the year-round navigation of steam driven boats; they were used as an 'ultimate sink' (Tarr 1996) to dispose of the tremendously increased private and industrial waste; rivers were drawn on to produce ever larger amounts of energy and they served as a main source of drinking water for the urban masses as well as a source for various industrial purposes (Jakobsson 2002).

These functions were impossible to fulfil as long as the rivers oscillated wildly between the extremes; instead, what was needed was, as the New York Times aptly phrased in 1895, "a happy mean between low water and flood". Thus, rivers were straightened, dredged, deepened and thus controlled much more effectively than ever before. "Without major rectification work", Mark Cioc (2002: 37) has pointed out, "the Rhine would never have been able to provide the regular water flow needed for irrigation, urban services, and year-round transportation" (cf. Blackbourn 2006; Bernhardt 2016). In a similar vein yet more than a century later, the

Los Angeles River was almost completely paved after several floods had caused massive destruction in the 1930s. Over 25 years and by the use of more than three million barrels of concrete, the Army Corps of Engineers transformed the river into a trench (Price 2008: 545-546). The Chicago River was even made to reverse its flow towards the Ohio and Mississippi River system so that the waste of the metropolis no longer polluted Lake Michigan, which was a major source of drinking water for the city (Cronon 1991: 249-250).

Industrialised rivers also developed into infrastructural corridors that gathered many functions such as telecommunication and power lines, streets, railroad tracks, and, of course, the river itself. The nodes of this infrastructural network were mostly located in cities and consisted of gas and water works, pumping stations, warehouses, river harbours as well as a vast amount of new bridges (Lübken 2007).

Rivers as Sites of Hazard

As much as cities located at rivers were sites of opportunity they were also sites of hazard. Settlements were founded at or near rivers for a reason, especially in the absence of other reliable and efficient means of transportation. But the increasing urban utilisation of rivers came at a cost. Floods and droughts, river-borne diseases and pollution have plagued river cities for millennia (Weintritt 2009). However, urban patterns of vulnerability and resilience to such hazards have changed significantly in the modern era.

Already in the early 19th century, droughts became a severe economic problem for many merchants in the eastern half of the United States. When, in the summer of 1818, the water level of the Ohio River was so low that navigation was all but impossible, one contemporary editor in Pittsburgh complained that "at this moment there is probably near a million worth of merchandise laying along our shores". Many harbour cities along the Upper Ohio River suffered badly as a result of this drought (Johnson 1991: 185-186).

If droughts posed huge problems for many riverine cities, especially before rivers were transformed into mere channels, flooding was an ever bigger challenge because it tended to happen more frequently and affected larger parts of society. Changing patterns of land-use in the floodplains certainly contributed to this vulnerability. While, for example, agricultural damage still played a large role during the devastating flood of the Middle Rhine in 1784, damage to industrial and infrastructural facilities was much more prominent in the 'flood of the century' in 1882/83 (Weichselgartner 2000: 123). Riverine cities accumulated social vulnerability and economic damage potential. Bridges, for example, often located in cities, turned out to be extremely vulnerable to high water levels. Sometimes, like during the 1913 flood of the Miami River in Ohio, hundreds of them collapsed during a single flood (Bigelow 1913; Lübken 2007). Also, a large number of industrial facilities was affected by floods. Water-intensive industries, often located in or near urban areas, like breweries, distilleries, dyeing mills or paper works, were especially vulnerable to flooding (Mutz 2007). Along the Saar, a tributary to the Rhine, all factories near the river had to be closed temporarily in 1882. At *Villeroy & Boch*, a huge ceramics manufacturer, the water entered the facilities so quickly that the operating teams did not even have enough time to shut down the machines. Throughout the Saarland, coal-mines had to stop their production after water had penetrated the shafts. Production loss amounted to more than 37.500 tons of coal in just a few days.

As a consequence of these developments, floods, from the late 19th to the mid 20th century, became more and more of a national problem. Individual cities and even states or regions were increasingly overburdened with the challenges of relief, flood control and reconstruction. Central governments took over many of these responsibilities and acted as risk managers of last resort (Moss 2002). In the United States, for example, new legislation transferred much of the power to prepare for and cope with disasters to the national government. In 1936, flood control was made a federal responsibility. Disaster relief was added to the tasks of the Federal government in 1950, and in 1968, the National Flood Insurance Program further intensified the centralisation of risk management (Lübken 2014: 254).

Finally, urban rivers were a transmitter of disease, especially at a time when urban sewage systems were more and more overwhelmed by the influx of a rapidly growing population. London's Thames River is arguably the most notorious historical example and has been immortalised by the writings of Charles Dickens (Kneitz 2016). The widespread belief that diseases were caused by miasma, i.e. by bad or foul air, prevented contemporaries from addressing the real causes of water-born epidemics until the mid-19th century. Diseases such as dysentery, typhoid, and, most importantly, cholera, regularly killed thousands of urbanites. Only with the advent of the 'sanitary city' in the late 19th century (Melosi 2008) and the adoption of germ theory to explain and fight the spreading of diseases could the outbreak of water-borne diseases be prevented. In Hamburg alone, during a cholera outbreak in 1892, almost 10.000 people died of the disease. However, Hamburg was an unusual case as most cities had already adopted other forms of sewage treatment by the time (Evans 1987).

Rivers and Power Structures

Rivers are not neutral infrastructural facilities that provide 'ecosystem services'. They are also instruments by which power can be exerted in various ways. Metropolises like London, Paris or Vienna have made use of 'their' rivers to control the hinterland by, for example, safeguarding their provision with wood (Barles 2017). More recently, cities like Los Angeles, San Francisco, and Las Vegas, have tapped water from drainage basins hundreds of miles away to foster rapid growth in a semi-arid environment (Soll 2013). Sometimes, this had severe ecological and social consequences in the areas from which the water was taken. The city of Los Angeles, for example, siphoned off water from California's Owens Valley, more than 200 miles away, cutting off local farmers of their water supply and draining Lake Owens (Steinberg 2002: 137, 166). Urban flood control, too, often relies on measures that are located upstream or downstream of a city—either by the construction of reservoirs at its headwaters or by flooding spillways and 'sacrificing' rural areas in order to protect a city (Lübken 2014: 184; Welky 2011: 166-167).

Urban rivers are also connected to issues of power and environmental justice by the distribution of environmental risk because disadvantaged parts of the population are often pushed into marginal environments such as swamps, bayous, ravines, or, for that matter, river floodplains. Thus, different parts of the population are affected by natural extreme events in different ways. Despite the often told myth that natural catastrophes act as a social equaliser, environmental risk has in most cases been unevenly distributed along the lines of class, gender, age, race, etc. As Jennifer Bonnell has pointed out, there is a close relationship between marginal environments and marginalised populations. She noted that only a few studies in the field of environmental inequality "investigate the congregation of marginalised populations in already degraded spaces or in urban borderlands" (2014: 78). Toronto's Don Valley, for example, where flooding was a constant menace, was as a place for squatters in the 1830s, a camp site for Roma families in the 1910s and 1920s, and a 'Hobo jungle' during the depression years of 1930/31. All of these groups were extremely mobile (or mobilised) and rather poor.

Also, the devastating impact of floods has been used as a pretext and a welcome opportunity to change the social composition of the urban population in the affected areas. In Cincinnati, Ohio, for example, Ernest P. Goodrich (1937), a New York City engineer who had been hired as an advisor to the Cincinnati City Planning Commission, viewed the devastating flood of the Ohio River in 1937 as "a unique opportunity [...] to reappraise the whole city plan, to amend and improve it where such is found desirable, and thus to provide for an even better future Cincinnati". Thus, the flood was used as a means to transform the waterfront area and rebuild it according to the needs of high modernism, including the construction of highways, parks, stadiums as well as the clearance of so-called slums.

While not all of these goals were realised, the social structure of the area changed fundamentally. Residents of the bottoms lived 'on borrowed time', the Cincinnati Times-Star noted on April 16, 1952. Sooner or later they would have to leave.

Restoration

Many rivers have been polluted to such a degree that they were literally 'sacrificed' to function as sewers for industrial and urban waste. Others, like the Fez River in Morocco, were buried underneath a parking lot (Hornstein 2017) or even completely filled, such as the Erdre River in Nantes (Massard-Guilbaud 2017). The Rhine had become a 'biological graveyard' (Disco 2017: 356) by the 1970s. As a result, many cities abandoned their rivers during the 19th and 20th centuries. In some cases, like in Los Angeles, citizens were surprised that their city actually had a river. "[Los] Angelenos have lost their fifty-one-mile river in plain sight—and can't see the essential daily connections from the river to their lives," as Jennifer Price has noted (2008: 549).

But the deteriorating conditions of urban rivers also triggered a movement to restore urban waterways to a more or less 'natural' state. Several major urban environmental catastrophes, such the infamous Cuyahoga River fire in 1969 (Stradling/Stradling 2008) and the storehouse fire of the Sandoz chemical plant in Basel and the subsequent pollution of the Rhine in 1986 (Cioc 2002: 182), certainly contributed to the notion that urban rivers were in need of 'rewilding' and 'renaturing' (McCool 2010). River restoration, however, is a complex endeavour and has taken many different forms, especially in cities, where the number of stakeholders is much higher than in rural areas. Where smaller urban creeks have been covered by streets and buildings, they have to be discovered first before they can be physically uncovered, daylighted and then be 'restored' (Pinkham 2000).

The attempts to restore urban rivers were facilitated by the fact that many urban waterfront areas had lost their economic significance as a result of deindustrialisation and new transportation technologies. Following a model that had been developed by port cities like London (Docklands), Baltimore (Inner Harbor) and Hamburg (Hafencity), many river cities also see the rejuvenation of their waterfronts, including the restoration of rivers, as a means to attract businesses, housing, and tourists to formerly abandoned areas (Beyer 2017: 253-255). Thus, urban river restoration is an ambivalent process. While it contributes to a heightened awareness of the value of 'nature in the city' and offers many amenities that come with access to urban waterfronts for many town dwellers, it is also a development that encourages gentrification.

Conclusions

Rivers have played a crucial role for the development of many cities. Closely tied to technological innovations, urban waterways and their larger river systems tremendously extended the spatial range of economic and social interactions, they shaped and defined the urban hinterland and were a key factor of the urban metabolism—both as an avenue for the transportation of resources and waste, and as a resource in its own right. Rivers in cities were sites of opportunity and sites of hazard. The many benefits that urban societies reaped from 'their' rivers came at the cost of the risk of flooding (and to a lesser extent droughts), pollution, and disease. While some urban dwellers were explicitly and intentionally taking the risk, others were pushed into hazardous situations and vulnerable livelihoods. Thus, while rivers certainly cleared many different developmental paths for urban society, they were also heavily transformed by the latter. Today, hardly any river flows unmodified through a city. Most urban rivers are embanked, channelised, and regulated in a myriad ways. Even 'restored' rivers represent a highly engineered environment that fulfils the needs of an urban society rather than representing a natural landscape. In the future, many river towns will face new challenges as anthropogenic climate change will affect the patterns of rainfall and run-off as well as the number and intensity of extreme events.

References

Barles, Sabine (2017): "The Seine as a Parisian river: Its imprint, its ascendancy, and its mutual dependencies in the eighteenth through the twentieth century." In: Martin Knoll/Uwe Lübke/Dieter Schott (eds.), Rivers lost, rivers regained: Rethinking river-city-relations, Pittsburgh: University of Pittsburgh Press, pp. 46-62.
Beck, Ulrich (1986): Risikogesellschaft: Auf dem Weg in eine andere Moderne, Frankfurt a.M.: Suhrkamp.
Bernhardt, Christoph (2016): Im Spiegel des Wassers: Eine transnationale Umweltgeschichte des Oberrheins, 1800-2000, Cologne/Weimar/Vienna: Böhlau.
Beyer, Antoine (2017): "The transport function versus post-industrial identities: To what extent does urban restructuring threaten the river transport capacities of the Rhine ports?" In: Ralf Banken/Ben Wubs (eds.), The Rhine: A transnational economic history, Baden-Baden: Nomos, pp. 253-279.
Bigelow, Lewis S. (1913): The 1913 flood and how it was met by a railroad, Pittsburgh: HardPress.
Bigham, Darrel E. (1998): On Jordan's banks: Emancipation and its aftermath in the Ohio river valley, Lexington/Kentucky: University Press of Kentucky.

Blackbourn, David (2006): The conquest of nature: Water, landscape, and the making of modern Germany, New York/London: W.W. Norton and Company.

Bonnell, Jennifer L. (2014): Reclaiming the Don: An environmental history of Toronto's Don river valley, Toronto: University of Toronto Press.

Castonguay, Stéphane/Evenden, Matthew (eds.) (2012): Urban rivers: Remaking rivers, cities, and space in Europe and North America, Pittsburgh/PA: University of Pittsburgh Press.

Cioc, Mark (2002): The Rhine: An eco-biography, 1815-2000, Seattle/London: University of Washington Press.

Colten, Craig E. (2005): Unnatural metropolis: Wrestling New Orleans from nature, Baton Rouge: Louisiana State University Press.

Cronon, William (1991): Nature's metropolis: Chicago and the Great West, New York/London: Norton & Company.

Disco, Nil (2017): "The power of positive thinking: From the chemicals convention to the Rhine action plan, 1970-1990." In: Ralf Banken/Ben Wubs (eds.), The Rhine: A transnational economic history, Baden-Baden: Nomos, pp. 355-378.

Evans, Richard J. (1987): Death in Hamburg: Society and politics in the cholera years 1830-1910, Oxford: Clarendon Press.

Febvre, Lucien (2006): Der Rhein und seine Geschichte, Frankfurt a.M.: Campus.

Goodrich, Ernest P. (1937): Outline of city planning commission investigation concerning the Cincinnati flood problem and the effect on the comprehensive city plan, prepared by Ernest P. Goodrich, consulting Eengineer, Cincinnati/Ohio: University of Cincinnati Archives, Alfred Bettman Papers, pt. I, Box 7, Folder 19.

Guillerme, André (1983): Les temps de l'eau: La cité, l'eau et les techniques, Nord de la France, fin IIIe siècle-début XIXe siècle, Seyssel: Editions du Champ Wallon.

Gumprecht, Blake (1999): The Los Angeles River: Its life, death, and possible rebirth, Baltimore: Johns Hopkins University Press.

Hausmann, Guido (2009): Mütterchen Wolga: Ein Fluss als Erinnerungsort vom 16. bis ins frühe 20. Jahrhundert, Frankfurt a. M.: Campus.

Hornstein, Shelley (2017): "Union is a raging river, or remembering Fez as the river remembers." In: Martin Knoll/Uwe Lübke/Dieter Schott (eds.), Rivers lost, rivers regained: Rethinking river-city-relations, Pittsburgh: University of Pittsburgh Press, pp. 312-330.

Jakobsson, Eva (2002): "Industrialization of rivers: A water system approach to hydropower development." In: Knowledge, Technology and Policy 14/4, pp. 41-56.

Johnson, Leland R. (1991): "Engineering the Ohio." In: Robert L. Reid (ed.), Always a river: The Ohio River and the American experience, Bloomington: Indiana University Press, pp. 180-209.

Kelman, Ari (2003): A river and its city: The nature of landscape in New Orleans, Berkeley/Los Angeles: University of California Press.

Kneitz, Agnes (2017): "Polluted Thames, declining city: London as an ecosystem in Charles Dickens's 'Our Mutual Friend'." In: Martin Knoll/Uwe Lübken/Dieter Schott (eds.), Rivers lost, rivers regained: Rethinking river-city-relations, Pittsburgh: University of Pittsburgh Press, pp. 216-234.

Knoll, Martin/Lübken, Uwe/Schott, Dieter (eds.) (2017): Rivers lost, rivers regained: Rethinking river-city-relations, Pittsburgh: University of Pittsburgh Press.

Lübken, Uwe (2014): Die Natur der Gefahr: Überschwemmungen am Ohio River im 19. und 20. Jahrhundert, Göttingen: Vandenhoeck & Ruprecht.

Lübken, Uwe (2007): "'Der große Brückentod': Überschwemmungen als infrastrukturelle Konflikte im 19. und 20. Jahrhundert." In: Jahrbuch für Universalgeschichte 58/1, pp. 89-114.

Massard-Guilbaud, Geneviéve (2017): "The city whose rivers disappeared: Nantes, 1850-1950." In: Martin Knoll/Uwe Lübke/Dieter Schott (eds.), rivers lost, rivers regained: Rethinking river-city-relations, Pittsburgh: University of Pittsburgh Press, pp. 85-106.

McCool, Daniel (2010): "Implementing river restoration project." In: Marcus Hall (ed.), Restoration and history: The search for a usable environmental past, New York/London: Routledge.

Melosi, Martin (2008): The sanitary city: Environmental services in urban America from colonial times to the present, Pittsburgh: University of Pittsburgh Press.

Melosi, Martin (1993): "The place of the city in environmental history." In: Environmental History Review 17/1, pp. 1-23.

Moss, David A. (2002): When all else fails: Government as the ultimate risk manager, Cambridge/Mass./London: Harvard University Press.

Mutz, Mathias (2007): "Naturale Infrastrukturen im Unternehmen: Die Papierfabrik Kübler & Niethammer zwischen Umweltabhängigkeit und Umweltgestaltung." In: Saeculum 58, pp. 59-87.

New York Times (1895): "Vagaries of the Ohio", November 24.

Pinkham, Richard (2000): Daylighting: New life for buried streams, Snowmass/Colorado: Rocky Mountain Institute.

Price, Jennifer (2008): "Remaking American environmentalism: On the banks of the L.A. River." In: Environmental History 13, pp. 536-555.

Pritchard, Sara B. (2011): Confluence: The nature of technology and the remaking of the Rhône, Cambridge/Mass./London: Harvard University Press.

Rada, Uwe (2013): Die Elbe: Europas Geschichte im Fluss, Munich: Siedler.

Schott, Dieter (2014): Europäische Urbanisierung (1000-2000): Eine umwelthistorische Einführung, Cologne/Weimar/Vienna: Böhlau.

Soll, David (2013): Empire of water: An environmental and political history of the New York City water supply, Ithaca/NY: Cornell University Press.

Steinberg, Theodore (2002): Down to earth: Nature's role in American history, New York: Oxford University Press.

Stradling, David/Stradling, Richard (2008): "Perceptions of the burning river: Deindustrialization and Cleveland's Cuyahoga River." In: Environmental History 13/3, pp. 515-535.

Tarr, Joel (1996): The search for the ultimate sink: Urban pollution in historical perspective, Akron/Ohio: University of Akron Press.

Trotter, Joe William (1998): River Jordan: African American urban life in the Ohio Valley, Lexington/Kentucky: The University Press of Kentucky.

Tvedt, Terje/Oestigaard, Terje (2014): "Urban water systems: A conceptual framework." In: Terje Tvedt/Terje Oestigaard (eds.), A history of water. Series III, Vol.I: Water and Urbanization, London/New York: I.B.Tauris, pp. 1-21.

Weichselgartner, Jürgen (2000): "Hochwasser als soziales Ereignis: Gesellschaftliche Faktoren einer Naturgefahr." In: Hydrologie und Wasserbewirtschaftung 44/3, pp. 122-131.

Weintritt, Otfried (2009): "The floods of Baghdad: Cultural and technological responses." In: Christof Mauch/Christian Pfister (eds.), Natural disasters, cultural responses: Case studies toward a global environmental history, Lanham et al.: Lexington, pp. 165-182.

Welky, David (2011): The thousand-year flood: The Ohio-Mississippi disaster of 1937, Chicago: Chicago University Press.

White, Richard (1995): The organic machine: The remaking of the Columbia River, New York: Hill and Wang.

Winiwarter, Verena/Schmid, Martin (2008): "Umweltgeschichte als Untersuchung sozionaturaler Schauplätze? Ein Versuch Johannes Colerus 'Oeconomia' umwelthistorisch zu interpretieren." In: Thomas Knopf (ed.), Umweltverhalten in Geschichte und Gegenwart, Tübingen: Attempo, pp. 158-173.

Winiwarter, Verena/Schmid, Martin/Dressel, Gerd (2013): "Looking at Half a Millennium of Co-existence. The Danube in Vienna as Socio-Natural Site." In: Water History 5, pp. 101-119.

Wittfogel, Karl A. (1957): Oriental despotism: A comparative study of total power, New Haven/Connecticut: Yale University Press.

Worster, Donald (1985): Rivers of empire: Water, aridity, and the growth of the American West, New York: Pantheon.

Zeisler-Vralsted, Dorothy (2014): Rivers, memory, and nation-building: A history of the Volga and Mississippi Rivers, New York: Berghahn.

Urban Energy Consumption, Mobility and Environmental Legacies

Christian Zumbrägel

Energy History—Where are we?

The field of energy history is crucially relevant to many of the most pressing issues of our time. Since the Fukushima nuclear accident in Japan in 2011 and the subsequent change of course in German energy policy, reflections on both energy provision and consumption have increasingly gained in political, economic and social importance (Kalmbach 2017: 49). In this context, 'Energiewende' has become a ubiquitous term in Germany. On the international level the notion of a wholesale 'energy transition' is being discussed—the shift from one regime of energy provision to another. It aims for developing a nuclear-free energy supply while substantially lowering carbon dioxide emissions in order to mitigate climate change. The ongoing debates on energy as a multi-layered issue have also promoted a growing interest in energy history.

Museums are presenting new exhibitions to show how energy has transformed our lives and landscapes over the past centuries.[1] Historians are increasingly engaging in energy research and broadening the interdisciplinary field of energy studies by providing manifold historical analyses (Kupper et al. 2017b: 143).[2] The growing numbers of energy-oriented international conferences and workshops as well as recently launched research initiatives[3] reinforce the impres-

---

1 Some museums of technology and industry prepared special exhibitions about energy: for example the Deutsche Museum in Munich (https://www.deutsches-museum.de/en/exhibitions/special-exhibitions/energiewenden/) and the exhibition The Age of Coal; see the review of the exhibition with references to other exhibitions on energy: Lackner 2018.
2 Internationally, historical research on energy is not exclusively associated with historical studies. These issues are an integrated part of the interdisciplinary fields of energy studies, energy humanities and transition studies.
3 This includes the "HoNESt—History of Nuclear Energy and Society" project (http://www.honest2020.eu) or the working group dedicated to "The Energy Challenge in Historical Perspective" as part of the "Tensions of Europe" network (https://www.tensionsofeurope.eu/the-energy-challenge-in-historical-perspective/). Moreover, the networks "Energy History" (http://histecon.fas.

sion of a stronger interest in the topic.[4] The field of energy history, however, is not only influenced by debates about current energy policy, but is also affected by recent changes in methodological approaches. Traditional energy history has been situated at the crossroads where economic and infrastructure history meet up with the history of technology. More recently, research on environmental history has contributed to the discipline as well—driven by influential concepts such as Christian Pfister's '1950s syndrome', which links human energy consumption to the environmental imprint of human societies (1995).

For about three decades, the city has increasingly come to stand at the centre of energy-historical research (Irsigler 1991; Schott 1997). Cities have a special place in the flows of energy that circulate between societies and their environments. The concentration of economic and urban activities early on rendered cities the major centres of energy accumulation and consumption. The precondition for an extensive use of energy, however, was the constant influx of energy sources from nearby or remote surrounding areas. As transport technologies had enabled access to these energy sources, they diversified and accelerated the consumption of energy in cities leading to substantial changes in the daily lives of urban residents. Over the course of the centuries, waterways and railways, canals and grids have completely transformed the relationships between cities and their hinterlands.

This article sheds light on the correlations between environmental issues and the provision and consumption of energy in Western urban areas. For doing so, it points out how cities have organised their flows of energy and how this has led to tensions and path dependencies in both the political and environmental domain. After an introduction to some 'classical' perspectives that locate energy history within the framework of the networked city (I), the article discusses how patterns of energy consumption, transport and environmental legacies have emerged on the scale of cities: Here, specific forms of energy consumption in private households are analysed (II). The rise of new energy needs that developed with the growing urban middle-class culture brought about new patterns of energy consumption. Next, the article focuses on urban transport technologies with the help of which cities gained access to both nearby and remote surrounding areas in order to ensure and control energy flows (III). The formation and growth of regional, national and global networks of energy transport was stimulated by the massive demand of energy. As a result, the environmental impacts of cities expanded significantly while the environmental integrity of the surrounding countryside, from

---

harvard.edu/energyhistory/index.html) and "Material Cultures of Energy (MCE)" (http://www.bbk.ac.uk/mce/) should be mentioned.

4 Notably (and in contrast to the above), there is no professorship explicitly related to the historical analysis of energy in the German research landscape.

which cities drew their resources and into which they deposited their waste, gradually deteriorated (IV).

In the course of this exposition, the article provides an overview of recent literature on the energy history of the 19th and 20th centuries focusing on German, European and North American perspectives and topics. More recent work, which has dealt with preindustrial energy history or the energy transition from premodern to modern industrial society, is referred to selectively.

For a long time, energy-historical narratives have concentrated on looking at the conditions and consequences of the transition to the energy regime based on fossil fuels. This research trajectory was influenced most strongly by Rolf Peter Sieferle, a well-known German historian on energy-related issues (2001 [1982]). Sieferle identified a fundamental transition at the turn of the 19th century. In premodern times, energy was produced by burning wood, charcoal or peat for heating, and harnessing wind, water or human and animal muscle power for the vast majority of mechanical energy. Sieferle called this the 'solar energy regime' because it depended on the energy provided by the sun that both created organic material through photosynthesis and generated the kinetic energy exploited by wind- and waterpower. In the late 18th century the shift to fossil fuels allowed England, and later other countries, to break free from the limitations of annual solar energy flows. At this point energy became generated from what Sieferle calls the 'subterranean forest': first, coal fired the industrialisation, and later oil became essential for the economic growth in the 20th century.

The Subterranean Forest is a stimulating but controversial work (for criticism see: Uekötter 2007: 61-62). It presents the long period from the Neolithic Revolution to the late 18th century as relying on a uniformly solar-based energy regime.[5] In Sieferle's story the 'subterranean forest' is seen as the main agent of energy and resource transformation in the process of industrialisation. As a result, the transition to the 'fossil energy regime' appears more sudden than it actually was. It neglects the continuity of preindustrial energy sources—like water, wind and other alternative forms of renewable energy—and that one energy regime did not spring fully formed into the place of another. These questions about continuities and periodisation are addressed in the final section of the article.

In recent years a growing amount of energy-historical studies have contributed to a more nuanced view of the processes of the last three centuries. Some of these studies are introduced in the following sections. In contrast to Sieferle, these studies rarely aim to categorise the entire human history of humanity into a small number of distinct stages of energy provision. Instead, more recent energy histories focus on particular regions at specific times to point their readers to the manifold forms of energy production and use throughout history. By clus-

---

5 Similar periodic characterizations can be found in: Mumford 1934; Debeir et al. 1989; Smil 2017.

tering together contemporary publications and projects that shed light on these geographic and temporal characteristics of energy-related processes, this article seeks to contribute to a re-reading of classical accounts of energy history.

Classical Perspectives: Cities and Networks

For a long time, accounts of energy history focused primarily on processes of energy provision. Historians of economics and technology explored the structural conditions that gave rise to innovations in energy technology—often in connection with the institutional foundations of energy provision for economies and societies. Political aspects such as the influence of public authorities and the development of large energy companies were especially emphasised (Stier 2000: 478-480; Zängl 1989).

Since the 1990s, studies of energy history in the 19th and 20th centuries have, by contrast, dealt mainly with aspects of cultural history (van Laak 2012: 17). For example, historians focused on daily lives and symbolic representations to examine the popularisation of electricity. Other authors investigated the cultural perception of electricity at the turn of the 20th century (Gugerli 1996; Osietzki 1996). In the course of this, cities of the Western world emerged early on as relevant objects of research because they were the central locations involved in the appropriation of electricity. In her dissertation *Elektrifizierung als Vision* historian Beate Binder explored the perceptions that city dwellers developed at the start of the 20th century in the face of the still new phenomenon of electricity. The electrification of transport and communication structures, in particular, turned electricity into a symbol for modernisation and urbanisation. At the same time, critics called attention to the negative side-effects of the new form of energy. They criticised the increasing traffic, the visual appearance of the city (e.g. a skyline cut up by electric cables) and the expansion of nightlife and crime due to electric lighting (Binder 1999). The development of electricity, and its public representation, contributed to profound changes in the socio-economic and cultural realities of urban environments as Ute Hasenöhrl has outlined in a recent review essay on the history of lightning technologies (2014).

The tendency to focus on cultural perspectives was inspired by general trends in historical studies and by pertinent works emerging from the history of technology. Among these, Thomas P. Hughes's seminal works marked a key point of reference. As Hughes pointed out in the introduction to *Networks of Power*, "Power systems are cultural artifacts" (1983: 2). Hughes described the evolution, function and stability of electricity networks as complex processes. In doing so, he did not limit his study to technical artefacts but included social, economic and political patterns. He clarified how actors, technologies and institutions interacted over time in order to develop and sustain 'Large Technological Systems' (LTS) such as electricity networks. Hughes's approach was much debated. For example, scholars criticised the concept of LTS for overemphasising the importance of centralised systems, neglecting the agency of actors beyond the powerful 'system-builders' and attributing too much determinism to path dependency and linear development from the invention to the stabilisation of a system (Zumbrägel 2015; Hasenöhrl/van der Straeten 2017: 372-375).

Hughes introduced the concept of 'technological styles' in order to describe technological differences in the urban context. For each of his three case studies—Chicago, London and Berlin—he identified local or urban conditions that contributed to specific adaptations of emerging technological systems. Here, Hughes emphasised the influence of social (and also natural) components on the construction and growth of national electricity systems. The development of these networks was not only determined by technical and economic factors. Cultural values and political decisions played as great a role as the principles of the energy market, institutional structures and legislative constraints. Geographical factors, too, affected the growth of systems (Hughes 1983: 462; cf. also Heymann 1998). Overall, the concept of 'technological styles' drew attention to the regional peculiarities of large-scale technical systems and has been included in a number of later histories of energy and infrastructures.

The concept of LTS inspired many scholars and stimulated research on energy history. Based on Hughes's work, electrification became one of the most investigated topics in urban history and the history of technology. Inspired by *Networks of Power*, Dieter Schott developed the concept of the 'Die vernetzte Stadt'. Schott interpreted the introduction of networks to provide urban households with necessities of daily life like drinking water, wastewater removal, gas lighting, and electricity as a response to the crisis in early modern urban development caused by increasing traffic and hygienic problems. The interconnection of these infrastructures in European cities around 1900 resulted in the complex system of the 'networked city', in which power grids and vehicles for urban transport like electric trams became inseparably intertwined and transformed the socio-economic and cultural realities of urban environments (Schott 1999; Hård/Misa 2008).

For decades, historians largely explained the electrification through the lens of large-scale power plants, grids and cities. Even in much recent work on the history of electricity, energy companies appear as the most relevant actors. Further studies focus on conflicts between the centralised electricity sector and decentralised supply strategies (Gilson 1994; Döring 2012), while yet others investigate how small-scale power plants have contributed to the electricity system (Löwen 2015). Still other historians ask in which ways the networked structures of today's plants and grids fit into political and economic contexts since the 1970s (Ehrhardt 2017).

To sum up, on the one hand Hughes's LTS concept provides historians with a useful framework to describe the rise, expansion and resilience of modern energy systems in Western urban societies. Moreover, it explains the complex interplay between technical networks and social aspects. On the other hand, Hughes's systemic approach has several limitations when it comes to tracing energy flows beyond large-scale systems.

Private Energy Consumption (in Cities)

Hughes's work, along with most histories of electricity, focused on production and analysed how electricity was generated and distributed across growing networks. Even when socio-economic patterns were addressed, research rarely examined the private use of energy. In the last decades, however, research into the history of energy has turned to the consumption side of the story. Among the first to do so, David Nye extended Hughes' work by looking at consumers in both households and small industries (1990). The book *Past and Future Energy Societies* takes on the perspective of the electricity consumer (Zachmann 2012: 7-11). The collection investigates how electricity and its appliances were appropriated in households, how they influenced everyday life and were, in turn, altered by consumers.

Emphasising the experiences of ordinary women and men rather than the activities of inventors and entrepreneurs, these user-centred stories pay explicit attention to private urban households. They show how private energy consumption affected different aspects of urban lifestyles and how it virtually created the image of the modern city. In her study of energy consumption in West German households after World War II, Sophie Gerber examines how electrical appliances affected urban living. She points out a fact that remains paradoxical up to the present day: private electricity consumption continually increased during the second half of the 20th century, even though the energy efficiency of electrical devices continually improved (Gerber 2014: 12-16). A 'coalition of wasters' ('Koalition der Verschwender'), which included representatives from the energy sector, appliance producers, and politicians as well as consumer groups and energy users, promoted the electrification of households. This resulted in today's availability of abundant energy and new lifestyles of the 'high-energy society' ('Hochenergiegesellschaft') (ibid: 320; Zachmann 2012: 7).

Studies on household electrification not only emphasised the creative power that electricity brought to urban lifestyles. They also pointed to resistive processes that were tied to the appropriation of new electrical devices. Focusing on the implementation of hot water tanks that the Berlin-based company Bewag rented to private households during the interwar period, Nina Lorkowski demonstrated that the expectations of energy companies often collided with traditional daily routines. For example, energy consumers rarely used the boilers for their daily hot water needs, as the companies intended; rather, they turned them on only during the traditional bathing day on the weekend, when the entire family, one after the other, took a bath in the warm water from a single tankful (Lorkowski 2019). Under certain conditions consumers resisted the marketing strategies of the electricity companies. This is reflected by the fact that long-proven energy technologies continued to play a role in private households even after electrification. Such was the case in West Germany, where even in the late 1950s more coal and gas stoves were in use than electric ones (Trentmann 2016: 24). In fact, energy sources such as coal and gas continued to play a role in everyday urban energy consumption particularly for purposes of cooking and heating. Reasons for the slow diffusion of modern electricity were not only its high costs, but also the fact that from the late 1880s onwards three competing technological systems were available, each of which had particular advantages and drawbacks (for a history of urban gas applications cf. Schott 2015: 283-286). The increasing access to electricity by urban households normalised perceptions about the availability of vast amounts of energy. At the same time, the dependence of energy consumption on complex and vulnerable infrastructures only became apparent in cases of system failures. As David Nye remarks in his history of blackouts in the USA, "people notice electricity only in its absence" (2010: 12; cf. also Baldwin 2004).

To sum up, user-centred studies have pointed out that urban energy consumption can only be understood as the result of a negotiation between representatives from the energy sector, appliance producers, politicians and, importantly, consumers. Developments in the energy sector have not always been determined by top-down processes. These studies instead highlight the agency of urban inhabitants. They were rarely passive beneficiaries of grids and electrical devices. Consumers have played significant active roles in previous energy transitions and have intervened in energy matters through bottom-up processes. This was particularly the case when they themselves both produced and consumed electricity—for example, in small plants powered by renewable energies. The significance of these 'small system builders' or 'user-producers' for the transformation of energy technologies has generally been too little illuminated (van der Vleuten et al. 2016: 1499-1500; Schott et al. 2016). This is in part due to the difficulties of finding adequate historical sources. Daily experiences and routines of ordinary consumers have left far fewer traces in writing than the activities of inventors, entrepreneurs and electricity suppliers.

This complex linking of production, distribution and consumption of energy is important for understanding the structures and processes of today's energy regime. Whereas centralised large-scale power plants and electricity networks dominated the Western European energy sector from the 1920s to the 1990s, today's shift to renewable energies is characterised by tendencies favoring the "relocalization of energy production" and relies on a number of small-scale solutions

(Schott 2019: 136). This development calls for concrete action on local and regional levels. It remains to be clarified exactly what 'user-producers' can contribute to realising climate protection goals. If research into energy history seeks to deliver relevant contextual knowledge for recent energy issues, though, historians should ask how daily energy consumption itself became a crucial factor in the mix—or, as historian Christopher Jones has proposed: "If we believe that many little things can add up to something big [...] we should give more critical attention to bottom-up policies directed towards residential markets" (2011: 817).

Energy on the Move

Energy, mobility and transport are intricately interdependent. Against this background it is remarkable, as historian Victor Seow (2014: 113) points out, "how little attention" historians have paid to these "close links" between energy and its movement. However, more recent energy histories have shown a broader interest in questions of mobility and transport.

Historical developments related to energy can be described by looking at different forms of mobility and transport. First, people and tools have moved to locations of energy provision. Second, energy sources themselves have been transported to people. Technologies like canals, railways or grids transported the energy harnessed on rivers, in coal mines or in densely forested areas to urban and industrial centres.

Early on, energy resources concentrated in expanding urban areas that depended on energy supply for their continued growth. In doing so, energy demands of cities reshaped much of the rural world (Irsigler 1991: 309; Schott 2014: 12). Urban needs for home heating and lighting were crucial drivers in moving energy from sites of production to sites of consumption (Radkau 1997; Knoll 2007). By the 18th century local woodlands in Vienna could no longer supply sufficient quantities of wood as fuel for the rapidly growing population. The city resorted to large-scale engineering measures to expand supply chains for wood further upstream along the Danube. Private entrepreneurs set up technical devices to facilitate wood transport to log-driving creeks and navigable streams in order to fuel Vienna's energy metabolism (Krausmann 2013; Zumbrägel 2014). Such large-scale technological efforts aimed at meeting urban energy demands exemplify the tendency to 'urbanize nature' since early modern times (Schott et al. 2019: 5-7).

The first strategy, the movement of energy-intensive work towards energy sources, has a long tradition as well. For centuries manufacturers brought their raw materials and tools to places where energy was produced (Periman 2004: 852). Before the spread of steam power, abundant power was to be found in extended woodlands, windy areas and especially along watercourses in mountainous regions, where waterpower was exploited to drive mechanical operations, and wood, peat or charcoal were available as sources of heat. In rural areas, the harnessing of renewable energy resources often led to a decentralised distribution of commercial activities along small creeks in forested areas (Schott 1997: 12-13).

Since the 1990s, historians of technology as well as economic and environmental historians have described these tendencies of decentralisation in different traditionally commercial regions. In doing so, they have pointed out that the steam engine rarely catalysed the take-off phase of industrialisation in these areas. The paper manufacturers in the German Alps, the textile industry of New England and the Po valley of Italy provide well studied examples: Early American and European industrialisation relied upon waterpower (Jones 2010: 470; Steinberg 2001; Parrinello 2018: esp. 656-668). In his study *Fossil Capitals* (2016) Andreas Malm demonstrated that in early 19th century Britain the adoption of coal and steam by manufacturing industries only slowly replaced their reliance on waterpower. Decades after James Watt perfected his steam engine, thousands of British spinning and weaving factories located in the hilly uplands near Manchester were still using traditional energy sources. Contrary to the popular views expressed in Sieferle's Subterranean Forest, Malm argues that the gradual shift to fossil fuels did not occur because newly designed engines fired by coal were cheaper, easier to handle or more reliable. The coal-fired steam engine was instead an instrument used to solve certain socio-economic problems associated with industrialisation. Returning to the themes of transport and mobility, Malm explained that water-powered mills had to be located at sites of flowing water—usually in rural areas—where the pool of potential workers was small. By contrast, steam-powered mechanical energy could be located in urban areas, where a huge pool of workers was within easy reach. Thus, the steam engine's high degree of mobility helped concentrate production and capital at the most profitable sites—particularly in the urban agglomerations where cheap labour was abundant.

Energy sources as wind and water continued to play a role in industrial energy regimes as indicated by quantitative reconstructions of energy metabolism (Kander et al. 2013). In the long run, however, the increasing mobilisation of mineral energy sources allowed societies to break free from the limitations of preindustrial solar flows. This also led to remarkable expansions in the transport sector. The construction of canals and railroads reduced transport costs and became an important driving force for industrialised sectors such as steel production, mining, and engineering in England and beyond (Wrigley 2010: chap. 4). As fossil fuels became more widely exploited in the industrial age, a system emerged in which coal was channeled in increasing quantities along rail or water ways. These intersections of energy flows and transport patterns in modern energy systems are at the centre of Christopher Jones's book *Routes of Power*. Jones argues that "transport systems were not simply passive conduits between producers and users" (2014: 4). Rather, canals, pipelines, railway tracks and transmission lines were instrumental in cultivating an increasing demand for different energy sources. The result was what Jones has called "landscapes of intensification." An increasingly dense network of transport technologies distances between centres of energy production and consumption. These processes gave rise to the familiar modern energy landscapes with cities as their nodes.

The emerging networks led to a steady decline transport costs. In the 19th century canals and railways made it feasible to supply industrial and urban centres with coal from several hundred kilometres away. In the 20th century pipelines and tankers for natural gas and oil transport, and especially grids, reproduced this pattern. Around 1900 the transmission of alternating current electricity enabled the distribution of energy over long distances and across national borders (Lagendijk 2016). Focusing on the emergence of national grids in North America, historian Julie A. Cohn has shown how many different visions, actors, technological components and local subnetworks shaped its expansion. These power structures did not develop nearly as uniformly as the notion of a 'grid' implies (2017: ix-xii). Yet, in many ways the transportation of energy over long distances was as challenging as the production of the energy itself. Recent studies have focused on the vulnerability and lack of reliability of these components of technological systems, which had to be constantly maintained and repaired to ensure a smooth flow of energy (Hirsh/Jones 2014: 109; Lagendijk/van der Vleuten 2013).

Coal, one of the main energy sources of the 19th century, was increasingly replaced by petroleum and later nuclear energy and natural gas in the 20th. Still, coal's share in the primary production of energy up until today has only decreased in relative, not in absolute terms (Edgerton 2008: 120-122). In contrast to coal, fluid petroleum could be used more flexibly and e transported more cheaply over large distances. The expansion of oil consumption ushered in unprecedented economic growth, evident in the United States before and in Europe and the rest of the world after World War II (Graf 2014: chap. 2). Since oilfields were irregularly distributed around the world, a global network emerged to extract, refine and distribute petroleum. Oil drilling equipment, refineries, pipelines, ocean tankers and gas stations together formed new 'landscapes of intensification' which have served the international flows of natural gas and petroleum in industrial areas as well as in everyday life (Melsted/Pallua 2018; Högselius 2013). These modern transport technologies were themselves powered by massive amounts of energy (Seow 2014: 113). The expansion of these infrastructures contributed to a rationalisation and automation of energy transport as historian Timothy Mitchell has pointed out in *Carbon Democracy*. Mitchell considers the political transformations induced by the shift from a coal-based social system to one based on oil as motivated by a strategic move to reduce structural weakness and safeguard the circulations of fossil energy against disturbances due to human error or strikes (2011: 29-42).

The mobilisation of energy in increasing quantities entailed not only the use of different energy sources but also new spatial relations between cities and their hinterlands. While the consumption of energy in metropolises such as Vienna and Paris around 1800 was served by very few sources of energy—mostly wood and waterpower from the nearby streams and forests—in the course of the 19th and 20th centuries the hinterland that served cities needs became "ever more global and simultaneously ever more diffuse" (Knoll 2017: 104; Kim/Barles 2012). The cities' hunger for energy was fed from ever more remote areas of the world. According to these processes, hierarchies beneath the level of cities shifted over the course of the centuries. Early modern towns lost power and influence when the development of energy flows directed toward the cities excluded them; or when energy of the hinterland ran short, as happened to cities situated among remote mountains and specialising in ore-smelting or salt-mining. For these energy-intensive operations they required massive amounts of wood that over time simply ran out (Radkau 1997: 57-60; Zumbrägel 2014). With the growth of what Carola Hein (2018) has called the 'global petroleumscape', other cities gained in strategic importance. Port cities like Rotterdam became central nodes and gateways precisely on account of the worldwide oil trade.

Environmental Consequences of (Urban) Energy Consumption

The mobilisation of energy in increasing quantities, the growing demand and the emergence of 'landscapes of intensification' were inextricably linked to environmental disruptions. Extraction, transport and burning of fossil fuels were dirty, toxic and ecologically intrusive operations. The mining of coal resulted in the re-routing, sealing and leaching of water veins and in the subsidence of land surfaces. The environmental consequences of lignite mining were at first more evident since surface mining turned landscapes into sandy wastelands (Uekötter 2015; Brüggemeier 2018: 109-122). Wherever coal was washed or burned, effluents, soot and smoke not only polluted water, land and air but had an extensive impact on the health and lifestyles of (urban) populations. Historians have analysed the interrelations between coal, society and the environment in early industrialised cities of Great Britain (Platt 2005; Thorsheim 2006; Tomory 2012). In their environmental histories of London and Manchester—once dubbed the 'chimney of the world'—William M. Cavert and Stephen Mosley described the profound effects of fossil fuel dependence for public health, the urban environment and daily lifestyles (Mosley 2001; Cavert 2016). In Victorian England, clothing and furniture fashions came to favour dark and heavy colours partly because of the difficulties of constantly cleaning white fabrics. Moreover, air pollution and reduced amounts of sunshine made spending time outside unattractive, so that domesticity became a significant part of everyday life (Mosley 2001: 71-74; cf. also Schott 2015: 209-

211). Not only the burning of fossil fuels but even the burning of traditional energy sources such as wood has had harmful environmental and sanitary consequences. Sarah Mittlefehldt has demonstrated this in a recent essay in which she links a wood burning power plant developed in Flint (Michigan, USA) to the issue of 'environmental justice'. The negative effects of the industrial-scale biomass power system in Flint tended to concentrate in urban areas that lacked political power. Poor and nonwhite residents were disproportionately emissions of carbon monoxide and toxic chemicals such as lead into the air (Mittlefehldt 2018).

Oil, a negligible pollutant before 1900, became the number one source of pollution during the 20th century. With the emergence and expansion of the 'global petroleumscape', its environmental effects achieved global dimensions. According to environmental historian John McNeill, no process was more influential in "world environmental history" than "the triumph of oil" (2000: 628). The example of oil demonstrates how decisions made by states, corporations and individuals in one region or country of the world can result in the polluting of landscapes on the other side of the globe. Extraction and transport disfigured entire regions within a few decades; explosions of offshore drilling rigs like 'Deepwater Horizon' in the Gulf of Mexico in 2010, tanker accidents, and a long series of pipeline leaks have permanently damaged both marine and terrestrial ecosystems across the globe.

While fossil fuels earned themselves an environmentally harmful image, electricity was often viewed as clean and pure. This can be seen in 20th century debates about the exploitation of nuclear power and hydroelectricity—also known as 'white coal'—in which the contrast to dirty coal, hygienic connotations, and metaphors of cleanliness played an important role (Blackbourn 2013: 14; Lehmann 2016: 74). However, in most cases electricity was merely 'hiding the fire', since it was largely produced by burning coal. This is especially true for the USA during second half of the 20th century, where the development and prevalence of nuclear power was limited in comparison to most European countries. This absence of transition caused disruptive impacts on the environment as the electricity network continues to rely on fossil fuels (Lifset 2019). The most profitable sites of electricity production were often located far from potential customers. With increasing distances through the expansion of networks and grids, the ecological consequences caused by electricity became ever less visible to people in urban and industrial centres (French 2017: 3-19).

The negative impacts of energy production in places far removed from its consumption are also exemplified in the transformation of rivers into 'organic machines', as historian Richard White has phrased it (1995; Miller/Warde 2019: 464-466). Marc Landry has examined the legacies of exploiting white coal in the case of the Alps, where run-of-river plants and large hydro-electrical storage installations serve as an important element in Europe's electricity supply. Landry traces the ecological consequences of hydropower, particularly the transformation of Alpine landscapes and water regimes. The destruction of watersheds for the purpose of harnessing vast amounts of energy included the upsetting of the rivers' water balance, the displacement and straightening of streams and the construction of artificial lakes, dams and grids in sensitive natural habitats (Landry 2015: 440-443). In some European cases, the transformation of rivers into energy landscapes stimulated the rise of environmental consciousness and prompted early environmental activism (Schoder/Schmid 2017). Following French's argument, environmentally disruptive infrastructures have come to dominate the Alpine landscape and yet are hardly visible in the places where the energy is consumed.

By now, a sizable literature has analysed hydroelectric power from both a technological and an environmental perspective in several cultural and natural contexts. Julia Tischler (2014) described similar environmental challenges with concerning the Kariba Dam Scheme in the Central African Federation. Heather Hoag (2013) and Kate Showers (2009) presented studies on East and West Africa while Sunila Kale (2014: 456) discussed the hydroelectrification of British India. Taken together, these studies are examples of the strong preference to concentrate on hydroelectric schemes when investigating energy histories of the Global South. In doing so, they problematise the transfer of Western energy technologies like dams and run-of-river plants that often resulted in unexpected, devastating ecological and social costs for local people and ecologies (Beattie/Morgan 2017: 42).

Due to the massive material throughput of the urban energy metabolism, the environmental impact of cities has expanded significantly both in spatial terms and in scope. While cities themselves made progress in terms of safety, lifestyle and health during the 19th and 20th centuries, surrounding hinterlands gradually deteriorated. But even within cities the relationships between energy consumption, socio-economic processes and environmental effects have shifted over the past centuries. The drastic increase in energy consumption after World War II, powered by cheap energy (especially petroleum), fundamentally changed the lifestyle of the majority of West Europeans and opened up new opportunities in what Christian Pfister summed up with the term '1950s syndrome' (Pfister 2003: 84). The first steps into the oil economy thus generated unpredicted interrelationships between energy consumption, and the pollution of air, water and soil.

Energy Challenges in Historical Perspective: Continuities vs. 'Energy Transitions'

Energy transitions are prevalent in today's public discourse. This concerns topics as fuel price fluctuations, environmental or security concerns, technological change, or better energy access. Such issues also affect historical scholarship on energy. Recent contributions to energy history rarely miss to touch upon the current energy transition. Scholars debate the consequences of our dependence on fossil fuels both for societies and environments and question the legacies of the processes that led to it (Quivik 2017: 866). The strengthened ecological awareness since the 1970s has contributed to research interests in alternative energy paths beyond coal and oil. Recently, historians have drawn more and more attention to the history of alternative forms of renewable energy (e.g. Abelshauser 2014; Hesse 2016: 126). However, industrial energy transitions are immediately associated with fossil fuels and historical research on modern energy regimes is still dominated by studies of the fossil fuel dependence of the Western world (e.g. Mitchell 2011; Shulman 2015; Malm 2016; Johnson 2014). Christopher Jones even talks about a recent 'petromyopia', what means an overrepresentation of studies concerned with the history of oil and fossil fuel transitions. On the one hand, understanding the routes and legacies of our current dependence on oil is important for engaging with the complex emerging challenges of sustainable development, heritage, policy-making and future regimes that look beyond oil. In this sense, 'petromyopia' offers new perspectives for general discussions addressing the role of energy in the 21st century. On the other hand, 'petromyopia' fails to highlight other important aspects of the social and cultural dimensions of energy in the 19th and 20th centuries (Jones 2016).

The predominant concern with 'energy transitions'[6] entails distortions on many levels: Sieferle's emphasis on the shift from solar to fossil energy regimes (2001) is a case in point for the frequent focus on discontinuities in energy history. Energy-historical research still engages primarily with the transformation that drove the Industrial Revolution described as shifts from 'solar' to 'fossil' or 'organic' to 'mineral' energy regimes (Jones 2014: 3; cf. also Unger 2013; Miller/Warde 2019: 466-468). Additionally, several quantitative studies have explored changes in energy provision and consumption during the transition from one energy regime to another. Such quantitative reconstructions have been extensively carried out for the cases of Vienna and Paris (Kim/Barles 2012; Krausmann 2013).

To be sure, current energy histories generally remark that such transitions were gradual processes that lasted for hundreds of years—years in which past, present and future regimes coexisted or were superimposed in hybrid ways (Kupper 2017a: 13-14). Shifts from wood to coal or oil did not occur as revolutionary turnarounds. They took place over long periods of time and were often fitful, uneven, and frequently contradictory. Still, the focus on transitions renders invisible important dynamics that took place in different regions of the world at different times, progressing at different speeds and with different rates of adoption. In

---

6 Research on historical energy transitions is not only carried out in historical disciplines but also in environmental, social and economic science: Melosi 1982; Allen 2012; Araújo 2014; Labussière/Nadaï 2018; Melsted/Pallua 2018.

transition research, constant factors are seldom at the centre of interest. From a historiographic perspective, the continuities in energy history seem less impressive than the drivers of change.

In fact, however, the persistence of what is usually labelled 'old' and 'outmoded' is easily overlooked and neglected in energy history: While fossil fuels are more immediately associated with the industrial energy transition than water, preindustrial energy sources did continue to play a role in industrial energy regimes for a long time. This was the case in many traditional commercial regions such as the hilly valleys of Western Germany, where long-proven energy technologies such as waterwheels remained crucial to industry until the 1930s and 1940s—despite the fact that water turbines and hydroelectric facilities were widely available (Zumbrägel 2018: 30). As was shown above, waterpower represents an interesting example of this kind of continuity, which was and still is particularly significant in certain geographical regions (Parrinello 2018). In some European coastal regions old tidal mills and windmills continued to function well into the 20th century to regulate water supply systems and effectively decentralise energy producers (Charlier/Menanteau 1997: 182; Hesse 2018: 9-10).

In some cases, these continuities have to do with labour traditions. Sometimes the durability of an engine or knowledge about its functioning played a role; sometimes simple cost-benefit calculations tipped the balance in favor of keeping old energy technologies running. In other cases, it was the existing infrastructural setting or effects of the environment which were responsible for this persistence. Trust in familiar energy forms and technologies could also account for such persistence as Ruth Sandwell (2017) has shown with regard to the electrification of rural areas in Canada. In Western Canada many households resisted the promotional efforts of electricity companies and instead stuck to traditional energy sources up until World War II. Not least in times of war or crisis, 'user-producers' in rural areas have repeatedly found new applications for long-proven engines: for example when owners of small mills in times of resource scarcity revamped their outmoded engines and hooked them up to electric generators (Kupper/Pallua 2016: 44-48; Federmann 1924: 27), or when engineers developed new ways to use wood or biomass to create electricity (Mittlefehldt 2018) or to power vehicles, as some Swedish motorists did when facing shortages of raw materials during World War II (Kaijser 2018).

Sometimes new technologies were simply too unreliable to be adopted or were not compatible with existing local structures. Studies in global infrastructure and energy history have made this point by analysing processes of transcultural transfer of technologies. In the 20th century, both urban and rural inhabitants of regions in Africa, Asia and Latin America developed their own decentralised structures of energy utilisation. Thus, they maintained a high level of resilience in energy provision. In Nigeria, for example, petrol and diesel generators became an essential part of the energy supply for urban dwellers who lacked access to centralised electricity networks (Larkin 2015).

Albeit such decentralised energy systems are surprisingly persistent in the face of large-scale infrastructures of energy supply, they remain below the radar of historical research. One reason for this is that the interpretative frameworks were developed to analyse the establishment and growth of modern networks—primarily focused on Western cities. Classical concepts like LTS or the 'networked city' are able to describe the expansion of electricity grids in the 20th century. Yet, when tracing energy paths beyond the beaten track of centralised systems, the analytical strengths of systemic frameworks are severely limited. Recent accounts in the fields of global history of technology and infrastructure history have questioned the usefulness of these Western-centric concepts to phenomena in the Global South. They have asked how we can tell the stories of people and places that are often made invisible by LTS. Thus, historians are developing new terms and approaches to describe processes of technological appropriation in foreign cultural contexts and rural areas characterised by specific socio-economic and natural conditions (Hasenöhrl 2018: 12-14). Recent and future research on energy history will also benefit from these transcultural perspectives. They elucidate how 'user-producers' in informal settlements have developed decentralised energy systems as alternatives to missing, failing or idle electric networks. Beyond grids, cities and centralised structures of the Western world, the energy history of the 19th and 20th centuries is still to be written.

References

Abelshauser, Werner (2014): "Der Traum von der umweltverträglichen Energie und seine schwierige Verwirklichung." In: Vierteljahresschrift für Sozial- und Wirtschaftsgeschichte 101, pp. 49-61.

Allen, Robert C. (2012): "Backward into the future: The shift to coal and implications for the next energy transition." In: Energy Policy 50, pp. 17-23.

Araújo, Kathleen (2014): "The emerging field of energy transitions: Progress, challenges, and opportunities." In: Energy Research and Social Science 1, pp. 112-121.

Baldwin, Peter C. (2004): "In the hearth of darkness: Blackouts and the social geography of lighting in the gaslight era." In: Journal of Urban History 30/5, pp. 749-768.

Beattie, James/Morgan, Ruth (2017): "Engineering edens on this rivered earth: A review article on water management and hydro-resilience in the British Empire, 1860s-1940s." In: Environment and History 23/1, pp. 39-63.

Binder, Beate (1999): Elektrifizierung als Vision: Zur Symbolgeschichte einer Technik im Alltag, Tübingen: Tübinger Vereinigung für Volkskunde.

Blackbourn, David (2013): "The culture and politics of energy in Germany: A historical perspective." In: RCC Perspectives 4, pp. 1-23.

Brüggemeier, Franz-Josef (2018): Grubengold: Das Zeitalter der Kohle von 1750 bis heute, Munich: C. H. Beck.

Cavert, William M. (2016): The smoke of London: Energy and environment in the early modern city, Cambridge: Cambridge University Press.

Charlier, Roger H./Menateau, Loic (1997): "The saga of tide mills." In: Renewable and Sustainable Energy Reviews 1/3, pp. 171-207.

Cohn, Julie A. (2017): The grid: Biography of an American technology, Cambridge, Mass.: MIT Press.

Debeir, Jean-Claude/Deléage, Jean-Paul/Hémery, Daniel (1989): Prometheus auf der Titanic: Geschichte der Energiesysteme, Frankfurt a.M.: Campus.

Döring, Peter (2012): "Dezentralisierung versus Verbundwirtschaft: Die Diskussion um die Regulierung der Elektrizitätswirtschaft im Vorfeld des Energiewirtschaftsgesetzes von 1935." In: Hendrik Ehrhardt/Thomas Kroll (eds.), Energie in der modernen Gesellschaft, Göttingen: Vandenhoeck & Ruprecht, pp. 119-148.

Edgerton, David (2008): The shock of the old: Technology and global history since 1900, London: Profile Books.

Ehrhardt, Hendrik (2017): Stromkonflikte: Selbstverständnis und strategisches Handeln der Stromwirtschaft zwischen Politik, Industrie, Umwelt und Öffentlichkeit (1970-1989), Stuttgart: Franz Steiner.

Federmann, Paul (1924): "Ausbau kleiner Wasserkräfte nach dem Kriege." In: Deutsche Wasserwirtschaft 19, pp. 27-30.

French, Daniel (2017): When they hid the fire: A history of electricity and invisible energy in America, Pittsburgh: University of Pittsburgh Press.

Gerber, Sophie (2018): Küche, Kühlschrank, Kilowatt: Zur Geschichte des privaten Energiekonsums in Deutschland, 1945-1990, Bielefeld: transcript.

Gilson, Norbert (1994): Konzepte von Elektrizitätsversorgung und Elektrizitätswirtschaft: Die Entstehung eines neuen Fachgebietes der Technikwissenschaft zwischen 1880 und 1945, Stuttgart: GNT.

Graf, Rüdiger (2014): Öl und Souveränität: Petroknowledge und Energiepolitik in den USA und Westeuropa in den 1970er-Jahren, Munich: De Gruyter.

Gugerli, David (1996): Redeströme: Zur Elektrifizierung der Schweiz. 1880-1914, Zürich: Chronos.

Hård, Mikael/Misa, Thomas J. (eds.) (2008): Urban machinery: Inside modern European cities, Cambridge, Mass.: MIT Press.

Hasenöhrl, Ute (2018): "Rural electrification in the British Empire." In: History of Retailing and Consumption 4/1, pp. 10-27.

Hasenöhrl, Ute (2014): "Neue Perspektiven auf die Geschichte der Beleuchtung und der Nacht: Ein Forschungsbericht." In: Neue Politische Literatur 59/1, pp. 88-112.

Hasenöhrl, Ute/van der Straeten, Jonas (2016): "Connecting the Empire: New research perspectives on infrastructures and the environment in the (post)colonial world." In: NTM 24/4, pp. 355-391.

Hein, Carola (2018): "Oil spaces: The global petroleumscape in the Rotterdam/The Hague Area." In: Journal of Urban History 44, pp. 887-929.

Hesse, Nicole (2018): "Under pressure: Low-tech wind energy landscapes in times of energy transitions, 1880-1930.", paper for the Conference: "How new are the renewables? Historicizing energy transitions", Munich, 21-23 February 2018, unpublished manuscript.

Hesse, Nicole (2016): "Windwerkerei: Praktiken der Windenergienutzung in der frühen deutschen Umweltbewegung." In: Technikgeschichte 83/2, pp. 125-150.

Heymann, Matthias (1998): "Signs of Hubris: The shaping of wind technology styles in Germany, Denmark, and the United States, 1940-1990." In: Technology and Culture 439, pp. 641-670.

Hirsh, Richard/Jones, Christopher (2014): "History's contributions to energy research and policy." In: Energy Research & Social Science 3, pp. 106-111.

Högselius, Per (2013): Red gas: Russia and the origins of European energy dependence, New York: Palgrave Macmillan.

Hoag, Heather J. (2013): Developing the rivers of East and West Africa: An environmental history. London: Bloomsbury Academic.

Hughes, Thomas P. (1983): Networks of power: Electrification in western society. 1880-1930, Baltimore: Johns Hopkins University Press.

Irsigler, Franz (1991): "Bündelung von Energie in der mittelalterlichen Stadt: Einige Modellannahmen." In: Saeculum 42, pp. 308-318.

Johnson, Bob (2014): Carbon nation: Fossil fuels in the making of American culture, Lawrence: University Press of Kansas.

Jones, Christopher F. (2016): "Petromyopia: Oil and the energy humanities." In: Humanities 5/2, pp. 1-10.

Jones, Christopher F. (2014): Routes of power: Energy and modern America, Cambridge: Harvard University Press.

Jones, Christopher F. (2011): "The carbon-consuming home: Residential markets and energy transitions." In: Enterprise & Society 12/4, pp. 790-823.

Jones, Christopher F. (2010): "A landscape of energy abundance: Anthracite coal, canals, and the roots of American fossil fuel depedence." In: Environmental History 15/3, pp. 449-484.

Kaijser, Arne (2018): "Driving on wood: The Swedish transition to power gas during WWII", paper for the Conference: "How new are the renewables? Historicizing energy transitions", Munich, 21-23 February 2018, unpublished manuscript.

Kale, Sunila (2014): "Structures of power: Electrification in colonial India." In: Comparative Studies of South Asia, Africa and the Middle East 34/3, pp. 445-475.

Kalmbach, Karena (2017): "Revisiting the nuclear age: State of the art research in nuclear history." In: Neue Politische Literatur, 62/1, pp. 49-69.

Kander, Astrid/Malanima, Paolo/Warde, Paul (2013): Power to the people: Energy in Europe over the last five centuries, Princeton, NJ: Princeton University Press.

Kim, Eunhye/Barles, Sabine (2012): "The energy consumption of Paris and its supply areas from the eighteenth century to the present." In: Regional Environmental Change 12, pp. 295-310.

Knoll, Martin (2017): "Energie und Geschichte." In: Siedlungsforschung 34, pp. 99-110.

Knoll, Martin (2007): "Von der prekären Effizienz des Wassers: Die Flüsse Donau und Regen als Transportwege der städtischen Holzversorgung Regensburgs im 18. und 19. Jahrhundert." In: Saeculum 58, pp. 33-58.

Krausmann, Fridolin (2013): "A city and its hinterland: Vienna's energy metabolism 1800-2006." In: Martin Schmid et al. (eds.), Long term socio-ecological research: Studies in society-nature interactions across spatial and temporal scales, New York: Springer, pp. 247-268.

Kupper, Patrick (2017a): "Energy and progress: Understanding energy transitions from a world history perspective." In: Christina Newinger/Christina Geyer/Sarah Kellberg (eds.), Energie.wenden: Energy transitions as chance and challenge in our time, Munich: oekom, pp. 12-15.

Kupper, Patrick/Melsted, Odinn/Pallua, Irene (2017b): "On Power: Neue Literatur zur Energiegeschichte." In: NTM 25, pp. 143-158.

Kupper, Patrick/Pallua, Irene (2016): Energieregime in der Schweiz seit 1800, Bern: Bundesamt für Energie BFE.

Lackner, Helmut (2018): "Ausstellungsbesprechung: Das Zeitalter der Kohle: Eine europäische Geschichte. Eine Ausstellung des Ruhr Museums und des Deutschen Bergbau-Museums in der Kokerei Zollverein in Essen." In: Technikgeschichte 85/3, pp. 203-215.

Lagendijk, Vincent (2016): "Europe's Rhine power: Connections, borders, and flows." In: Water History 8/1, pp. 23-39.

Lagendijk, Vincent/van der Vleuten, Erik (2013): "Inventing electrical Europe: Interdependences, borders, vulnerabilities." In: Per Högselius/Anique Hommels/Arne Kaijser/Erik van der Vleuten (eds.), The making of Europe's critical infrastructure: Common connections and shared vulnerabilities, New York: Palgrave Macmillan, pp. 62-101.

Labussière, Olivier/Nadaï, Alain (2018): Energy transitions, New York: Palgrave Macmillan.

Landry, Marc (2015): "Environmental consequences of the peace: The Great War, dammed lakes, and hydraulic history in the eastern Alps." In: Environmental History 20/3, pp. 422-448.

Larkin, Brian (2015): "Ambient infrastructures: Generator life in Nigeria." In: Technosphere Magazine, September 30, 2017 (https://technosphere-magazine.hkw.de/article1/cd07bf50-921e-11e6-9341-7d6509c7f586/76704180-91e7-11e6-8d22-0bf4eeadcfb0).

Lehmann, Philipp N. (2016): "Infinite power to change the world: Hydroelectricity and engineered climate change in the Atlantropa Project." In: The American Historical Review 121/1, pp. 70-100.

Lorkowski, Nina (2019): Warmes Wasser – Weiße Ware: Energiewende im Badezimmer 1880-1939, Paderborn: Ferdinand Schöningh, unpublished manuscript.

Löwen, John-Wesley (2015): Die dezentrale Stromwirtschaft: Industrie, Kommunen und Staat in der westdeutschen Elektrizitätswirtschaft 1927-1957, Berlin: De Gruyter.

Malm, Andreas (2016): Fossil capital: The rise of steam power and the roots of global warming, London: Verso.

McNeill, John (2000): Something new under the sun: An environmental history of the twentieth-century world, New York: W. W. Norton.

Melosi, Martin (1982): "Energy transitions in the nineteenth century economy." In: George H. Daniels/Mark H. Rose (eds.), Energy and transport: Historical perspectives on policy issues, Beverly Hills: Sage Publications, pp. 55-69.

Melsted, Odinn/Pallua, Irene (2018): "The historical transition from coal to hydrocarbons: Previous explanations and the need for an integrative perspective." In: Canadian Journal of History 53/3, pp. 395-422.

Mitchell, Timothy (2011): Carbon democray: Political power in the age of oil, London: Verso.

Mittlefehldt, Sarah (2018): "Wood waste and race: The industrialization of biomass energy technologies and environmental justice." In: Technology and Culture 59/4, pp. 875-898.

Mosley, Stephen (2001): The chimney of the world: A history of smoke pollution in Victorian and Edwardian Manchester, London: White Horse Press.

Mumford, Lewis (1934): Technics and civilization, New York: Harcourt, Brace and Co.

Nye, David E. (2010): When the lights went out: A history of blackouts in America, Cambridge, Mass.: MIT Press.

Nye, David E. (1990): Electrifying America: Social meanings of a new technology, 1880-1940, Cambridge, Mass.: MIT Press.

Osietzki, Maria (1996): "Das symbolische Kapital der Technik: Ein kulturhistorischer Blick auf die Elektrifizierung." In: Burkhard Dietz/Michael Fessner (eds.), Technische Intelligenz und 'Kulturfaktor Technik': Kulturvorstellungen von Technikern und Ingenieuren zwischen Kaiserreich und früher Bundesrepublik Deutschland, Münster: Waxmann, pp. 87-104.

Parrinello, Giacomo (2018): "Systems of power: A spatial envirotechnical approach to water power and industrialization in the Po valley of Italy, ca. 1880-1970." In: Technology and Culture 59/3, pp. 652-688.

Periman, Richard D. (2004): "Energy flow in early industrial world." In: Encyclopedia of Energy 1, pp. 849-858.

Pfister, Christian (2003): "Energiepreis und Umweltbelastung: Zum Stand der Diskussion über das 1950er Syndrom." In: Wolfram Siemann/Nils Freytag (eds.), Umweltgeschichte: Themen und Perspektiven, Munich: C.H. Beck, pp. 61-86.

Pfister, Christian (ed.) (1995): Das 1950er Syndrom: Der Weg in die Konsumgesellschaft, Bern: Haupt.

Platt, Harold (2005): Shock cities: The environmental transformation and reform of Manchester and Chicago, Chicago/London: University of Chicago Press.

Quivik, Fredric (2017): "Steam and power." In: Technology and Culture 58/3, pp. 866-868.

Radkau, Joachim (1997): "Das Rätsel der städtischen Brennholzversorgung im hölzernen Zeitalter." In: Dieter Schott (ed.), Energie und Stadt in Europa: Von der vorindustriellen 'Holznot' bis zur Ölkrise der 1970er Jahre, Stuttgart: Franz Steiner, pp. 43-75.

Sandwell, Ruth W. (2017): "People, place and power: Rural electrification in Canada, 1890-1950." In: Paul Brassley/Jeremy Burchardt/Karen Sayer (eds.), Transforming the countryside: The electrification of rural Britain, London/New York: Routledge, pp. 178-204.

Schmid, Martin/Schoder, Angelika (2017): "Where technology and environmentalism meet: The remaking of the Austrian Danube for hydropower." In: Hrvoje Petrić/Ivana Žebec Šilj (eds.), Environmentalism in central and southeastern Europe: Historical perspectives, New York: Lexington Books, pp. 3-21.

Schot, Johan (2016): "The roles of users in shaping transitions to new energy systems." In: Nature Energy 1, pp. 1-7.

Schott, Dieter (2019): "Energizing European cities: From wood provision to solar panels. Providing energy for urban demand, 1800-2000." In: Tim Soens/Dieter Schott/Michael Toyka-Seid/Bert De Munck (eds.), Urbanizing nature: Actors and agency (dis)connecting cities and nature Since 1500, New York: Routledge, pp. 135-156.

Schott, Dieter (2014): Europäische Urbanisierung: 1000-2000, Cologne/Weimar/Vienna: Böhlau.

Schott, Dieter (1999): Die Vernetzung der Stadt: Kommunale Energiepolitik, öffentlicher Nahverkehr und die 'Produktion' der modernen Stadt. Darmstadt

– Mannheim – Mainz. 1880-1918, Darmstadt: Wissenschaftliche Buchgesellschaft.

Schott, Dieter (1997): "Einführung." In: Dieter Schott (ed.), Energie und Stadt in Europa: Von der vorindustriellen 'Holznot' bis zur Ölkrise der 1970er Jahre, Stuttgart: Franz Steiner, pp. 7-42.

Schott, Dieter/Soens, Tim/Toyka-Seid, Michael/De Munck, Bert (2019): "Introduction: Did cities change nature? A long-term perspective." In: Dieter Schott/Tim Soens/Michael Toyka-Seid/Bert de Munck (eds.), Urbanizing nature: Actors and agency (dis)connecting cities and nature Since 1500, New York: Routledge, pp. 3-25.

Seow, Victor (2014): "Fuels and flows: Rethinking histories of transport and mobility through energy." In: Transfers 4/3, pp. 112-116.

Showers, Kate B. (2009): "Congo river's Grand Inga hydroelectricity scheme: Linking environmental history, policy and impact." In: Water History 1/1, pp. 31-58.

Shulman, Peter A. (2015): Coal and empire: The birth of energy security in industrial America, Baltimore: Johns Hopkins University Press.

Sieferle, Rolf-Peter (2001): The subterranean forest: Energy systems and the industrial revolution, Cambridge: White Horse Press.

Sieferle, Rolf-Peter (1982): Der unterirdische Wald: Energiekrise und Industrielle Revolution, Munich: C.H. Beck.

Smil, Vaclav (2017): Energy and civilization: A history, Cambridge: The MIT Press.

Steinberg, Theodore (1991): Nature incorporated: Industrialization and the waters of New England, Cambridge: Cambridge University Press.

Stier, Bernhard (2000): "Die neue Elektrizitätsgeschichte zwischen kulturhistorischer Erweiterung und kommunikationspolitischer Instrumentalisierung." In: Vierteljahresschrift für Sozial- und Wirtschaftsgeschichte 87, pp. 477-487.

Thorsheim, Peter (2006): Inventing pollution: Coal smoke and culture in Britain since 1800, Athens, Ohio: Ohio University Press.

Tischler, Julia (2014): "Whose Power? Energie und Entwicklung in der Spätkolonialzeit am Beispiel des Kariba-Staudamms in der Zentralafrikanischen Föderation." In: Birte Förster/Martin Bauch (eds.), Wasserinfrastrukturen und Macht von der Antike bis zur Gegenwart, München: De Gruyter, pp. 266-286.

Tomory, Leslie (2012): "The environmental history of the early British gas industry, 1812-1830." In: Environmental History 17/1, pp. 29-54.

Trentmann, Frank (2016): Materielle Kultur und Energiekonsum: Verbraucher und ihre Rolle für eine nachhaltige Entwicklung, Munich: oekom.

Uekötter, Frank (2015): "Bergbau und Umwelt im 19. und 20. Jahrhundert." In: Klaus Tenfelde/Stefan Berger/Hans-Christoph Seidel (eds.), Rohstoffgewinnung im Strukturwandel: Der deutsche Bergbau im 20. Jahrhundert (Geschichte des deutschen Bergbaus. Bd. 4), Münster: De Gruyter, pp. 539-563.

Uekötter, Frank (2007): Umweltgeschichte im 19. und 20. Jahrhundert, Munich: Oldenbourg.

Unger, Richard W. (ed.) (2013): "Energy transitions in history: Global cases of continuity and change." In: RCC Perspectives 2.

van der Straeten, Jonas (2015): "Electrification in Tanzania from a historical perspective: Discourses of development and the marginalization of the rural poor." In: Martina Schäfer (ed.), Micro perspectives for decentralized energy supply: Proceedings of the international conference, Berlin: Universitäts-Verlag der TU Berlin, pp. 156-161.

van der Vleuten, Erik (2016): "Small-scale hydropower in the Netherlands: Problems and strategies of system builders." In: Renewable and Sustainable Energy Reviews 59, pp. 1493-1503.

van Laak, Dirk (2012): "Unter Strom: Über Dynamos und politische Dynamik." In: Hendrik Ehrhardt/Thomas Kroll (eds.), Energie in der modernen Gesellschaft: Zeithistorische Perspektiven, Frankfurt a.M./New York: Vandenhoeck & Ruprecht, pp. 17-31.

White, Richard (1995): The organic machine: The remaking of the Columbia River, New York: Hill & Wang.

Wrigley, Edward A. (2010): Energy and the English industrial revolution, Cambridge: Cambridge University Press.

Zängl, Wolfgang (1989): Deutschlands Strom: Die Politik der Elektrifizierung von 1866 bis heute, Frankfurt a.M.: Campus.

Zachmann, Karin (2012): "Past and present energy societies: How energy connects politics, technologies and cultures." In: Nina Möllers/Karin Zachmann (eds.), Past and Present energy societies: How energy connects politics, technologies and cultures, Bielefeld: transcript, pp. 7-45.

Zumbrägel, Christian (2018): 'Viele Wenige machen ein Viel': Eine Technik- und Umweltgeschichte der Kleinwasserkraft (1880-1930), Paderborn: Ferdinand Schöningh.

Zumbrägel, Christian (2015): "Dreißig Jahre danach: Thomas P. Hughes' Networks of Power als Leitkonzept der Stadt- und Technikgeschichte." In: Informationen zur modernen Stadtgeschichte 1, pp. 93-98.

Zumbrägel, Christian (2014): "Die vorindustriellen Holzströme Wiens: Ein sozionaturales großtechnisches System?" In: Technikgeschichte 81, pp. 335-362.

Animals in Urban-Environmental History

Dorothee Brantz

Are there animals in the library? At first sight this might appear like a rather preposterous question; after all the library is probably one of the most human mind-centred places. Here, even human bodies are reduced to vehicles for the transmission of ideas, so how could this be a place for animals (apart from the proverbial bookworm)? Actually, libraries are full of animals. Just because no one has ever bothered to count the spiders, bugs, and perhaps even mice etc. that inhabit libraries, this does not mean that they are not there. But more to the point, libraries are full of books that deal with animals. In almost any field of enquiry, be it literature, medicine, art, geography, biology, history, medicine, or philosophy, animals play an important role in the (con-)textualisation of ideas about life. Indeed, libraries are becoming places where a growing number of scholars are mining a wide variety of sources in order to think and write about animals.

Libraries point to the multiplicity of human-animal engagements on a number of levels ranging from the physical to the representational. They attest to how animals are represented in textual sources, how they are narrated by scholars, and of course how actual animals share this space. What is true for the library also applies to other areas of urban life, e.g., the street, the restaurant, the university. The interactions of humans and animals have added to the historical wealth of the urban fabric. In what follows, I will pursue a 'what was—what is—what could be' approach to sketch how animals were slowly but surely integrated into historical—and particularly urban-environmental—scholarship over the past four decades.

Animals in Urban-Environmental History

Animals have always been part of urban history. Since the ancient period, the construction of cities, the mobility of urban societies, as well as the provision of human populations with food, clothing and other goods heavily depended on animals, their labour power and material products. Cities were (and still are) filled with animals and their representations. Until well into the 20th century, horses served as the main means of transport. Donkeys, dogs, camels, elephants and many others also served that purpose. The physical shape of cities was deeply dependent on these animals and their ability to transport heavy materials for the construction of cities or the removal of trash. Pets, circus and zoo animals of all kinds were purposefully brought to cities to accompany and entertain people. Millions of specimen were hunted all over the world to fill the exhibition halls and research laboratories areas of curiosity cabinets, natural history museums, and universities. Livestock was herded to cities to feed people, cows to give their milk. Countless free roaming animals, including birds, fish, rabbits, monkeys, rats etc. have inhabited cities alongside human populations. Not to forget the millions of insects, bugs and other small creatures that thrived particularly in cities. Their presence added to the biological diversity of cities, but also to environmental pollution (e.g., stench, water pollution, excrement) or even to the spread of contagious diseases. Together, these animals contributed to each city's distinct urban ecosystem, to the sights, sounds, and smells of the city in its distinct seasonal variations.

This centuries-long engagement left countless primary source materials about urban animals ranging from political treatises and medical reports to technical manuals; from artistic representations to handbooks on urban hygiene to private accounts, photographs, films, and statistical assessments. Despite this wealth of sources, urban historians were not particularly interested in how animals affected the development of cities because cities were commonly regarded as 'man-made' spaces created solely through human intentions and for human purposes. In the beginning, even environmental historians followed this line of argument by refusing to view cities as legitimate areas for environmental investigations (Worster 1988; Meisner Rosen/Tarr 1994; Hays 1993; Hays 1998). Despite this initial reluctance, urban-environmental history has become an established subfield of environmental history, not the least because it highlighted some of the unintended consequences of urbanisation such as the massive production of waste and water pollution as well as factors beyond human control (Tarr 1996; Melosi 2000; Platt 2004; Luckin/Massard-Guilbaud/Schott 2005; Schott/Toyka-Seid 2008; Schott 2014). In many of these accounts, animals are mentioned, but the interest in urban animals actually grew out of another field of study, namely cultural history.

Cultural historians always showed a great interest in the representation of the hitherto underrepresented, i.e., women, minorities, and eventually animals. The study of the historical relations between humans and animals started with pet culture and much of the history of pets was, not surprisingly, an urban story. The pioneering historians in this field examined how dogs, parrots, monkeys, cats etc. captured the boudoirs and private homes of (bourgeois) urbanites in London, Paris and other large metropoles (Ritvo 1989; Kete 1994; Robbins 2002; Mason 2005). Indeed, they often described the emergence of pet cultures in distinct reference to bourgeois attempts at social distinction. Other cultural institutions like zoos have also been discussed in relation to the emergence of bourgeois urban culture (Klös/Frädrich/Klös 1994; Akerberg 2001; Dietrich/von Engelhardt/Rieke-Müller 2001; Baratay 2002; Rothfels 2002; Hanson 2004; Ash 2008; Miller 2013). Apart from specific architectural manifestations, these histories have also heightened our understanding of the troubled presence of the exotic and colonial in urban centres. Generally, the urban dimension has been pronounced in all kinds of histories regarding human-animal relations even if these publications did not explicitly address the urban context (Rothfels 2002; Brantz/Mauch 2010; Krüger/Steinbrecher/Wischermann 2014; Spannring 2015). One could argue that the 'animal turn' has, to some extent, coincided with an 'urban turn' (Ritvo 2004; Ritvo 2007; Brantz 2008; Wischermann 2009).

The question of class provided another key theme in the first urban-environmental histories of human-animal relations. For instance, Clay McShane's and Joel Tarr's (2007) study of urban horses examined the impact of social class on the engagement with and treatment of horses in 19th century Boston. The understanding of animals as part of the provisioning of cities, the emergence of particular hygiene regimes, urban entertainment, and everyday life has brought forth a broad array of studies in recent years, for instance on slaughterhouses (Brantz 2003; Lee 2008; Pacyga 2015; Nieradzik 2017). Specific animals, most notably dogs (McKenzei 2008; Wang 2012; Pearson 2017), but also rats (Sullivan 2004) have received scholarly attention to show how urban societies integrated those animals that were desired, while it excluded those deemed threatening. In general, the history of human-animal relations has enhanced our critical understanding of urban regimes of inclusion and exclusion, both with regard to historical urban practices across the centuries and also with regard to theory and method-oriented historiographical debates.

Current Outlooks

In current research, environmental and cultural perspectives increasingly converge due to the spectrum of sources used, but also because of the conceptual frameworks that are employed. Recent edited volumes about animals in urban history attest to this spectrum of perspectives (Atkins 2012; Dean/Ingram/Sethna 2017; Hauck et al. 2017). Moreover, the last years saw the emergence of a growing number of animal histories of particular cities, for instance about London (Velten 2013), New York (McNeur 2015), or Seattle (Brown 2016). In general, one could argue that animals are finding their way into mainstream history because an increasing number of urban histories mention animals as part of the historical urban-environmental and socio-cultural landscape.

Conceptually, the question of agency plays a particularly central role in this regard (Hribal 2007; Pearson 2015; Pearson 2017; Wirth et al. 2016). In a posthumanist move, scholars are questioning the human-centred conception of agency to call for a more inclusive understanding of who shapes (urban) environmental and social developments. The argument is transformative in that it seeks to broaden the spectrum of actors and hence the understanding of social inclusion. Geographers were among the first to insist that animals cannot simply be viewed in light of (human) representations, but that they should be regarded as independent, practice-oriented (urban) actors (Philo/Wilbert 2007). The question of urban agency might point towards new directions in thinking about the environmental integration of cities more generally (de Munck et al. 2019). With regard to animals, the concept of agency opens up new methodological approaches but also ethical concerns (Brantz 2017).

Another innovative direction in thinking about the relation between animals and human society is the concept of liminality or 'limianimality' as proposed by Clemens Wischermann and others (Wischermann 2017; Wischermann/Steinbrecher/Howell 2018). Focusing on the 'betwixt and between' spaces and times, this perspective calls into question the traditional boundaries between humans and animals to further expose the constructed nature of pre-modern and modern binaries from multiple animate perspectives like stray dogs, bats, backyard birds to name but a few. The edited collection *Animal History in the Modern City* (Wischermann/Steinbrecher/Howell 2018) brings together hitherto separate animate universes to question underlying taxonomies, such as domesticated and wild, city and countryside, or inside and outside. The contributions to this multi-perspective volume transgress chronological boundaries, bringing together the early modern and modern periods. They also transcend geographical boundaries reaching from Europe across the Atlantic to the Americas, and across the Mediterranean to Africa, thus offering a thought-provoking perspective on how such innovative scholarship can work.

Apart from new conceptual approaches, the field has also witnessed the evolution of particular sub-genres. A good example of this is the history of zoological gardens. Whereas earlier histories tended to focus on the actual institution of zoos and their internal developments, recent histories read zoos in the context of larger urban developments (Wessely 2008; Bruce 2017; Roscher 2018). Another sub-genre where existing narratives are taken up and pushed in new directions is the study of urban wildlife. The study of urban wildlife has been a topic for popular accounts for quite some time, but in recent years it is gaining scholarly attention in light of heightened concerns about biodiversity. Cities are increasingly recognised as a space where non-domesticated animals play an important role in everyday life. Scholarly as well popular publications discuss the presence of wild animals in urban settlements and the consequences for humans and urban ecologies (Ineichen 1997; Biehler 2011; Biehler 2013; Benson 2013; Kegel 2013; Van Horn 2015; Lotzkat 2016).

Some Future Possibilities

Having looked at the developments of human-animal studies in urban-environmental history since the emergence of the field in the 1990s, one might wonder what some possible directions for the future of this field might be. In what follows, I would like to point to some possibilities, particularly as they present themselves in relation to questions of scope and scale. Firstly, there is a need to broaden our geographical scope: thus far, most histories have focused on Europe and North America, even more specifically on the major cities of these two continents. Thus, there is a need to move to other continents as well as down the scale towards smaller cities in Europe and North America. There is a growing number of scholars studying Australia (Franklin 2006; Gaynor 2004; Gaynor 2007), different regions in the Middle East (Mikhai 2014) and Africa (Swart 2010; Krüger 2014; Speitkamp/ Zehnle 2014; Gißibl 2016). However, there are still few specifically urban-environmental accounts of human-animal relations for these and other regions of the world. Expanding our geographic scope will broaden our understanding of the local specificities and also of the distinctions in the physical presence, cultural interpretations, and ecological consequences of animals in urban areas. This would enable us to build a more global perspective on urban human-animal relations.

Secondly, another potentiality lies in the shift of the temporal scope. We need to move beyond the modern period and explore deeper into the past. The pioneering work of Erica Fudge (2006; 2013; 2018) has opened many venues into the study of human-animal relations in the early modern period, thus far primarily in Britain (cf. Crane 2012; Tague 2015). Even more to the point, Aline Steinbrecher's (2009) research documents the significance of animals for early modern urban development (cf. Turnbull 2010). At the same time, we still have few studies that investigate the medieval and ancient periods, when animals played a crucial role in the construction and provision of cities as well as for the entertainment of urbanites. In general, a more epoch-transgressing perspective might be fruitful. Apart from such long historical timespans, other environmentally driven temporalities, like the seasons or night and day, promise new insights into the interactions of humans and non-humans in urban spaces. (Urban) environments are shaped by seasonal differences that enforce an alternative— circular—temporality that overlays linear historical development. It seems to be obvious that cities provide different environments in the summer and in winter, but empirical research on this issue still remains scarce. Similarly, the long geological timespans currently discussed in regard to the concept of the 'antrhopocene' refer to a temporal dimension that reaches far beyond the usual historical epochs historians work with (Chakrabarty 2018). Thinking about temporal scales in an environmental context, we need to consider a broader range of natural temporalities.

Lastly, few studies investigate the different patterns of movement and behaviour among urban animals—the swarms, the hives and herds, the migratory paths in and through cities as well as the conflicts among different kinds of animals in the city. So far, this has been the domain of animal ecologists, but historians have recently entered into dialogue with ecologists. On the level of urban research, this might have the potential of looking more closely at animal behaviour and exploring the creation of distinct urban places for animals—anything from architectural measures to ward off birds to the rise of urban bird sanctuaries, dog parks, pet groomers and insect hotels. Urban-environmental scholars have contributed a great deal to a broader vision of the urban landscape, but we still have a way to go to promote a more relational understanding of urban co-habitation and a truly multispecies society (Haraway 2003; Wolf 2009). The question remains, and it is not just a scholarly one, how we create a more inclusive urban environment where animals are regarded as integral rather than as marginal and where they are considered for their own sake and not just in relation to human intentionality. Thinking of cities as ecosystems means recognising the urban as a multispecies society—as a zoöpolis (Wolch/Emel 1998). In the age of climate change this appears paramount in order to protect or even promote local urban biodiversity (Gandy 2018), but also to enhance our awareness of the global consequences of urban living.

References

Akerberg, Sofia (2001): Knowledge and pleasure at Regent's park: The gardens of the zoological society of London during the nineteenth century, Umea: Umea University Press.
Ash, Mitchell (ed.) (2008): Mensch, Tier und Zoo: Der Tiergarten Schönbrunn im internationalen Vergleich vom 18. Jahrhundert bis Heute, Vienna: Böhlau.
Atkins, Peter (ed.) (2012): Animal cities: Beastly urban histories, Burlington: Ashgate.
Baratay, Eric (2002): Zoo: A history of zoological gardens in the west, London: Reaktion Books.
Benson, Etienne (2013): "The urbanization of the eastern gray squirrel in the United States." In: Journal of American History 100, pp. 691-710.
Biehler, Dawn (2013): Pests in the city: Flies, bedbugs, cockroaches, and rats, Seattle: University of Washington Press.

Biehler, Dawn (2011): "Embodied wildlife histories and the urban landscape." In: Environmental History 16, pp. 445-450.

Brantz, Dorothee (2017): "Assembling the multitude: Questions about agency in the urban environment." In: Urban History 44, pp. 130-136.

Brantz, Dorothee (2008): "Die 'animalische Stadt': Die Mensch-Tier-Beziehung in der Urbanisierungsforschung." In: Informationen für Moderne Stadtgeschichte 2008, pp. 86-100.

Brantz, Dorothee (2003): Slaughter in the city: The establishment of public abattoirs in nineteenth-century Paris and Berlin, Ann Arbor: Proquest/UMI Press.

Brantz, Dorothee/Mauch, Christof (eds.) (2010): Tierische Geschichte: Die Beziehung von Mensch und Tier in der Kultur der Moderne, Paderborn: Schöningh.

Brown, Frederick (2016): The city is more than human: An animal history of Seattle, Seattle: University of Washington Press.

Bruce, Gary (2017): Through the lion gate: A history of the Berlin Zoo, New York: Oxford University Press.

Chakrabarty, Dipesh (2018): "Anthropocene time." In: History and Theory 57, pp. 5-32.

Crane, Susan (2012): Animal encounters: Contacts and concepts in medieval Britain, University of Pennsylvania Press.

de Munck, Bert/Soens, Tim/Schott, Dieter/Toyka-Seid, Michael (eds.) (2019): Urbanizing nature: Actors and agency (dis)connecting cities and nature since 1500, New York: Routledge.

Dean, Joanna/Ingram, Darcy/Sethna, Christabelle (eds.) (2017): Animal metropolis: Histories of human-animal relations in urban Canada, Calgary: University of Calgary Press.

Dietrich, Lothar/Engelhardt, Dietrich von/Rieke-Müller, Annelore (eds.) (2001): Die Kulturgeschichte des Zoos, Berlin: VWB.

Franklin, Adrian (2006): Animal nation: The true story of animals and Australia, Sydney: University of New South Wales Press.

Fudge, Erica (2018): Quick cattle and dying wishes: People and their animals in early modern England, Ithaca: Cornell University Press.

Fudge, Erica (2013): "The animal face of early modern England." In: Theory, Culture and Society 30, pp. 177-198.

Fudge, Erica (2006): Brutal reasoning: Animals, rationality and humanity in early modern England, Ithaca: Cornell University Press.

Fudge, Erica (ed.) (2004): Renaissance beasts: Of animals, humans, and other wonderful creatures, Urbana: University of Illinois Press.

Gandy, Matthew (2018): "Cities in deep time: Biodiversity, metabolic rift and the urban question." In: City 22, pp. 96-105.

Gaynor, Andrea (2007): "Animal agendas: Conflict over productive animals in twentieth-century Australian cities." In: Society and Animals 15, pp. 29-42.

Gaynor, Andrea (2004): "Animal husbandry and house wifery? Gender and suburban household production in Perth and Melbourne, 1890-1950." In: Australian Historical Studies 36, pp. 238-254.

Gißibl, Bernhard (2016): "The conservation of luxury: Safari hunting and the consumption of wildlife in 20th-century east Africa." In: Bernd-Stefan Grewe/Karin Hofmeester (eds.), Luxury in global perspective: Commodities and practice, Cambridge: Cambridge University Press, pp. 261-298.

Gißibl, Bernhard (2016): The nature of German imperialism: Conservation and the politics of wildlife in colonial east Africa, New York/Oxford: Berghahn.

Haraway, Dona (2003): The companion species manifesto, Chicago: University of Chicago Press.

Hanson, Elizabeth (2004): Animal attractions: Nature on display in American zoos, Princeton: Princeton UP.

Hauck, Thomas/Stefanie Hennecke/André Krebber/Wiebke Reinert/Mieke Roscher (eds.) (2017): Urbane Tier-Räume, Berlin: Reimer.

Hays, Samuel P. (1998): "The role of urbanization in environmental history." In: Samuel P. Hays (ed.), Explorations in environmental history, Pittsburgh: University of Pittsburgh Press, pp. 75-84.

Hays, Samuel P. (1993): "From the history of the city to the history of urbanized society." In: Journal of Urban History 19, pp. 3-25.

Hribal, Jason C. (2007): "Animals, agency, and class: Writing the history of animals from below." In: Human Ecology Review 14, pp. 101-112.

Ineichen, Steffen (1997): Die wilden Tiere in der Stadt: Zur Naturgeschichte der Stadt, Zürich: Waldgut.

Kegel, Bernhard (2013): Tiere in der Stadt: Eine Naturgeschichte, Munich: Dumont.

Kete, Kathleen (1994): The beast in the Boudoir: Petkeeping in nineteenth century Paris, Berkeley: University of California Press.

Klös, Heinz-Georg/Frädrich, Hans/Klös, Ursula (1994): Die Arche Noah an der Spree: 150 Jahre Zoologischer Garten in Berlin, Berlin: FAB.

Krebber, André/Roscher, Mieke (eds.) (2011): "Themenheft 'Tiere und Geschichtsschreibung'." In: Werkstatt Geschichte 56.

Krüger, Gesine (2014): "Das koloniale Tier: Natur-Kultur-Geschichte." In: Thomas Forrer/Angelika Linke (eds.), Wo ist Kultur? Perspektiven der Kulturanalyse, Zürich: vdf, pp. 73-94.

Krüger, Gesine/Steinbrecher, Aline/Wischermann, Clemens (eds.) (2014): Tiere und Geschichte: Konturen einer Animate History, Stuttgart: Steiner.

Lee, Paula Young (ed.) (2008): Meat modernity and the rise of the slaughterhouse, New Hampshire: University Press of New England.

Lotzkat, Sebastian (2016): Landflucht der Wildtiere: Wie Wildschwein, Waschbär, Wolf und Co. unsere Städte erobern, Hamburg: Rowohlt.

Luckin, Bill/Massard-Guilbaud, Geneviève/Schott, Dieter (eds.) (2005): Resources of the city: Contributions to an environmental history of Europe, Aldershot: Ashgate.

Mason, Jennifer (2005): Civilized creatures: Urban animals, sentimental culture, and American literature, 1850-1900, Baltimore: The Johns Hopkins University Press.

McKenzie, Kirsten (2008): "Dogs and the public sphere: The ordering of social space in the early nineteenth-century Cape Town." In: Lance van Sittert/Sandra Swart (eds.), Canis Africanis: A dog history of Southern Africa, Leiden: Brill, pp. 91-111.

McNeur, Catherine (2015): Taming Manhattan: Environmental battles in the Antebellum city, Cambridge: Harvard UP.

McShane, Clay/Tarr, Joel (2007): The horse in the city: Living machines in the nineteenth century, Baltimore: Johns Hopkins University Press.

Meisner Rosen, Christine/Tarr, Joel Arthur (eds.) (1994): "The importance of an urban perspective in environmental history." In: The Journal of Urban History, 20, pp. 299-310.

Melosi, Martin (2000): The sanitary city: Urban infrastructure in America from colonial times to the present, Baltimore: Johns Hopkins University Press.

Mikhail, Alan (2014): The animal in Ottoman Egypt, New York: Oxford UP.

Miller, Ian Jared (2013): The nature of the beasts: Empire and exhibition at the Tokyo imperial zoo, Berkeley: University of California Press.

Nieradzik, Lukasz (2017): Der Wiener Schlachthof St. Marx: Transformation einer Arbeitswelt zwischen 1851 und 1914, Göttingen: Vandenhoeck & Ruprecht.

Pacyga, Dominic (2015): Slaughterhouse: Chicago's Union Stockyard and the world it made, Chicago: University of Chicago Press.

Pearson, Chris (2017): "History and animal agencies." In: Linda Kalof (ed.), Oxford Handbook of Animal Studies, Oxford: Oxford UP.

Pearson, Chris (2017): "Stray dogs and the making of modern Paris." In: Past & Present 1/234, pp. 137-172.

Pearson, Chris (2015): "Beyond 'resistance': Rethinking nonhuman agency for a 'more-than-human' world." In: European Review of History: Revue européenne d'histoire 22, pp. 709-725.

Philo, Chris/Wilbert, Chris (eds.) (2000): Animal spaces, beastly places: New geographies of human-animal relations, London: Verso.

Platt, Harold (2004): Shock cities: The environmental transformation and reform of Manchester and Chicago, Chicago: University of Chicago Press.

Roscher, Mieke (2018): "Liminality in the post-war zoo: Animals in East and West Berlin, 1955-1961." In: Clemens Wischermann/Aline Steinbrecher/Philip Howell (eds.), Animal history in the modern city: Exploring Liminality, London: Bloomsbury, pp. 201-219.

Roscher, Mieke (2015): "Von einer Geschichte mit Tieren zu einer Tiergeschichte" In: Reingard Spannring/Karin Schachinger/Gabriela Kompatscher/Alejandro Boucabeille (eds.), Disziplinierte Tiere? Perspektiven der Human-Animal Studies für die wissenschaftlichen Disziplinen, Bielefeld: transcript, pp. 75-100.

Rothfels, Nigel (2002): Savages and beasts: The birth of the modern zoo, Baltimore: Johns Hopkins University Press.

Schott, Dieter (2014): Europäische Urbanisierung, 1000-2000: Eine umwelthistorische Einführung, Cologne/Weimar/Vienna: Böhlau.

Schott, Dieter/Toyka-Seid, Michael (eds.) (2008): Die europäische Stadt und ihre Umwelt, Darmstadt: Wissenschaftliche Buchgesellschaft.

Speitkamp, Winfried/Zehnle, Stephanie (eds.) (2014): Afrikanische Tierräume: Historische Verortungen, Cologne: Köppe.

Steinbrecher, Aline (2009): "Die gezähmte Natur in der Wohnstube: Zur Kulturpraktik der Hundehaltung in frühneuzeitlichen Städten." In: Sophie Ruppel/Aline Steinbrecher (eds.),'Die Natur ist überall bey uns': Mensch und Natur in der Frühen Neuzeit, Zürich: Chronos, pp. 125-143.

Sullivan, Robert (2004): Rats: Observations on the history and habitat of the city's most unwanted inhabitants, New York: Bloomsbury.

Swart, Sandra (2010): Riding high: Horses, humans and history in South Africa, Johannesburg: Wits UP.

Tague, Ingrid (2015): Animal companions: Pets and social change in eighteenth-century Britain, University Park, Pennsylvania: Pennsylvania State University Press.

Tarr, Joel (2010): "Urban environmental history." In: Frank Uekötter (ed.), The turning points of environmental history, Pittsburgh: University of Pittsburgh Press, pp. 72-89.

Tarr, Joel (1996): In search for the ultimate sink: Urban pollution in historical perspective, Akron: University of Akron Press.

Turnbull, Alexandra (2010): "The horse in landscape: Animals, grooming, labour and the city in the seventeenth-century Netherlands." In: Queen's Journal of Visual and Material Culture 3, pp. 1-24.

Van Horn, Gavin (2015): City creatures: Animal encounters in the Chicago wilderness, Chicago: University of Chicago Press.

Velten, Hannah (2013): Beastly London: A history of animals in the city, London: Reaktion Books.

Wang, Jessica (2012): "Dogs and the making of the American state: Voluntary association, state power, and the politics of animal control in New York City, 1850-1920." In: Journal of American History 98, pp. 998-1024.

Wessely, Christina (2008): Künstliche Tiere: Zoologische Gärten und urbane Moderne, Berlin: Kadmos.

Wirth, Sven/Laue, Anett/Kurth, Markus/Dornenzweig, Katharina/Bossert, Leonie/Balgar, Karsten (eds.) (2016): Das Handeln der Tiere: Tierliche Agency im Fokus der Human-Animal Studies, Bielefeld: transcript.

Wischermann, Clemens (2017): "Liminale Leben(s)räume: Grenzverlegungen zwischen urbanen menschlichen Gesellschaften und anderen Tieren im 19. und 20. Jahrhundert." In: Urbane Tier-Räume, Berlin: Reimer, pp. 15-31.

Wischermann, Clemens/Steinbrecher, Aline/Howell, Philip (eds.) (2018): Animal history in the modern city: Exploring liminality, London: Bloomesbury.

Wolch, Jennifer/Jody Emel (1998): Animal geographies: Place, politics and identity in the nature-culture borderlands, London: Verso.

Wolf, Cary (2009): What is posthumanism? Minneapolis: University of Minnesota Press.

Worster, Donald (1988): "Doing environmental history." In: Donald Worster (ed.), The ends of the earth: Perspectives in modern environmental history, New York: Cambridge University Press, pp. 289-308.

Mobilities, Migration and Demography

Martin Knoll and Reinhold Reith

In his programmatic monograph advocating a new mobility paradigm in social sciences, sociologist John Urry (2007: 3) choses the example of 360.000 passengers, who are statistically flying on board of an aircraft in the air space above the territory of the USA at any given time 24/7. By this, he wants to illustrate the new dimension of mobility today's societies have reached on a global scale. With a grain of salt one could argue that the population of a medium sized city is in the sky above the USA at any moment, practicing a high impact type of mobility which predominantly connects urban centers, which requires an elaborate system of mobile and immobile infrastructures and which is a powerful agent in globalizing societies and economies as well as in 'urbanizing nature' (Soens et al. 2019). Related discussions, such as the one on the Great Acceleration or the Anthropocene (McNeill/Engelke 2014) address some of the topics bridging the areas of research between urban and environmental history. This scholarly interest in a fundamental change in the social ecology of 19th and 20th century industrialised societies, can thus not only be linked to interdisciplinary mobilities studies but also to discussions within historical demography and migration history on positions such as Wilbur Zelinsky's (1971) hypothesis of a mobility transition, which assumes that there "are definite, patterned regularities in the growth of personal mobility through space-time during recent history, and these regularities comprise an essential component of the modernization process." (ibid: 221-222). Zelinsky's hypothesis has been widely discussed and criticised for drawing a too static picture of societies before 1800 (Lucassen/Lucassen 2009). And our chapter argues for a long term perspective as well to avoid shortcomings.

Where all scholarly debates on Great Acceleration, Anthropocene, and Mobility Transition merge, is the diagnosis that indeed there is "something new under the sun" (McNeill 2000) in the way 19th and 20th century industrialized and urbanised societies organise their economies, their mobilities, their social ecologies and not least, their cities.

However, to understand, what in fact is 'new under the sun', it is necessary to carefully trace back the long term developments in premodern centuries, and to take stock of the findings of different disciplines such as historical geography, historical demography, migration history, mobilities studies, urban and environmental history. Trying to do this within the framework of a volume aiming at a concise overview over concepts of urban-environmental history is a kind of endeavour, as this is linking debates which in many cases have not been linked until now. But this endeavour may also point to a desideratum: Research should better integrate the fields of mobilities and migration into the research of urban-environmental history.

The tight links between the topics of migration and urbanisation might be hardly surprising, as already long before 1800—and increasingly thereafter—migration to cities took a considerable share of the totality of all migration processes (Lucassen/Lucassen 2009: 352, 359-362). However, two other aspects of obviously multifaceted interconnections are still largely disconnected in academic research: the histories of environment and migration. Marco Armiero and Richard Tucker (2017) have tried to fill this gap. According to them, apart from some exceptions, environmental historians "have not been significantly active in studying the history of mass migrations, nor have the historians of migration ever been interested in the environment." (ibid: 5) Armiero and Tucker have no doubt that this bias is all but reasonable, as migrants "are themselves nature on the move." (ibid: 9) And they point to the fact that the environmental history of migration—contradicting Turnerian style historiography with its extra urban focus on 'frontiers' and 'wilderness' (see the introductory chapter of this volume)—is mainly dealing with urban phenomena: "The frontier was not only somewhere west of the Mississippi in America or wherever 'wild nature met civilization.' There was also an urban frontier where immigrants were pushed to live." (ibid: 8). But investigating cities on the move entails much more than studying migrations and mobilities of individuals and groups, it also has to do with infrastructures and a reassessment of city-hinterland-relations.

Migration, Urban Demography and Urbanisation: Advocating the Long Term Perspective

Older and more recent research positions agree regarding the demographic findings on the development of the city in the Late Middle Ages and the Early Modern Period and assume that the cities could not reproduce themselves well into the 19th century. Massimo Livi Bacci has named 'unsafe living conditions' and Arthur Imhof 'unsafe lifetime' as the causes of the high mortality rate, with two-thirds to three-quarters of deaths caused by infectious diseases (Bacci 1999; Imhof 1988). Last but not least, the plague caused massive population losses (Pfister 2007; Reith 2011). Medium and large cities had high mortality rates. The pattern was characterised by high death and low birth rates and a generally advanced age of marriage.

Population losses due to diseases and outbreaks of epidemics affected cities more than rural areas (Imhof 1975: 226). Urban populations were regularly decimated by diseases during the middle ages and the early modern period well into the 19th century (Knittler 2000: 47). Historians give the structural density of the urban population and the associated hygienic conditions as the main reasons for the high mortality rates. It were the liberal bourgeois historians of the 19th and 20th centuries, who coined a negative image of the early modern city (Knittler 2000: 11). This old school of research drew a somewhat distorted picture of the early modern city as site staring at dirt. However, this image was fundamentally criticised by Ulf Dirlmeier among others (1981a/b), and later on by Annette Kinzelbach (1995). While the narrative of the dirty premodern city is still present in many recent publications, its shortcomings are obvious. The plague, to name but one example, disappeared in the 17th/18th century, when population growth in the 18th century made urban coexistence increasingly dense.

The consequence of the demographic findings are: growth and regeneration of the cities were only possible through immigration, though even demographers like Artur E. Imhof believed that our early modern ancestors had seldom left the boundaries of their villages (Imhof 1981: 35-36). In 1983, Steve Hochstadt pointed to the persistence of the image of an immobile pre-industrial society: "Premodern Germans are still described as immobile in most general demographic studies. Even city populations are considered exceptionally stable [...] Only with industrialization did German society become mobile." (Hochstadt 1983: 197-198). In 1988, Gerhard Jaritz and Albert Müller criticised that socio-historical representations inspired by the theory of modernisation had repeatedly described the development of pre-modern into modern society as a radical increase in mobility—on the backdrop of a "spatially stable, immobile pre-modern society" (Jaritz/Müller 1988: 12). It was only in the 1990s, that the perspective of migration as a "normal and structural element of human societies throughout history" (Lucassen/Lucassen 1997: 9) became internationally accepted on the basis of more recent research (Lucassen 1987; Page Moch 1992; Canny 1994; Hoerder 2000).

The *Encyclopedia of European Migration and Minorities* sums up the new state of research in terms of terminologies and concepts to the effect that the traditional approach to the complex phenomena of migration, which is oriented towards state borders and state measures, is more and more succeeded by action-theoretical or process-oriented approaches (Bade et al. 2012; Hoerder/Lucassen/Lucassen 2012: xxv).

There is consensus that even in the centuries after the great migratory movements of the Middle Ages, numerous groups and individuals were on the move in late medieval and early modern Europe: Merchants, pilgrims, craftsmen, artists, scholars, students, clerics, mercenaries, Jews, beggars and other marginalised people (Jaritz/Müller 1988; Gilomen et al. 2000). Social historical research has become increasingly interested in migration with a focus on immigration into the city. Initially, the focus was on groups that were forced to migrate due to religious persecution, such as the French Huguenots, the Flemish Protestants, or even the Salzburg emigrants, although the founding of 'exulterous cities' also occurred from time to time (Scoville 1960). Heinz Schilling sees denominational migration as a specific type of migration, as a large "trans-European migration" (Schilling 1992: 68).

Despite all the difficulties, the analysis of the citizens' books reveals a high level of immigration into the cities and the contours of citizen migration (Schwinges 2000: 25). Data for 24 municipalities, both large cities such as Berlin, Frankfurt, Cologne and also other cities of the 17th and 18th centuries, show that the 'typical' citizenry consisted almost equally of immigrants and natives. The highest proportion of foreigners and immigrants among the new citizens was recorded in Prague in the period between 1618-53 with 87 per cent (Hochstadt 1983: 199). The admission of women as citizens was most widespread in the south of the Reich (Studer 2000: 40). However, the 'citizens' usually represented a minority of the urban population in the early modern period. Hochstadt estimates the proportion of citizens at 10 to 15 per cent; however, with their families they accounted for 40 to 60 per cent of the population. The proportion of second-class citizens (with families) who had acquired the 'small citizenship' as residents or incolates is estimated at 20 to 40 per cent of the urban population. The group of non-citizens was apparently more mobile, and the proportion of immigrants was higher among this group: in 1675, 74 per cent of the 'Beisassen' (inhabitants without citizenship) in Würzburg were immigrants, while the figure for citizens was only 57 per cent. In 1700, two thirds of the inhabitants of Frankfurt am Main came from outside the city, but only half of the citizens had immigrated (Hochstadt 198: 203). The quantitative relationship of the group of citizens to the group of 'second-class' citizens was certainly a result of the given community's 'foreign policy'. In Upper Germany the acquisition of citizenship was apparently more difficult than in Lower Germany. Individual cities—such as Hamburg—, for example, pursued a relatively open, pro-alien policy (Schaser 1995: 149).

Hochstadt has advocated the thesis that, "mobility reached extraordinary proportions" at the bottom of the social ladder. Thus, he focused on the group of servants of both sexes, whose share of the urban population he estimated at 10 to 15 per cent, as well as the group of apprentices and journeymen, whose share he estimated at 5 per cent (Hochstadt 1983: 202f). Hochstadt estimates can be regarded as minimum values (cf. Ehmer/Reith 2002).

In spite of the shift in the weighting between urban and rural areas in the early modern period, education and employment were still concentrated in the cities, although the weighting between cities and their hinterland had shifted (Schilling 1993; Knittler 2000). Large as well as small cities depended on the influx of servants, and the surrounding regions played an important role as a reservoir of labor (Eder 1990: 216; Dürr 1995/2001; Wagener 1996: 120-27).

The migration of craftsmen and specialists and in particular the journeyman migration has been documented since the 14th century and has thus met with great scholarly interest. Already Georg Schanz, who had evaluated the oaths of the journeymen in Konstanz at Lake Constance for the period from 1489 to 1579, noticed "a colorful confusion" regarding the origin (Schanz 1877: 335) of the men. He concluded that direction and extension of journeyman migration from and to Constance were different according to trades and extended after 1540 "to all cardinal points over the whole German Empire". The extent of immigration and emigration was an indicator of the economic importance of a city (ibid: 343).

Tramping provided the impetus for the development of journeymen associations—originally after the great plague—and Epstein remarked, "although poor documentation and historiographical prejudice has cast journeymen mobility into the shadows, markets in itinerant skilled labour were a fundamental feature of pre-modern European crafts" (Epstein 2004: 251). Tramping, however, was a specifically Central European phenomenon, and a Europe-wide comparison must take into account other forms of migration: In the Alps, the Pyrenees, or even in northwestern Germany, there were networks of circular and chain migration from certain rural communities etc. that specialised in a specific commercial activity and supplied urban markets and their hinterland. When a certain level of urban concentration had been reached, as in early modern mega-cities like London or Paris, labour markets developed without formal arrangements (for the dominance of the capitals after 1500, cf. Schott 2014: 157-192).

In the 18th century, an inter-regional tramping system developed even in regions with a high level of urbanisation and economic integration—as in northern Italy and the Netherlands, and there was no migration comparable to tramping in these areas. In Central Europe, journeyman organisations were established in the Middle Ages to overcome the asymmetries of the market in connection with the numerous small and medium-sized towns. Where political fragmentation was great, they developed strongly, and the guilds as well as the authorities had little control over them (Epstein 2004). One consequence of immigration was that predominantly foreign workers were employed in the cities—and that the cities and the urban economy were also dependent on immigration. This enabled the journeymen to leave the city in case of conflict. For Western and Central Europe, Prak et al. (2018) have pointed out that family members were, with some exceptions, a minority among guild members and apprentices.

The duration of the temporary immigration of servants and journeymen was very different: some moved on after a short stay, others settled down after having lived in the town for several years. Most students also immigrated on a temporary basis: University cities, as educational institutions, had a strong attraction for students coming from regions beyond the city and its hinterland (Hahn 2012: 87-88), with small and medium-sized cities in particular being regarded as classic university cities. In many cases, the matriculation registers provide information about the origin of the students (Matschinegg 2014). It was precisely the eventual closure of a university that revealed its significance for the city. This applied particularly to the economic potential, as well as the cultural significance and educational opportunities offered by these institutions (Leiser 1979; Höroldt 1979; Reith 2012). However, the divide between the history of education and universities on the one hand and the history of migration on the other still has to be closed.

Although the miners' settlements were sometimes close to the deposits or the mining operations, the mining towns were a special type of town (Kaufhold/Reininghaus 2004). These were settlements or markets without formal privileges but they were the core of the mining region. Early modern metal ore mining shows a certain proximity to the city. Already in the high Middle Ages, mining towns such as Goslar, Freiberg, Iglau and Kuttenberg emerged. Numerous mining towns developed in the course of the so-called Great Mining boom in the transition from the Late Middle Ages to the Early Modern Period. In the Erzgebirge, Schneeberg was initially a haphazard settlement, while Annaberg and Marienberg, with their checkerboard topography, were planed and built under the control of territorial rulers (Kratzsch 1972). Mining had a high labour demand and the fluctuation was high depending on the yield or the drying up of the deposits, especially as the miners enjoyed freedom of movement. Schwaz in Tyrol, with its 20.000 inhabitants, was the second largest city in the Habsburg Empire in the 16th century. Only Vienna was larger than this mining centre. (Ebner 1989). The *Schwazer Bergbuch* (1556) reflects the influx from various regions. The miners were "ain gesamblt volck" ("a mixed bunch") (Stöger 2006, 172-173). Some mining towns fell into disrepair and as a result, miners turned to other occupations and new centres—such as Kongsberg in Norway—and Russia also recruited workers in the 17th/18th century. The settlements in the Banat in the 18th century were sometimes founded due to forced migration, as well as in Salzburg in 1525, then 1686/91, and finally in 1732 by the expulsion of the Protestant miners of Dürrnberg (Stöger 2006).

In hard coal mining, the formation of districts was more pronounced, but it was not necessarily urban. For example, it was not until the 1850s that the boom phase began in the German Ruhr area, where the coal and steel industry remained dominant until the 1960s. On the one hand there was an urban sprawl in the landscape, on the other an unprecedented speed of growth of the cities, which made any urban planning seem outdated the day after it had been decided (Tenfelde 2004: 125). However, the Ruhr area only grew concentrically around a few cities at the beginning, and since 1850 it has developed polycentrically, with the period between 1880 and 1930 being regarded as the city formation phase.

The infrastructure in particular had to be provided for the rapidly growing mining cities that had been built according to plan: These initially included fortifications such as the town wall and town towers, the town hall, the granary, church buildings (altars), schools, a slaughterhouse, the hospital, bathhouses and baths, pharmacy and cemetery. At first, for example, the mining towns in the Erzgebirge were composed of wooden buildings, which were soon replaced by massive stone buildings, whereby most of the private houses were also supplied with piped drinking water (Kratzsch 1972: 46). Artificial moats and canals were built to supply wood. In Annaberg and Marienberg there were even small bathing facilities in many private houses. Urban construction and building supervision played a central role (Fouquet 1999 in general). Most of the building regulations were apparently based on experiences with conflagrations and plague epidemics; this is indicated, for example, by the fire regulations in the mountain towns of the Erzgebirge mountains—such as Marienberg (1536).

One will be able to analyse these developments in the framework of the comprehensive paradigm urbanisation, which increasingly replaces the older concept of urbanisation as a sub-process of a modernisation that began in the 18th century and was oriented towards the Anglo-Saxon perspective of a "history of the way Europe was urbanized" (Knittler 2000: 51-72). Fouquet (1999) therefore evaluates the public building activity as push factor and part of the inner urbanisation process noticeable in the second half of the 15th century, which accelerated from the beginning of the 16th century until the end of the 17th century. Cities like Augsburg experienced a real "urbanistic metamorphosis" at the beginning of the 17th century (Roeck 1985).

The classic master narrative or verdict that it was not until the 19th century that the central areas of water supply and sanitation were able to catch up with the services of antiquity has meanwhile become obsolete (Reith 2011: 124).

Mobilising Urban-Environmental History

There is an ambivalence inherent to the metaphor of social or urban metabolism (cf. Barles in this volume). The conception of flows and streams of matter and energy blurs the fact that these materials and humans, which constitute urban life do not simply 'flow'. There are actors, practices, infrastructures, but also economic constellations, legal systems and policies, which ensure transport, travel, supply and discharge. And along with mobilised materials, microbes, and bodies, there are perceptions, and images on the move, all of them shaping and being shaped by urban environments. The more complex this constellation is, the more it creates an urban technosphere (Otter in this volume). Colin G. Pooley (2017) has argued "that the sub-disciplines of transport history, migration history and mobilities studies too rarely interact directly with each other, and that there is much to be gained from the integration and cross-fertilisation of different approaches." (ibid: 251). We would like to second Pooley's claim, but also to widen it: There is the need to establish stronger links between urban-environmental history, historical studies of transport, mobility and migration, and particularly the recently flourishing interdisciplinary mobilities studies in social sciences. We use the term 'mobilities' intentionally as a plural form. While the established historiography of migration uses the terms 'mobility' and 'migration' more or less synonymously (Lucassen/ Lucassen 2008), recent mobilities research applies a broader concept of mobility, encompassing all forms of movements of people, goods, and information, migration being one aspect amongst others.

Concerning urban environment and migration, Marco Armiero and Richard Tucker (2017) underline the importance of the urban dimension for the environmental history of migrations. To add just one example, by taking seriously the potential of this perspective, urban-environmental history becomes aware of the multiple interconnections between the shape of urban topographies and social and ethnical segregation. "What were the Italian backyards, full of vegetables, rabbits and chickens," Armiero and Tucker (2017: 9) ask,

> if not a different appreciation of land and natural resources and a porous space blending work, living, and leisure times? The constructivist style can contribute to urban-environmental history, rethinking ecologically the ethnic enclaves, exploring how immigrants understood and activated urban commons, including garbage, that is, a space traditionally occupied by immigrant workers.

From this appreciation of questions of urban social ecology it is only a small step to the integration of questions of health and environmental (in)equalities into the investigation (Armiero/Tucker 2017: 10; Massard-Guilbaud/Rodgers 2011), the latter for example materializing in segregation processes within the cities and also in their ever more fluid hinterlands (cf. Platt 2005; Frioux 2009).

But what about the links between urban-environmental history and the highly dynamic field of social science based mobilities studies? What are the conceptual and analytical intersections? What impulses can mobilities studies give to urban-environmental history? A recent review essay by Peter Merriman and Lynne Pearce (2017) on *Mobility and the humanities*, which does not deal with nature-society-relations at any point, raises doubts that they can do this. These doubts, however, are not justified. Büscher, Sheller, and Tyfield (2016) point at what they call "mobility intersections", which "lead to a radical rethinking of how to study emergent social processes, including multiple mobile-cum-immobile socio-technical and socio-natural phenomena" (ibid: 490). They are convinced that mobilities research calls for intersectionality of different approaches or even a comprehensive postdisciplinary approach due to the complexity of the topic (ibid: 487). Given the broad interdisciplinarity, which has been characterising environmental history from its beginning, this can be read as an invitation for joint efforts in postdisciplinary scholarship.

Second, Büscher, Sheller, and Tyfield advocate special attention for "the gendered, racialized, and differentially embodied (im)mobilities of inequality; or the making of 'good mobilities' and 'good cities'; or the uneven mobilities of disaster vulnerability and climate adaptation" (ibid: 487). Albeit not explicitly developed in their agenda, these topics invite a historical long term perspective without exception. Büscher, Sheller, and Tyfield further contextualise mobility as an aspect of social ecology, dealing with categories like sustainability and referring to the Anthropocene debate (ibid: 488).

Finally, and once more implicitly delimiting common ground between the perspectives of mobilities studies and environmental history, they highlight the relevance of a materiality centred approach:

> The nuanced sensitivity to materials, spaces, and sensations developed within architecture and design resonates with research into situational mobilities and the mobilities design involved in their unfolding. It makes it possible to take departure in concrete and specific mobile situations and how materialities shape interactions at multiple scales, including large-scale environmental impacts; such as the 'politics of pavements' which explore how their impermeabilty to rain shapes how pavements interact with the dynamics of extreme weather. (ibid: 490)

While approaches driven by new materialism have already been established in urban-environmental history (cf. Otter 2010), mobilities' research interest for the tensions between mobility and immobility may guide new insights if more systematically applied in historiography. Every infrastructure established to enable mobility, is at the same time creating immobility. Roads, railtracks, but also wires and tubes mobilizing people, materials, energy, and information, are erected at the price of fixing material and capital at a certain place and limiting the mobility of dwellers resident near buildings erected for this purpose. The limited flexibilities of such systems play a critical role in this context, not yet sufficiently analysed by urban-environmental history. To give one example: tourism, maybe the type of mobility of highest global impact today, seasonally leads to drastically fluctuating human populations. Local infrastructure systems for provision, discharge and housing have to be capable of accommodating the peaks while being expensive to maintain all year round. From the point of view of urban-environmental history this can be traced back well into 19th century, when Belle Époque tourism with its luxury hotelry created a first elitist blueprint for mass tourism (cf. Humair 2011, for the example of Lake Geneva and the making of a tourism industry within a highly urbanised region).

Further, social science based mobilities studies are right to highlight the question of (dis-)connection. Ever expanding networks enabling intensified connectivity necessarily create 'small worlds' of those disconnected (Sheller/Urry 2006: 216), a question of obvious relevance for the discussions on environmental justice and centre-periphery-problems.

To summarise the potential of mobilities studies approaches for urban-environmental history, the most important benefit is that this body of theories tries to overcome the shortcomings of older static or sedentarist perspectives and underlines the necessity of approaches which adequately take phenomena of mobility, fluidity, and hybridity into consideration, while at the same time not falling into the contrary, namely nomadic theory's celebration of the opposite of sedentarism: nomadism and deterritorialisation (ibid: 210). Sheller and Urry give an example for the shortcomings of earlier, more static theories:

> Yet sociology's view of urban life failed to consider the overwhelming impact of the automobile transforming the time-space 'scapes' of the modern urban/suburban dweller. Industrial sociology, consumption studies, transportation studies, and urban analyses have been largely static [...] failing to consider how the car reconfigures urban life, with novel ways of dwelling, travelling, and socialising in, and through an automobilized time-space [...] (ibid:. 209).

The automobile, probably 20th century's most momentous technical product with respect to society and nature (McNeill 2000), also stands in the focus of urban-environmental history for good reasons. While earlier means of transportation already intensively interacted with the development of urban environments (Mende 2006), the automobile in fact exposed an unprecedented transformative power. Even if not all the radical planning concepts to create automobile cities were realised (cf. Flonneau 2006 for Paris), the automobile conquered urban space, outplaced other types of mobility, caused pollution, noise, and nuisances and—probably most importantly—was the most important driver in the making of suburbia. Once again: the move of dwellers to the green fringes of cities was by no means new, as the better off in late 19th century metropolises had already benefited from the growing commuting distances bridged by horse tram, tramways, and suburban trains. But what happened in the making of "car country" United States (Wells 2012) from the interwar years on and in Europe after World War II, was of a completely new dimension, leading to the situation that for example in Switzerland around the millennium there were 114 square meters of space per capita dedicated to road traffic, while only a third of that space was dedicated to housing (Winiwarter/Knoll 2007: 238). Avenues, streets, roads, and carparks began to cover growing shares of landscape in and outside the cities. Local ecosystems and land use systems turned into residential housing. Similar processes affected the development of decentralised industrial zones. Analysing the related problems, Swiss historian Christian Pfister described a "mobility spiral" (1995: 92): The omnipresence of motorised traffic and concomitant environmental problems caused a 'shortening reaction' of those suffering from traffic. Escaping into supposedly 'natural' leisure regions these travellers triggered the development as well as the pollution of these regions. The example of motor traffic and the making of suburbia is a significant example for the necessity of searching for the actors behind mobility related metaphors like 'flows' and 'streams': it was about politics, and lobbying when the US federal government fuelled the boom of car dependent housing at the urban fringes with heavily subsidizing highway construction after World War II. The Federal-Aid Highway Act from 1956 foresaw a 90 per cent funding for 41.000 miles of super highways, a system designed by highway engineers "almost entirely without consulting city planners or public transportation officials", as Christopher W. Wells (2012: 254) noted. In the US, the post World War II housing boom in an overwhelming majority brought a hitherto unthinkable number of single family houses into car dependent suburbs.

What are the limits of the 'mobilities paradigm' recently promoted in the social sciences? Once more, the answer is not that surprising, as it comes from historians: By stressing the unprecedented nature of today's mobile society and due to their origin in modernisation theory, mobilities studies neglect the long term perspective and therefore underestimate the epistemic value of tracing back long term trajectories well into premodern times in order to better understand, what in fact is 'new under the sun' in 19th and 20th century urbanisation. What has been shown in the first part of this chapter for migration and urban demography, also applies to the wider context of city and mobilities: We need a clear understanding of the preceeding phenomena and the long term trajectories to get a comprehensive understanding of the more recent transformation processes.

The re-negotiation of city-hinterland-relations under the auspices of leisure and tourism may serve as an example. Seen from a historical long term perspective, urbanites and 'classical' theorists of city-hinterland-relations, such as Johann Heinrich von Thünen (1783-1850), had developed a clear understanding of the functional ties between the city and related regions, be it in terms of trade, land use, provision (of the city with resources and labour), or discharge—in short: all factors that urban-environmental historians tend to summarise under the category of urban metabolism (Barles/Knoll 2019; Barles in this volume). But well back into pre-modern times, city dwellers also visited the adjacent landscapes for leisure purposes, nobility maintained rural residences outside the city walls, less privileged at least undertook trips—such as the one on Easter, which is an important theme in Johann Wolfgang von Goethe's Faust drama, first published in 1808.

These mobility relations changed fundamentally in the course of 19th and 20th century urbanisation, and contemporaries were aware of this change. A notice by a local observer somewhat ironically commenting on the numerous Munich skiers crowding the Brauneck summit in Lenggries, Upper Bavaria in the 1930s, may serve as an example. Referring to the earlier role of this alpine region as supplier of wood, which was floated down the river Isar to Munich, the author noted that while earlier wood from Lenggries was transported to Munich, now the Munich urbanites brought wood [i. e. their skis, M. K.] to the region (Kuisle 1999: 96-97).

In the beginning, it were mainly regions in the near vicinity of cities that became urbanised by tourism, but later on, this also became true for more and more remote destinations. The mountainous regions of the Austrian Wienerwald are a telling example for the multifaceted transformations rural regions underwent in late 18th and early 19th century due to the growing leisure mobility of urban dwellers (cf. Matzka 2007). In the case of Wienerwald, however, the history was one of a downturn of tourism following the crisis of the metropolis after World War I, when the capital lost its role of being the centre of an empire covering large parts of Europe. But tourism and leisure mobility initiated another process in the Wienerwald: the integration of what had long been a destination for temporary touristic stays, into a residential suburbia of the nearby metropole.

In a dialectical process urbanites, namely the bourgeois middleclass, and their associations, explored landscapes in their search for an anti-urban retreat, explored landscapes, made them accessible by organizing the construction of roads, pathways, and accommodation, and last but not least tried to implement their values and lifestyles there (Anderson 2012). For the example of Seattle and its environs Matthew Klingle once asked, whether the relations between the city and its leisure hinterland were characterised by fair play (Klingle 2006)—a more than necessary question.

Conclusions

Cities are on the move. For centuries, they have been attracting migrants. Port towns have been hubs for long distance migration. Cities are centres of trade and nodes of communication. They are destinations and markets for tourism. Urban life is characterised by tempo and dynamism. Has urban history sketched a too static image of the city in history? Has urban-environmental history—albeit working with metaphors like metabolism or co-evolution, which imply fluidity and motion—failed to fully acknowledge the manifold forms of mobilities shaping the making of the modern city?

The discussion of this chapter has taken stock of two strands of research: the history of migration and the interdisciplinary mobilities studies. The former represents a historical subdiscipline, whose findings have aptly helped to disprove concepts of supposedly static, and sedentary premodern societies. The latter, based in the social sciences, also suggests to overcome sedentarist perspectives. However, in its emphasis of the unprecedented character of 20th and 21st century mobilities it tends to underestimate the role of long term precursor processes. Urban-environmental history can learn from both of these inputs to give dimensions like migration, mobility, tourism, and transport more room in historiography, as cities were and are on the move.

References

Anderson, Ben (2012): "The construction of an alpine landscape: Building, representing and affecting the Eastern Alps, c. 1885-1914" In: Journal of Cultural Geography 29/2, pp. 155-183.

Armiero, Marco/Tucker, Richard (2017): "Introduction: Migrants in environmental history." In: Marco Armiero/Richard Tucker (eds.), Environmental history of modern migrations, Florence: Taylor and Francis, pp. 1-15.

Bade, Klaus J./Emmer, Pieter C./Lucassen, Leo/Oltmer, Jochen (eds.) (2011): The encyclopedia of migration and minorities in Europe: From the 17th century to the present, Cambridge/New York: Cambridge University Press.

Bade, Klaus J./Emmer, Pieter C./Lucassen, Leo/Oltmer, Jochen (eds.) (2007): Enzyklopädie Migration in Europa: Vom 17. Jahrhundert bis zur Gegenwart, Paderborn/Munich: Ferdinand Schöningh.

Barles, Sabine/Knoll, Martin (2019): "Long-term transitions, urban imprint and the construction of hinterlands." In: Tim Soens/Dieter Schott/Michael Toyka-Seid/Bert de Munck (eds.): Urbanizing nature: Actors and agency (dis)connecting cities and nature since 1500, New York: Routledge, pp. 29-49.

Büscher, Monika/Sheller, Mimi/Tyfield, David (2016): "Mobility intersections: Social research, social futures." In: Mobilities 11/4, pp. 485-497.

Canny, Nicholas (ed.) (1994): Europeans on the move: Studies on European migration 1500-1800, Oxford: Clarendon Press.

Dirlmeier, Ulf (1981): "Umweltprobleme in deutschen Städten des Spätmittelalters." In: Technikgeschichte 48, pp. 191-205.

Dirlmeier, Ulf (1981): "Die kommunalpolitischen Zuständigkeiten und Leistungen süddeutscher Städte im Spätmittelalter (vor allem auf dem Gebiet der Ver- und Entsorgung)." In: Jürgen Sydow (ed.), Städtische Versorgung und Entsorgung im Wandel der Geschichte, Stuttgart: Jan Thorbecke, pp. 113-150.

Dohrn-van-Rossum, Gerhard (2004): "Migration – Innovation – Städtenetze: Ingenieure und technische Experten." In: Mathieu Arnoux/Pierre Monnet (eds.),

Le technicien dans la cité en Europe occidentale 1250–1650, Rome: École française de Rome, pp. 291-307.

Dürr, Renate (1995): Mägde in der Stadt: Das Beispiel Schwäbisch Hall in der Frühen Neuzeit, Frankfurt a.M.: Campus.

Dürr, Renate (2001): "Die Migration von Mägden in der frühen Neuzeit." In: Marita Krauss/Holger Sonnabend (eds.), Frauen und Migration, Stuttgart: Franz Steiner, pp. 117-132.

Ebner, Herwig (1989): "Österreichische Bergbaustädte und Bergmärkte im Mittelalter und in der frühen Neuzeit." In: Jahrbuch für Regionalgeschichte 16 I, pp. 57-72.

Eder, Franz (1990): Geschlechterproportion und Arbeitsorganisation im Land Salzburg 17.-19. Jahrhundert, Vienna/Munich: Verlag für Geschichte und Politik and Oldenbourg.

Ehmer, Josef (2011): "Quantifying mobility in early modern Europe: The challenge of concepts and data." In: Journal of Global History 6, pp. 327-338.

Ehmer, Josef/Reith, Reinhold (2002): "Die mitteleuropäische Stadt als frühneuzeitlicher Arbeitsmarkt." In: Peter Feldbauer/Michael Mitterauer/Wolfgang Schwentker (eds.), Die vormoderne Stadt: Asien und Europa im Vergleich, Vienna/Munich: Oldenbourg, pp. 232-258.

Epstein, Stephan R. (2004): "Labour mobility, journeyman organisations and markets in skilled labour Europe, 14th–18th centuries." In: Mathieu Arnoux/Pierre Monnet (eds.), Le technicien dans la cité en Europe occidentale, 1250-1650, Rome: École française de Rome, pp. 251-269.

Flonneau, Mathieu (2006): "Notre Dame of Paris challenged by the car: Between the secular and the 'sacred'." In: Gijs Mom/Laurent Tissot (eds.), Road history: Planning, building and use, Neuchâtel: Ed. Alphil, pp. 133-161.

Fontaine, Laurence (1996): History of pedlars in Europe, Durham: Duke University Press Books.

Fouquet, Gerhard (1999): Bauen für die Stadt: Finanzen, Organisation und Arbeit in kommunalen Baubetrieben des Spätmittelalters. Eine vergleichende Studie vornehmlich zwischen den Städten Basel und Marburg, Cologne/Weimar/Vienna: Böhlau.

Gilomen, Hans-Jörg/Head-König, Anne-Lise/Radeff, Anna (eds.) (2000): Migration in die Städte: Ausschluss – Assilmilierung – Integration – Multikulturalität, Zurich: Chronos.

Hahn, Sylvia (2012): Historische Migrationsforschung, Frankfurt a.M./New York: Campus.

Hochstadt, Steve (1983): "Migration in preindustrial Germany." In: Central European History 16, pp. 195-224.

Hoerder, Dirk (2000): "Metropolitan migration in the past. Labour markets, commerce, and cultural interaction in Europe, 1600-1914." In: Journal of International Migration and Integration 1, pp. 39-58.

Hoerder, Dirk/Lucassen, Jan/Lucassen, Leo (2011): "Terminologies and concepts of migration research." In: Klaus J. Bade/Pieter C. Emmer/Leo Lucassen/Jochen Oltmer (eds.), The encyclopedia of migration and minorities in Europe: From the 17th century to the present, New York: Cambridge University Press, pp. XXV-XXXIX.

Höroldt, Dieter (1979): "Zur wirtschaftlichen Bedeutung der Universitäten für ihre Städte." In: Erich Maschke/Jürgen Sydow (eds.), Stadt und Hochschule im 19. und 20. Jahrhundert, Sigmaringen: Jan Thorbecke, pp. 25-76.

Humair, Cédric (2011): "The hotel industry and its importance in the technical and economic development of a region: The Lake Geneva case (1852-1914)." In: Journal of Tourism History 3 (3), pp. 237-265.

Imhof, Arthur E. (1988): Von der unsicheren zur sicheren Lebenszeit: Fünf historisch-demographische Studien, Darmstadt: Wissenschaftliche Buchgesellschaft.

Imhof, Arthur E. (1975): "Demographische Stadtstrukturen in der frühen Neuzeit: Gießen und seine Umgebung im 17. und 18. Jahrhundert als Fallstudie." In: Zeitschrift für Stadtgeschichte, Stadtsoziologie und Denkmalpflege 2, pp. 190-227.

Imhof, Arthur E. (1989): Die gewonnenen Jahre: Von der Zunahme unserer Lebensspanne seit dreihundert Jahren oder von der Notwendigkeit einer neuen Einstellung zu Leben und Sterben, Munich: C. H. Beck.

Jaritz, Gerhard/Müller Albert (eds.) (1988): Migration in der Feudalgesellschaft, Frankfurt a.M./New York: Campus.

Kinzelbach, Annemarie (1995): Gesundbleiben, Krankwerden, Armsein in der frühneuzeitlichen Gesellschaft: Gesunde und Kranke in den Reichsstädten Überlingen und Ulm, 1500-1700, Stuttgart: Franz Steiner.

Klingle, Mathew (2006): "Fair play: Outdoor recreation and environmental inequality in twentieth century Seattle." In: Andrew C. Isenberg (ed.), The nature of cities. Rochester, New York: University of Rochester Press, pp. 122-156.

Knittler, Herbert (2000): Die europäische Stadt in der Frühen Neuzeit: Institutionen, Strukturen, Entwicklungen, Vienna/Munich: Oldenbourg.

Kratzsch, Klaus (1972): Bergstädte des Erzgebirges: Städtebau und Kunst zur Zeit der Reformation, Munich: Schnell & Steiner.

Kuisle, Anita (1999): "Eine Bahn für die Münchener: Die Geschichte der Bergbahn aufs Brauneck." In: Franziska Lobenhofer-Hirschbold (ed.), Ziemer zu Vermithen: Von Berchtesgaden bis Zillertal, Aspekte der touristischen Entwicklung von 1850–1960, Großweil: Freilichtmuseum des Bezirks Oberbayern, pp. 96-106.

Leiser, Wolfgang (1979): "Die Stadt und der Verlust ihrer Universität." In: Erich Maschke/Jürgen Sydow (eds.), Stadt und Hochschule im 19. und 20. Jahrhundert, Sigmaringen: Jan Thorbecke, pp. 77-90.

Livi Bacci, Massimo (2000): The population of Europe: Making of Europe, Oxford: Wiley-Blackwell.

Lucassen, Jan (1987): Migrant labour in Europe, 1600-1900: The drift to the North Sea, London: Routledge.

Lucassen, Jan/Lucassen, Leo (eds.) (2005): Migration, migration history, history: Old paradigms and new perspectives, Bern: Peter Lang.

Lucassen, Jan/Lucassen, Leo (2008): "Mobilität." In: Friedrich Jäger (ed.): Manufaktur –1 Naturgeschichte, Stuttgart: Metzler, rows 624-644.

Lucassen, Jan/Lucassen, Leo (2009): "The mobility transition revisited, 1500-1900: What the case of Europe can offer to global history." In: Journal of Global History 4/03, pp. 347-377.

Massard-Guilbaud, Geneviève/Rodger, Richard (eds.) (2011): Environmental and social justice in the city: Historical perspectives, Cambridge: White Horse Press.

Matschinegg, Ingrid (2004): "Universitäre Massenquellen (Matrikel, Akten)." In: Josef Pauser/Martin Scheutz/Thomas Winkelbauer (eds.), Quellenkunde der Habsburgermonarchie (16.-18. Jahrhundert): Ein exemplarisches Handbuch, Vienna: Böhlau, pp. 714-724.

Matzka, Christian (2007): Tourismus im Wienerwald 1850-1914: Die Entstehung einer Freizeitregion vor den Toren der Großstadt, vom Bau der Eisenbahnen bis zum Ersten Weltkrieg, St. Pölten: Niederösterreichisches Institut für Landeskunde.

McNeill, John Robert (2000): Something new under the sun: An environmental history of the twentieth-century world, London: The Penguin Press.

McNeill, John Robert/Engelke, Peter (2014): The great acceleration: An environmental history of the anthropocene since 1945, Cambridge, Massachusetts/London: The Belknap Press of Harvard University Press.

Mende, Michael (2006): "Vehicle design and the metropolitan avenue, 1850-1960." In: Gijs Mom/Laurent Tissot (ed.): Road history: Planning, building and use, Neuchâtel: Ed. Alphil, pp. 187-204.

Merriman, Peter/Pearce, Lynne (2017): "Mobility and the humanities." In: Mobilities 12/4, pp. 493-508.

Moch, Leslie Page (1992): Moving Europeans: Migration in Western Europe since 1650, Bloomington: Indiana University Press.

Otter, Chris (2010): "Locating matter: The place of materiality in urban history." In: Tony Bennett/Patrick Joyce (eds.): Material powers: Cultural studies, history and the material turn, London: Routledge.

Pfister, Christian (2007): Bevölkerungsgeschichte und historische Demographie 1500-1800, Munich: Oldenbourg.

Pfister, Christian (ed.) (1995): Das 1950er Syndrom: Der Weg in die Konsumgesellschaft, Berne: Verlag Paul Haupt.

Pooley, Colin G. (2017): "Connecting historical studies of transport, mobility and migration." In: The Journal of Transport History 38/2, pp. 251-259.

Prak, Maarten/Crowston, Clare/De Munck, Bert/Kissane, Christopher (2018): "Access to the trade: Monopoly and mobility in European craft guilds, 17th and 18th Centuries." In: Economic History Working Papers 88365, London School of Economics and Political Science, Department of Economic History.

Reith, Reinhold (2012): "Stadt und Universität in historischer Perspektive." In: Reinhold Reith (ed.), Die Paris Lodron Universität Salzburg: Geschichte – Gegenwart – Zukunft, Salzburg: Müry Salzmann, pp. 210-222.

Reith, Reinhold (2011): Umweltgeschichte der Frühen Neuzeit, Munich: Oldenbourg.

Reith, Reinhold (2008): "Circulation of skilled labour in late medieval and early modern central Europe." In: Stephan R. Epstein/Maarten Prak (eds.), Guilds, innovation and the European economy, 1400-1800, Cambridge: Cambridge University Press, pp. 114-142.

Schanz, Georg (1877): Zur Geschichte der deutschen Gesellen-Verbände, Leipzig: Duncker & Humblot.

Schaser, Angelika (1995): "Städtische Fremdenpolitik im Deutschland der Frühen Neuzeit." In: Alexander Demandt (ed.), Mit Fremden leben: Eine Kulturgeschichte von der Antike bis zur Gegenwart, Munich: C. H. Beck, pp. 137-157; 270-278.

Schilling, Heinz (2004): Die Stadt in der Frühen Neuzeit, Munich: Oldenbourg.

Schilling, Heinz (1992): "Die niederländischen Exulanten des 16. Jahrhunderts: Ein Beitrag zum Typus der frühneuzeitlichen Konfessionsmigration." In: Geschichte in Wissenschaft und Unterricht 43, pp. 67-78.

Schubert, Ernst (2011): "Musicians, showmen, jugglers, and acrobats in Central Europe in the early modern period." In: Klaus J. Bade/Pieter C. Emmer/Leo Lucassen/Jochen Oltmer (eds.), The encyclopedia of migration and minorities in europe: From the 17th century to the present, Cambridge/New York: Cambridge University Press, pp. 580-582.

Schwinges, Rainer Christoph (2000): "Bürgermigration im Alten Reich des 14. bis 16. Jahrhunderts." In: Hans-Jörg Gilomen/Anne-Lise Head-König/Anna Radeff (eds.), Migration in die Städte: Ausschluss – Assilmilierung – Integration – Multikulturalität, Zurich: Chronos, pp. 17-37.

Schwinges, Rainer Christoph (1986): Deutsche Universitätsbesucher im 14. und 15. Jahrhundert: Studien zur Sozialgeschichte des Alten Reiches, Stuttgart: Steiner Verlag Wiesbaden.

Scoville, Warren Candler (1960): The persecution of Huguenots and French economic development 1680-1720, Berkeley/Los Angeles: University of California Press.

Sheller, Mimi/Urry, John (2006): "The New Mobilities Paradigm." In: Environmental Planning A 38 (2), pp. 207-226.

Soens, Tim/Schott, Dieter/Toyka-Seid, Michael/deMunck, Bert (eds.) (2019): Urbanizing nature: Actors and agency (dis)connecting cities and nature since 1500, New York: Routledge.

Studer, Barbara (2000): "Adelige Damen, Kauffrauen und Mägde: Zur Herkunft von Neubürgerinnen in spätmittelalterlichen Städten Süddeutschlands und der Schweiz." In: Hans-Jörg Gilomen/Anne-Lise Head-König/Anna Radeff (eds.), Migration in die Städte: Ausschluss – Assilmilierung – Integration – Multikulturalität, Zurich: Chronos, pp. 39-55.

Tenfelde, Klaus (2004): "Bergbau und Stadtentwicklung im Ruhrgebiet im 19. und 20. Jahrhundert." In: Karl Heinrich Kaufhold/Wilfried Reininghaus (eds.), Stadt und Bergbau, Cologne/Weimar/Wien: Böhlau, pp. 117-134.

Urry, John (2012): Mobilities, Cambridge: Polity Press.

Wagener, Silke (1996): Pedelle, Mägde und Lakaien: Das Dienstpersonal an der Georg-August-Universität Göttingen 1737-1866, Göttingen: Vandenhoeck.

Wells, Christopher W. (2014): Car country: An environmental history, Seattle: University of Washington Press.

Winiwarter, Verena/Knoll, Martin (2007): Umweltgeschichte: Eine Einführung, Cologne/Weimar/Vienna: Böhlau.

Zelinsky, Wilbur (1971): "The Hypothesis of the Mobility Transition." In: Geographical Review 61/2, pp. 219-249.

Heritage, Renewal and the Construction of Identity in Urban History

Michael Toyka-Seid

What Jan Morris (2001) in her recollections of Trieste has termed the "meaning of nowhere" can be perceived in many contemporary cities. There is a feeling that globalisation and the necessities of capitalist progress have eroded the characteristics of historic places and surroundings (Le Galés 2002). The urge to become 'modern' and thus interesting for people and businesses always on the move (Philo/Kearns 1993; Frank 2011) tends to blur the historic dynamics which have made the cities in former times and which have been part of the collective memory of urban inhabitants ever since. Not surprisingly, over the last years there has been a tendency to turn back the tide and to re-live and re-invent the 'old' in the modern city (Schott 2010). When Eric J. Hobsbawm and Terence Ranger introduced the term 'invention of tradition' into the social sciences (Hobsbawm/Ranger 1992) they were primarily interested in the interplay of ritual and symbolism in historical thinking. However, many traces of their concept can easily be detected in the re-discovery and re-invention of the city in the early 21st century.

A rather early example for the attempt to bring back the 'old' into a city imprinted by modernity is the old English port town of Bristol (Toyka-Seid 2003a). As will be argued in the second section of this article, Bristol can be seen as a rather early example of attempts to rehabilitate what is 'old' in cities and to bring back a sense of history and identity to the inhabitants in the course of those endeavours. The various forms in which historians and urban researchers have looked at the different ways urban identities have been constructed and invented in the last decades will be subject of the following first section.

Shaping Urban Identities

When thinking about urban identities it is essential to recollect the debates about urbanity as a specific way of urban life triggered by Louis Wirth's seminal deliberations in the 1930s (Wirth 1938). Those disputes reached new heights with the experience of loss and post-war reconstruction of many European cities in the times of the Second World War. The debate on rebuilding Europe's 'lost cities' had repercussions throughout Europe and beyond (Diefendorf 1993; Ward 2002; Clapson/Larkham 2013). This was particularly true for Germany, where the experience of the National-Socialist regime precluded nostalgic claims to rebuild an allegedly better urban past (Beyme 1987; Kocka 1997). What resulted was the 'second destruction' of the cities in the immediate post-war modernisation (Schleich 1978), guided by the principle of a city made for cars and not for men (Reichow 1959; Bernhardt 2017).

The execution of the modernity paradigm by planners, architects and municipal administrators not only changed the physical face of cities. It also undermined the feelings of belonging by the urban inhabitants and thus spurred another outburst of critical commentaries in the late 1950s and early 1960s. The need to safeguard the alleged roots of urban identities was now put in the centre of the argument. The question posed by authors like Jane Jacobs (1961) and Alexander Mitscherlich (1963) was taken up publicly and effectively by the German journalist and urbanist Wolf Jobst Siedler, who lamented "the eclipsing of the intrinsic real [...], which only allows an emotional urban experience" (Siedler 1964; translation MTS).

Those explorations into the conditions of urban identities provoked a deliberate political move to safeguard the historical fabric and meaning of cities in the 1970s. With the 'European Heritage Year', proclaimed by the European Council in 1975, for the first time an international convention expressed the recognition of the value of urban ensembles, of the plurality of monuments worthy of protection and of the importance of the participation of the urban population in the process of safeguarding the urban past (Falser et al. 2015). The question what constitutes urban heritage and how this should be maintained, preserved and not least kept alive has since then engaged urban planners, architects, sociologists and historians alike and is mirrored in a multitude of theoretical approaches and interpretations (Graham 2002; Bandarin/van Oers 2012). In an article published a few years ago, Hans-Rudolf Meier has pondered over the practical importance heritage conservation has gained in this process as a 'guiding tool' (Leitinstrument) for urban development (Meier 2013).

The debate initiated in the immediate post-war years by sociologists and urban activists was put on an even wider footing by urban researchers from different disciplines in the 1990s. An important opening was suggested by French historian and urban theorist Françoise Choay. In her analysis *L'allegorie du patrimoine* (1992) she emphasised the ability of urban buildings and places to entrench people in their urban surrounding and the necessity to think about different levels of historicity when talking about the built urban past. Choay's analysis represents an early attempt to think together the idea of physical space, urban feeling and urban memories in the process of shaping urban identities. In Choay's succession authors broached the idea of a specific urban habitus (Lee 2002; Lindner 2003), underlined the importance of heterogeneity, density and acceleration of time for the perception of cities (Massey 1999) or sought for the distinctive urban in the collective memories of cities (Boyer 1996; McDowell 2008).

All those approaches to define what lies at the root of urban identity building have found substantial continuation in subsequent scientific efforts. An important expansion in this debate, representing a new way of looking at the immanent mechanics behind the different tracks taken by cities and their inhabitants to create, construct and invent a specific urban identity, was presented in recent years with the concept of an 'Intrinsic Logic of Cities', developed in an interdisciplinary research effort at Darmstadt University of Technology (Gehring 2008; Löw 2008). The fact that apparent differences exist in the ways in which cities act and react, sense and communicate, deal and distribute their material and immaterial resources, had long been attentively observed by urban researchers. Starting point for the 'intrinsic logic'-approach of looking at cities thus were those obvious divergences, which—this is the guiding idea of the concept of an 'intrinsic logic'—all have their identifiable roots in a broad sample of physical, social and cultural imprints, which can be identified on the local level.

Not surprisingly, long before the 'intrinsic logic'-approach urban historians have taken account of the multitude of stampings which have made cities distinguishable in history and helped to develop an urban identity. Equally less surprising the built heritage of cities played a major role in almost all of the explanations found in history. Actually, the questions of why heritage should be preserved and which heritage this should be have been a matter of conservationist and urban planning debates since the first codification of buildings worthy of protection in the Venice Charter of 1964. In more recent years questions regarding the value of 'inconvenient' historic buildings have been raised (Huse 1997; Macdonald 2009) and the need and entitlement to reconstruct old and forlorn monuments has been questioned (von Buttlar et al. 2010). The last turn in this dispute has been the currently very popular 'invention' of old buildings, as can be seen in the neighbourhood of Dresden's Frauenkirche or the new 'Altstadt' of Frankfurt/Main (Vinken 2011). Apart from such rather debatable developments it of course remains one of the most important questions in the context of urban identity creation how the often 'dissonant heritage' can be managed and made fruitful for different groups of urban dwellers (Ashworth/Tunbridge 1996; Saretzki 2016).

Historical research into the remodelling of what is considered to be 'old' in cities has been widespread and far-reaching over the last years. Thus it soon became obvious that the safeguarding of European cities' heritage after 1975 not only included the historical core areas of the cities. The rapidly vanishing factories, railway stations and production sites in the former industrial areas of the cities were of particular interest almost from the beginning (Soyez 2016; Graham et al.

2000; Oevermann/Mieg 2014). In Germany the transformation of the Ruhr area into a huge post-industrial and cultural site since 1989 created particular interest (Ganser 1999) and can still be seen today as a role model for dealing with derelict industrial sites. Housing experiments like the community buildings of the 'Rote Wien' (Schwarz et al. 2019) or the physical remains of the Garden City movement (Ward 2011) also found new appreciation in this period. However, from the point of view of historical research, the most striking examples for the re-invention of the historical city can be found in the inauguration of a new era of the relations between cities and open waters in the last decades of the 20th century. Proximity of rivers and streams and access to water had been at the beginning of urban life in Europe and have accompanied the eventful fate of the respective cities all over Europe ever since (Janssens/Soens 2018; Jakobsson 2018). In the last quarter of the 20th century the rediscovery and rehabilitation of the core areas near the historical arteries of the cities again marked the starting point for new urban experiences, founded on the remains of the old city.

The redevelopment of marinas, riverbanks and urban waterfronts, the 're-naturing' of small rivers and streams and manifold attempts to create re-usages for harbour areas and dilapidated warehouses have figured prominently on the agenda of urban rehabilitation in recent years. Century-old European cities, but also rather young urban foundations like Singapore, Shanghai or Montreal have participated in this process (Broeze 1989; Hawley 2011; White 1995). The tendency to look for the historical connections between cities and their water-related environment also included the search for cultural representations and appropriations (Schubert 2003; Goodbody/Wanning 2008; Knoll et al. 2016). Last but not least, the study of the relationship between city and water increased the understanding of the spatial dimension of urban rehabilitation and the physical and mental re-invention of cities (Schott 2007; Castonguay/Evenden 2010; Otter 2010).

Bristol—an Example for Urban Heritage Management and Identity Creation

It was its proximity to open water which stood at the beginning of the history of Bristol, founded as 'Bridgstow', the place at the bridge on the confluence of rivers Avon and Frome, in the 11th century (Little 1991; MacDonald 1995). At the centre of the economic rise of the city lay the overseas harbour, sheltered from the open sea by the gorge of the River Avon. In the industrial age Britain's 'Second City' lost ground, exemplified by the failure to install a 'floating harbour' in the centre of the town to open Bristol's traditional harbour for the vessels of the 'Iron Age' (Poole 2013). But despite the fact that industrialisation and urbanisation had brought about major changes in the build-up environment of the city, the visual presence of a sea-bound city remained intact. The historical nucleus of the city was still discernible in the first half of the 20th century, and civic pride in Bristol over the centuries had a strong pillar in the city's visual presence. It was echoed by many testimonies of visitors to the city who enthused about the interplay of topography and built environment (Batty 1986). The centrepiece of this perception of a historic port town constituted the visual and mental omnipresence of the harbour, lined by brick warehouses, merchants' halls, cranes and church spires. Early photographs of Bristol taken at the turn from the 19th to the 20th century recall this feeling of a 'City of the Sea' (Beeson 2013).

Even so there was a feeling in the early 20th century that the city had to refresh its picturesque pre-modern outlook and adapt to the necessities of a new age, characterised by new modes of transport and easy accessibility of the central business district. The new thinking found its most striking expression in the inter-war years with the transformation of the most famous ensemble of historic buildings in the centre of the city. Bristol's Queen Square got "literally in the path of progress" (Evening News April 25, 1993). The Square, hailed by contemporaries as a masterpiece of urban planning and thoughtful layout in the late 17th century, with its Georgian buildings and tree-lined crossing, had added urban grandeur to the shipyards, warehouses and piers dominating maritime Bristol (Ralph 1979; Toyka-Seid 2003). The decision of the Civic Council in 1935 to build a new circuit road trespassing the historic centre included a thoroughfare which was to cross the Square from its north-western to its south-eastern corner. The heated public debate would not stop the city fathers: Trees were removed, a diagonal axis across the square was laid out and more than 20 families were removed from their homes—"an example in the kind of sacrifice that we are having to make in the interest of traffic." (Correspondence Bristol Evening World, June 30, 1937)

Worse was to come with German air raids hitting the city shortly into the Second World War. But the 'Blitz' also opened opportunities for planners and urban decision-makers in the immediate post-war era (Hasegawa 1992). In the years after the Second World War, Bristol became an example for the rapid and thoroughgoing 'modernisation' of British cities, quite in tune with the tide of modernist urban planning in the years after the Charter of Athens (Domhardt 2012). The measures taken by the councillors and urban planners were altering the face of the old city and confused the mental maps of the inhabitants (Ackland et al. 1989). Roads, parking lots and high-rise buildings dwarfed what was left of the traditional building stock, blocked thoroughfares and familiar views and levelled the topography of the urban space. It was in those years that a leading architects' association in the city even considered plans to build a five meter high pedestrian way through the city, leaving space for the rapidly increasing number of motorised vehicles (Bristol Architects' Forum 1960).

The tide turned in the 1970s, forced by local groups determined to withstand the omnipotence of planners and local politicians and trying to establish alternative visions for the built legacy of the city and its representation. But to stir up public opinion, it needed the outrage about plans advocated by the civic architect in 1966 to fill up the by now commercially useless river basin and to build new streets and community housing on the covered River Avon.

Initially the project found widespread support in the strong 'modernist' section of the urban population. A correspondent to the *Evening Press* mocked the "present sentimental preoccupation with waterways and warehouses which gave the city its unique character but have largely outlived their usefulness." (Evening Press, April 17, 1968) But soon the local opposition united on this issue of historical forgetfulness. A powerful local initiative to rescue the River Avon and its surroundings assembled, heritage groups, architectural societies and the local press started to support the fight against the plans of the town council and demanded to orientate urban planning and rehabilitation at "community as a whole" (Bristol Planning Group 1968: 30). In spring 1973, after more than five years of fierce debate, the city officials skipped all plans to remodel the historical harbour area.

Looking at the reasons for the radical change in dealing with the physical heritage of Bristol, it is evident that a substantial part of the population after twenty years of post-war rebuilding had become discontent with this 'march to modernity'. Equally important however was the widespread unease about the loss of historical appearance and feeling of belonging in a place that had drastically changed its face in the course of only a few decades. Pride in the built environment of the historic city had been a constant feature of Bristol's self-perception and representation, even after the damage inflicted by the war. When the pride of Bristolians was shaken by the modernist rage of economy-oriented urban development, the inhabitants revolted. Of course they did so in the context of widespread dissatisfaction about the economic crisis since the late 1960s and the lacking chances of political participation for the majority of the people in a rather rigid political system. But equally important was the changed climate of opinion with regard to questions of the historical identity of cities, promoted by the international movement for the protection of historical buildings in the early 1970s. The 'Fight for Bristol' in the 1970s provides a clear indication that matters of urban memory and identity were capable to stir up political commitment and thus become attractive for rather different sections of the urban society. Like in many other cities which started to deal with their built past in this period, urban rehabilitation and conservation turned out to be matters above party politics and affiliation (Priest/Cobb 1980).

Since the upheavals of the 1970s, the idea of constructing a 'new' city image based on 'Bristol's glorious past' has increasingly gained acceptance and support by political decision-makers, urban experts and civic society alike. Following the decision of the city fathers to abandon the idea of a comprehensive re-planning of the historic harbour area, a five-year-plan for urban conservation came into force in 1977. Historic buildings like the neo-romanesque Arnolfini Building were renovated and dedicated to new purposes. Even more important, the destruction of old and decrepit buildings was stopped. In the 1990s Bristol celebrated its rebirth as a 'City of the Sea' with the major event of a 'Festival of the Sea', celebrating the jubilee of the Bristol-sponsored journey of John Cabot to the Americas half a millennium before. Since then the annual harbour festival has become a hallmark of the city's efforts to strengthen civic collective memory and identity formation. In 2015 the Harbour Festival also stood in the centre of Bristol's activities as European Green Capital, showcasing the latest developments in the attempt to change the self-representation of the historic merchant city (Bristol Harbour Festival 2019). Behind all those endeavours lies the idea that the material heritage of the city not only embodies the memory of times long bygone, but that the physical remains convey lost meaning and history as well (Steets 2011).

There are other signs as well for the triumph of a by now widely adopted historically based self-esteem of the city which could not have gained this importance without the intervention of civil society half a century before. The restoration of the historic confluence of Avon and Frome around eight hundred years after the little rivulet Frome had been covered up to allow Bristol's commercial growth in the 12th century, the dismantling and disappearance of some of the concrete highrise structures built in the 1960s to mark Bristol's 'rise' in those years (Evening Post April 24, 1961) and not the least the reconstruction of Queen Square to its former architectural glory in recent years have added to Bristol's re-invented historical appearance. The fact that currently more than one and a half million inhabitants and tourists enter the formerly enclosed urban space every year to admire the rejuvenated Georgian facades, to listen to open-air-concerts or to participate in the annual petanque league run may be seen as a proof that historical imagery not necessarily has to get in the way of the modern appropriation of the city. Historical verifiability, even if it is only an allegedly one, serves the wishes of a travelling tourist class and has the potential to develop its own 'historical reality' (Lindner 2006; Groebner 2013; Groebner 2018). But 'old' Bristol nowadays is not only a place for tourists or idle city strollers. Quite to the contrary the administration in recent years has not only succeeded to build new living quarters in old warehouses, but also erected subsidised housing in close proximity to the old harbour area, thus safeguarding the interests of modern urbanites and the lower levels of urban society likewise—an approach followed by many urban rehabilitation schemes in Great Britain and other countries (Toyka-Seid 2017). Urban identity as can be seen in Britain's formerly 'Second City' may need the physical proof of historic buildings and urban arrangements, but it also needs the constant offer to participate in this history conveyed in old buildings and spaces and the feeling of belonging to the city. The Bristol example can show that shaping an urban identity cannot be left to politicians and planners. It needs the participation of the urban population in this process, it needs the articulation of different opinions and the input and acceptance of the people who have to live with the consequences of the re-living and re-invention of the city's built and remembered history, as it was postulated in the New Urban Agenda of UN Habitat III in Quito 2016. The fascination of the physical space of the historic city remains, even in times when modern urban theoreticians postulate ideas of the smart and virtual city (Rötzer 1995; Mitchell 1995; Schrenk et al. 2019). Cities will remain places for people who live, work and deal with their cities. It will be the task of future generations of urban historians to judge in which way the re-invention of the city as a place of urban memory and history in the early 21st century has contributed to the sustainability of cities (Schott/Toyka-Seid 2010).

References

Ackland, Mary (1989): The sixties in Bristol, Bristol: Redcliffe.
Ashworth, G. J./Tunbridge, J. E. (1996): Dissonant heritage: The management of the past as a resource of conflict, New York: Wiley.
Bandarin, Francesco/Oers, Ron v. (2012): Reconnecting the city: The historic urban landscape approach and the future of urban heritage, Oxford: Wiley.
Batty, J. H. (1986): Bristol observed: Visitors' impressions of the city from domesday to the Blitz, Bristol: Redcliffe.
Beeson, Anthony (2013): Central Bristol through time, Bristol: Amberley Publishing.
Bernhardt, Christoph (2014): "Längst beerdigt und doch quicklebendig: Zur widersprüchlichen Geschichte der 'autogerechten Stadt'." In: Zeithistorische Forschungen 14, pp. 526-540.
Betjeman, J. (1961): The most beautiful city in England, Daily Telegraph 8.5.1961.
Beyme, Klaus v. (1987): Der Wiederaufbau: Architektur und Städtebaupolitik in beiden deutschen Staaten, Munich/Zürich: Piper.
Boyer, Christine (1996): The city of collective memory: Its historical imagery and architectural entertainment, Cambridge, Mass.: MIT Press.
Bristol Architects' Forum (1969): Forum's Bristol plan, Bristol.
Bristol harbour festival 2019: (https://www.bristolharbourfestival.co.uk/about-history).
Bristol Planning Group (1968): The central area and its waterways, Bristol County Library Acc. Nr. B24572.
Broeze, Frank (ed.) (1989): Brides of the sea: Port cities of Asia from the 16th to the 20th centuries, Queensland: University of Hawaii Press.

Buttlar, Adrian v. (ed.) (2010): Denkmalpflege statt Attrapenkult: Gegen die Rekonstruktion von Baudenkmälern: Eine Anthologie, Basel: Birkhäuser.

Byrne, Eugene (2013): Unbuilt Bristol: The city that might have been, 1750-2050, Bristol: Redcliffe.

Castonguay, Stephane/Evenden, Matthew (2012): Urban rivers: Remaking rivers, cities and space in Europe and North America, Pittsburgh: University of Pittsburgh Press.

Clapson, Mark/Larkham, Peter (eds.) (2013): The Blitz and its legacy: War-time destruction to post-war reconstruction, Farnham: Taylor & Francis.

Choay, Francoise (1992): L'allegorie du patrimoine, Paris: Seuil.

Diefendorf, Jeffry (1993): In the wake of war: The reconstruction of German cities after World War II, New York: Oxford University Press.

Domhardt, Konstanze Sylva (2012): The Heart of the City: Die Stadt in den transatlantischen Debatten der CIAM 1933-1951, Zürich: GTA.

Falser, Michael/Lipp, Wilfried/ICOMOS Austria (eds.): (2015): Eine Zukunft für unsere Vergangenheit/A Future for Our Past/Un Avenir pour Notre Passé. Monumenta III, Vienna: Hendrik Bäßler.

Ferguson, G. (1989): "The high rise, concrete city." In: Mary Ackland (ed.), The sixties in Bristol, Bristol, pp. 27-31.

Frank, Sybille (2011): "Stadtmarketing." In: Martina Löw/Georgios Terizakis (eds.), Städte und ihre Eigenlogik: Ein Handbuch für Stadtplanung und Stadtentwicklung, Frankfurt a.M./New York: Campus, pp. 37-46.

Ganser, Karl (1999): Liebe auf den zweiten Blick: Internationale Bauausstellung Emscher Park. Dortmund: Harenberg.

Gehring, Petra (2008): "Was heißt Eigenlogik? Zu einem Paradigmenwechsel für die Stadtforschung." In: Helmuth Berking/Martina Löw (eds.), Die Eigenlogik der Städte: Neue Wege für die Stadtforschung, Frankfurt a.M./New York: Campus, pp. 153-168.

Goodbody, Axel/Wanning, Berbeli (2008): Wasser – Kultur – Ökologie, Göttingen: V&R Unipress.

Graham, Brian (2002): Heritage as knowledge: Capital or culture? Urban Studies 39:5-6, pp. 1003-1017.

Graham, Brian/Ashworth, G. J./Tunbridge, J. E. (2000): A geography of heritage: Power, culture and economy, London: Routledge.

Groebner, Valentin (2018): Retroland: Geschichtstourismus und die Sehnsucht nach dem Authentischen, Frankfurt a.M.: Fischer.

Groebner, Valentin (2013): "Touristischer Geschichtsgebrauch. Über einige Merkmale neuer Vergangenheiten im 20. und 21. Jahrhundert." In: Historische Zeitschrift 296.2, pp. 408-428.

Hasegawa, Junichi (1992): Replanning the blitzed city centre: A comparative study of Bristol, Coventry and Southampton 1941-1950, Buckingham: Open University Press.

Hawley, Steven (2011): Recovering a lost river: Removing dams, rewilding salmons, revitalizing communities, Boston: Beacon Press.

Hobsbawm, Eric/Ranger, Terence (eds.) (1992): The invention of tradition, Cambridge: Cambridge University Press.

Huse, Norbert (1997): Unbequeme Baudenkmäler: Entsorgen? Schützen? Pflegen? Munich: C.H. Beck.

Jacobs, Jane (1961): The death and life of great American cities, New York: Pimlico.

Jakobsson, Eva (2018): "Stockholms's changing waterscape: A long-term perspective on a city and its flowing water." In: Tim Soens/Dieter Schott/Michael Toyka-Seid/Bert De Munck (eds.), Urbanizing nature: Actors and agency (dis)connecting cities and nature since 1500, New York: Routledge, pp. 197-216.

Janssens, Ric/Soens, Tim (2018): "Urbanizing water: Looking beyond the transition to water modernity in the cities of the lower Low Countries, 13th to 19th centuries." In: Tim Soens/Dieter Schott/Michael Toyka-Seid/Bert De Munck (eds.), Urbanizing nature: Actors and agency (dis)connecting cities and nature since 1500, New York: Routledge, pp. 89-111.

Knoll, Martin/Lübken, Uwe/Schott, Dieter (eds.) (2017): Rivers lost—rivers regained: Rethinking city-river relationships, Pittsburgh: University of Pittsburgh Press.

Kocka, Jürgen (1997): "Wider die Idealisierung der historischen Stadt." In: Michael Mönninger (ed.), Stadtgesellschaft, Frankfurt a.M.: Suhrkamp, pp. 97-100.

Le Galés, Patrick (2002): European cities: Social conflicts and governance, Oxford: Oxford University Press.

Lee, L. (2002): "Relocating location: Cultural geography, the specificity of place and the city habitus." In: Jim McGuigan (ed.), Cultural methodologies, London: SAGE Publications, pp. 126-141.

Lindner, Rolf (2006): "The 'Gestalt' of the urban imaginary." In: European Studies 23, pp. 35-42.

Lindner, Rolf (2003): "Der Habitus der Stadt: Ein kulturgeographischer Versuch." In: PGM. Zeitschrift für Geo- und Umweltwissenschaften 147.2, pp. 46-53.

Löw, Martina (2008): "Eigenlogische Strukturen: Differenzen zwischen Städten als konzeptionelle Herausforderung." In: Helmuth Berking/Martina Löw (eds.), Die Eigenlogik der Städte: Neue Wege für die Stadtforschung, Frankfurt a.M./New York: Campus, pp. 33-54.

MacDonald, Peter (1995): Bristol: The most beautiful, interested and distinguished city in England, Bristol: Petmac Publications.

Macdonald, Sharon (2009): Difficult heritage: Negotiating the Nazi Past in Nuremberg and Beyond, Oxford/London: Routledge.

Massey, Doreen (2006): "Keine Entlastung für das Lokale." In: Helmuth Berking (ed.), Die Macht des Lokalen in einer Welt ohne Grenzen, Frankfurt a.M./New York: Campus, pp. 25-31.

McDowell, Sara (2008): "Heritage, memory and identity." In: Brian Graham/Peter Howard (eds.), The Ashgate research companion to heritage and identity, Aldershot: Ashgate, pp. 37-54.

Meier, Hans-Rudolf (2013): "Denkmalschutz als Leitinstrument der Stadtentwicklung?" In: Forum Stadt H. 1, pp. 35-51.

Mitchell, William J. (1995): City of bits: Space, place and the infobahn, Cambridge, Mass.: Cambridge University Press.

Mitscherlich, Alexander (1963): Die Unwirtlichkeit unserer Städte: Anstiftung zum Unfrieden, Frankfurt a.M.: Suhrkamp.

Morris, Jan (2001): Trieste and the meaning of nowhere, London: Faber.

Oevermann, Heike/Mieg, Harald A. (eds.) (2014): Industrial heritage sites in transformation: Clash of discourses, London/New York: Routledge.

Otter, Chris (2010): "Locating matter: The place of materiality in urban history." In: Tony Bennett/Patrick Joyce (eds.), Material powers: Cultural studies, history and the material turn, London: Taylor & Francis, pp. 38-59.

Philo, Chris/Kearns, Gerry (eds.) (1993): Selling places: The city as cultural capital. Past and present, Oxford: Pergamon.

Poole, Steve (ed.) (2013): A city built upon the water: Maritime Bristol 1750-1900, Bristol: Redcliffe.

Priest, Gordon (1972): A high buildings policy for Bristol. BCS Pamphlet No. 1, Bristol; Bristol County Library B25879.

Priest, Gordon/Cobb, Pamela (1980): The fight for Bristol: Planning and the Growth of Public Protest, Bristol: Redcliffe Press.

Ralph, E. (1997): "Queen Square." In: Bristol & West County Illustrated News, April.

Reichow, Hans Bernhard (1959): Die autogerechte Stadt: Ein Weg aus dem Verkehrs-Chaos, Ravensburg: Maier.

Rötzer, Florian (1995): "Die Telepolis: Urbanität im digitalen Zeitalter." In: Ullrich Schwarz (ed.), Risiko Stadt? Hamburg: Bollmann, pp. 176-189.

Saretzki, A. (2016): "Die vermarktete Stadt: Städtisches Kulturerbe aus marketingtheoretischer Sicht." In: Informationen zur modernen Stadtgeschichte 1, pp. 66-74.

Schleich, Erwin (1978): Die zweite Zerstörung Münchens, Stuttgart: Steinkopf.

Schott, Dieter (2016): "The taming of the Soar: Leicester transforms its river environment." In: Richard Rodger/Rebecca Madgin (eds.), Leicester: A modern history, Lancaster: Carnegie Publishing, pp. 115-136.

Schott, Dieter (2007): "Stadt und Fluss: Flüsse als städtische Umwelten im 19. und 20. Jahrhundert." In: Bernd Herrmann (ed.), Beiträge zum Götinger Umwelthistorischen Kolloquium 2004-2006, Göttingen: Universitätsverlag, pp. 145-162.

Schott, Dieter (2004): "Zukunft und Geschichte der Stadt: Stadtrepräsentationen im 20. Jahrhundert." In: Georg Iggers/Dieter Schott/Hanns H. Seidler/Michael Toyka-Seid (eds.), Hochschule – Geschichte – Stadt: Festschrift für Helmut Böhme, Darmstadt: wbg Academic, pp. 319-341.

Schott, Dieter/Toyka-Seid, Michael (2010): "Stadt und Nachhaltigkeit." In: Informationen zur modernen Stadtgeschichte 2, pp. 7-21.

Schenk, Manfred/Popovich, Vasiliy V./Zeile, Peter/Elisei, Pietro/Beyer, Clemens/Ryser, Judith (2019): Is this the real world? Perfect smart cities vs. real emotional cities, Vienna: Competence Center of Urban and Regional Planning.

Schubert Dirk (2003): "Aus der Geschichte lernen? Hafen- und Uferzonen im Wandel." In: Informationen zur modernen Stadtgeschichte 2, pp. 34-42.

Schwarz, Werner Michael/ Spitaler, Georg/ Wikidal, Elke (eds.) (2019): Das Rote Wien – 1919-1934: Ideen, Debatten, Praxis, Vienna: Birkhäuser.

Siedler, Wolf J./Niggemeyer, Elisabeth/Angress, Gina (1964): Die gemordete Stadt: Abgesang auf Putte und Straße, Platz und Baum, Berlin: Herbig.

Soyez, Dietrich (2016): "Industriekultur als städtisches Erbe und lebendige Präsenz." In: Informationen zur modernen Stadtgeschichte 1, pp. 53-65.

Steets, Silke (2011): "Architektur." In: Martina Löw/Georgiuos Terizakis (eds.), Städte und ihre Eigenlogik: Ein Handbuch für Stadtplanung und Stadtentwicklung, Frankfurt a.M./New York: Campus, pp. 133-140.

Toyka-Seid, Michael (2019): "The roots of the sustainable city: The visible waters of the city in modern Mainz and Wiesbaden." In: Tim Soens/Dieter Schott/Michael Toyka-Seid/Bert De Munck (eds.), Urbanizing nature: Actors and agency (dis)connecting cities and nature since 1500, New York: Routledge, pp. 290-300.

Toyka-Seid, Michael (2003a): "Bristol – Köln." In: Helmut Böhme/Arnold Körte/Michael Toyka-Seid (eds.), Wohnen – Planen – Bauen: Erneuerung historischer Kernstädte in Südostasien und Europa im historisch-architektonischen Vergleich, Darmstadt: WBG, pp. 19-74.

Toyka-Seid, Michael (2003b): "From urban harmony to civil strife: Civic pride, urban representation and the changing fate of Queen Square in Bristol." In: Andreas Fahrmeir/Elfie Rembold (eds.), Representation of British cities: The transformation of urban space 1700-2000, Berlin: Philo, pp. 90-107.

Vinken, Gerhard: "Lokale Sinnstiftung – Die Bedeutung der Denkmale." In: Helmuth Berking/Martina Löw (eds.), Die Eigenlogik der Städte: Neue Wege für die Stadtforschung, Frankfurt a.M./New York: Campus, pp. 73-82.

Ward, Stephen (2002): Planning the twentieth century city: The advanced capitalist word, Chicester: Academy Press.

Ward, Stephen (2011): The garden city: Past, present and future, London: Routledge.

White, Richard (1995): The organic machine: The remaking of the Columbia river. New York: Hill & Wang.

Wirth, Louis (1938): "Urbanism as a way of life." In: American Journal of Sociology 44.1 (July), pp. 1-24.

Urban Heritage and Urban Development

Rebecca Madgin

Debates concerning the relationship between heritage and urban development have spanned centuries.[1] These debates have recently intensified as cities across Europe have increasingly wrestled with the ways in which their historic environment can be considered in the context of achieving sustainable urban development. Furthermore, the rapid urbanisation of countries such as China and India has added a further dimension to debates concerning the contemporary relevance of historic buildings. These debates reached their clearest expression, in terms of international practice, through the introduction of the *Historic Urban Landscapes* (HUL) approach by UNESCO in 2011 (Bandarin and van Oers 2012). The report emphasised the role of historic buildings within the broader context of urban development. However, this report, which provides a framework for historic cities, is not new in identifying the relationship between heritage and development (Sonkoly 2017). As this chapter will illustrate, academic research from across a number of different fields, including urban history, urban studies, archaeology, architecture, planning history and critical heritage studies, has consistently sought to examine the ways in which historic buildings have been considered within urban development strategies. The chapter will consider first the relationship between urban change and urban conservation and second the extent to which urban conservation has moved from the margins to the mainstream of urban development and sustainability strategies. This discussion also touches on some key ideas and debates that have framed research as well as the ways in which the literature has evolved over time.

---

1 This work was supported by the Arts and Humanities Research Council [grant number AH/P007058/1].

Preservation, Conservation and Heritage

This chapter considers the role of historic buildings within urban development across time and place. To achieve this a number of different terms have to be used in order to stay true to their original usage. More specifically, the terms preservation, conservation, and heritage are used within this chapter. These terms have been used synonymously within existing literature, but they are subject to differing definitions in an international context. As Jokilehto explained in his seminal work on architectural conservation, the theory behind restoration and preservation continually differed between countries and time periods (1999). For example, in America the term preservation is used to describe a process that in the United Kingdom would be called conservation. Similarly, heritage can mean an inheritance, or it can refer more literally to natural, built, cultural, intangible and tangible assets.

For clarification, when the term preservation is used in this chapter it is defined as a process by which no modernisation of the building occurs except for necessary maintenance works in which original materials reflecting the historic integrity of the building are used. Conservation is also subject to much debate concerning the exact extent and type of change made to the historic building. For the purposes of this chapter, conservation is used to describe the adaptive re-use of a historic building. This can mean that the building's interior and/or its structure are modernised in order to fulfil a contemporary use. Heritage is used in a literal, rather than figurative sense, and applies to both built heritage and the memories and meanings that are embedded within historic places.

Reacting to Loss: The Emergence of Preservation and Conservation

The city is a palimpsest of traditions, history, thoughts and memories which is constantly being changed and re-negotiated by urban stakeholders. The pace and scale of urban development demands that value judgements are made on the existing built environment. Investigating why buildings should be retained in the face of change reveals their value to contemporary society. As Miller stated "so long as there is no suggestion of change, no perception of threat" then the meanings invested in a place "tend to remain implicit and unexpressed" (2003: 29). However, in times of rapid change, the past is ascribed with a contemporary value as the "continued existence of familiar surroundings may satisfy a psychological need, which even if irrational, is very real. Nothing gives more tangible assurance of stability than bricks and mortar." (Hubbard 1993: 363)

Recognising the value of heritage has traditionally been provoked by the threat of change and in particular the pace and scale of urban change. Indeed, the lived experience of the pace and scale of urban change acted as a catalyst for the development of both the preservation and conservation movements in the UK. *Antiquaries*, a pioneering work by Roey Sweet, conveyed the public outcry against the demolition of medieval town walls and historic buildings because they were said to embody the "collective memory and the communal identity of the town or city" (2004: 295). The relationship between urban change and antiquarian action was further demonstrated in Australia as Davison explained how fire damage to colonial buildings in Sydney motivated the lawyer-antiquarian J.M. Forde to research the history of the city (Davison and McConville 1991). The theme of reacting to loss remained present in a more formal way in the 19th century in the UK as the Society for the Protection of Ancient Buildings (SPAB), one of the earliest formal preservation societies, wanted to "[t]urn public attention to the intrinsic value of our ancient buildings, and the grievous loss we incur by their destruction" (SPAB 1874). Ashworth, one of the leading scholars in the study of urban heritage, believed this backlash against destruction was a reaction to the 'crude forces' of urbanisation and industrialisation and thus drew a further connection between urban change and the desire to protect historic buildings. As such the early preservation movement in the UK focussed predominantly on rural, pre-industrial artefacts and desired a nostalgic evocation of the 'rustic idyll' (Ashworth 1991: 16).

This relationship between preservation and urban change developed further as a result of World War II, when wartime destruction provided both the opportunity and the necessity to re-configure urban space. Early work within urban history highlighted the existence of a dichotomy in approaches to post-war reconstruction: to reconstruct, or to embrace modernism and build new. This field of research has been led by Jeffry Diefendorf's corpus of work on European cities (1990), and the lens has more recently been widened to include cities in Japan (Hein et al. 2003) and China (Lincoln 2015). Further work in a UK context led by Larkham (2003) and Pendlebury (2004) demonstrated how planners failed to recognise the significance of historic buildings within reconstruction plans as they favoured created overtly modernist plans.

Notwithstanding the grandiose plans of the immediate post-war period, there was however a cultural hangover concerning the scale of destruction of the existing environment. Jörg Arnold, whilst not writing specifically about urban heritage, used diaries to examine the emotional impact of loss in German cities and the ways in which it impacted on post-World War II reconstruction planning (2011). This theme, concerning the psychological dimension of urban destruction, was also found within Grenville's seminal work in which she demonstrated the horror of losing historic buildings in a UK town: "I read [...] with horror of the proposed pulling down of Worcester brick by brick [...] Worcester is an old and faithful city and its charm lies in its ancient streets and buildings and lack of modern structures [...] The idea is nothing short of a scandal" (Grenville 2007: 455). Grenville's work was markedly different to the majority of published research on the link between heritage and reconstruction. She followed Giddens' notion of ontological security, defined as "the confidence that most human beings have in the continuity of their self-identity and the constancy of the surrounding social and material environments of action" (Giddens 1990: 92), and its relationship to the preservation of historic buildings.

In the context of widespread loss it thus is no coincidence that ideas to enshrine heritage protection in legislation emerged as a global concern during the 1940s. In France, for example, this occurred under the Vichy Regime with the law of February 25, 1943 which amended the 1913 *Monuments Historiques* to protect both the monument and its surrounding area. Many of the formal listing systems, however, developed in the immediate aftermath of World War II. The key period across the globe seems to have been 1945-49 which saw the creation of the Town and Country Planning Act in the UK, and the formation of the New South Wales National Trust in Australia and the National Trust for Historic Preservation in the United States. This was likely no coincidence as Lesh, working in the context of 20th century Australia, and Swenson, working in the context of 19th century Europe, both emphasised the importance of the transnational flow of ideas in shaping legislative protection (Lesh 2018; Swenson 2013). Furthermore, the global circulation of ideas concerning heritage protection was further supported at the supranational level by charters such as the *Convention for the Protection of Cultural Property in the Event of Armed Conflict* (1954), which sought to enshrine the importance of retaining the historic environment within international practice.

Despite this raft of legislation, threats to the historic environment continued into the 1960s. However, this time the threat came not from wartime damage, but from urban planning initiatives that favoured comprehensive redevelopment. Again, the tensions between history and modernity identified by Larkham and Pendlebury were evident, but this time resulted in the backlash against the modernist architecture of the 1960s (Klemek 2011) and the principles of modern planning (Jacobs 1961). Crucially, this period saw a number of grassroots campaigns mounted by local communities to stop what they saw as the annihilation of their way of life in and amongst a familiar environment. Alongside polemics such as *The Sack of Bath* (1973) were emotionally laden texts which pleaded with urban planners to retain historic buildings. Gomme and Walker recognised that Glasgow, a great proponent of comprehensive redevelopment, "will not survive a massacre of buildings which define it" and exhorted that "preservation of isolated special monuments is not enough"; if we "want Glasgow to remain Glasgow, we must [...] consult the genius of the place in all" (1968: 255). Running alongside such arguments were high-profile campaigns in a range of cities across Europe and America, perhaps most famously, the campaign to prevent the demolition of Les Halles in Paris and Penn Station in New York. Jane Jacobs was involved in a number of these campaigns in New York and her published work in this period is a crucial, yet overlooked, aspect of the urban heritage field. Jacobs' seminal work *The Death and Life of Great American Cities* (1961) sought to "attack [...] the principles and aims that have shaped modern, orthodox city planning and rebuilding" by offering a different approach to urban planning and one that noticed the role that old buildings could play within this (Jacobs 1961: 3). However, whilst Jacobs stated that "cities need old buildings so badly it is probably impossible for vigorous streets and districts to grow without them", she was more concerned with facilitating different economic needs and not with preservation for preservation's sake (1993: 244). The key element of Jacobs' work for the development of the urban heritage field was her ability to see historic buildings as an integral element of the urban jigsaw rather than individual monuments. Furthermore, Jacobs' work introduced the economic and emotional value of urban heritage to a wider audience. In recent years Jacobs' work has been heavily criticised, largely for seemingly pre-empting gentrification. But it does provide an early and formative account of the importance of the historic environment that stretches beyond the traditional focus on architectural and historic interest (Schubert 2014).

The 1960s are commonly acknowledged as the pivotal period for heritage protection both in Europe and beyond and the point at which a shift from protecting individual monuments towards protecting groups of buildings occurred and thus towards preventing the worst excesses of comprehensive redevelopment initiatives.

Again the global flow of ideas was seen with the creation of a number of similar laws across countries in a relatively short period of time. For example, the Loi Malraux (France, 1962), the creation of the National Historic Preservation Act (America, 1966), the Civic Amenities Act (UK, 1967), and Law 765 (Italy, 1967) each stressed the importance of conserving areas rather than single monuments. In France, the Loi Malraux created secteurs sauvegardé which were areas that contained a number of historically significant buildings. France is traditionally considered the leader in protecting groups of historic buildings, yet the USA has a longer tradition through efforts to preserve the Vieux Carre in New Orleans (1921) and Charleston (1931). However, the USA did not formally set up a national register of places and landmarks until 1966 and as such the Loi Malraux is commonly attributed as the first example of providing group protection. In many respects, the UK Civic Amenities Act was similar to the Loi Malraux as it also created conservation areas. However, whilst the 1967 Act was the first instance of a planning and protection policy in the United Kingdom to acknowledge the role of the historic environment in the urban future, it focused on preservation. Unlike the Loi Malraux, the Civic Amenities Act made no reference to finding a new use for a historic building. The change from preservation to conservation in France occurred much earlier than in Britain where finding new uses for old buildings did not become common until the consequences of the economic downturn of the 1970s.

These acts marked a dual shift in the evolution of European conservation and planning ideals. Firstly, as identified in influential works by Dobby (1978), Appleyard (1979), Kain (1981) and Larkham (1996), conservation now embraced areas rather than just individual buildings. Secondly, conservation areas and urban plans now offered a degree of protection from the comprehensive renewal programmes and introduced a policy, in theory at least, of valuing the historic environment within wider urban development policies.

Theoretically the development of legislative protection made it more difficult to demolish historic buildings. Indeed, this trend towards favouring the retention and re-use of historic buildings continued into the late twentieth century as conservation became one part of an urban survival strategy designed to ameliorate the impact of deindustrialisation in Western cities. In particular, the contraction of the manufacturing sector led to a reliance on what Hewison, in his seminal work *The Heritage Industry* (1987), perceived to be the last and only resource—heritage. The decline of the traditional industries left urban centres with no option but to recycle and re-present the past in an attempt to counter economic decline. Hewison's work focused on the use of industrial museums such as Wigan Pier in northern Britain. The phenomenon was also apparent with the use of former industrial structures as part of urban regeneration strategies.

Within this economic context, the historic environment was viewed as a catalyst for securing property-led urban regeneration. In many former industrial cities, historic buildings were converted into apartments, offices, bars, and restaurants. This reconceptualisation of the industrial legacy was an international issue with notable examples of restoring groups of historic buildings in the United States with Lowell National Heritage Park (1978), in France with the rehabilitation of the Le Blan complex in Lille (1980) and in Britain with Dean Clough in Halifax (1983). A focus on the area rather than an individual building was carried through from the 1960s to the 1980s, as the dual processes of deindustrialisation and depopulation in Western industrial cities led to a need for socio-economic diversification. As such, the 1980s saw the value of heritage tied much more firmly to its supposed economic value. Areas such as the Albert Dock in Liverpool, Castlefield in Manchester and the Jewellery Quarter in Birmingham used a combination of public and private sector funding to adaptively re-use their historic environment (Madgin 2010). Accompanying this shift was a focus on the role of heritage within place marketing strategies as cities sought to use their heritage as their unique selling point in order to attract both human and capital investment (Ashworth/ Kavaratzis 2011). The protection of heritage had now moved away from preventing loss towards a consideration of how conservation could aid the socio-economic transformation of cities at the turn of the twenty-first century.

Heritage and Sustainable Urban Development

> [...] the role of urban conservation as an aim of planning has also undergone a transformation, shifting it from the margins to the mainstream, and in this shift, urban conservation has become an inescapable element of the way cities remake themselves in the twenty-first century (Pendlebury/Strange 2011: 361).

Pendlebury and Strange recognised the ways which protection of urban heritage gradually became a central concern of urban development strategies in the English city during the latter decades of the twentieth century. In part, this was due to the evolution of legislation which itself was based on emotional reactions to the threat and reality of loss alongside the transnational circulation of ideas concerning heritage protection. This narrative was not restricted to the English city but was embedded in the internationally-focused *Historic Urban Landscapes* approach first outlined in 2011. This approach took the idea of mainstreaming within planning further to see heritage as an integral part of sustainable urban development. The HUL approach was derived from two core beliefs: First, existing planning systems failed to adequately consider heritage and second, the traditional approach to conservation is "no longer valid" and indeed is "rooted in nineteenth century ideology" which therefore "fails to provide a convincing definition of what historic values are appreciated by modern societies; excludes communities in the definition of heritage, and, above all, it does not allow the understanding and management of change" (Bandarin/van Oers 2014: 13). Alongside this, the HUL approach stated that there was a need to "better integrate and frame urban heritage conservation strategies within the larger goals of overall sustainable development" (HUL Recommendation 2011: 2). In essence the HUL approach went beyond mainstream planning to consider the ways in which heritage could contribute to sustainable development goals. This new approach moved away from the traditional veneration of the architectural and historic interest of historic buildings and towards a belief that the conservation of heritage could play a significant role in achieving sustainable urban development in its economic, social and environmental dimensions.

The relationship between heritage and sustainable urban development is one current focus of research, much of which is carried by scholars analysing the Historic Urban Landscapes approach (cf. Bandarin 2019: 13-16). At an international level, the ways in which the historic environment could contribute to sustainable urban development was made explicit through the UNESCO-statement that urban heritage is "a social, cultural and economic asset for the development of cities" (2011: 5). This position was supported by the UK Government as they maintained that

> [...] the historic environment is an asset of enormous cultural, social, economic and environmental value. It makes a very real contribution to our quality of life and the quality of our places. [...] It can be a powerful driver for economic growth, attracting investment and tourism, and providing a focus for successful regeneration (2010: 1).

At both a national and international level, urban heritage is therefore no longer at the margins of urban development or a problem to be solved. It has come to be seen as a panacea for a number of urban ills and as a mechanism to help realise sustainable urban development. Within this discourse the desire to see conservation as managing change rather than preventing loss is pre-eminent and as such focusses on the three dimensions of sustainability: economic, social and environmental development. This accords with the instrumentalisation of heritage into considering what it can *achieve* or how it can *contribute* to sustainable urban development or rather what *value* it has.

The values-based approach to heritage management grew out of the influential Burra Charter, first published in 1979. It promoted the cultural significance of historic places beyond their material fabric and was popularised by the Getty Conservation Institute through a series of reports (1999; 2000; 2002; 2005). This approach then worked its way into future international charters, most explicitly the Faro Convention (2005), and is currently seen as a crucial component of sustainable urban development. Within this context, identifying the values of heritage and how this can help realise sustainable urban development is crucial and, despite some critique, is now the dominant way of viewing the historic environment (Poulios 2010; Fredheim/Khalaf 2016). The below sections take three values of heritage: economic, social and environmental value to consider existing and emergent research themes.

Economic Value

Establishing the economic value of heritage has long preoccupied academics and practitioners. A fierce debate has raged surrounding the 'ambiguous relationship' between heritage and economic value (Ashworth 2002: 9). It has revolved around two questions: first, whether heritage should and could be commodified, and second, how to collect robust data that illustrate the economic value of re-used historic buildings. The first point relates to the traditional origins of the preservation movement and the desire to respect the aesthetic, architectural, and historic interest of heritage to recognise that "there is a strongly felt view that any attempt to attach economic values to heritage is at best a pointless irrelevance and at worst an unacceptable soiling of the aesthetically sublime with the commercially mundane" (Graham et al. 2000: 129). On the other hand, commentators have extolled the virtues of re-using historic buildings. Binney found that historic industrial buildings in the UK were "built to last, their load bearing walls are solid and made to carry massive floor loadings" (1990: 13). Furthermore, Binney stated that "they are extremely adaptable as the majority are laid out on an open plan and can be repaired and upgraded for a range of uses". The adaptive re-use of buildings therefore offered the chance for the private sector to be "handsomely rewarded by profit" (1990: 13). Contrary to these findings, Ashworth believed that "few historic buildings have been saved from demolition by dominantly economic arguments" yet did acknowledge that "listed commercial buildings hold their own in the property market and perform as investments as well as, if not better than, similar unlisted institutional buildings" (Ashworth 2002: 23). As such, establishing and publicising the economic value of heritage has recently been the subject of much research within academia and practice in the UK. These findings have focused on both historic residential buildings located within conservation areas (Ahlfeldt et al. 2012) but also the value of commercial historic buildings (Heritage Lottery Fund 2013).

Common across the findings is the identification of a heritage premium. In a residential context Ahlfeldt et al. found that houses in conservation areas in England sell, on average, for a premium of 23 per cent (2012: 5) whereas the Heritage Lottery Fund found that "[a]cross the UK, the businesses based in listed buildings are highly productive and make an estimated annual contribution to UK GDP of £47 billion and employ approximately 1.4 million people. This represents 3.5 per cent of the UK's 'gross value added' (GVA) and 5 per cent of total UK employment" (HLF 2013: 7). However, these positive findings are contradicted by other studies. For example, Labadi in her European-wide evaluation of the socio-economic impacts of heritage-led regeneration put forward the view that the evaluations she examined were often subject to what she terms "optimism bias" defined as "the demonstrated, systematic tendency for project appraisers to be overly optimistic about project costs, duration and benefits" (Department for Communities and Local Government 2007: 5, quoted in Labadi 2011: 106). It would appear that whilst evidence for the economic value of heritage is forthcoming, Ashworth's contention concerning the "ambiguous relationship" remains correct.

Social Value

The identification of social value and its use within urban management strategies is a key aspect of the *Historic Urban Landscapes* approach. The HUL moves the debate away from the veneration of the material fabric to embrace the ways in which social life relates to the existing urban structure. This approach marks an extension of a number of international charters such as the Burra Charter (1979), the Faro Convention (2005) and the Quebec Declaration (2008) in foregrounding the experiential dimensions of historic places (Madgin et al. 2018). As van Oers and Haraguchi stated "it is as much about buildings and spaces, as about rituals and values that people bring to the city." (2010: 14)

The HUL approach thus seeks to embed social values at the heart of urban change and marks an evolution from the legislative approach adopted in the 1960s. In sum, the HUL moves away from just seeing the value of heritage as aesthetic, architectural and historic and towards also respecting the rituals, cultural values, and experiences of people within the city. This approach is challenging for a heritage sector where legislation still privileges the architectural and the historic. Whereas some countries such as England do include communal and social value in their definition of what makes a historic place significant, legislation still statutorily requires only architectural and historic criteria to be met.

At the heart of the social value conundrum is a difficulty of defining what it is, let alone how best to capture it. Whilst national policies and international charters, such as the Burra Charter (1979; 2013) and Quebec Declaration (2008), have increasingly recognised a relationship between people and historic places, there has been very little agreement on which terminology to use. For example, intangible spirit, feeling, meaning, sense of place, identity or social and communal value have each been used within the discourse about people-historic place relationships. At the heart of each of the above terms is a desire to understand the components of the relationship between people and heritage (Wells 2015). Urban historians have largely neglected the social value aspects of urban heritage bar a few notable examples (Madgin et al. 2018; Pendlebury/Hewitt 2017; Gregory 2015). These works identified the ways in which a sense of belonging developed between people and the historic environment that motivated their desire to prevent the loss of historic spaces. Ideas surrounding the social value of heritage are much more developed within the field of critical heritage studies (Johnstone 1992; Emerick 2014; Jones/Leech 2015). There they are often used to further challenge the Authorised Heritage Discourse (AHD), developed by Laura Jane Smith (2006) and the notion of experts (Schofield 2014; Madgin/Taylor 2015).

One of the main issues with social value, especially in the context of urban development, is that it leads to "many unsupported claims as to its (heritage) value". Whilst statements such as "historic places foster community identity" and "historic places enrich our lives" may be true, "we lack sufficient evidence to understand, much less support them" (Wells 2015: 48). For example, Historic England acknowledged that communal and social values "are not always clearly recognised by those who share them" (2008: 31). Labadi took this further to lament the "erroneous assumption that rehabilitating historic urban areas with the aid of cultural or heritage projects always leads to an improvement for the local community" (2011: 112). Methodological innovation that can provide a robust evidence base has been forthcoming but despite this, asserting the relevance of qualitative data remains problematic both within academia and the wider heritage sector (Wells/ Stiefel 2018).

A final issue with the identification of social value is the further confusion of where it occurs in the heritage management cycle. Put differently, is social value an 'input', i.e. part of the criteria for designation and management, or an 'output', i.e. the social benefits of, for example, retaining a historic building or engaging with an urban heritage site. Much work in an academic context has sought to examine what social value is and how it can be used within designation and management strategies (Mayes 2018; Jones 2017; Wells 2017), whereas the wider heritage sector has focused on trying to identify the social benefits of engaging with heritage (Historic England 2018).

As with economic value, it appears that there is also an ambiguous relationship between social value and heritage. A number of claims have been made to support its existence and importance but these claims have not yet managed to challenge the traditional veneration of the physical fabric among legislators in many countries.

Environmental Value

> Generally, the literature dealing with the intersection of sustainable development and heritage is scant, and can perhaps be best characterized as thin and largely descriptive case studies (Bushell 2015: 503).

Sustainable urban development comprises a number of different facets: social, economic and environmental. Whilst the above sections demonstrate the increasing focus on economic and social value within research and practice, the place of environmental value is less secure. As Bushell acknowledges, the environmental value of urban heritage is an area that has not captured the attention of many academics. Partly this is due to the elusive concepts of sustainability, sustainable development, heritage and sustainable cities. Rodwell's seminal work, *Conservation and Sustainability in Historic Cities* (2007), acknowledges that the concept of sustainable cities is nebulous. He points to a 1994 definition which states that a sustainable city is "one in which its people and businesses continuously endeavour to improve their natural, built and cultural environments at neighbourhood and regional levels, whilst working in ways which always support the goal of global sustainable development" (2007: 111). This definition, Rodwell continues, aligns with the goals of Patrick Geddes and also Gustavo Giovannoni who both sought to see the city as an ecosystem. In a similar vein, Jacobs' work on New York also saw the city as an ecosystem and recognises the environmental value of walkable cities—a street pattern that is commonly seen within historic cities such as Rome and Edinburgh. Further, historic buildings are a source of embodied energy adding a further level of environmental value to the conservation of existing buildings.

Current debates within the context of environmental value centre on first how historic buildings can be rehabilitated in an environmentally friendly way, and second the ways in which historic cities already contribute to sustainable urban development. The work that does exist tends to focus on climate change and environmental sustainability rather than considering the role of heritage within the framework of sustainable urban development (Howard 2013; Heathcote et al. 2017). In addition, whilst there are a number of tools to assess the environmental value of historic buildings, research does not often examine the ways in which these buildings contribute to the environmental dimension of sustainable urban development (Fouseki/Cassar 2014) nor are the industry-standard tools, such as BREEAM, often used within heritage management (Shetabi 2015). Avenues for research may arise from the popularisation of the HUL approach as it seeks to shift the mindset away from individual buildings towards the urban landscape as a holistic entity. Contained within this is a desire to assess the sustainability of historic social, economic and environmental dimensions of sustainability and in particular to consider the resilience of historic cities (Bigio 2014). Rodwell's seminal work is now supported by a raft of publications that seek to examine the concept of sustainable development in the context of heritage (Labadi/Logan 2016; Leifeste/Stiefel 2018). However, as with social value, a shift in philosophy and attitude towards conservation needs to be matched by changes in practice. This is evident within Caitlin DeSilvey's work in which she puts forward a different management strategy that embraces loss as part of the heritage eco-system. DeSilvey puts forward the notion of 'curated decay' in which she suggests that we need to rethink how we preserve historic sites in what she terms "postpreservation", stating that it is "possible to look beyond loss to conceive ways of understanding and acknowledging material change" (2017: 1). This position returns the field to one that embraces the inextricable role of 'loss' within urban conservation and how different pressures—economic, social, environmental—can affect the ways in which built heritage is managed. Given the recent declaration of a 'climate emergency' it may well be that the narrative of loss that provoked much of heritage practice and policy in the nineteenth and twentieth century is further developed into the twenty-first century.

Conclusions: From Reactive to Proactive?

The field of urban heritage is diverse, incorporating different ontological assumptions and epistemological positions. Accordingly, this chapter has drawn on material from within urban history, urban studies, planning history, archaeology, architecture and critical heritage studies as well as from the wider built environment sector. The chapter has sought to provide both a retrospective view of changes to the legislative system in different cultural contexts as well as to show how both academic literature and professional practice have evolved since the middle of the twentieth century. Contained within this are some emerging themes that open up the prospective view for urban heritage studies. Crucially, as heritage is increasingly embedded within a values-based approach that now considers cities as urban landscapes rather than isolated buildings, future research could critique the economic, social and environmental values that are often attributed to heritage within policy rhetoric. If heritage has moved from the margins to the mainstream, then it has done so by shifting from primarily being 'reactive' in that it sought to mediate loss and manage the extent of change, towards being 'proactive' by seeking to place heritage at the centre of sustainable urban management strategies. Rather than focus on managing change, perhaps the future of urban heritage, both as a field of study and professional practice, will instead emphasise the need to manage continuity within broader sustainable urban development strategies.

References

Ahlfeldt, Gabriel M./Holman, Nancy/Wendland, Nicolai (2012): An assessment of the effects of conservation areas on value: (https://content.historicengland.org.uk/content/docs/research/assessment-ca-value.pdf).
Appleyard, Donald (1979): The conservation of European cities, Massachusetts: MIT Press.
Arnold, Jörg (2011): The allied air war and urban memory: The legacy of strategic bombing in Germany, Cambridge: Cambridge University Press.
Ashworth, Gregory John (2002): "Conservation designation and the revaluation of property: The risk of heritage innovation." In: International Journal of Heritage Studies 8/1, pp. 9-23.
Ashworth, Gregory John (1991): Heritage planning: Conservation as the management of urban change, Groningen: Geo Pers.
Ashworth, Gregory John/Kavaratzis, Mihalis (2011): "Why brand the future with the past? The role of heritage in the construction and promotion of place brand reputations." In: Frank M. Go/Robert Govers (eds.), International place branding yearbook, London: Palgrave MacMillan, pp. 25-46.
Bandarin, Francesco/Pereira Roders, Ana (2019): Reshaping urban conservation: The historic urban landscape approach in action, Singapore: Springer.
Bandarin, Francesco/van Oers, Ron (2012): The historic urban landscape: Managing heritage in an urban century, Chichester: Wiley Blackwell.

Bandarin, Francesco/van Oers, Ron (2014): Reconnecting the city: The historic urban landscape approach and the future of urban heritage, Chichester: Wiley Blackwell.

Bigio, Anthony Gad (2014): "Historic cities and climate change." In: Bandarin Francesco/van Oers, Ron (eds.), Reconnecting the city: The historic urban landscape approach and the future of urban heritage, Chichester: Wiley Blackwell, pp. 113-128.

Binney, Marcus/Machin, Francis/Powell, Ken (1990): Bright future, the re-use of industrial buildings, London: SAVE Britain's Heritage.

Bushell, Robyn (2015): "Heritage and sustainable development: Transdisciplinary imaginings of a wicked concept." In: Waterton, Emma/Watson, Steve (eds.), The palgrave handbook of contemporary heritage research, Hampshire: Palgrave Macmillan, pp. 492-506.

Council of Europe (2005): Council of Europe framework convention on the value of cultural heritage for society: (https://www.coe.int/en/web/conventions/full-list//conventions/rms/0900001680083746).

Davison, Grame/McConville, Chris (eds.) (1991): A heritage handbook, Sydney: Allen & Unwin.

De la Torre, Marta (2002): Assessing the values of cultural heritage: Research report, Los Angeles: Getty Conservation Institute.

Department for Communities and Local Government (2007): Regeneration: Adjusting for optimism bias in regeneration, projects and programmes. General Guidance Note, London: Department for Communities and Local Government.

DeSilvey, Caitlin (2017): Curated decay: Heritage beyond saving, Minnesota: University of Minnesota Press.

Diefendorf, Jeffry M. (1990): Rebuilding Europe's bombed cities, Basingstoke: MacMillan.

Dobby, Alan (1978): Conservation and planning, London: Hutchinson.

Emerick, Keith (2014): Conserving and managing ancient monument: Heritage, democracy, and inclusion, Woodbridge: Boydell & Brewer

Fergusson, Adam (1973): The sack of Bath, Salisbury: Compton Russell.

Fouseki, Kalliopi/Cassar, May (2014): "Energy efficiency in heritage buildings: Future challenges and research needs." In: The Historic Environment 5/2, pp. 95-100.

Fredheim, Harald L./Khalaf, Manal (2016): "The significance of values: Heritage value typologies re-examined." In: International Journal of Heritage Studies 22/6, pp. 466-481.

Getty Conservation Institute (2005): Values and heritage conservation, Los Angeles: Getty Conservation Institute.

Giddens, Anthony. (1991): Modernity and self-identity: Self and society in the late modern age, Cambridge: Polity.

Gomme, Andor/Walker, David (1968): Architecture of Glasgow, London: Lund Humphries.
Graham, Brian/Ashworth, Gregory John/Tunbridge, John E. (2000): A geography of heritage, power, culture and economy, London: Arnold.
Gregory, Jenny (2015): "Connecting with the past through social media: The 'beautiful buildings and cool places Perth has lost' Facebook group." In: International Journal of Heritage Studies 21/1, pp. 22-45.
Grenville, Jane (2007): "Conservation as psychology: Ontological security and the built environment." In: International Journal of Heritage Studies 13/6, pp. 447-461.
Heathcote, Jen/Fluck, Hannah/Wiggins, Meredith (2017): "Predicting and adapting to climate change: Challenges for the historic environment" In: The Historic Environment: Policy & Practice 8/2, pp. 89-100.
Hein, Carola/Diefendorf, Jeffry/Ishida Yorifusa (eds.) (2003): Rebuilding urban Japan after 1945, London: Palgrave Macmillan.
Heritage Lottery Fund (2013): New ideas need old buildings: (https://www.heritagefund.org.uk/sites/default/files/media/research/new_ideas_old_buildings_2013.pdf).
Hewison, Robert (1987): The heritage industry: Britain in a climate of decline, London: Methuen.
Historic England (2008): Conservation principles, policies and guidance: (https://content.historicengland.org.uk/images-books/publications/conservation-principles-sustainable-management-historic-environment/conservationprinciplespoliciesguidanceapro8web.pdf/).
Historic England (2018): Heritage and society 2018, Heritage Counts: (https://historicengland.org.uk/content/heritage-counts/pub/2018/heritage-and-society-2018-pdf/).
Howard, Andy J. (2013): "Managing global heritage in the face of future climate change: The importance of understanding geological and geomorphological processes and hazards." In: International Journal of Heritage Studies, 19/7, pp. 632-658.
Hubbard, Philip (1993): "The value of conservation: A critical review of behavioural research." In: Town Planning Review, 64/4, pp. 359-74.
ICOMOS (2013). The burra charter. (http://australia.icomos.org/wp-content/uploads/e-Burra-Charter-2013-Adopted-31.10.2013.pdf).
ICOMOS (2008): Québec declaration on the preservation of the spirit of place: (http://www.icomos.org/images/DOCUMENTS/Charters/GA16_Quebec_Declaration_Final_EN.pdf).
Jacobs, Jane (1993): The death and life of great American cities, New York: Random House.
Jacobs, Jane (1961): The death and life of great American cities, Middlesex: Penguin.

Johnston, Chris (1992): What is social value? Canberra: Australian Government and Publishing Service.

Jones, Siân (2017): "Wrestling with the social value of heritage: Problems, dilemmas and opportunities." In: Journal of Community Archaeology & Heritage 4/1, pp. 21-37.

Jones, Siân/Leech, Steven (2015): Valuing the historic environment: A critical review of existing approaches to social value, Swindon: AHRC.

Jokilheto, Jukka (1999): A history of architectural conservation, Oxford: Butterworth-Heinemann.

Kain, Roger (1981): Planning for conservation, London: Mansell.

Klemek, Christopher (2011): The transatlantic collapse of urban renewal, Chicago: University of Chicago Press.

Labadi, Sophia (2011): Evaluating the Socio-economic impacts of selected regenerated heritage sites in Europe: (http://openarchive.icomos.org/1238/1/Sophia_Labadi_2008CPRA_Publication.pdf).

Labadi Sophia/Logan, William (2016): Urban heritage, development and sustainability: International frameworks, national and local governance, London: Routledge.

Larkham, Peter J. (2003): "The place of urban conservation in the UK reconstruction plans of 1942-52." In: Planning Perspectives, 18/2, pp. 295-324.

Larkham, Peter J. (1996): Conservation and the city, London: Routledge.

Leifeste, Amalia/Stiefel, Barry L. (2018): Sustainable heritage: Merging environmental conservation and historic preservation, London: Routledge.

Lesh, James Phillip (2018): At the intersection of heritage preservation, urban transformation, and everyday life in the twentieth-century Australian city, University of Melbourne: Unpublished PhD Thesis.

Lincoln, Toby (2015): Urbanizing China in war and peace: The case of Wuxi county, Honolulu: University of Hawai'i Press.

Madgin, Rebecca (2010): "Reconceptualising the historic urban environment: Conservation and regeneration in Castlefield, Manchester, 1960-2009." In: Planning Perspectives, 25/1, pp. 29-48.

Madgin, Rebecca/Taylor, Michael (2015): "Who do heritage values belong to?" In: Context 142, pp. 12-14.

Madgin, Rebecca/Webb, David/Ruiz, Pollyanna/Snelson, Tim (2018): "Resisting relocation and reconceptualising authenticity: The experiential and emotional values of the southbank undercroft, London, UK." In: International Journal of Heritage Studies 24/6, pp. 585-598.

Mason, Randall (1999): Economics and heritage conservation, Los Angeles: Getty Conservation Institute.

Mayes, Thompson M. (2018): Why do old places matter? How historic places affect our identity and well-being, Maryland: Rowman & Littlefield.

Miller, Michael J. (2003): The representation of place: Urban planning and protest in France and Great Britain, 1950-1980, Aldershot: Ashgate.

Pendlebury, John (2004): "Reconciling history with modernity: 1940s plans for Durham and Warwick." In: Environment and Planning B: Planning and Design 31/3, pp. 331-348.

Pendlebury, John/Hewitt, Lucy (2018): "Place and voluntary activity in inter-war England: Topophilia and professionalization." In: Urban History 45/3, pp. 453-470.

Pendlebury, John/Strange Ian (2011): "Centenary paper: Urban conservation and the shaping of the English city." In: Town Planning Review 82/4, pp. 361-392.

Poulios, Ioannis (2010): "Moving beyond a values-based approach to heritage conservation." In: Conservation and Management of Archaeological Sites 12/2, pp. 170-185.

Rodwell, Dennis (2007): Conservation and sustainability in historic cities, Chichester: Wiley Blackwell.

Schofield, John (2014): Who needs experts? Counter-mapping cultural heritage, Abingdon: Ashgate.

Schubert, Dirk (2014): Contemporary perspectives on Jane Jacobs: Reassessing the Impacts of an urban visionary, Abingdon: Ashgate.

Shetabi, Linda (2015): Heritage conservation and environmental sustainability: Revisiting the evaluation criteria for built heritage, Proceedings of FABRIC, The Threads of Conservation, Australia ICOMOS Conference, Adelaide.

Smith, Laura Jane (2006): Uses of heritage, London: Routledge.

Society for the Protection of Ancient Buildings (1874): Manifesto: (https://www.spab.org.uk/about-us/spab-manifesto).

Sonkoly, Gábor (2017): Historical urban landscape, London: Palgrave Macmillan.

Sweet, Rosemary H. (2004): Antiquaries: The discovery of the past in eighteenth century Britain, London: Hambledon.

Swenson, Astrid (2013): The rise of heritage: Preserving the past in France, Germany and England, 1789-1914, Cambridge: Cambridge University Press.

UK Government (2010): The government's statement on the historic environment for England 2010: (https://webarchive.nationalarchives.gov.uk/+/http:/www.culture.gov.uk/images/publications/Acc_HeritageVision_Part1.pdf).

UNESCO (2011): HUL recommendation: (http://whc.unesco.org/uploads/activities/documents/activity-638-98.pdf).

UNESCO (2011): New life for historic cities: The historic urban landscape approach explained: (https://whc.unesco.org/document/123570).

UNESCO (1954): Convention for the protection of cultural property in the event of armed conflict: (http://www.unesco.org/new/en/culture/themes/armed-conflict-and-heritage/convention-and-protocols/1954-hague-convention/).

Van Oers, Ron/Sachiko, Haraguchi/World Heritage Centre and Historic Urban Landscape Initiative (2010): Managing historic cities, world heritage paper series No.27 (Paris, France: UNESCO World Heritage Centre): (http://whc.unesco.org/uploads/activities/documents/activity-47- 1.pdf).

Wells, Jeremy C. (2017): "Are we 'ensnared in the system of heritage' because we don't want to escape?" In: Archaeologies 13/1, pp. 26-34.

Wells, Jeremy C. (2015): "Making a case for historic place conservation based on people's values." In: Forum Journal 29/3, pp. 44-62.

Wells, Jeremy C./Stiefel, Barry L. (2018): Human-centered built environment heritage preservation, London: Routledge. [Web references last accessed 05/03/19]

Village—Small Town—Metropolis

Clemens Zimmermann

Conventionally, the 'size' of a town or settlement is seen as one of its most important features, which in comparative perspective also reveals the manifest qualities of a town. Different types of cities were already distinguished according to their size during antiquity. However, additional qualitative criteria were attached to this definition—the concept of the metropolis, for instance, has developed out of the ecclesiastic context characterising a city as a 'mother city' and bishopric see. Thus it seems appropriate to develop typologies in which size forms the basis and the main (although not the 'sole' effective) category. In urban research, the description of individual cases based on implicit or explicit arguments derived from their 'intrinsic logic' ('Eigenlogik') is often analysed in front of the backdrop of such typologies and ideal types. The history of each individual town, indeed each village, and the typological attributions applied here are intimately related to the history of urbanisation, which identifies overarching processes and elements that might not necessarily occur in every single community, but may be observed with significant frequency (Bernhardt 2012).

The following chapter will summarise the research on three types of settlement: the 'village', the 'small town' and the 'metropolis'. It will focus on the Western European—particularly German—context since the late 19th century. It sets out from an understanding of urban history that regards rural forms of settlement and the interrelations between towns and villages, resp. the relationship between a town and its hinterland, as an inherent part of its programme. Such town-hinterland relationships are visible in economic contexts, as the provisioning of towns was dependent on imports from outside and supplies from the surrounding area. This included the social metabolism of resources, such as running water which, in turn, required functioning waste-water systems. On the other hand, rural populations could expect to find certain services only in nearby towns. These towns were not only the primary outlets for produced goods but also cultural focal points and the seats of cultural institutions (Schott 2014: 65-88; Zimmermann 2001).

The Village—Definitions and Research Approaches

Approximately 15 per cent of the current population of the Federal Republic of Germany live in municipalities with less than 5000 inhabitants. Obviously, not all such communities would be called 'villages'. Semi-industrial settlements, conglomerates of a number of formerly autonomous villages or suburban communities, which may have developed around a 'village core', are part of this category of towns. Ever since the municipal reforms at the end of the 1960s, thousands of West German villages have vanished from the statistics simply by having been subsumed through mergers. For this reason, one of the tasks of research, both on the historical and present situation, is to investigate the essential spatial forms of social community construction associated with the village.

The study by Gertrud Hüwelmeier (1997) is one example of a folkloristic or ethnological perspective. It stresses the role of local associations in the 'social world' of a village, shared notions about belonging, otherness, continuities and discontinuities as well as solidarity. Accordingly, the village represents a social community, a socialisation space that sets itself apart from other villages by a specific historicity, which continually reproduces itself anew within conventional social conceptions—and has a characteristically strong orientation toward the inside. The aspect of community building is prominent here. Other more extensive accents are set by Gunter Mahlerwein (2009; 2016), who discusses not only the *village* but also rural 'communities' ('Gemeinden'). Their history is interpreted within the context of overarching sociocultural change, such as the diminishing integrative forces of traditional forms of community, pluralisation through immigration, the rise in education levels, the service sector and the welfare state. In addition, many of these rural communities have been drawn into the process of suburbanisation. Villages or—if one takes the political view extending beyond village borders—'rural municipalities' are entities of rural space which are in a constant state of change. They are also characterised by continuous mobility between villages as well as between villages and towns—up to the lifestyle of present-day suburbanites. For many people, life in village *and* town converge in everyday experience, such as for young people in professional training (Mahlerwein 2009; Mahlerwein 2016: 181-205; cf. Kersting/Zimmermann 2015).

Historically, villages appear as a special and relatively delimited form of social organisation. They are regulated by manorial or state norms, but are partly administered autonomously as a 'municipality', despite the regulatory ambitions of state administrators and interference by feudal lords. In this form of social organisation, the following concepts are especially important: 'commons', as collective forms of ownership and usage rights, and 'peasants', as social group. Village women and juveniles are particularly important groups, both as actors in household and market production as well as for the regular interactions between villages and towns. The association of the 'village' with 'communality' ('Gemeinschaft') in the work of Ferdinand Tönnies (1887) is of particular relevance in the historiography on villages. Based on this is the still widespread idea that the community of a village forms a specially intense communicative bond tuned toward social control. However, while the notion of a particularly intense communality appears as a prominent feature of villages from an outside view, this form of sociability also reflects economic necessities (Troßbach/Zimmermann 2006: 9-16, 239-241). Whilst a definition of 'village' for the 20th and early 21st centuries will continue to hinge on the notion of communality, the factor of mobility and migration will play a larger role (Mahlerwein 2009; 2016). Besides, other historical characteristics of the village, such as commons or the peasantry as a leading group, have lost their significance. However, already in the past, major free-tenant peasants did not always dominate the villages as much as assumed in conventional interpretations of communality. At times, minor bonded agricultural labourers and other lower agrarian strata played a leading role in the social organisation of villages. The plurality in social forms of village economies was considerably stronger than is reflected in conventional views about the 'peasant' village.

In the current debate about villages four aspects stand out:

First, Werner Nell and Marc Weiland (2014) contend that, while certainly villages have not ceased to exist as 'real' social entities, they have adopted a second imaginary existence—namely, in literature, cinema and other media. Not only is the lifeworld of villages reshaped in media, but the imaginations of non-villagers are also strongly influenced by these representations. However, current periodical literature, does not reference concrete village society but a territorially aspecific but extremely aesthetic 'countryside'. This illusionary figment appears to be highly attractive to a mainly female (big-)city readership (Nell/Weiland 2014; Zimmermann/Mahlerwein/Maldener 2018).

Second, it is important to consider diverging cultural conceptions about the appearance of villages. Widespread popular images of typical rural living, ranging from idyll to satirical depictions (Schalko 2015; Türschmann 2014), starkly contrast with empirical research that has highlighted diversity and dynamics *alongside* 'traditional' patterns and continuities as well as partial modernisation of social organisation. It may seem appropriate to contrast the culturally laden ideas to modernise village life as designs conceived by an 'urban' planning elite on the one hand, and local everyday life that follows 'rural' patterns on the other hand. Marcel Thomas (2018) has pointed out the conflicts in transition from 'village' to 'city' that resulted from this juxtaposition of cultural constructions. However, it remains questionable whether one should go so far as to polarise the cultural patterns of urbanity and rurality to such an extent, to disjoin them from their social bases and from living practices, and to interpret them solely as floating discourses and life styles. The fact is that—often idealised—conceptions of rurality reverberate back on village and town planning (Langner 2016).

Third, the discourse on the 'future of the village' has shaped the scholarly debate. Over the past few decades and in particular from the 1990s, thousands of villages have lost inhabitants, economic substance and innovative potential. The reason for this is not so much the new trend of re-urbanisation than processes of regional differentiation. As a result, a sharp divide between villages has emerged that is based on their geographical location. For example, there are villages where the only residents left are virtually all elderly (meeting their needs becoming increasingly precarious, however), while others profit from the influx of city dwellers and commuting professionals (Becker 1997: 52-69, 280-294; Die Zukunft der Dörfer 2011).

Fourth, research following the concept of 'rurality' that does not directly address villages as delimitable territorial units, but 'rustic' living and discourses based on a notion of 'the countryside', has questioned the supposedly now ubiquitous urbanity and the prevalence of urban lifestyles (Dirksmaier 2009). At least at the level of public infrastructure, forms of mobility and consumption, 'town' and 'countryside' are not as easily distinguished as some 50 or 100 years ago—especially in intermeshed metropolitan regions.

The Small Town—Attempts at a Definition

Compared to the quite complex, profoundly historical subject matter of the village and its rapidly changing characteristics in the 20th century, the small town (Kleinstadt) seems to be somewhat simpler to grasp. Considered statistically, according to the definitions in use since the international statistical conventions of 1871/1887, small towns have between 5000 and 10.000 residents. Still smaller ones fall under the category of 'country town' ('Landstadt'). Departing from this definition, it has become customary to distinguish small towns with respect to their local core functions and their economic and social specialisations, such as factory towns, mining towns or spa towns. Smaller towns are often characterised by such specific functions more clearly than larger cities that are usually more heterogeneous. For decades, a major strand in geographical research has concentrated on the question of how to measure the centrality functions of such small towns. It is largely assumed—and historical studies have substantiated the claim—that small towns and country towns assume much greater institutional and commercial importance than their modest numbers of inhabitants indicate because facilities such as medical surgeries and secondary schools, which served a broader hinterland, settled there. The proximity to a large city or the location within an agglomeration plays a role in this as well (Zimmermann 2003). On the one hand, consensus has largely been reached that many characteristics of mid-sized cities (Schmidt-Lauber 2010) equally apply to small towns. On the other hand, historical studies may include towns below the threshold of 5000 inhabitants, provided they meet other criteria conventionally defining small towns. Yet the small town stands out prominently against its surrounding villages and rural areas. Like the countryside or village, the small town continues to be determinable as an entity with definite qualities—in relation to its environs and to other towns.

According to the 19th century literary discourse the small town permitted more humane living by virtue of its reduced scale and pace. It was frequently depicted as the citizens' lost paradise. During the 20th century, this image was adjusted to reflect the tension between the critique of civilisation attached to life in large cities and the 'other' path to modernity that small towns seemed to offer. It appeared as a retreat and a place for individual resistance (Nowak 2013: 71-77; Hüppauf 2005).

Small-town representations of the 20th century vacillate between folkloristic illuminations and criticism of their anti-urbanity, between ideals and clichés, between visual authentification strategies and medial standardisation processes. In the case of the town of Bretten in Baden, Benita Luckmann (1970) described an atmosphere in which a critical reflection about the own past during National Socialism was suppressed. This was a typical external observation during the 1970s, soon to be followed by numerous explorations of small-town milieux. Such critical inquiries asked whether small towns, with their petty bourgeoisie and elites, had an affinity to National Socialism. Soon not only the potentials for resistance came to light but also continuities transcending both the caesura of 1933 and 1945 (Luckmann 1970; Stokes 1984; Klemp 1997; Minner 1999; Peters 2015). The debate about small towns' role in National Socialism points to a larger field of research that is concerned with processes of political mobilisation, the effects of deagrarianisation, continuities in worldview and cultural milieux (Gruttmann 2012).

Christine Hannemann and Carsten Benke (2002) concluded from extensive sociological field research in East Germany during the 1990s that the residents' assessment of the quality of life, the persistence of the local way of life and the manageable scale of small-town living was positive, although it could be perceived as restrictive. In current publications, the future development of small towns does not appear as negative throughout, but presents a picture that differs with the location of the towns. The greatest problems are seen to be vacant properties in pedestrian zones, migration into agglomerations and the competition to private stores by online shopping which, however, also massively affects larger towns (Gatzweiler 2012; Schrödel 2014; Beißwenger 2017).

The Metropolis—Definitions

From the point of view of the 20th century, a metropolis (within the European context) is a prominent big city of recognised economic prosperity, cultural diversity and innovative energy. It is recognised for its abundance of social and cultural institutions and serves as a role-model for urban development. The metropolis differs from the demographically defined 'big city' ('Großstadt', above 100.000 inhabitants), although the latter is equally important regionally as a centre of services, culture and economic development, especially in Germany with its polycentric structure of cities. It is also distinguished from the 'mega-city', which is currently understood as an agglomeration (including a core town) of a total of over 10 million inhabitants. The concept of the mega-city aims specifically at the phenomenon of rapid urbanisation in Latin America, Asia and Africa which has considerably broadened the horizon of recent urban research (Hoerning 2012; Schwentker 2006; Sander-Faes/Zimmermann 2018; on the metropolis as a municipal region: Saldern 2018).

A metropolis is characterised by a level of centrality beyond that of other big cities and operates as a node in an international network of communication and culture. It may not necessarily be the largest city, but its cultural uniqueness has historically been acknowledged as distinctive. It is generally agreed that a metropolis offers a high quality of life, in the sense of a rich and highly diverse urbanism, cultural offerings and entertainment, and the experience of different milieux.

In recent conceptualisations, the metropolis is increasingly defined as a culturally symbolic place within the context of a global economy of symbols. In this connection, the metropolis is a site that takes on a prominent function in the course of cultural globalisation and allegedly cultural homogenisation (Volgmann 2013: 21-30). A somewhat competing concept of the metropolis, the 'global city' (Sassen 1991), refers to a city noted for its commerce on a global scale, functioning as an international node in networks of trade, value addition and communication, but riven with serious social faults (Michel 2010). This concept of the metropolis, based on a cities' cultural and economic centrality, also fits in well with an environmental history perspective, in which these cities are the nodes of material flows (Schott 2014: 17-22, 174-178, 214-217; Bernhardt 2001).

The status of a metropolis is not definitely established. Its characteristics reflect the perception of available amenities, a specific atmosphere, and the image that residents as well as outsiders have of the city. Defined in this way, the status of a metropolis cannot be 'produced' at will, no matter how actively it is promoted. In most cases sociologists and historians practising in the field are quite unanimous about whether a given city has acquired the quality of a metropolis.

Friedrich Lenger (2013) has emphasised the ambivalent role of European metropolises in the process of modernisation. On the one hand, they served as role-models and pace-setters of modernism. On the other hand, the same processes aggravated problems of segregation and led to such contradictions as the factual "weakening of the central core" and a visionary "inner-city renaissance". With a particular focus on the history of social history and the history of the public sphere, Lenger analysed phases of expansion and crises, highlighted the role of infrastructure, city planning and art, and emphasised the formative role of migratory processes and urban social movements (cf. Lenger 2013, pp. 13, 245-272, 385-434, 516-552; cf. Zimmermann 2000; Behrends/Kohlrausch 2014). While many researchers have pointed out the historical achievements reached during the process of modernisation, the uniqueness, beauty and model character of metropolises, their social and environmental problems have again been recognised in recent analyses. Dieter Schott's study (2014) is exemplary in this regard. He presents the 'networked city' and the emergence of urban planning as a reaction to the environmental crises of the 19th century. Miserable living conditions, high mortality, inadequate basic amenities, and a lack of green spaces have led to a path of development that has culminated in the model of the 'sustainable city' at the end of the 20th century (Schott 2014: 275-345).

Desiderata of Research on Metropolis, Small Town and Village

A trend in metropolitan research that so far has only been taken up hesitantly is to reflect on the experiences of inhabitants. How exactly are private and increasingly normalised and commercialised public spaces bound together in a metropolis? How is the critical security situation perceived, particularly in the very largest cities? How do tenants cope with the massively rising rents and still devise forms of self-determined living? Village research likewise lacks studies on differing experiences, and particularly on perceptions of urbanity from a village perspective. In the context of small towns, research on perceptions of the 'subjective' experience is somewhat more developed. Through regular questionnaire surveys, on the one hand, and studies in literary and cultural sciences, on the other hand, we know more about this level of everyday life in small towns.

Although the 'agglomeration' established itself as a settlement type during the second half of the 20th century, superimposing itself upon former boundaries, it is highly remarkable that the different settlement types continue to exist, even inside such agglomerations. In addition, the formation of agglomerations has to be analysed more systematically in the context of regional development. As the formation of agglomerations is often related to the depletion of other regions, it is indeed an unbalanced and polarising development.

Furthermore, there is a lack of transnational or translocal studies going beyond comparative analysis, which focus on the relations between cities. For the future one must expect that especially in metropolitan research, historical aspects of migration will gain ground as well as the issue of multi-culturality. In the context of a transnational research agenda, more emphasis will also be placed on identifying the appropriate parameters of modernisation and modernity (Bechtel/ Galmiche 2008; Behrends/Kohlrausch 2014). With the rise of post-colonial studies particularly in the English-speaking world and the expansion of studies on global history, one should expect that post-colonial approaches will be applied more explicitly to the history of cities and urbanisation. Master narratives of European modernity are beginning to be questioned, while the experiences of 'the others' are being included in urban histories. This does not mean that models of European urban development will lose historical validity in other regions of the world, and that the conceptions of humane city design arising originally within the European context are becoming obsolete. However, it has to be acknowledged that ultimately the 'non-Western' world has significantly influenced European modernity, most palpably so in metropolises (Randeria 2000; Osterhammel 2010: 315-464). This implies that Western modernising campaigns are also falling within the scope of critical observation—for instance, the planning euphoria of the 1970s and the opposition to it (Haumann 2011; Zitzewitz 2014; Baumeister/Bonomo/Schott 2017).

All in all, the current debates on the history of cities and urbanisation show that typologies, such as the ones sketched above, are indispensable in order to arrive at differentiated and yet clear and comparable results. They depend on the premises made by researchers and on their contemporary ways of thinking about cities and settlements. As such the typologies of village, small town and metropolis are themselves subject to historical change. Besides, the boundaries between the different settlement types are becoming blurred by a growing array of material, social and communicative interdependencies and linkages that emerge between them. This focus on translocal connectivity seems to contradict the idea of conceptualising types of settlements according to their function. Nonetheless, it still makes sense to discuss the basic quantitative and qualitative characteristics that define the different types of urban sites. They continue to operate in different ways and with different effectiveness, and most of all, they continue to be experienced as distinguishable entities despite the levelling tendencies of globalisation.

References

Baumeister, Martin/Bonomo, Bruno/Schott, Dieter (eds.) (2017): Cities contested: Urban politics, heritage and social movements in Italy and West Germany in the 1970s, Frankfurt a.M./New York: Campus.

Bechtel, Delphine/Xavier Galmiche (eds.) (2008): Les Villes multiculturelles en Europe centrale, Paris: Belin.

Becker, Heinrich (1997): Dörfer heute: Ländliche Lebensverhältnisse im Wandel 1952, 1972 und 1993/95, Bonn: Forschungsgesellschaft für Agrarpolitik und Agrarsoziologie.

Behrends, Jan C./Martin Kohlrausch (eds.) (2014): Races to modernity: Metropolitan aspirations in eastern Europe 1890-1940, Budapest/New York: Central European University Press.

Beißwenger, Klaus-Dieter (2017): Online-Handel: Mögliche räumliche Auswirkungen auf Innenstädte, Stadtteil- und Ortszentren, Berlin: Deutsches Institut für Urbanistik.

Bernhardt, Christoph (ed.) (2012): "Urbanisierung im 20. Jahrhundert." In: Informationen zur modernen Stadtgeschichte 2, pp. 5-11.

Bernhardt, Christoph (ed.) (2001): Environmental problems in European cities in the 19th and 20th Century, Münster: Waxmann.

Die Zukunft der Dörfer (2011): Zwischen Stabilität und demografischem Niedergang, Berlin: Berlin-Institut für Bevölkerung und Entwicklung.

Dirksmaier, Peter (2009): Urbanität als Habitus: Zur Sozialgeographie städtischen Lebens auf dem Land, Bielefeld: transcript.

Gatzweiler, Hans-Peter (ed.) (2012): Klein- und Mittelstädte in Deutschland: Eine Bestandsaufnahme, Stuttgart: Bundesinstitut für Bau-, Stadt- und Raumforschung.

Gruttmann, Dörthe (2012): "Kleinstadt in der Moderne: Billerbeck im 20. Jahrhundert." In: Werner Freitag (ed.), Geschichte der Stadt Billerbeck, Bielefeld: Verlag für Regionalgeschichte, pp. 263-477.

Hannemann, Christine/Benke, Carsten (2002): Kleinstädte in Ostdeutschland: Welche Zukunft hat dieser Stadttyp? Berlin: Humboldt-Universität zu Berlin/Institut für Sozialwissenschaften.

Haumann, Sebastian (2011): 'Schade, daß Beton nicht brennt...' Planung, Partizipation und Protest in Philadelphia und Köln 1940-1990, Stuttgart: Steiner.

Hoerning, Johanna (2012): "Megastädte." In: Franz Eckart (ed.), Handbuch Stadtsoziologie, Wiesbaden: VS, pp. 231-262.

Hüppauf, Bernd (2005): "Die Kleinstadt." In: Alexa Geisthövel/Habbo Knoch (eds.), Orte der Moderne: Erfahrungswelten des 19. und 20. Jahrhunderts, Frankfurt a.M./New York: Campus, pp. 303-315.

Hüwelmeier, Gertrud (1997): Hundert Jahre Sängerkrieg: Ethnographie eines Dorfes in Hessen, Berlin: Reimer.

Kersting, Franz-Werner/Clemens Zimmermann (eds.) (2015): Stadt-Land-Beziehungen im 20. Jahrhundert: Geschichte- und kulturwissenschaftliche Perspektiven, Paderborn: Ferdinand Schöningh.

Klemp, Stefan (1997): 'Richtige Nazis hat es hier nicht gegeben': Nationalsozialismus in einer Kleinstadt am Rande des Ruhrgebiets, Münster: Lit.

Langner, Sigrun (2016): "Rurbane Landschaften: Landschaftsentwürfe als Projektionen produktiver Stadt-Land-Verschränkungen." In: Aus Politik und Zeitgeschichte 46/47, pp. 41-46.

Lenger, Friedrich (2013): Metropolen der Moderne: Eine europäische Stadtgeschichte seit 1850, Munich: Beck.

Luckmann, Benita (1970): Politik in einer deutschen Kleinstadt, Stuttgart: Enke.

Mahlerwein, Gunter (2009): "Modernisierung der ländlichen Gesellschaft in Deutschland: Der Beitrag der Suburbanisierung." In: Zeitschrift für Agrargeschichte und Agrarsoziologie 57/2, pp. 13-29.

Mahlerwein, Gunter (2016): Grundzüge der Agrargeschichte: Die Moderne (1880-2010), Vol. 3, Cologne/Weimar/Vienna: Böhlau.

Michel, Boris (2010): Global City als Projekt: Neoliberale Urbanisierung und Politiken der Exklusion in Metro Manila, Bielefeld: transcript.

Minner, Katrin (1999): Erinnerung und Modernität: Westfälische Ortsjubiläen im Dritten Reich, Münster: Ardey.

Nell, Werner/Marc Weiland (eds.) (2014): Imaginäre Dörfer: Zur Wiederkehr des Dörflichen in Literatur, Film und Lebenswelt, Bielefeld: transcript.

Nowak, Christiane (2013): Menschen, Märkte, Möglichkeiten: Der Topos Kleinstadt in deutschen Romanen zwischen 1900 und 1933, Bielefeld: Aisthesis.

Osterhammel, Jürgen (2010): Die Verwandlung der Welt: Eine Geschichte des 19. Jahrhunderts, 5th ed., Munich: Beck.

Peters, Christian (2015): Nationalsozialistische Machtdurchsetzung in Kleinstädten: Eine vergleichende Studie zu Quakenbrück und Heide/Holstein, Bielefeld: transcript.

Randeria, Shalini (2000): "Geteilte Geschichte und verwobene Moderne." In: Jörn Rüsen/Hanna Leitgeb/Norbert Jegelka (eds.), Zukunftsentwürfe: Ideen für eine Kultur der Veränderung, Frankfurt a.M./New York: Campus, pp. 87-96.

Saldern, Adelheid von (2018): "Los Angeles: Von der Metropolregion zur Global City Region." In: Stephan Sander-Faes/Clemens Zimmermann (eds.), Weltstädte, Metropolen Megastädte: Dynamiken von Stadt und Raum von der Antike bis zur Gegenwart, Ostfildern: Thorbecke, pp. 223-238.

Sander-Faes, Stephan/Clemens Zimmermann (eds.) (2018): Weltstädte, Metropolen, Megastädte: Dynamiken von Stadt und Raum von der Antike bis zur Gegenwart, Ostfildern: Thorbecke.

Sassen, Saskia (1991): The global city, New York et al.: Princeton University Press.

Schalko, David (2015): "Braunschlag": Television series in eight parts, Vienna: Hoanzl.

Schmidt-Lauber, Brigitta (ed.) (2010): Mittelstadt: Urbanes Leben jenseits der Metropole, Frankfurt a.M.: Campus.

Schott, Dieter (2014): Europäische Urbanisierung 1000-2000: Eine umwelthistorische Einführung, Cologne/Weimar/Vienna: Böhlau.

Schrödel, Gerrit (2014): Empirische Bestandaufnahme der deutschen Kleinstädte zu Beginn des 21. Jahrhunderts: Ein Siedlungstyp im sozioökonomischen Niedergang? Göttingen: Cuvillier.

Schwentker, Wolfgang (ed.) (2006): Megastädte im 20. Jahrhundert, Göttingen: Vandenhoeck & Ruprecht.

Stokes, Lawrence D. (ed.) (1984): Kleinstadt und Nationalsozialismus: Ausgewählte Dokumente zur Geschichte von Eutin 1918-1945, Neumünster: Wachholtz.

Thomas, Marcel (2018): "Making a town: Urbanity, rurality, and the politics of place in Ebersbach (Fils), 1945-1989." In: Journal of Urban History 44/6, pp. 1-19.

Tönnies, Ferdinand (1887): Gemeinschaft und Gesellschaft: Abhandlung des Communismus und des Socialismus als empirische Kulturformen, Leipzig: Fues.

Troßbach, Werner/Zimmermann, Clemens (2006): Die Geschichte des Dorfes: Von den Anfängen im Frankenreich zur bundesdeutschen Gegenwart, Stuttgart: Ulmer.

Türschmann, Jörg (2014): "Dorfchroniken: Wie TV-Serien von Menschen auf dem Land erzählen." In: Sabine Schrader/Daniel Winkler (eds.), TV glokal: Europäische Fernsehserien und transnationale Qualitätsformate, Marburg: Schüren, pp. 140-160.

Volgmann, Kati (2013): Metropole: Bedeutung des Metropolenbegriffs und Messung von Metropolität im deutschen Städtesystem, Detmold: Dorothea Rohn.

Zimmermann, Clemens (2003): "Die Kleinstadt in der Moderne." In: Clemens Zimmermann (ed.), Kleinstadt in der Moderne, Ostfildern: Thorbecke, pp. 9-27.

Zimmermann, Clemens (ed.) (2001): Dorf und Stadt: Ihre Beziehungen vom Mittelalter bis zur Gegenwart, Frankfurt a.M.: DLG-Verlag.

Zimmermann, Clemens (2000): Zeit der Metropolen: Urbanisierung und Großstadtentwicklung, Frankfurt a.M.: Fischer.

Zimmermann, Clemens/Mahlerwein, Gunter/Maldener, Aline (eds.) (2018): Landmedien und mediale Bilder von Ländlichkeit im 20. Jahrhundert, Innsbruck: Studienverlag.

Zitzewitz, Jutta von (2014): Die Stadt, der Highway und die Kamera: Fotografie und Urbanisierung in New York zwischen 1945 und 1965, Berlin/Munich: Deutscher Kunstverlag.

European Periphery

Rainer Liedtke

Whether something is central or peripheral depends entirely on the position of the observer. The historiography of urban Europe in the 19th and 20th centuries, and in particular with regard to urbanisation and environmental issues, shows a marked tendency to consider anything outside North Western and Central Europe as 'peripheral'. With a few exceptions, the development of Scandinavian, Southern, South Eastern and Eastern European cities has been of only secondary interest in academic discourses of European urban history. The field is still dominated by enquiries into the metropolises and smaller cities of Britain, the German-speaking lands, France and the Low Countries. This contrasts sharply with the great interest in Mediterranean towns and cities in the Middle Ages and Early Modern periods.

This chapter explores a small selection of recent research on Southern European urbanisation. The following overview does not claim to be comprehensive, but it should serve to give an impression of recent questions addressed in research on the urban development of Portugal, Spain and Italy, especially in the 20th century. Research on specific cities or countries has been included as well as some comparative studies looking at Southern Europe more broadly. The Euro crisis of the past decade, which has hit Southern Europe particularly hard, has not helped to strengthen academic and research structures in that area. However, it has prompted scholars, especially in the social sciences, to enquire more closely into the origins of a supposed North-South divide. Finally, this selection is limited to works written in English, which are accessible to a broader international readership. Research published in Italian, Spanish and Portuguese is obviously far more extensive. Studies that take into account the environmental history of cities in Southern Europe are scarce. With the exception of transport infrastructure, the environment is therefore rather peripheral in the writings on Southern European cities, which obviously also has to do with the very different experience of industrialisation.

A Peripheral Perspective

In a way, research on Southern Europe and other peripheral regions seems to portray cities in this region as catching up on achievements such as urban development, public housing and welfare, town planning, urban governance and civic society and, to a lesser extent, infrastructure. These topics have been discussed extensively over the past decades with regard to the self-defined 'centre' of Europe. We know a lot about housing, governance, infrastructure and so forth of London, Paris and Berlin as well as a number of second and third tier cities in the North-West of Europe, usually those that underwent significant industrialisation or were centres of government and power. However, applying the term 'catching up' would mean falling into the same trap as those scholars who have claimed to write about the 'European city' while regarding only a portion of the continent's urbanities (cf. Siebel 2004). Instead, Southern European developments should be considered in their own right. In some cases, a distinct Southern pattern is evident, while in others the process reveals characteristics representative of one country or simply an individual city. This has been stressed in many of the contributions to the path breaking collection of essays edited by Martin Baumeister and Roberto Sala (2015). While not dealing specifically with urbanisation, this collection identifies several aspects that have prevented a specific or at least independent 'peripheral' perspective on European developments. The contributions challenge the idea of promoting a uniting and continuously integrating Europe that leaves little room for 'aberrant' developments. Instead, the volume considers whether there was a specific path of Southern European modernisation, which differed from the supposedly 'normative' Anglo-American model. In doing so, the discursive power hierarchies imposed by the North-Western European 'core' over the 'periphery' become evident. Furthermore, most contributions to Baumeister and Sala (2015) question the perceived unity of the European South and provide ample evidence for the marked historical differences between the countries in the region.

One particular weakness affecting much research on the urbanisation of Southern Europe is the relative paucity of hard data. While incomplete or missing land registers make it difficult to ascertain ownership structures over time in many Southern cities, only a few recent studies address this problem. Chatel et al. (2017) turn to urban census data from France, Italy, Spain and Portugal, drawing on over 65.000 local units from population censuses between 1920 and 2010. Their research has established patterns of distribution and growth of population in various Southern European localities. They conclude that since the 1970s a distinct deconstruction and extension of cities in this region has occurred, leading to new forms of social organisation. This adds significantly to our understanding of urbanisation processes in this part of Europe, but more empirical studies of this kind are required to provide the foundations for further research.

Deficient Governance, Planning and Infrastructure

Well-ordered city planning, including the meaningful implementation of infrastructure not only for transportation but for all the utilities, such as water, gas and electricity, which developed during the 19th century, has probably been the single-most important characteristic of the modern 'European city'. While there is no lack of masterplans for most Southern European metropolises, there is very often an enormous discrepancy between official planning and its practical implementation. This means that in many Southern European locations water pipes, gas mains, electric cables or the city transportation network have been constructed and assembled in a rather piecemeal fashion, sometimes years after the hasty erection of dwellings, which provided at least some provisional accommodation for incoming migrants from the countryside. This classical topic of Southern urbanity has recently been analysed in the context of Italian city development. Percy Allum's (2003) study on Naples explains the enormous disparity between the drafting of masterplans and their at best partial implementation. He draws attention to the intricate relations between planners and politicians since the Second World War but also to the role of building speculation in the South Italian metropolis. This was a perennial problem in 20th century Southern Europe, and remains a problem today, highlighting the importance of personal relations in understanding urban formations.

The fact that land registers are often incomplete or even absent poses another challenge to planned development in many Southern European cities, as does multiple and conflicting ownership of usually small plots of building ground, a situation that has led to sometimes peculiar alliances. This has been shown in a study on planning in Turin, an Italian city that is not completely representative for Southern European developments because of the strong presence of an urban working class and a rather 'western' model of governance. Nevertheless, in his enquiry into urban governance in the context of city planning Gilles Pinson (2002) has been able to demonstrate that the interests of the Turin authorities and a multitude of smaller actors on the micro level have mutually reinforced each other to arrive at a rather effective mode of city planning. When looked at from the outside, this process appears fragmented and, at least to the Western European observer, chaotic because of the number of actors involved on different levels. However, this pattern, which is quite typical for many Southern European communities, could also strengthen the municipal institutions and enhance their legitimacy.

Nonetheless, city planning gone spectacularly wrong has also been a familiar feature of the Southern European urban experience. Post-war city ruins are a case in point, exemplified by unfinished public works in Italy. While not specifying the detailed background for such examples of administrative failure, Pablo Arboleda (2017) makes clear that usually rather obscure and singular political and economic circumstances involving a variety of actors occupied with urban planning and governance were responsible. Furthermore, expert knowledge and professional qualifications determined who was in charge of executing plans and allocating resources to a much lesser extent than in Western and Central Europe. Interpersonal relations defined processes of urban development and therefore shaped the structure of civic society on the local level in all of the Mediterranean.

What most studies fail to address is that in many instances citizens—either individually or as collective actors—often found ways to make up for the failures of official planning by creating alternative 'public works' on the local micro level, if only for their immediate neighbourhood. Once again, urban historians accustomed to Western developmental traditions regarded such action as 'illegal' and disordered. However, for many Southern European cities they were without alternative, especially during the period of accelerated urban growth from the 1950s to the 1970s. New arrivals from the countryside needed not only housing but also access to utilities such as water, gas and electricity and connection to the urban transport networks. To regard this as 'catching up' with Western European developments would be missing the point.

As in most European cities, the last third of the 19th century saw the beginning of a fundamental modernisation of urban public works also in the South. A study of Barcelona's water supply system between the 1860s and 1960s demonstrates that the city learned from international experiences but at the same time had to come to terms with problems specific for Southern Europe or Spain respectively (Guardia et al. 2014). These included droughts, unreliable communal authorities and patterns of governance, corruption, frequent regime changes and above all a city that had grown relatively uncontrolled since Ildefons Cerda had planned new urban districts in the most revolutionary style during the 1860s.

One of the defining characteristics of Barcelona's urban development that emerged in the 19th century and continued to be of great importance into the 20th century was the city's market system. Although running a system of city markets was the norm in any European metropolis, the Southern European experience differed from that of the North-West in the sense that large and permanent covered markets remained particularly significant until the age of the supermarket. While in highly industrialised countries public markets became less and less central for supplying the citizens with food and household items from as early as the late 19th century, such institutions continued to flourish in the South. In Barcelona they defined city quarters, served as important centres for social interaction and for the empowerment of women who often ran the stalls (Fava et al. 2016). Markets became landmarks and focal nodes of the city's neighbourhoods. In their vicinity, a dense network of commercial but also cultural activities evolved. Covered markets therefore remained a distinct urban characteristic in Southern Europe for much longer than in the rest of Europe, in the same way as 'life in the open' through the ample usage of public spaces for the conduct and display of social and cultural life.

Another highly interesting collection of essays on the same period explores the mutual influence of the development of natural sciences and Barcelona's urban infrastructure (Hochadel et al. 2016). The focus here moves away from the usual elite-based discourse involving only a few central institutions to a more public or 'civic' approach exploring manifestations of science in different parts of the city. Contributions deal with public parks, dental clinics, sanitation and electricity, underground medical treatment or Spiritism and how they shaped various parts of the city. This volume therefore points to Barcelona as a modern, future-oriented metropolis, which nevertheless incorporated a utilitarian yet conservative outlook on scientific developments on the everyday level.

While studies on the development of port cities, particularly the Portuguese cities as Atlantic transit points are plentiful for the Early Modern period, Research on the subsequent periods is much scarcer. Magda Pinheiro (2009) provides a very useful English language overview of the development of Lisbon in the time after it had lost much of its colonial grandeur. Focusing on urban transport networks, her article explains that communal and state institutions only cared for the development of the central core of the city, while the provision of housing and infrastructure to the ever-growing suburbs and outlying areas were left to private developers. Interestingly, but not uncharacteristic for Southern Europe, railways, which were pivotal to the development of most North-Western European cities, only played a minor role in Lisbon, where short distance electric tramways served for transportation in the inner city.

In front of this backdrop, immigration from the countryside created huge problems for Lisbon throughout the 20th century, when public works usually lagged behind the development of dwellings. In spite of the existence of urban masterplans, many citizens needed to take the initiative themselves if they wanted adequate living quarters. Lisbon is thus a textbook case reflecting virtually all Southern European cities. Masterplans had been produced for both of Portugal's major cities, Lisbon and Porto, during the 1930s, as the detailed account by Teresa Marat Mendes and Vitor Oliveira (2013) outlines. This development came in the consolidation phase of the Salazar dictatorship and demonstrates the importance the regime attributed to an orderly development of the urban form. Influenced by French planning practices in particular, the new General Urban Development Plans were up to international standards, including zoning, regulatory codes and the integration of health and hygiene measures. Rationalism, which on paper was full of good intentions, guided the planning process; in practise, though, the economic means to realise it were insufficient, with the plans also failing to account for the massive enlargement of the cities due to internal migration.

Finally, a fascinating study of the development of urban infrastructure connected to the Olympic Games of 1960 in Rome deserves to be mentioned. Simon Martin (2017) explores the organisation of the games, building activities and general urban revival in the context of Italy's larger national goal to dissociate itself from its fascist past, much like West Germany did with the 1972 Olympics in Munich. At the same time, the games were seen as a chance for the ruling Italian Christian Democratic Party not only to strengthen its political following but also to fill the pockets of contractors it associated with. The article concludes that the change to rebrand and modernise the eternal city was clearly forsaken and that the Games only provided minimal change in the urban fabric of Rome.

Challenges of Rapid Urban Growth

Migration from the countryside was one of the forces that drove the tremendous changes many Southern cities underwent since the 1950s. This transformation is charted in a collection of essays on Italian cities edited by John Foot and Robert Lumley (2004). They show that internal migration, as well as international immigration, changed urban identities and cultures. Focusing on Milan and Turin in particular, the individual contributions demonstrate that urban development changed notably between the phase of accelerated industrialisation during the 1950s and 1960s and the onset of deindustrialisation in the 1980s, a phase that continues to this day. In particular, in the cultural sphere, the old established boundaries of the city, some stemming from the time of the Northern Italian city-states, were challenged by new or revised forms of cultural production, including architecture, the role of central squares, the perception of urban crime or the creation of urban literature. However, the contributions to Foot and Lumley (2004) represent only a partial image of urban reality in a country where some regions have much in common with the well-known urban history of North-Western European cities. What is important to remember here is that the established connection between industrialisation and urbanisation does not function in the same way in Southern Europe, where there were very few regions characterised by heavy industry and only some which thrived during the second wave of industrialisation. Therefore, urban growth in the South was and remains a phenomenon that needs to be regarded outside the industrialisation paradigm.

Nonetheless, the history of towns in Southern Europe that do exist because of industrialisation is relevant for the understanding of Southern European urban history. This story also needs to be heard, if only to correct the image that 'the South' was a latecomer in urban development. Such a case is Sesto San Giovanni, north of Milan's city centre, which since the late 19th century grew into one of the country's pre-eminent centres of industrial production. Valerio Varino's (2016) study tells a story that is reminiscent of the history of classic 'industrial villages' in the German Ruhr Area or the English Midlands. Within a relatively short period of time, when the town's population surged, a close-knit urban community emerged, while the development of public services and the formation of an urban civil society lagged behind.

Coping with the Legacy of Authoritarian Regimes

During the 1920s (Italy and Portugal) and 1930s (Greece and Spain), dictatorships were established in all Southern European countries, which was not all that uncommon for inter-war Europe in general. While Italian Fascism and the Greek military dictatorship did not survive the Second World War, autocratic regimes remained in power in Spain and Portugal until the mid-1970s, with another short-lived dictatorship in Greece between 1967 and 1974. These political conditions are very significant particularly in the context of research on urbanisation in Spain and Portugal.

Research on urban Spain, especially on the 20th century, has overwhelmingly focused on Barcelona, and the publications regarded here reflect this. Partially this is due to the good availability of sources about the Catalonian capital. However, another probably more important reason is the interest researchers have shown in Barcelona during the Franco dictatorship as a city that was historically much more hostile to the regime than the political power centre Madrid. Finally, together with the Basque region, the city was and remains the most heavily industrialised part of Spain. Among the topics that have interested urban historians of Spain most, welfare and housing stand out. Both constituted connected fields in which the short-lived pre civil war republic, but in particular the dictatorship, were highly active in order to have a formative and controlling impact on society. It is therefore not surprising that, in stark contrast to much of the research in other parts of Europe, endogenous forces in the field of housing, urban planning and welfare policies play a much larger role in Spain and have been far better researched than, for example, grass roots initiatives and self-help activities by urban dwellers. This is shown conclusively in José Maria Cardesín's essay (2016). Instead of looking at city plans and city planners independently, most studies start by investigating the political influence on urban development, maybe with a side-glance at exogenous economic factors which of course determined the leeway regimes and also planners had in an economically rather limited environment.

The Republican period before the Civil War, which has drawn less attention from urban historians than the following dictatorial decades, was nevertheless highly influential for the post-war period, as a highly interesting study on this 'urban transition' demonstrates (Carmona et al. 2017). The urban housing market was already much stretched by incoming peasants during the 1920s and 30s, with demand for the construction of dwellings soaring. However, the article shows that housing supply was also substantially increased. From this, the authors conclude that there was a rather responsive policy of creating new dwellings at affordable prices on the communal level. The flight from the countryside, however, was not nearly as severe in Spain as in other Southern countries during the decades after the Second World War. While the Spanish dictatorship may be blamed for devising all kinds of methods to control its citizens, it apparently did what it could under the strained economic conditions to create new, if not always terribly attractive dwellings in the rapidly growing conurbations.

The extremely stable Salazar dictatorship shaped Portugal's urban politics and planning even beyond its end in the mid-1970s. An empirical study demonstrates the persistence of interpersonal networks that outlasted the transition to democracy (De Almeida 2017). While the initial, freely held local elections swept away almost all of the old political guard, this democratisation was only superficial. De Almeida argues that city dwellers were willing to participate in local government and voted into office a diverse group of experts and non-experts from different social backgrounds, who had not been tainted by overt allegiance to the old regime. However, many could not retain their positions in future elections when clientelist considerations, the perennial political feature in all of Southern Europe, began to influence local politics again. While it was true that 'ordinary people' initially assumed control, old networks of acquaintance and material and immaterial indebtedness took over again. Such observations on the legacies of dictatorship might also explain why in Southern Europe civic society and urban governance followed a logic that was different from that of North-Western Europe.

Conclusions

There is far less research on urbanisation in Southern Europe than on cities in the North-West of the Continent. Some very good research is being ignored not only in international comparisons, but also by experts in the various national histories because it is not written in English. Nevertheless, the notion that this research 'on the periphery' has to catch up with what has been established about the urban North-West of Europe is plainly wrong. Instead, urban societies from Portugal to Greece (and including Turkey in some respects) have found ways of coping with historical developments and the resulting challenges that differed markedly from the 'common' European story. This includes the region's economic development and migratory patterns, but also the markedly different political structures and experiences, such as clientelism and the legacies of dictatorship that lasted well into the second half of the 20th century. Historical research specifically addressing environmental issues in Southern European cities is only in its infancy. This reflects the widespread disregard for such topics in society and politics in these countries.

We are definitely lacking studies that elaborate on the commonalities and differences of the Southern European urbanisation experience as a sort of counter story to the established narrative of the 'European city' that only portrays development to the north of the Pyrenees, the Alps and the Balkans. A broader perspective on European urban history that recognises the specificity of the Southern regions will be able to move beyond the established interpretations of urban development.

References

Allum, Percy (2003): "The politics of town planning in post-war Naples." In: Journal of Modern Italian Studies 8, pp. 500-527.
Arboleda, Pablo (2017): 'Ruins of modernity': The critical implications of unfinished public works in Italy. In: International Journal of Urban and Regional Research 41, pp. 804-820.
Baumeister, Martin/Sala, Roberto (eds.) (2015): Southern Europe? Italy, Spain, Portugal and Greece from the 1950s until the present day, Frankfurt a.M.: Campus.
Cardesín, José Maria (2016): "Housing and welfare in Spain from the Civil War to present times." In: Urban History 43, pp. 285-305.
Carmona, Juan/Lampe, Markus/Rosés, Joan (2017): "Housing affordability during the urban transition in Spain." In: The Economic History Review 70, pp. 632-658.
Chatel, Cathy/Esteve, Albert/Henneberg-Matí, Jordi/Morillas-Torné, Mateu (2017): "Patterns of population and urban growth in southwest Europe, 1920-2010." In: Journal of Urban History 43, pp. 1021-1040.
De Almeida, Map (2017): "The revolution in local government: Mayors in Portugal before and after 1974." In: Continuity and Change 32, pp. 253-282.
Fava, Nadia/Guàrdi, Manel/Oyón, José L. (2016): "Barcelonas food retailing and public markets, 1876-1936." In: Urban History 43, pp. 454-475.
Foot, John/Lumley, Robert (eds.) (2004): Italian cityscapes: Culture and urban change in contemporary Italy, Exeter: University of Exeter Press.
Guardia, Manel/Rosselló, Maribel/Garriga, Sergi (2014): "Barcelona's water supply, 1867-1967: The transition to a modern system." In: Urban History 41, pp. 415-434.
Hochadel, Oliver/Nieto-Galan, Agusti (eds.) (2016): Barcelona: An urban history of science and modernity, 1888-1929, Abingdon: Routledge.

Marat Mendes, Teresa/Oliveira, Vitor (2013): "Urban planners in Portugal in the middle of the twentieth century: Étienne de Groër and Antão Almeda Garrettin." In: Planning Perspectives 28, pp. 9-111.

Martin, Simon (2017): "Rebranding the republic: Rome and the 1960s olympic games." In: European Review of History 24, pp. 58-79.

Pinheiro, Magda (2009): "Lisbon: From the nineteenth century capital city to the metropolis: The role of transport networks." In: Ralf Roth (ed.), Städte im europäischen Raum: Verkehr, Kommunikation und Urbanität im 19. und 20. Jahrhundert, Stuttgart, pp. 87-107.

Pinson, Gilles (2002): "Political government and governance: Strategic planning and the reshaping of political capacity in Turin." In: International Journal of Urban and Regional Research 26, pp. 477-493.

Siebel, Walter (ed.) (2004): Die europäische Stadt, Berlin: Suhrkamp.

Varino, Valerio (2016): "Building an industrial society: Welfare capitalism in the 'city of factories'." In: European Review of History 23, pp. 724-750.

Urban-Environmental Perspectives in History Teaching

Noyan Dinçkal and Detlev Mares

'Teaching' is not a concept of urban-environmental history; thus, the question whether urban-environmental concepts can enhance historical learning processes might seem arbitrary. May not any historical subject become an object of teaching?

The specific teaching value of concepts of urban-environmental history is threefold. First, the conceptual dimension itself resonates with fundamental considerations of current history teaching, both at school and university levels. In many places, current approaches to the teaching of history aim to initiate learners into the operations of historical thinking. Rather than cramming students with facts and figures, they are encouraged to develop their 'competences' in order to solve 'problem-oriented' questions. This calls for the deliberate application of concepts and categories which help to arrange the vast arrays of historical information into meaningful narratives (Rüsen 2013: 156-166). Therefore, we will examine in which respects concepts from urban-environmental history may contribute to this didactic purpose.

Second, the concerns of urban-environmental history touch on relevant issues of current public debates. They resonate with concerns about the future of urban life and environmental problems and link up to more comprehensive perspectives on social and economic development. This makes the issues addressed in urban-environmental history relevant for all kinds of questions that deal with the current and future interrelationship of urban life and the environment (Dinçkal/Mares 2011). By dissolving the dichotomy implied in the alleged division between the 'culture' and 'nature', some concepts from urban-environmental history hold the potential to reshape the basic categories with which learners approach their surroundings and thus allow them to reflect on their individual position in ongoing processes of socio-ecological change.

Third, concepts of urban-environmental history offer opportunities to relate local experiences to larger, even global contexts. As soon as the concepts are discussed not only theoretically, but also using the concrete example of the city on the doorstep, the familiar environment can become the starting-point for the scrutiny of more general trends and patterns. In this context, teaching urban-environmental history can also benefit from source material available at the local level, often inviting to pursue explorative forms of teaching, such as projects organised in partnership with local museums or archives (cf. Evenden 2009; Lewis 2004). However, it is important not to assume that learners automatically have an interest in their local environment (cf. John 2018: 48-50). In most cases, interest in the local environment must first be raised. In such constellations, the use of concepts from urban-environmental history for the design of teaching units allows teachers to transcend the local situation by giving a broader resonance to local experiences.

In the following chapter, we ask in what respects the concepts of urban-environmental history, which have been introduced in this volume, might contribute to the aims of history teaching. In order to suggest possible answers to this question, we proceed in two steps. First, we will briefly summarise our understanding of the core aims of history teaching, based on some ideas discussed in German history didactics; then we will relate these fundamentals to concepts of urban-environmental history.

Concepts, Competences and Problems

'To think historically' does not only involve the knowledge of facts but the capacity to construct meaningful narratives, based on a methodologically appropriate discussion of source material and prior interpretations of history. In order to be 'meaningful' in this sense, historical narratives have to, among other aspects, relate historical detail to larger categories, which structure the plethora of information from the past according to questions of relevance (Schreiber 2016: 119-129). The questions are of particular relevance if they emerge from problems which connect to current issues. In order to develop the capacity to build such narratives, history didactics has started to direct much attention at 'competences'. In Germany alone, more than a half-dozen models for defining and arranging historical competences have been suggested (Barricelli et al. 2012). Despite their differences, they share some similar assumptions and aims: Learners should be enabled to render judgment on complex historical questions. This implies the capacity to evaluate historical settings and come to conclusions about causes and effects at work in historical situations, but it also includes the ability to apply the conclusions drawn from historical considerations to current challenges (Zülsdorf-Kersting 2016).

In order to achieve these aims of history teaching, didactic theory recommends starting from asking questions which constitute problems rather than sticking with chronology. As far as the definition of the term is concerned, 'problem' refers to different dimensions of teaching history. First of all, it refers to any teaching arrangement which starts from the observation of some unusual, surprising or not self-explaining fact. This instigates a structured learning process in several stages, from identifying the problem, grappling with ways of tackling it (involving the use of historical source material) and devising a solution. Since this process requires argument rather than the mere description of past processes, 'problems' constitute an intellectual challenge to learners and call for a negotiation of complex contexts (Hensel-Grobe 2012: 53-59; Pandel 2013: 340-343).

'Problem-oriented' and 'competence'-based approaches are not singular to history teaching, since prompting learners to develop structured arguments is at the heart of teaching in many disciplines. However, there are more specific dimensions to problem-related learning in history. Beyond referring to any problem-centred question identified in class, a historical 'problem' has to be embedded in wider social and theoretical issues. For example, experiences from the life-world of learners, especially social constellations that may challenge identities and norms of behaviour, are dealt with as core problems of the 'big' questions of modern society, such as inequality, poverty, injustice, climate change, challenges of democracy. The same goes for reflections on the main categories of historical and political thinking, through which relevant information is distinguished from less relevant information, real from fictional narratives or in which different stages in historical processes are identified (Barricelli 2011: 84-85).

In which respects might concepts of urban-environmental history contribute to initiate learning processes along the lines sketched out so far? We would like to focus on two potential benefits:

First, the life-world of learners is currently pervaded by debates about environmental issues. In 2019, 'Fridays for Future', an international movement of young people for political action on climate change, seems to have inspired a new generation of environmental activism. The elections to the EU parliament in the same year saw a moderate rise of parties campaigning on similar issues. Many of the initiatives were, not exclusively but to a large extent, urban phenomena, thus highlighting the challenge of combining sustainable ways of resources management with urban life styles and locating these issues close to the concerns of pupils and students. Integrating concepts from urban-environmental history into teaching thus links existing calls for increasing the environmental dimension in history teaching to current concerns (cf. e. g. Schwartz 2006).

Second, beyond current political drama, concepts of urban-environmental history may contribute to develop more sophisticated thinking on the relationship between 'culture' and 'nature'. Frequently, both are seen as opposed or at least different spheres, with human 'culture' and the artificial ways of urban life damaging or destroying an idealised, harmonious 'nature' best left independent of human interference. However, as Martin Melosi (in this volume) observes, "cities are only artificial in our eyes if humans themselves are excluded from the natural world." And yet, such binary myopia informs much thinking on the relationship between urban life and natural environment. Many of the concepts of urban-environmental history introduced in this volume dispute such dichotomies. Instead, they negotiate the line between 'nature' and 'city' or 'society', the 'cultural' and 'natural' worlds. With respect to material aspects, such as resources and waste management, circulatory and metabolic approaches link the urban and extra-urban spheres in processes of exchange which show both sides depending on each other (Barles and Weber in this volume). The concept of the 'technosphere' tackles the binary division head-on by observing the effects of technological development even in places that might appear as nature 'untouched' by human interference. Instead, as Chris Otter (in this volume) remarks, humans themselves, "in fact, are artefacts of the technosphere." Apart from analysing material effects, some concepts, such as the concept of 'socio-natural sites' (Winiwarter/Schmid in this volume), have been put to good use in understanding visual representations of urban and environmental constellations, emphasising the cultural dimension inherent in the construction of images of urban and natural life (Knoll 2013). Thus, concepts from urban-environmental history challenge much received thinking, facilitating fresh perspectives among learners and serving the general purpose of training students in the reflected use of categories in historical thinking. This might go so far as to reveal contradictions in learners' own ways of life, e. g. a careless use of energy resources while protesting against climate change at the same time.

Concepts as Perspectives

While the application of concepts from urban-environmental history heeds the calls of academic history didactics, many practitioners find the explicit application of theoretical concepts rather ambitious, given the limits of many actual teaching arrangements, not the least the lack of time. Such objections are not to be ignored. However, attempts to integrate theory into history teaching are not without precedent (cf. e. g. Guse et al. 2015), and concepts from urban-environmental history may make a promising addition to such efforts. Moreover—and more important—our argument does not necessarily call for involving learners with the details of theory. More crucial is the fact that concepts from urban-environmental history offer perspectives on history that may inform the planning of teaching arrangements in a more implicit mode. If perspectives such as overcoming the dichotomous thinking about 'culture' and 'nature' are applied to history teaching, they can be discussed on the basis of much of the regular (source) material used in class.

In this way, the learners' capacities for conceptual thinking can be developed without tiresome reference to the details of particular concepts. If learners are inspired to overcome the dichotomous view of urban and environmental relationships, their perspective may be sharpened even without explicit recourse to the underlying concepts. Thus, by applying perspectives derived from the concepts, learners will develop the capacity to transcend crude binary thinking, even if the theoretical foundation may not be explicitly discussed. The theoretical depth can be adjusted according to the capacities of the particular learners' groups, whose abilities might be developed over the course of time.

If understood as a perspective on history, the use of concepts from urban-environmental history in history teaching fundamentally shapes the angle of approaching basically any teaching (and source) material. Thus, many sources are available, since using the concepts is not limited to particular material but—as a specific perspective—may guide learners' approaches to all kinds of material. In the rest of the paper, we will use some examples to illustrate this thought.

Some Examples for the Urban-Environmental Perspective in History Teaching

The concept of 'urban metabolism' offers a first approach for tackling the dichotomy between 'culture' and 'nature' while at the same time bringing the material side of urban-environmental history to the fore: raw materials, such as water and wood, enter the city from the countryside; waste materials, such as sewage or smoke emissions, return to the countryside. By its focus on the metabolism of the city, the approach describes the consumption of resources in the city as well as the conversion of materials. This also reveals the 'colonisation' of the surrounding countryside by the city, e.g. through the depletion of resources or environmental pollution (Fischer-Kowalski 1997; Barles in this volume). On the other hand, however, cities never appear to be merely resource-consuming parasites—after all, they themselves produced raw materials to an extent not to be underestimated. For example, cotton and linen rags were used to make paper, or animal bones were processed into bone charcoal, which in turn was used in sugar refineries. In the modern city, this complex interplay of importing and converting material and energy resources is inextricably linked with the functioning of large-scale supply systems such as the modern central water supply or sewage disposal through the sewage system (Barles 2005; Schott 2014: 174-178, 189-199).

Dieter Schott (2013b) has suggested an arrangement of source material to teach the concept of urban metabolism by highlighting the role of rivers in mobilising resources for the cities. Using the example of Regensburg in the German state of Bavaria, he demonstrates shifts in the city's outreach into its surroundings. In the 1830s, the traditional supply of timber and firewood along the Danube river came under stress when a new canal allowed cities at a greater distance to participate in the provision of wood from regions which had up to then been the main suppliers of Regensburg. Timber prices in Regensburg increased, causing debates about tapping into new resources along new ways of transport. Different actors with different interests, such as wood traders, urban consumers and the administration of state forests, shaped these debates (ibid: 62-68). This example enables learners to recognise the social construction of resources management, thus underlining the mutual dependence of urban and environmental dimensions from a metabolic perspective.

The concept of 'socio-natural sites' also attempts to overcome the dichotomy of nature and human agency by establishing an epistemological framework which manages to include both. Its champions combine perspectives from other approaches, such as practice theory and evolutionary theory, in order to arrive at a set of categories that transcend common essentialisms of nature, society and human agency (Winiwarter/Schmid in this volume). If applied to representations of urban-environmental constellations, learners can be made to engage with and question the very dichotomy of nature and human agency. By asking whether such a clear divide can be maintained, valuable learning processes may be inaugurated. Since some research has focused on the representation of socio-natural sites in visual sources, the approach easily combines with the analysis of pictures in class. As an example, take the famous image of Munich in the Schedelsche Weltchronik of 1493 (available with Commons License on: https://de.wikipedia.org/wiki/Datei:Schedel-weltchronik-muenchen.jpg).

The city is shown from the East, from an elevated position across the river Isar, which takes up about a quarter of the picture, with the bent bridge over the river given pride of place (cf. Knoll 2013: 223-225). The upper half of the picture is covered by the impressive outline of the city with its major churches. If we ask for the relationship between nature and human life, however, it is the area between the river and the city walls that is of the greatest interest. Here we see many examples for the close interconnection between river and urban economy (cf. Lübken in this volume). The picture shows rafts and wood stacks by the river bank in great detail. There are also several signs of commercial activity, such as mills and warehouses. For travellers, the area between city walls and the river is clearly demarcated by both a bridge and a city gate.

By analysing the picture from the perspective of socio-natural interrelations, learners will be motivated to question the dualism of an urban, man-made and a natural environment. For example, rafts made of wood are part of both the natural and the human sphere. Their mere existence invites the refutation of the dichotomy of both spheres and calls for an integrated approach. This is just one example for a set of questions that can be raised by basically any visual representation of urban environments. For teaching purposes, the approach can yield more results if a series of representations of one city in different periods of time or a set of comparative pictures of different urban-environmental arrangements are introduced to learners. In either way, learners can experience cities as sites of a symbiosis between human and natural environments, and thus they are encouraged to ask questions about the relationship between both.

The symbiosis and its problems become particularly clear when the focus is on urban risks and resilience (Collet in this volume). On the one hand, due to their dense settlement and building structure, cities have always been fragile formations, susceptible to fires, wars, floods or epidemics. At the same time, however, cities are among the most persistent historical phenomena. This permanence and resilience points beyond mere natural factors. It has to be recognised that natural disasters, such as fires or floods, were results of a "fatal combination of natural and social factors", as Dominik Collet (in this volume) emphasises and that "risks are in fact socially constructed and embedded into the cultural fabric of city life". In teaching, risk and resilience raise some central questions that refer directly to the socio-natural interdependencies of cities. Above all, the resilience concept places cities in relation to their ecological framework and, in this context, also takes the constant flow of material and immaterial resources into account. In addition, questions of risk and resilience also refer to current problems. In particular, the growing threat posed by global climate change, which aggravates the effects of floods and storms among others, puts the questions of human agency and human interference in natural processes at the centre of current debates. The resilience perspective therefore offers many opportunities to combine historical observations with current debates and to ask how former societies reacted to similar risks.

This interdependence of human and natural environment can be addressed in many more ways, for example in how the reduction of environmental risk played a vital part in urban life. In London, the great fire of 1666 destroyed almost 80 per cent of the city's surface area, and this only one year after the plague had killed about 80.000 people. Dieter Schott (2013a: 300-302) describes the reactions to this fire and makes clear how the fire led to important changes in the urban organisation and appearance of the city. Only then were the first land registers introduced, house types standardised, wooden ornaments banned and fire prevention measures such as firewalls introduced. Similar to London, this modernisation effect can also be seen in Istanbul. In the capital of the Ottoman Empire many aspects of urban transformation in the second half of the 19th century—the remodelling of the streets, building codes, the required building materials, and the erection of central water supply works—were related to the impact of nightmarish fires. In this way, Istanbul's old fabric of streets and lanes disappeared almost completely (Dinçkal 2008: 56-57).

However, when questions of urban resilience are discussed in a technicist manner at the level of material and infrastructural adaptation alone, central aspects of social inequality and environmental justice are neglected in the historical understanding of urban risks. As a rule, the entire urban population does not suffer in the same way from the consequences of urban catastrophes. The burdens and risks are unequally distributed among the population. Factors such as social inequality or racism have shaped the experience of urban disasters (Vardy/Smith 2017).

The recent example of Hurricane Katrina, which devastated New Orleans in 2005, shows that it was not only the risks of being affected by such disasters that depended on factors such as race, gender and class. In addition, the limitations of classical success narratives can also be problematised when analysing the ways in which such events were coped with from an urban-environmental history perspective. The hurricane was followed by a radical redesigning of New Orleans' building structure and, as a result, a comprehensive change in its urban social structure. The lock-outs from social housing in the inner city as a result of the structural redesign of the city and the subsidised construction of model settlements for higher-income residents particularly affected the poor, African Americans, and the elderly. For many New Orleans residents, the disaster did not end after the hurricane, but began after it (Baade/Baumann/Matheson 2007; Sims 2010). By considering such contexts, some of the 'big' problems of society singled out by history didactics can enter history teaching.

Conclusions

Integrating urban-environmental perspectives into history teaching does not cover all aspects of human and environmental relationships. However, most approaches avoid the pitfalls of focussing too closely on received narratives of modernity which either interpret urban-environmental concerns in a triumphalist context of man's victory over nature or construct narratives of decay and degradation. Of course, such narratives may be attached to the interests described here, although the history of environmental ideas shows that they have never reigned undisputed and must not be applied without careful reflection (cf. Probst 2019). The emphasis deriving from the concepts of urban-environmental history offers a perspective for history teaching which is much more open to the complex relationships of human and natural interactions than many of the linear narratives. Learners are thus enabled to arrive at a more sophisticated understanding of historical processes rather than being stuck in simplifying story lines. By applying perspectives from urban-environmental history, teaching can go a long way to overcome dichotomous approaches which are common in conventional interpretations and may distort the complexities of underlying reality (Culver 2014). At the same time, dealing with urban-environmental history can highlight the complexity and also the sometimes fragile foundations of urban development and current resource management by addressing the underlying historical structures and decisions (cf. Sörlin 2011; Rosen/Tarr 1994).

Although our chapter has mainly dealt with the modern European city, it goes without saying that many of the arguments for teaching urban-environmental history can also easily be applied to non-European urban scenarios, if they are adapted to the specific historical experiences and current challenges (Gandy 2014). The solutions and problems of the European cities must not be misjudged as the only valuable or deserving cases of urban-environmental history, but they provide examples for possible negotiations with some of the fundamental problems of urban life.

References

Baade, Robert A./Baumann, Robert/Matheson, Victor (2007): "Estimating the economic impact of natural and social disasters, with an application to hurricane Katrina." In: Urban Studies 44, pp. 2061-2076.

Barles, Sabine (2005): "A metabolic approach to the city: 19th and 20th century Paris." In: Dieter Schott/Bill Luckin/Geneviève Massard-Guilbaud (eds.), Resources of the city: Contributions to an environmental history of modern Europe, Aldershot: Ashgate, pp. 28-47.

Barricelli, Michele/Gautschi, Peter/Körber, Andreas (2012): "Historische Kompetenzen und Kompetenzmodelle." In: Michele Barricelli/Martin Lücke (eds.), Handbuch Praxis des Geschichtsunterrichts, vol. 1, Schwalbach: Wochenschau, pp. 207-235.

Barricelli, Michele (2011): "Problemorientierung." In: Ulrich Mayer/Hans-Jürgen Pandel/Gerhard Schneider (eds.), Handbuch Methoden im Geschichtsunterricht, Schwalbach: Wochenschau, 3rd edition, pp. 78-90.

Culver, Lawrence (2014): "Confluences of nature and culture: Cities in environmental history." In: Andrew C. Isenberg (ed.), The Oxford Handbook of Environmental History, Oxford: Oxford University Press, pp. 553-572.

Dinçkal, Noyan/Mares, Detlev (2011): "Die Stadt als vernetztes System: Didaktische Möglichkeiten im Schnittfeld von Stadt-, Umwelt- und Technikgeschichte." In: Geschichte in Wissenschaft und Unterricht 62, pp. 92-105.

Dinçkal, Noyan (2008): "Arenas of experimentation: Modernizing Istanbul in the late Ottoman Empire." In: Mikael Hård/Thomas J. Misa (eds.), Urban machinery: Inside modern European cities, Cambridge, Mass.: MIT Press, pp. 49-69.

Evenden, Matthew (2009): "Environmental history pedagogy beyond history and on the web." In: Environmental History 14, pp. 737-743.

Fischer-Kowalski, Marina (1997): Gesellschaftlicher Stoffwechsel und Kolonisierung von Natur: Ein Versuch in Sozialer Ökologie, Amsterdam: Gordon & Breach.

Gandy, Matthew (2014): The fabric of space: Water, Modernity, and the urban imagination, Cambridge, Mass./London: MIT Press.

Guse, Klaus-Michael/Kraft, Claudia/Groth, Daniel/Schäfer, David (2015): "Making sense of postcolonial theories and applying them to the relationship between eastern and western Europe." In: Uta Fenske/Daniel Groth/Bärbel Kuhn/Klaus-Michael Guse (eds.), Colonialism and decolonization in national historical cultures and memory politics in Europe: Modules for history lessons, Frankfurt a.M.: Peter Lang, pp. 101-109.

Hensel-Grobe, Meike (2012): "Problemorientierung und problemlösendes Denken." In: Michele Barricelli/Martin Lücke (eds.), Handbuch Praxis des Geschichtsunterrichts, Schwalbach: Wochenschau, pp. 50-63.

John, Anke (2018): Lokal- und Regionalgeschichte, Frankfurt a.M.: Wochenschau.

Knoll, Martin (2013): Die Natur der menschlichen Welt: Siedlung, Territorium und Umwelt in der historisch-topographischen Literatur der Frühen Neuzeit, Bielefeld: transcript.

Lewis, Michael (2004): "This class will write a book: An experiment in environmental history pedagogy." In: Environmental History 9, pp. 604-619.

Pandel, Hans-Jürgen (2013): Geschichtsdidaktik: Eine Theorie für die Praxis, Schwalbach: Wochenschau.

Probst, Milo (2019): "Freiheit im Einklang mit der Natur: Fortschritt und Naturbeziehungen bei Elisée Reclus (1830-1905)." In: Historische Anthropologie 27, pp. 125-143.

Rosen, Christine M./Tarr, Joel A. (1994): "The importance of an urban perspective in environmental history." In: Journal of Urban History 20, pp. 299-310.

Rüsen, Jörn (2013): Historik: Theorie der Geschichtswissenschaft, Cologne/Weimar/Vienna: Böhlau.

Schott, Dieter (2013a): "Katastrophen, Krisen und städtische Resilienz: Blicke in die Stadtgeschichte." In: Informationen zur Raumentwicklung 4, pp. 297-309.

Schott, Dieter (2013b): "Stadt und Fluss: Zentrale Dimensionen städtischer Umweltgeschichte." In: Bärbel Kuhn/Astrid Windus (eds.), Umwelt und Klima im Geschichtsunterricht, St. Ingbert: Röhrig Universitätsverlag, pp. 57-76.

Schott, Dieter (2014): Europäische Urbanisierung (1000-2000): Eine umwelthistorische Einführung, Cologne/Weimar/Vienna: Böhlau.

Schreiber, Waltraud (2016): "Historische Kompetenzen in Theorie, Empirie und Pragmatik." In: Wolfgang Hasberg/Holger Thünemann (eds.), Geschichtsdidaktik in der Diskussion: Grundlagen und Perspektiven, Frankfurt a.M.: Peter Lang, pp. 113-151.

Schwartz, Robert M. (2006): "Teaching environmental history: Environmental thinking and practice in Europe: 1500 to the present." In: The History Teacher 39, pp. 325-354.

Sims, Benjamin (2010): "Disoriented city: Infrastructure, social order, and the police response to hurricane Katrina." In: Stephen Graham (ed.), Disrupted cities: When infrastructure fails, New York/London: Routledge, pp. 41-53.

Sörlin, Sverker (2011): "The contemporaneity of environmental history: Negotiating scholarship, useful history, and the new human condition." In: Journal of Contemporary History 46, pp. 610-630.

Vardy, Mark/Smith, Mick (2017): "Resilience." In: Environmental Humanities 9, pp. 175-179.

Zülsdorf-Kersting, Meik (2016): "Historische Urteilsbildung: Theoretische Klärung und empirische Besichtigung." In: Wolfgang Hasberg/Holger Thünemann (eds.), Geschichtsdidaktik in der Diskussion: Grundlagen und Perspektiven. Frankfurt a.M.: Peter Lang, pp. 197-223.

Authors

Barles, Sabine, professor of urban planning at Université Paris 1 Panthéon Sorbonne, France. Her research focuses on urban environment, urban technology and the interactions between societies (especially cities) and nature in both contemporary and historical (from 18th century onwards) terms. In particular, she addresses the questions of urban metabolism, environmental imprints, territorial ecology and socio-ecological trajectories.

Bernhardt, Christoph, head of department for historical research and deputy director of the Leibniz-Institute for Research on Society and Space in Erkner near Berlin. He teaches as an associate professor for modern and contemporary history at Humboldt University Berlin. His main fields of research are European urban and environmental history.

Brantz, Dorothee, professor of modern urban history and director of the Center for Metropolitan Studies at Technische Universität Berlin. Her areas of expertise include urban-environmental history, human-animal studies, the history of warfare, and the history of photography. She has published widely on urban human-animal relations. Currently she is working on a project about seasons in the city.

Collet, Dominik, professor for environmental history at the University of Oslo. He works on climate history, socionatural disasters and material cultures of knowing in early modern Europe. He is the author of *Die doppelte Katastrophe: Klima und Kultur in der europäischen Hungerkrise 1770-1772* (Vandenhoeck & Ruprecht, 2019) and a founding member of the Oslo School for Environmental Humanities (OSEH).

Dinçkal, Noyan, professor for modern European history of knowledge and communication at the University of Siegen. His main fields of interest are the cultural history of technology and science, as well as urban-environmental history. His publications include *Sportlandschaften. Sport, Raum und (Massen-)Kultur in Deutschland 1880-1930* (Vandenhoeck & Ruprecht, 2013).

Haumann, Sebastian, assistant professor at Darmstadt University of Technology. He has held research and teaching positions at University of Düsseldorf, the University of Pennsylvania, the University of Leicester and Jena University. His research in urban and environmental history focusses on resources and urban planning. He has recently completed a study on 'critical' raw materials in the age of industrialisation.

Knoll, Martin, professor for the history of European Regions at the University of Salzburg, Austria. His research interests include environmental history, tourism history and the historical change of city-hinterland-relations. With Uwe Lübken and Dieter Schott he has co-edited a collected volume on city-river-relations *Rivers lost—rivers re-gained* (University of Pittsburgh Press, 2017), with Sabine Barles he contributed a chapter on *Long-Term Transitions, Urban Imprint and the Construction of Hinterlands* in *Urbanizing Nature* (Routledge, 2019).

Liedtke, Rainer, professor and chair of European history (19th and 20th century) at the University of Regensburg. He has studied at the universities of Bochum, Warwick and at St. Antony's College, Oxford and holds a D.Phil. in modern history from Oxford University. He has taught at the University of Michigan, Berlin University of Technology, University of Gießen, University of Kiel and Darmstadt University of Technology. His interests include comparative European history, urban history, the history of modern Greece and the historical experience of the Jews in modern Europe.

Lübken, Uwe, professor of American history at Ludwig-Maximilians-University, Munich. He has held teaching and research positions at the universities of Cologne, Munich, Münster and at the German Historical Institute in Washington, DC. He has published on (American) transnational history and the history of natural hazards and catastrophes. His publications include a history of flooding of the Ohio River (Vandenhoeck & Ruprecht, 2014) and co-edited volumes on urban fires (University of Wisconsin Press, 2012), the management of natural resources (Berghahn Books, 2014) and city-river relations (Pittsburgh University Press, 2016). His current work explores the intersections of mobilities and the environment.

Madgin, Rebecca, professor of urban studies at the University of Glasgow, is an urban historian who works broadly on the relationship between heritage and place-making. More specifically, her research examines the emotional and economic values of heritage in the context of urban redevelopment initiatives. She has published work on examples of heritage-led redevelopment initiatives in the twentieth and twenty-first centuries using examples drawn from the UK, Europe and China.

Mares, Detlev, senior lecturer at the Institute of History at Darmstadt University of Technology. He works on modern British history, history of radical politics and didactics of history.

Melosi, Martin V., Cullen Professor Emeritus and founding director of the Center for Public History at the University of Houston, Texas, USA. He is a specialist on the history of the urban environment. His latest book, *Fresh Kills: A History of Consuming and Discarding in New York City*, will be published by Columbia University Press in January 2020.

Otter, Chris, associate professor of history at Ohio State University. He is the author of *The Victorian Eye: A Political History of Light and Vision in Britain, 1800-1910* (University of Chicago Press, 2008) and *Diet for a Large Planet: Industrial Britain, Food Systems, and World Ecology* (University of Chicago Press, 2020).

Reith, Reinhold, professor of economic, social and environmental history at the University of Salzburg, Austria. His major interests and empirical research concern artisans, merchants, wages, labour, consumption, environment and technology. His publications include a textbook on early modern environmental history *Umweltgeschichte der Frühen Neuzeit* (Oldenbourg Wissenschaftsverlag, 2011) and a commented edition of 18th century merchants' accountbooks *Haushalten und Konsumieren. Die Ausgabenbücher der Salzburger Kaufmannsfamilie Spängler von 1733 bis 1785* (Stadtarchiv und Statistik der Stadt Salzburg, 2016).

Schanbacher, Ansgar, researcher and scientific coordinator in the research programme "Nachhaltigkeit als Argument" ("Sustainability as an argument") at Göttingen University. He studied history, economics, Polish language and literature in Leipzig and Lublin (Poland) and was a postgraduate (Dr. phil.) at the Göttingen Research Training Group Interdisciplinary Environmental History. His current research focuses on natural hazards and natural resource management in early modern cities.

Schmid, Martin, associate professor at the Center for Environmental History (ZUG), Institute of Social Ecology, Department for Economics and Social Sciences, University of Natural Resources and Life Sciences Vienna (BOKU). Trained in archaeology and history at the University of Vienna (Mag. phil. 2002, Dr. phil. 2007), 2014 venia legendi in environmental history at Alpen-Adria-Universität Klagenfurt. Carson Fellow at the Rachel Carson Center for Environment & Society, LMU and Deutsches Museum in Munich in 2011. Deputy director of the Institute of Social Ecology 2016-17, founding member (2003) and director of ZUG in 2010.

Toyka-Seid, Michael, has worked as research associate at Darmstadt University of Technology on projects on urban renewal and rehabilitation in European and Southeast Asien cities and on visible waters in cities in the context of an interdisciplinary research on ways to urban sustainability. He has published on the history of sanitation and public health, on the history of noise and the the environment in cities. At current he is working as a language trainer for refugee children.

Weber, Heike, professor for history of technology at Techniche Universität Berlin. Her main research lies at the intersection of consumption history, environmental history and history of technology. She has worked on 20th century everyday technologies (e.g. household appliances, media technologies, mobile electronic devices). Currently, she studies the history of waste, recycling and repair, thereby pushing history of technology beyond its traditional focus on production, consumption and use towards issues of obsolescence, decay and disposal.

Winiwarter, Verena, was appointed professor of environmental history at Alpen-Adria-Universität Klagenfurt in 2007, and holds the same position at Vienna University of Natural Resources and Life Sciences since 2018, when the Institute of Social Ecology was moved there. First trained as a chemical engineer, she holds a PhD in environmental history from Vienna University and was granted the venia legendi in Human Ecology in 2003 at Vienna University. Since 2016, she is a full member of the Austrian Academy of Sciences, Chairperson of the Commission for Interdisciplinary Ecological Studies (OEAW), President of ICEHO, founding member of ESEH and member of the advisory boards of the Centre for Environmental History (University Tallinn), Deutsches Museum (München) and Technisches Museum Wien.

Zimmermann, Clemens, senior professor for cultural and media history, Saarland University. His publications include *Lets Historize it. Jugendmedien im 20. Jahrhundert* (Böhlau, 2018); *Europäische Medienstädte* (Röhrig 2017); *Journalism and Technological Change* (Campus, 2014); *Industrial Cities. History and Future* (Campus, 2013).

Zumbrägel, Christian, postdoctoral researcher at Technische Universität Berlin. His areas of expertise include the history of technology and environmental history with a particular focus on history of renewable energies, raw materials and maintenance and repair. He obtained his PhD from Darmstadt University of Technology. His PhD thesis *'Viele Wenige machen ein Viel'– Eine Technik- und Umweltgeschichte der Kleinwasserkraft (1880–1930)* (Schöningh 2018), won book prizes of the Association of German Engineers (VDI), the Georg-Agricola-Gesellschaft (2017) and the Gesellschaft für Geschichte der Wissenschaften, der Medizin und der Technik e. V. (GWMT).

Acknowledgements

This volume would not have been possible without the support of many people. In particular, the editors would like to thank Stefanie Gatzka and Petra Grieshofer, who did most of the copy-editing work on the chapters. Several chapters were translated into English or needed English language editing, which was provided by Ann M. Hentschel and Sascha Möbius.

For financial support, we thank the University of Salzburg (Rectorate and History Department).

Historical Sciences

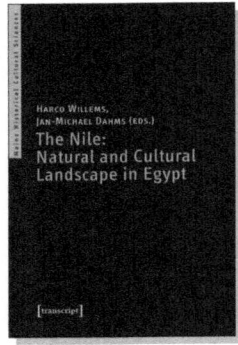

Harco Willems, Jan-Michael Dahms (eds.)
The Nile: Natural and Cultural Landscape in Egypt

2017, 374 p., pb., numerous partly col. ill.
29,99 € (DE), 978-3-8376-3615-4
E-Book available as free open access publication
ISBN 978-3-8394-3615-8

Gesa zur Nieden, Berthold Over (eds.)
Musicians' Mobilities and Music Migrations in Early Modern Europe
Biographical Patterns and Cultural Exchanges

2016, 432 p., pb., numerous partly col. ill.
34,99 € (DE), 978-3-8376-3504-1
E-Book available as free open access publication
ISBN 978-3-8394-3504-5

Laura Meneghello
Jacob Moleschott – A Transnational Biography
Science, Politics, and Popularization in Nineteenth-Century Europe

2017, 490 p., pb.
49,99 € (DE), 978-3-8376-3970-4
E-Book: 49,99 € (DE), ISBN 978-3-8394-3970-8

All print, e-book and open access versions of the titles in our list are available in our online shop www.transcript-verlag.de/en!

Historical Sciences

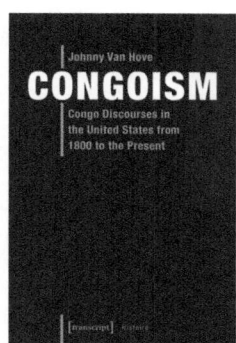

Johnny Van Hove
Congoism
Congo Discourses in the United States from 1800 to the Present

2017, 360 p., pb., numerous ill.
39,99 € (DE), 978-3-8376-4037-3
E-Book: 39,99 € (DE), ISBN 978-3-8394-4037-7

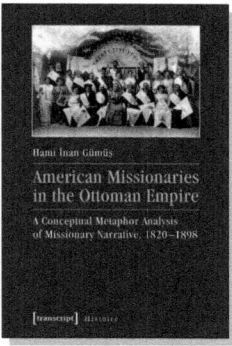

Hami Inan Gümüş
American Missionaries in the Ottoman Empire
A Conceptual Metaphor Analysis of Missionary Narrative, 1820-1898

2017, 260 p., pb.
34,99 € (DE), 978-3-8376-3808-0
E-Book: 34,99 € (DE), ISBN 978-3-8394-3808-4

Jörg Rogge (ed.)
Killing and Being Killed: Bodies in Battle
Perspectives on Fighters in the Middle Ages

2017, 272 p., pb.
29,99 € (DE), 978-3-8376-3783-0
E-Book available as free open access publication
ISBN 978-3-8394-3783-4

All print, e-book and open access versions of the titles in our list are available in our online shop www.transcript-verlag.de/en!